AN ELOQUENT PICTURE GALLERY

The South African portrait photographs of Gustav Theodor Fritsch, 1863–1865

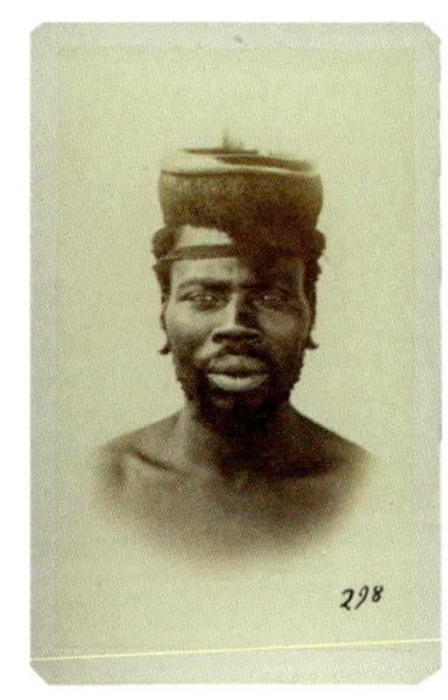
298
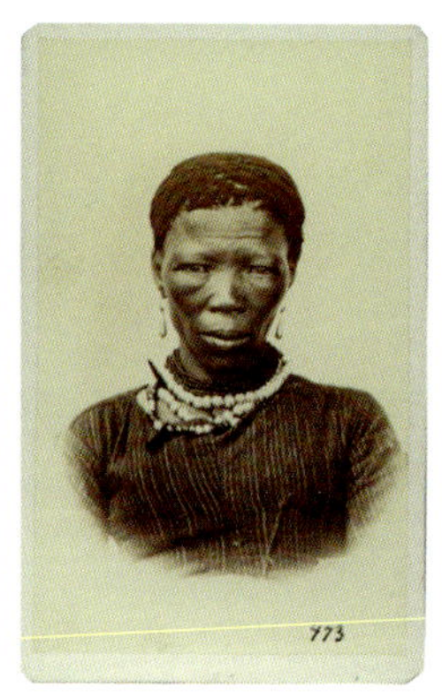
773
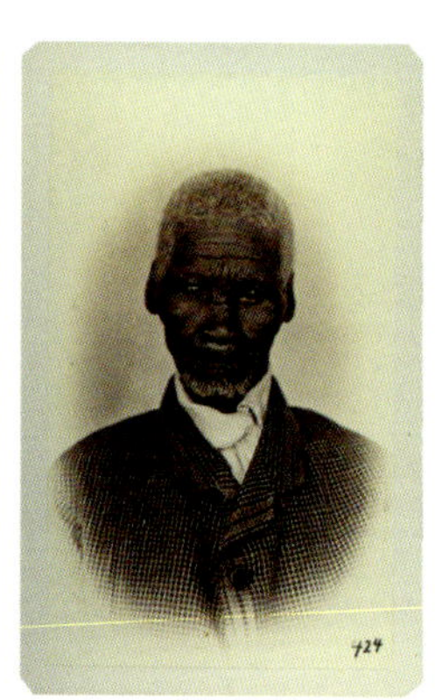
724
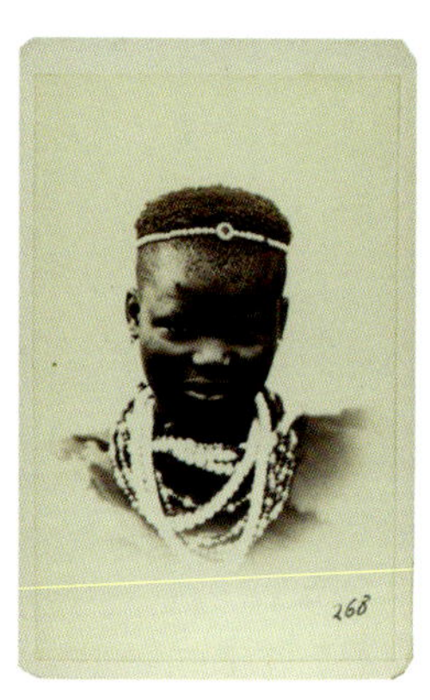
268
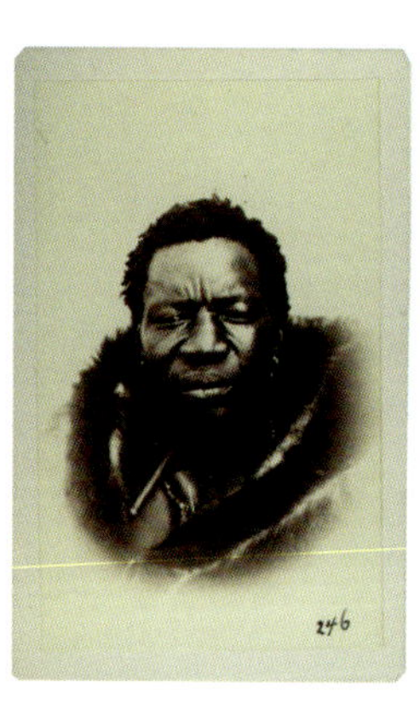
246
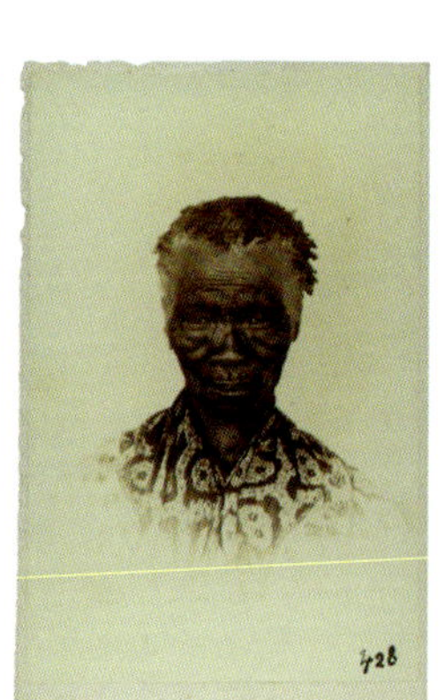
728

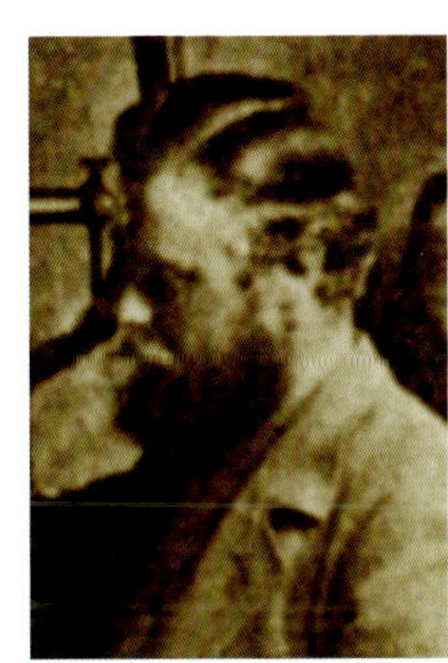

AN ELOQUENT PICTURE GALLERY

The South African portrait photographs of Gustav Theodor Fritsch, 1863–1865

Edited by
Keith Dietrich and Andrew Bank

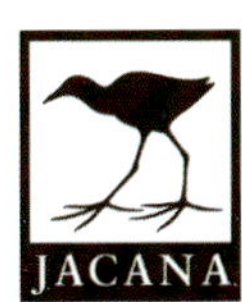

First published by Jacana Media (Pty) Ltd in 2008

10 Orange Street
Sunnyside
Auckland Park 2092
South Africa
+2711 628 3200
www.jacana.co.za

ISBN 978-1-77009-641-7

Design and layout: Keith Dietrich and Natascha Griessel
Set in Optima
Printed by CTP Book Printers
Job no. 000810

See a complete list of Jacana titles at www.jacana.co.za

CONTENTS

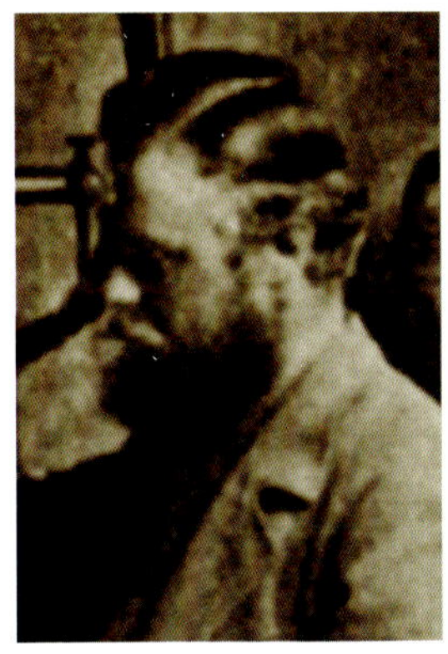

Acknowledgements

This book has been the product of two periods of intense activity during which we have accumulated personal and institutional debts. We were both warmly hosted, each for some weeks, by Dr Angelica Tunis, curator of the Africa Department of the Museum of Ethnology, Berlin, on separate visits to Berlin some six or seven years ago. Angelica gave us open access to the photographic collection. Christine Stelzig, who had drawn up the index to the collection, generously shared information, and the Director of the African Collection, Dr Peter Junge, kindly granted us permission to reproduce Fritsch's southern African portrait photographs, which form the centrepiece of this volume. We are also grateful to National Library of South Africa, Cape Town, for permission to reproduce material from its Visual Collection.

Without the financial support of the National Arts Council of South Africa, this publication would simply not have been possible. Thanks also to the Research Sub-Committee A at Stellenbosch University, the National Research Foundation of South Africa, which provided financial support for background research, Mimi Seyffert of the J.S. Gericke Library at Stellenbosch University, and Claus Heydenrych, Marelize van Zyl and Annemi Conradie for their assistance with research and translation. We are grateful to Natascha Griessel for the layout of this book.

Special thanks to Walter Köppe for translating texts from Fritsch's books and one of the essays from German, Linde Dietrich for assistance with translation and hours of editorial work, and Anja Macher for translation work. We are deeply grateful to Linde and Anja for their patience, encouragement and emotional support during the long and interrupted gestation of the book. Our thanks to Russell Martin of Jacana Media, who took on this book in an act of faith and patiently saw it through to completion in that trusting spirit.

Keith Dietrich and Andrew Bank
September 2008

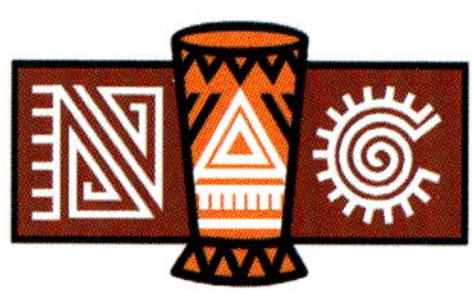

National Arts Council of South Africa

Preface Keith Dietrich

In 1863, a year after completing his degree in medicine at the University of Berlin, the 25-year-old Dr Gustav Theodor Fritsch embarked on an expedition to South Africa at his own expense with a view to conducting an anthropological study of the indigenous people of the region. Fritsch's journey was primarily motivated by his scientific interests, particularly in comparative anatomy and anthropology. At a time when many conflicting theories were being advanced in the area of race studies, he sought to reach his own conclusions by conducting primary research in the field. His background in the natural sciences also equipped him to conduct detailed botanical, entomological, ornithological and zoological observations.

Fritsch's three-year expedition through southern Africa gave rise to two major publications, namely his *Drei Jahre in Süd-Afrika. Reise-skizzen nach Notizen des Tagesbuchs zusammengestellt* (Three Years in South Africa: Travel Sketches Compiled from Notes in a Journal, hereafter referred to as *Drei Jahre*), which was published in 1868, and his *Die Eingeborenen Süd-Afrika's ethnographisch und anatomisch beschreiben* (The Natives of South Africa Anatomically and Ethnographically Described, hereafter referred to as *Die Eingeborenen*), which was published in 1872. While his travel account, *Drei Jahre*, was aimed at a broader public readership and therefore written in a more popular and conversational vein, *Die Eingeborenen* is a scholarly publication that stemmed from his academic interest in anthropology, and particularly the anatomy and customs of the indigenous inhabitants of the country.

Compared to earlier traveller-scientists who visited South Africa, such as Peter Kolb, Anders Sparrman and William Burchell, Fritsch's contribution to the anthropological literature on indigenous people from southern Africa was unique. He was an accomplished photographer and collected a comprehensive body of photographic records on his travels that were used as source material for the illustrations in his *Drei Jahre* and *Die Eingeborenen*, and for the etchings in his *Atlas*, which accompanied *Die Eingeborenen*. The photographs include portrait and full-length studies of individuals, images of groups of people, scenes of African and colonial settlements, and landscapes.

Of all these, it is the portraits that far outnumber the rest, and despite their anthropological intention, the quality of the portraits is quite extraordinary.

Fritsch's books and articles have never been translated into English and only a few of his photographs have been published. The material, therefore, remains relatively unknown and his research on South Africa has consequently not been given any exposure. The primary aim of this book, therefore, is to bring together a comprehensive collection of Fritsch's southern African photographs, particularly his portraits.

Fritsch's travel account is by no means a dispassionate narration by an *unbefangene Beobachter* (detached observer), as he often refers to himself. Throughout his work the reader is reminded that the subjective experiences and observations of the writer form the main focus of the volume. Yet his descriptions bring to life the interaction of groups and their idiosyncrasies in a period of social and cultural transformation and adaptation, something that is often missing in contemporary travel accounts, in which African cultures are usually described as static and timeless. Notwithstanding the state of flux in this transitional period of colonial history, when the power and traditional way of life of local communities was being considerably eroded and undermined, the presence of the local people is asserted through the medium of photography.

Today we recognise that the cultural diversity of South Africa constitutes one of our major national assets. This book sets out to draw on this dynamic by uncovering the rich resources within our cultural heritage, particularly works of cultural and historical importance from overseas collections, and making them accessible to the South African public. The 234 of Gustav Fritsch's South African photographs reproduced in this book were retrieved from the Ethnologisches Museum, Staatliche Museen zu Berlin, Stiftung Preußischer Kulturbesitz (from the collection of the BGAEU) (EM-SMB). Four of his South African portraits have also been sourced from the National Library of South Africa Visual Collection, Cape Town Campus (NLSA), and one has been sourced from the Berlin Society for Anthropology, Ethnology and Prehistory (BGAEU).

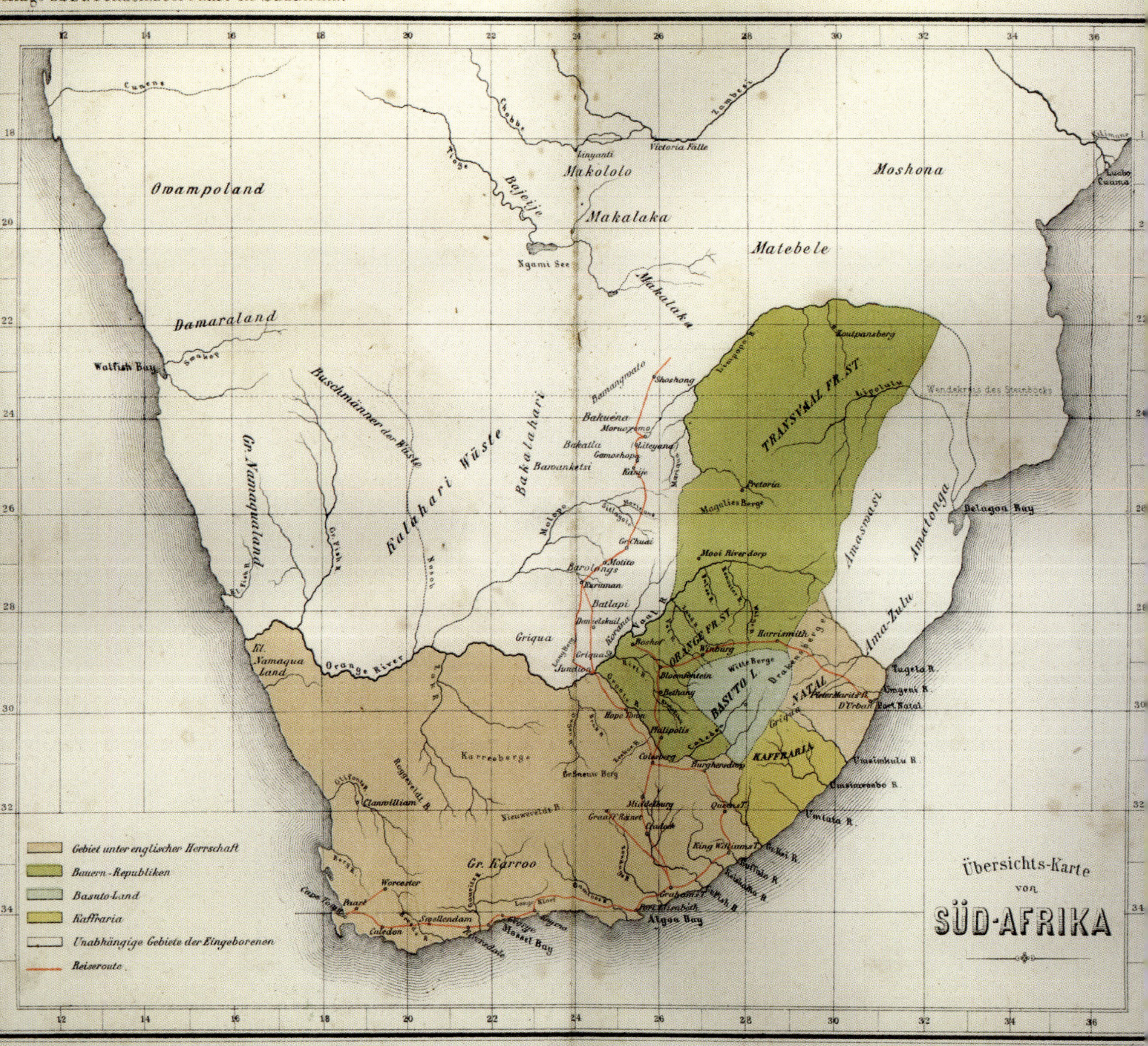

▲ This map of southern Africa plots Fritsch's route (shown in red) on his two expeditions during his three years of travel in the region. (*Drei Jahre in Süd-Afrik*

Introduction
The life and photographic career of
Gustav Theodor Fritsch, 1838–1927

Andrew Bank

We know frustratingly little about the private life of Gustav Theodor Fritsch. For a man who came to play a prominent role as a scientist and public intellectual in Berlin for some fifty years – from the 1860s through to the 1910s – he left remarkably few remains with which to piece together any coherent story about his personal development or inner life. This is as true of visual as of documentary records. Ironically, while we know a considerable amount about the photographic ideas of Fritsch and about the many hundreds of photographs that he took during his career, there are just a few photographic images in which he himself appears.

The only surviving portraits of Fritsch are two cabinet-size prints that feature in one of the 39 albums in the Africa Department of the Museum of Ethnology in Berlin. This album (no. 21) was compiled by Richard Neuhauss, then photographic archivist of the Berlin Society for Anthropology, Ethnology and Prehistory. It is entitled 'Pictures of African Researchers' and contains portraits of the leading Africanists of Fritsch's generation. The two images of him were taken by different photographers, probably a few years apart – one by J.C. Schaarwächter in October and the portrait reproduced here by Carl Günther just a few years later.[1] There is a severe consistency about these portraits, both of which feature the jacket, the substantial grey beard, the askant glance and a distant gaze.

The only other photograph of Fritsch that we have been able to trace is one in which he appears in a group portrait of members of the Berlin Society for Anthropology, Ethnology and Prehistory probably taken around 1880, to judge from the approximate age of Fritsch in this photograph (he was about 40).[2] Here we can make out a jacket, parted hair and full beard, but given the shadow on his face and his downward glance, there is no means of making eye contact with the subject, of eliciting more sense of personality from this photograph. The closest we get to an image of Gustav Fritsch as a young man and Fritsch as the photographer of the elegant 'picture gallery' of southern African portraits which are the centrepiece of this book comes in an illustration in his travelogue, *Drei Jahre in Süd-Afrika*, published in Breslau in 1868, two years after his return from his three-year-long African travels. This is one of a few illustrations in which Fritsch the travelling scientist, or 'impartial observer' as he described himself in the Preface, is inserted into the foreign landscape to which he introduced his popular German readership. The image was reworked from a photograph, possibly one taken in the field by an assistant. It shows the author (who is not mentioned in the caption) examining a protea specimen plucked from one of the flowering bushes that feature in the foreground of this landscape. The angle from which we see Table Mountain in the background suggests that the photograph on which this illustration was based was taken on the lower slopes of Lion's Head, most likely in the late months of 1863 shortly after Fritsch's arrival in Cape Town. There is enough similarity with the Fritsch of the late 1870s photograph to confirm that this is indeed the traveller's self-image. Here he is attired in the manner of the gentleman traveller with jacket, walking stick and hat for protection against the African sun.

Such then are the visual fragments. What of the documentary traces? The libraries and archives in Berlin, unfortunately, contain no collection of private papers for Fritsch, comparable to the collections of his more famous colleagues in the Berlin Society, like Rudolf Virchow or Felix von Luschan.[3] One of Fritsch's granddaughters has kept a few letters that he wrote to his mother from southern Africa in 1864 and 1865, but this is all we have in the way of private papers.[4] The only more substantial source of data is a single official form on which Fritsch recorded information about his life. He was then in his early eighties, as the form was filled in on his eventual retirement after more than fifty years of work at the King Frederick William University in Berlin (today's Humboldt University).[5] Given the format, the information consists primarily of personal achievements and, as such, is more revealing of the public than the private man.

Fritsch's handwritten inscription dedicating a copy of his travelogue, *Drei Jahre*, to Wilhelm Bleek, c.1869.

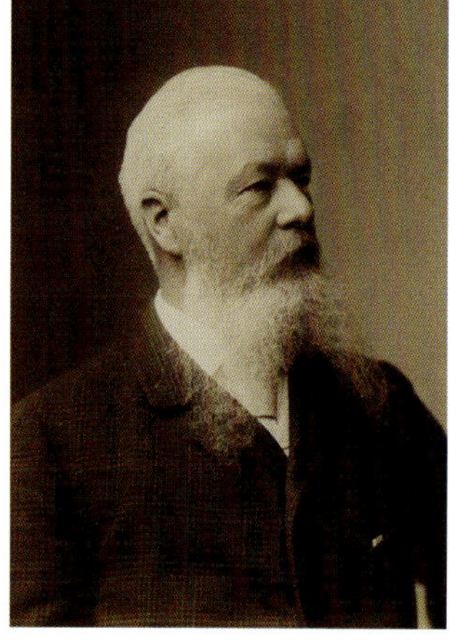

Gustav Fritsch, Berlin, early 1900s (EM-SMB/21/P11193).

Here we read (and the occasional brief biographical sketch confirms)[6] that Gustav Theodor Fritsch was born on 5 March 1838 in Cottsbus. His home town lay about a hundred kilometres downstream and south-east of 'Athens on the Spree', as Berlin was then often known. From biographical sketches we learn that Fritsch's father was a land surveyor named Ludwig and that his mother's name was Sophie. We know that his father died in 1841 when the young boy was just three years of age. He was therefore raised by his mother,[7] which helps to explain the deep sense of personal debt expressed towards her in the acknowledgement on the title page of his southern African travelogue, 'To a loyal mother dedicated with heartfelt gratitude'.

The pink form in the university archive relates that Gustav began school at a gymnasium in Cottsbus, as one might expect, but then moved – perhaps in his early teens – to the Marie-Magdalena Gymnasium in the larger town of Breslau, two hundred kilometres east of Cottsbus and close to the Polish border. He matriculated here in 1857 and then at the age of 19 enlisted for a year in the Prussian army as a volunteer infantryman. In all likelihood his regiment, the 2nd Regiment of the Guards, would have been stationed in Breslau.

In 1858 the 20-year-old Gustav Fritsch enrolled to study natural science at the University of Breslau. His early studies in this field are the clue to explaining the focus of one of his first published articles, that documenting the insect life of southern Africa.[8] After a few years Fritsch moved first to Heidelberg University and then to Berlin University, where he studied medicine. He graduated for the first part of his medical degree at Berlin University on 9 August 1862 with a dissertation on the spinal cord. It was only after his return from his southern African travels that Fritsch was awarded his full degree after submitting a 46-page *Habilitation* on the characteristics of microcephalics (people born with unusually small skulls and brains), a topical subject among his future anthropological colleagues.[9]

The most detailed inventory of achievements in this late-life retrospective features under the subheading 'military career'. During his second year of study at university, Fritsch passed an officer's examination. Eight days after arriving back from his travels in southern Africa, Fritsch enlisted to fight in the war against Austria. From June to September 1866 he was based in a battalion in Breslau, rising to the rank of Second Lieutenant. Fritsch proudly recorded the string of military honours that he was awarded after the Austro-Prussian War. Four years later, when Prussia went to war with France, Fritsch re-enlisted. He served as an officer in an infantry regiment from 24 July 1870 until 23 March 1871, and recalled his participation in the sieges of Strasbourg and Paris. He was again rewarded with military honours, and was eventually promoted to the rank of First Lieutenant in 1873.

The document also contains bare details about Gustav Fritsch's family life. He married Helen Hirt, daughter of the publisher of his 1868 travelogue and his subsequent scientific study on southern Africa, *Die Eingeborenen Süd-Afrika's* (1872). We can speculate that Fritsch met his future wife while negotiating about the publication of his first book. Though he was close on 30, his future wife Helen was still a teenager, being only 18 years old when the book was published. Their first child, a daughter named Hildegard, was born in 1873. Their second child, Erich, was born in April 1876 and would become an artist in later life. Fritsch's comment in the margin next to his name – 'insecure and sickly' – suggests (in the early 1920s at least) a sense of parental disappointment. We can only guess whether Erich's choice of profession was part of his father's dismissive attitude, for Fritsch's published writings in his later years reveal a deep distaste for modern art and, in particular, what he saw as the highly distorted representations of the body by modern artists. Railing against modern art movements was a prominent theme of his writings of the

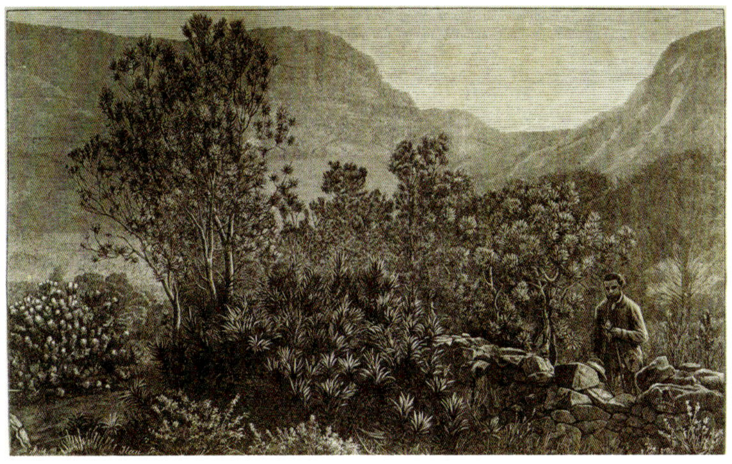

◀ Wood engraving of Fritsch (*Drei Jahre*, Fig. 2).

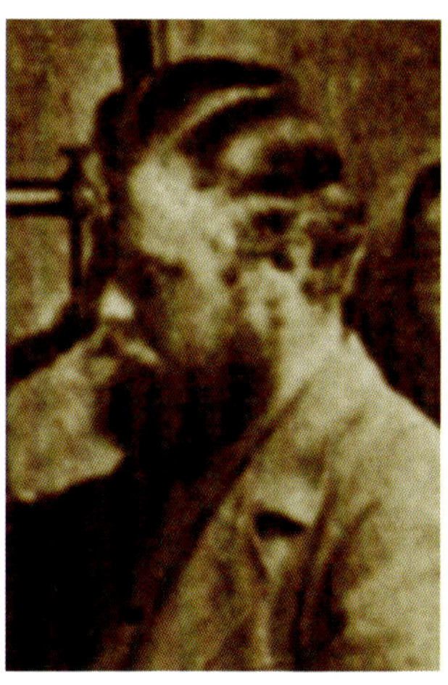

Gustav Fritsch, about 40 years old, from a group photograph of members of the Berlin Society for Anthropology, Ethnology and Prehistory (T. Theye (ed.), *Der geraubte Schatten*)

1890s and early 1900s.[10] The Fritsches' third child, another daughter named Editha, was born in June 1878. She later married an officer in the Prussian Army, but was left widowed by the early 1920s, most probably during the First World War. We also learn that Fritsch was married for 44 years: his wife Helen herself died in 1915 when he was 77 years of age.

The papers in the university archive are silent on Fritsch's career as a photographer, the aspect of his career that most closely concerns us in this book. For information on his photography and associated travels and academic career, we are forced to turn to his published writings, beginning with his southern African travelogue. Here we learn that he left Plymouth on a self-funded expedition to southern Africa in August 1863, a year after his graduation ceremony in Berlin. He had already spent some time reading in the libraries of Berlin, Paris and London. After arriving in Cape Town in early September, he stayed at a German guest house in the centre of town and spent a further few months reading documents and published works in the Grey Library, curated by his more famous fellow graduate from Berlin, Wilhelm Bleek. Michael Godby suggests in his essay in this volume that there is little evidence of a warm relationship between the two men, especially as Fritsch made no mention of Bleek in his travelogue but did mention others whom he met at the South African Library, notably Edward Layard, the curator of the South African Museum (then housed in the same building). However, we do know that Fritsch later donated at least 48 prints of his southern African portraits to the Grey Library and an inscribed copy of his travelogue to Wilhelm Bleek shortly after its publication. The inscription in Fritsch's handwriting reads: 'Dedicated by the Author to his Esteemed Friend, Dr Bleek'. Wilhelm Bleek's co-researcher and sister-in-law, Lucy Lloyd, used the high-quality illustrations in this very copy of the travelogue as a way of accumulating vocabulary in the highly complex /Xam language in the early days of their now famous research project on /Xam language and folklore.[11]

We also know that Bleek effusively promoted Fritsch's later scientific study on southern Africa, *Die Eingeborenen Süd-Afrika's*, and especially his photographic portraiture in a review written for readers of the local intellectual journal, the *Cape Monthly Magazine*. While he had quibbles about the misspelling of Grey (as 'Gray') and elements of Fritsch's system of racial classification, there is no doubting the laudatory tone. 'The present work gives the results of his scientific anthropological studies, on account of which he undertook the expedition. The author, who is an excellent photographer, took himself on his travels the photographs of more than a hundred natives, representatives of different races; each head being in profile and *en face*. Most of these photographs (specimens of which can be seen in the Grey Library, to which the author kindly presented a good many) were afterwards etched in copper, and thus form the magnificent atlas accompanying the letter-press text of this work. We particularly direct our readers' attention to this part of the work, as it is one which even those who do not understand German can fully appreciate. But the fact is that the author has with great industry collected, arranged, and gone through the great mass of the existing published (and even much unpublished) material, for a knowledge of the Natives of South Africa south of the tropic of Capricorn; and, in consequence, his work has become an indispensable compendium for any one who may in any way occupy himself with the anthropology and ethnology of these regions.'[12]

Most of Fritsch's 'native portraits' were taken during his first, year-long expedition, from November 1863 until November 1864, which took him through the Eastern Cape, the Orange Free State and into Natal. In a rare private letter, written by Gustav Fritsch to his mother from Cape Town on 1 February 1865, the month before he

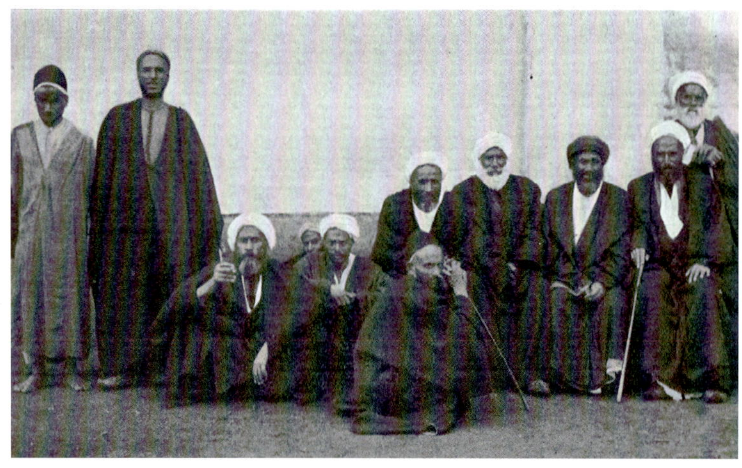

'Mixed population of the Delta, from own photograph', 1881. (G. Fritsch, *Aegyptische Volkstypen der Jetztzeit*, Fig. 5).

embarked on his second expedition, from March 1865 until the end of 1865, which took him through the northern regions of the Cape Colony and into Bechuanaland, Fritsch reported that he had already accumulated most of his portrait collection. He had brought together 179 photographs (here referring to the portraits), as well as 52 stereoscopes and 60 landscapes.[13] We might speculate, then, that he ended up taking close to 300 portrait photographs in all.

In the first part of this book, Keith Dietrich presents 234 of Fritsch's South African photographs. All but five of these photographs have been sourced from the photographic collection of the Berlin Society for Anthropology, Ethnology and Prehistory kept in the Africa Department of the Museum of Ethnology in Berlin.[14] The photographs from the Museum of Ethnology are archived in Albums 13, 15, 18, 28, 30 and 32. Album 13 contains 126 full-negative reprints of Fritsch's South African photographs that formed part of Carl Dammann's *Anthropologisch-ethnologisches Album in Photographien herausgegeben mit Unterstützung aus der Sammlung der Berliner Anthropologischen Gesellschaft* (1874). In so doing, Dietrich seeks to set up the archive of images in a new way, grounding them firmly in an African context. By tracking down and retrieving these images of a highly eclectic range of peoples of southern Africa from their fragmentary appearances in six albums hidden away in a small storeroom of a museum in an outlying suburb of Berlin, Dietrich seeks to re-appropriate these images and re-present them in newly contextualised form. In the present volume, the photographs are ordered (not by 'racial type', as Fritsch would do in his 1872 study, or by album, as they are encountered in the museum), but in the sequence in which they were taken, a sequence of places and photographic occasions that can be reconstructed, often in some detail, by a close reading of the narrative of the journey that Fritsch worked up from the field-notes he made on site. In general, Dietrich's

essay highlights the ambiguity and complexity in Fritsch's relationship towards the subjects that sat before his lens. It is also suggestive of the ways in which the original portraits somehow exceed the boundaries initially imposed upon them by Fritsch. They allow us to uncover, in some cases more than others, small stories of African people whose lives and appearances are documented nowhere else.

The year after his return to Berlin in 1866 (and following his active service in the Prussian military), Fritsch was appointed as an assistant in the Anatomy Department at the King Frederick William University. On 31 August 1871, he was appointed as a full-time lecturer in the Anatomy Department and three years later a Professor. (In 1893 he would be appointed as an Honorary Professor, only retiring eventually under pressure from the university authorities in March 1921 at the age of 83!)[15] In his early years in the Anatomy Department, Fritsch worked under Professor C.B. Reichert, co-editor of the medical journal *Anatomische Physiologische Wissenschaft*. It was here that Fritsch published his first article on anatomy, based on work he had done with Eduard Hitzig on the localisation of brain functions, the findings of which his co-author promoted as 'a new kind of phrenology'.[16]

It was, however, in the anthropological community, in particular that of the Berlin Society of Anthropology, that Fritsch found his true intellectual home. While he published in a wide range of other journals in his early years, including medical, geographical, entomological and photographic journals, his ideas were increasingly tested out on his anthropological peers in Berlin. Fritsch was a founder member of the Berlin Society of Anthropology in 1869 and served as the organisation's assistant secretary in the early 1870s. He would remain a highly vocal presence within this organisation for some 40 years. It is in his articles in its journal, *Zeitschrift für Ethnologie*, and his frequent addresses at

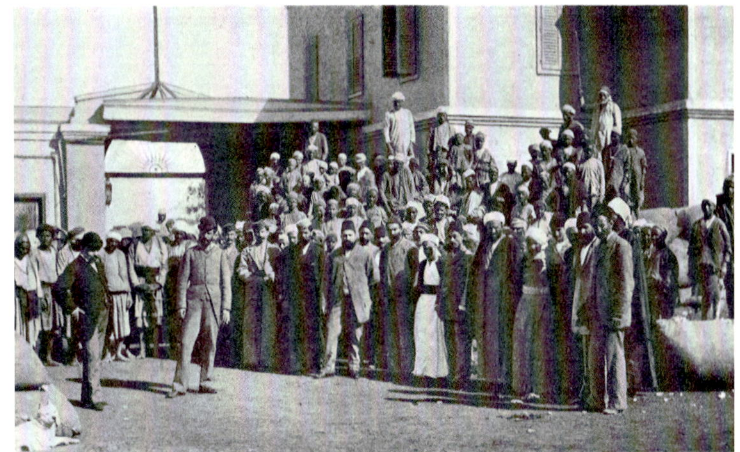

'Cotton farmers of the Delta, from own photograph', 1881. (G. Fritsch, *Aegyptischen Volkstypen der Jetztzeit*, Fig. 4).

its meetings, the proceedings of which were published in its pages, that we can most accurately track the photographic career of Gustav Fritsch. I think of his photographic career in three overlapping phases, each associated with a different attitude towards the people who were the main subjects of his anthropological photographs.

The first phase was the southern African photographic work of the mid-1860s, which forms the focus of the first part of this volume and the essays by Michael Godby and Andrew Bank in the second. One of the central issues raised in these two essays is how the 'honorific' portraits that Fritsch took during his two years of travels, many of African chiefs and mission converts, relate to the racial attitudes expressed in his travelogue. Godby argues that the artistic tradition in which Fritsch located his portraits of 'racial types' encouraged this 'honorific' framing of his subjects at a time before the 'repressive' aspect of portrait photography had developed. This, Godby suggests, is how we can square the 'honorific' portraits with the often dismissive attitudes towards Africans expressed in the text of his travelogue. My own essay proposes that the racial attitudes Fritsch expressed in his travelogue were still relatively open-ended and consistently ambiguous. While there is certainly evidence of stereotyping and expressions of frustration with Africans whom he encountered, my reading of the narrative suggests that it is not out of keeping with the 'honorific' tradition in which he cast his portraiture. I attempt to highlight the degree of Fritsch's curiosity and engagement with African culture, particularly in the latter stages of his journey, contrasting this 'ethnological' (or culturally oriented) attitude and the tone in his writing style with the much harsher and strongly physical emphasis of his anthropological writing in his scientific study of 1872, *Die Eingeborenen*, where the portraits were re-presented and interpreted in the text according to bodily characteristics rather than culture.

Although the photographic work of Fritsch was confined to the mid-1860s, he remained the Society's unofficial expert on southern African history and ethnology during subsequent decades, often presenting his portrait photographs and travel illustrations at meetings. On the eve of the publication of *Die Eingeborenen*, at the December 1871 meeting, Fritsch gave a public presentation of his southern African portrait photographs, commenting in detail on the processes of their production and defending the integrity of the process of translation from photograph to etching. During the 1870s Fritsch commented frequently on the physical characteristics and rock art of the Bushmen, including remarks about the veracity of a portrait photograph of Wilhelm Bleek's main informant, //Kabbo, which had come before the Society through Bleek's old mentor, Richard Lepsius, and on his conviction that certain rock art drawings located by missionaries in Damaraland were indeed the work of Bushmen.[17] On the occasion of a 15-year-old Sotho boy being presented before the Society at a meeting in 1873 (one of many such *Völkerschauen*),[18] Fritsch provided his peers with a detailed account of the history of the Sotho up to recent times.[19] At the time of the Anglo-Zulu War, Fritsch presented background information on the history and ethnography of the Zulu, including the story of the rise of Shaka. There was a visual dimension to his presentation on 21 February 1880: 'Mr Fritsch discusses the end of the Zulu wars by using many photographs and drawings.'[20] It is likely that his own portraits of the Zulu, focusing on their hair-styling practices, were among the illustrative materials that he used.

There is also evidence that Fritsch exploited fresh opportunities to recycle his southern African photographic collection and present them to new audiences. A fellow member of the Free Photographic Association, founded in Berlin in 1889, later reported on Fritsch's fresh presentation of his southern African portraits at the Museum of

Ethnology in Berlin in November 1893: 'Based on the great success of this and subsequent evenings the wish for a large electrical projector to be installed in a big auditorium was expressed by the Free Photographic Association. Because of the links with the Berlin Society for Anthropology and the Royal Museum of Ethnology, the projector was finally installed in the auditorium of the Museum of Ethnology and on 20 November 1893, it enabled an "old African", our chairman Professor Gustav Fritsch, to herald the new era of projector evenings with his talk "South Africa 30 years ago".'[21]

Fritsch's other acknowledged area of expertise was photography. The importance of visual methods in the emerging German anthropological community is still open debate. While Andrew Zimmerman has argued that visual methods were at the very centre of the anthropological approach of the new German school, and that of Berlin in particular, Andreas Broeckmann's essay in this volume advocates a more cautious attitude. In his analysis, Fritsch's advocacy of a new theory of photography and his declarations of the anthropological potential of photography ran against, rather than with, the German anthropological grain from the 1870s onwards. Broeckmann demonstrates that Fritsch developed a sophisticated visual theory as he came to promote the superiority of photographic over other visual forms of documentation, the importance of close collaborative relationships between photographers and the scientists or publishers who produced drawings based on their photographs, and a very precise set of guidelines for the taking of anthropological and ethnographic photographs in a handbook for travellers published in 1875. This included contributions by Fritsch's more famous scientific peers like Rudolf Virchow and Adolf Bastian. Fritsch's essay in this collection, which also looked at the use of the microscope by travellers, was republished with very little alteration in the 1888 and 1906 editions of this collection, suggesting that he remained an acknowledged expert in the field of photography. It also suggests, as Broeckmann argues, that there was relatively little interest among the German anthropological community in updating these guidelines despite the obvious and momentous changes in photographic technology over these three decades.

Whereas southern Africa had been the focus of his photographic work in the 1860s, the Orient (broadly conceived) became the focus of what I interpret as the second phase of Fritsch's career as an anthropological photographer from the 1870s through to the 1900s. During this period he expanded beyond the genre of individual portraiture. His anthropological photographs of the peoples of the Orient came to include the genres of group portraiture and micro-photography.

His first work in this new phase may be dated to 1874, when he led a Prussian expedition to Persia. While astronomical observations were the primary goal of this journey, Fritsch used the opportunity to expand his portfolio of images of 'racial types'. When he reported back to the Berlin Society 'On the present-day habits and physical characteristics of the Tribes [*Völker*] of the Orient',[22] he presented an illustrated lecture which included photographs of market scenes and architecture as well as numerous portraits of 'racial types' in Persia. He expressed regret at not having acquired more such images, which he attributed variously to the shyness of his subjects and the Persian cultural practice of restricting visits to an hour before sunset.[23]

Some six years later, Fritsch embarked on a photographic field-trip to Egypt. Fritsch had visited Egypt once before, in 1868, as a member of an earlier astronomical expedition to observe a solar eclipse. But his trip had been cut short by illness and I have been unable to find evidence of any surviving photographs from 1868. The photographs that Fritsch took in 1881 represent a departure from the genres of individual portraiture and landscape photography that he had accumulated on his journey through southern Africa. A large brown rectangular box in the Africa Section of the Berlin Museum of Ethnology contains a selection of these images: 12 cabinet-size prints pasted (probably by Richard Neuhauss) on to three cardboard sheets, each headed 'Egypt'. Apart from a photograph of a market scene taken in Esneh and another entitled 'Town Djellal. Upper Egypt', the remaining prints were all taken in the town of Al-Mansurah, a hundred kilometres north of Cairo on the Nile Delta. Most of them were shot at a particular cotton factory, Firma Planta & Company. The photographs variously show street scenes outside the factory, factory workers (identified as fellahin) collecting their wages at a counter with lines of men and lines of women in separate photographs, and group portraits of cotton farmers who had recently delivered their produce to the factory. Fritsch reproduced two of these group portraits in his later book on the 'races of Egypt', along with the unusual scene of the diverse employees of the factory standing in the street outside the building, with cotton bales framing the image. His comments in the accompanying text suggest the ambiguity between a 'racial reading' of the group portrait and his decision to present a complex and mixed scene of social and economic interaction. 'The photograph is attached because I cannot think of a better way to illustrate in one single glance the remarkable and mixed races of the Delta. We can see in the foreground the slim figure of the manager of the factory, a Greek, to his left his accountant a Swiss, on the right towards the back the technician a German, between and towards the back a few Italians as well as the mixed but recognisable group of Levantines, on the far right in the front an Armenian, adjoining these on top of the terrace-like cotton bales are to be found the majority of the Fellahin workers, right at the back towers an Arab overseer who directs with a steady hand a stick to calm the agitated masses.'[24]

It is tempting to speculate that the last three photographs in the series, household scenes from what the captions identify as 'A fellahin settlement in Al-Mansurah', were taken in the households of the factory workers. The captions to these prints, like 'Fellahin at a mealtime (Al-Mansurah, Delta)', suggest an unusual preoccupation with the ordinary in what come closest to 'fieldwork-type' photographs of a modern anthropological kind.

Fritsch's work as a travelling photographer in the Orient still displays a degree of eclecticism and diversity. He wrote articles in the *Zeitschrift für Ethnologie* on the representation of the human body in the antique sculpture of Persia and the portrait character of Ancient Egyptian monuments.[25]

Fritsch's second major expedition to Egypt was undertaken in 1898–1899 with much more narrowly racial scientific motives in mind. From the mid- to late 1880s onwards, in the context of Germany's colonisation of Africa and other parts of the world (a development that Fritsch outspokenly supported), his racial ideology had become more rigid, arguably more extreme than that of most of his scientific peers in the Berlin Society. He was now almost obsessively preoccupied with obtaining photographic data on the physical anthropology of non-European 'races'.

In 1904 Fritsch published the results of his photographic expedition in a study entitled *Ägyptische Volkstypen der Jetztzeit* (1904). The book featured 52 members of the 'Egyptian races' photographed in naked and in full-body form, each in front, rear and side profile view. Following the precedent he had established in his southern African *Atlas*, published over thirty years earlier, Fritsch presented the 'races' in a hierarchy from what he considered to be the most evolved to those he considered least evolved. In southern Africa the series had proceeded from the Zulu down to the Bushmen. In the case of North Africa this racial hierarchy ran from the Levantine down to the Arabic and Egyptian and ending up with the 'Negroid racial type'. The captions suggest that many of these subjects were photographed at hospitals in Cairo and Alexandria. Fritsch expressed his gratitude to the European doctors at these institutions for allowing him access to subjects who, one might assume, had no rights of refusal, and for taking photographs along the guidelines that he had set out. The bodily evidence of this institutional context is visible from the diseases of a number of those photographed, from syphilis to skin disorders.

Fritsch's obsession with the naked bodies of non-Europeans is also evident from his compilation of an album of 375 photographs of *Aktstudien* (nude studies) that he compiled around the turn of the century. To the naked portraits of the races of Egypt, he added naked and often erotic images of men and women, many taken by himself on his tours of the Orient in 1903–1904 and 1906. There are many photographs of women from Egypt, India, the East Indies and Japan. Some 30 of these women are identified in the captions as *Freuden-mädchen* (prostitutes). In 1919 Fritsch donated what had hitherto presumably been a private (and perhaps secret) album to the Berlin Society for Anthropology.[26]

Prisoners rather than hospital patients or sex workers were the subjects (or, in this instance undoubtedly, the objects) of Fritsch's next major photographic project in the field of racial science. Here his photographic work was on a microscopic level, by now a very well-established genre in the medical sciences like anatomy. While Fritsch had promoted the scientific value of micro-photography as early as 1869, he only systematically applied micro-photography to racial classification after the turn of the century, on the basis of data gathered during his two expeditions. In 1903–1904 Fritsch was primarily interested in acquiring micro-photographic evidence of retinas. In his anatomical work on the Andaman Islands over ten days in December 1904, he analysed the retinas of recently deceased male prisoners from 'this veritable laboratory of Indian humankind', arguing in his later published study, *Über Bau und Bedeutung der Area centralis des Menschen* (1908), that retinal characteristics were an important marker of racial difference.[27]

Michael Hagner's essay in this volume analyses Gustav Fritsch's application of micro-photography to the racial classification of hair. Hagner notes that while Fritsch had first published on this subject in 1885 at a time when his anthropological peers in the Berlin Society for Anthropology, like Rudolf Virchow, were also keenly preoccupied with the examination of the hair types of different races, his micro-photographic work in this field culminated in the publication of two 'splendid folios with costly plates' in 1912 and 1915: *Das Haupthaar und seine Bildungsstätte bei den Rassen des Menschen* and *Die menschliche Haupthaaranlage*. Here again his collections of samples in the field provided the raw materials for his racial theory. In this case some of the data derived from the 45 scalps that Fritsch had collected on his travels through India, China, Japan and Australia during his second world tour of 1906.

The third and final phase in the photographic career of Gustav Fritsch, as I have charted it, saw a shift in focus from African and Oriental 'Others' to the European Self. Fritsch's clearest statement on this new direction in his photographic and theoretical work is appropriately expressed in the pages of an 1894 issue of the *Zeitschrift für Ethnologie*. 'For many years it has pained me deeply that in a circle of men who have made it their mission to study humanity that no possibility has presented itself to get to know ourselves, to establish the foundation against which to conduct proper comparisons. It is of no use to see the odd example of foreign races in nature or in photographs because one cannot discern the unusual or deviant as long as we do not know what we ourselves look like.'[28]

His first major attempt to 'get to know the self' was developed in his 1899 study entitled *Die Gestalt des Menschen*. Fritsch set out here to define what he termed 'the normal-ideal person',[29] by deriving a model of perfect body proportions from classical sources, notably from the theory of proportions set out by the Greek sculptor

Polyclitus. As Annette Lewerentz argues in her essay in this volume, Fritsch then used this abstract model as the basis for constructing his own idealised model of bodily proportions, or what he referred to as a 'canon' or 'key of proportions' (*Proportionsschlüssel*). Once this abstract 'canon' had been defined, and the book includes a detailed illustration of this ideal, the bodily configurations of different races could be tested against this 'norm'. Fritsch's primary interest, however, was in the bodies of contemporary Europeans, who seemed to resemble this classically derived norm most closely. The appendix to his book featured 25 plates, which tracked the progression from abstract classical models to the 'normal-ideal' bodies of German athletes whom Fritsch had photographed. Plates 7–12 presented a figure identified by the captions as the Borghese warrior from all possible angles, variously showing skeletal formation, musculature and classical posture. Plates 13–16 then presented a powerful male model variously throwing or balancing a very large rock above his head, in an obvious visual echo of the outstretched posture of the Borghese warrior. Plates 20 and 21 then presented male and female models in an active photographic sequence: 'Walking man (from Muybridge)' and 'Dancing woman (from Muybridge)'.[30] These sequences completed the projection of an abstract model from classical sources into active, living European subjects on the eve of the twentieth century.

The concept of 'racial beauty' implicit in this earlier work became the organising idea of Fritsch's 1911 study, *Nackte Schönheit*. Here we can clearly see that Fritsch had made the transition from photography as science to photography as (racially motivated) art. As Lewerentz emphasises, the photographs of European bodies that Fritsch presented in *Nackte Schönheit* were no longer taken according to any scientific guidelines, let alone those which he himself had so meticulously laid out in his contribution to a 1875 handbook for travellers and which he had followed in his own photographic work in Egypt in 1898 and 1899. As the book's title indicated, a much more abstract sense had by now come to serve as the model of racial measurement and comparison. Significantly enough, Fritsch challenged not only what he saw as the near heretical productions of the modern art movement, but also what he came to consider as an excessive reliance on measurement by physical anthropologists and racial theorists. Whereas he had taken 55 measurements on a single skull in his 1872 study of the 'Native races of South Africa', in 1911 he complained about the dangers of being 'swamped with numbers'.[31] Indeed, Michael Hagner's notion that Fritsch's late turn to micro-photography was an admission of the failure of his earlier quantitative scientific model may be applied equally to his late turn to abstract concepts like the 'canon of proportions' and 'racial beauty'.

As noted earlier in this essay, Fritsch was forced to retire in 1921. He died six years later in Berlin, seemingly a poor man despite his colourful and ostensibly successful career. A letter from his widowed daughter enquired from the authorities at the Frederick William University whether they would pay for her father's funeral. In view of his 52-year-long career, they agreed to do so.

In conclusion, what light does this story of Fritsch's life and career throw on the photographs reproduced in the pages that follow, and in particular on the portraits of the peoples of southern Africa that are the centrepiece of this book? How are we to view visual images produced by a photographer who set out with (at least partly) racial motives in mind and whose racism became increasingly rigid and extreme in his later life, to the extent that his racial thinking by the 1910s and 1920s would have been perfectly in keeping with that of the Nazi ideologues of the new generation?

The first defence of what might be seen as a controversial attempt to resurrect the life and work of an extreme racist is that his photographic output needs to be clearly periodised, as I have sought to do in this introduction. While there remains some debate as to exactly how open Fritsch's racial attitudes were during the first, southern African phase of his photographic work, there is no doubt that his attitudes then were still ambiguous and (at least in my analysis) relatively fluid. The portrait photographs reproduced in the first part of this book were taken with mixed motives: partly as a quest to compile a portfolio of 'racial types', and also partly (I would argue) as a way of celebrating the diversity and complexity of the peoples and cultures encountered on his travels.

The second reason for showcasing these portrait photographs is that, regardless of the exact motives of the man who hid behind the cloth, he was (as Wilhelm Bleek acknowledged at the time) an 'excellent photographer'. It is as well to remember that these portraits were taken no more than 25 years after the invention of photography, and that they compare very favourably in quality to the best portrait photographs of that early phase in the history of photography. Perhaps because of his scientific training, Fritsch was highly adept at the technically demanding process of taking fieldwork photographs, and the lasting appeal of his visual images is testimony to his skills at mixing chemicals, developing prints and carrying out all the demanding tasks required in this precarious early phase of camera-work.

The third reason, one that numerous essays in this volume touch upon (especially that of Lize van Robbroeck most fully and eloquently), is that the photographs – in their very indexical recording of all that came before the lens – spill over, metaphorically speaking, from their frames. As the visual theorist Elizabeth Edwards demonstrates, anthropological photographs have a performative quality, an agency that allows them to transcend the cross-cultural containment associated with a specific photographic occasion in the past. Edwards proposes that we adopt a highly fluid concept of framing.[32] The very ability of the camera to capture the unwanted – in Fritsch's case, this was sometimes the clothing or cultural ornaments worn by his southern

African subjects – encourages this sense of visual images spilling over or somehow exceeding their frames and contexts of construction.

Finally, the portrait photographs that Fritsch took are rare historical documents. In a period in which visual images of Africans are extremely rare and precious – those of European settlers somewhat less so by the mid-1860s – Fritsch produced, regardless of his intentions, a remarkable and unique historical record. For the vast majority of the Africans he photographed, his visual images are the only evidence we have of what they looked like, evidence that can serve as a starting point in piecing together some of the small stories contributing to the complex tapestry that is the history of the southern African interior during the middle decades of the nineteenth century. Surely it would be a great sadness if such a record were to remain buried away in albums in a storeroom in Berlin rather than being re-presented as a fresh and rich archive of African photographs.

ENDNOTES

1   Richard Neuhauss was an anthropological photographer with extensive experience of fieldwork in Egypt. He reordered the Berlin Society for Anthropology's photographic collection in 1908 at a time when the collection consisted of some 12,000 photographs. The number of photographs increased to 17,950 photographs in 1914 and then at a much more moderate rate during the interwar period, numbering 22,771 photographs by 1939. For these figures and an analysis of the history of the collection, see T. Theye, 'Einige Neuigkeiten zu Leben und Werk der Brüder Carl Victor und Friedrich Wilhelm Dammann', *Mitteilungen aus dem Museum für Völkerkunde Hamburg*, 24–25 (1994–1995), 247–204. Today there are 39 albums from the Society's collection stored in the Africa Section of the Berlin Museum of Ethnology dating from the period 1863–c.1940, suggesting that Fritsch's southern African portraits are perhaps the earliest of the photographs in this collection. See C. Stelzig, *Inhaltsverzeichnis der Alben der Berliner Gesellschaft für Anthropologie, Ethnologie und Urgeschichte* (Berlin, 1995).

2   T. Theye (ed.), *Der geraubte Schatten. Photographie als ethnographisches Dokument* (Munich and Berlin, 1989).

3   In his incisive study of *Anthropology and Antihumanism in Imperial Germany* (Chicago and London, 2001), Andrew Zimmerman draws extensively on the collections of private papers left by these leading figures in the Berlin anthropological community.

4   See the essay by Anne Leweretz in this volume.

5   Humboldt University Archive, Registry, Personal files, F, no. 51, vol. 1 (1874–1927), 14 pp.

6   See *Neue Deutsche Biographie*, vol. 5 (Berlin, 1960); O. Spohr, 'Gustav Fritsch' in C.J. Beyers (ed.), *Dictionary of South African Biography* (Cape Town, 1977), 311–312; I. Hilton, 'Introduction' in G. Fritsch, *A German Traveller in Natal* (Durban, 1992), 9–15.

7   *Neue Deutsche Biographie*, vol. 5 (Berlin, 1960); see also Hilton, 'Introduction', 9.

8   G. Fritsch, 'Das Insektenleben Süd-Afrika's', *Berliner Entomologischen Zeitschrift*, 14 (1867).

9   See A. Lewerentz, 'Der Mediziner Gustav Fritsch als Fotograf', *Baessler Archiv* (2001), 272–273. On the anthropological interest in microcephalics, see Zimmerman, *Anthropology and Antihumanism*, 75–77.

10   See the essay by Anne Lewerentz in this volume.

11   On the use of the visuals in Fritsch's *Drei Jahre* in the dialogue between Lucy Lloyd and the first main informant in their work on /Xam language and literature, /A!kunta, in September 1870, see A. Bank, *Bushmen in a Victorian World: The Remarkable Story of the Bleek-Lloyd Collection of Bushman Folklore* (Cape Town, 2006), 87–95.

12   W.H.I. Bleek, 'Dr. Fritsch's Natives of South Africa', *Cape Monthly Magazine*, 6 (March 1873), 173.

13   Letter from Gustav Fritsch to his mother, Cape Town, 1 February 1865, in the possession of Maria Schwabe, as cited Annette Lewerentz, pers. comm., July 2008. My thanks to Annette Lewerentz for this reference.

14   Four of his South African portraits have also been sourced from the National Library of South Africa Visual Collection, Cape Town Campus, while one has been sourced from the Archive of the Berlin Society for Anthropology, Ethnology and Prehistory kept in Charlottenburg, Berlin.

15   Humboldt University Archive, Personal files, F, no. 51, vol. 1 (1874–1927).

16   Their findings were based on experiments conducted on applying electricity to the brains of dogs. Andrew Zimmerman cites their work as evidence of the strongly physical orientation of the Berlin anthropologists of the late 1860s and early 1870s (see Zimmerman, *Anthropology and Antihumanism in Imperial Germany*, 53–54).

17   For an analysis of Fritsch and the Berlin Society of Anthropology's comments on the //Kabbo portrait, see Bank, *Bushmen in a Victorian World*, 186–189; on his comments on Bushman rock art, see the English translation of his article by H.C. Schunke in G. Fritsch, 'Rock paintings existing near !Ameib in Damaraland, South Africa', *Cape Monthly Magazine*, 18 (April 1879), 1–6.

18   On these Völkerschauen, see especially Zimmerman, *Anthropology and Antihumanism*, 'Exotic spectacles in the global context of German anthropology', 15–37.

19   *Zeitschrift für Ethnologie*, 5 (1873), Record of Proceedings 14.6.1873, 103-5.

20   *Zeitschrift für Ethnologie*, 12 (1880), 295.

21   Goerke cited in Theye, *Der geraubte Schatten*, 68.

22   *Zeitschrift für Ethnologie*, 8 (1876), 160-4.

23   *Zeitschrift für Ethnologie*, 7 (1875), 63.

24   G. Fritsch, *Ägyptische Volkstypen der Jetztzeit: Nach anthropologischen Grundsätzen aufgenommene Aktstudien* (Wiesbaden, 1904).

25   See, for example, G. Fritsch, 'Die Baudenkmäler in Persien', *Zeitschrift für Ethnologie*, 9 (1877), 224–229; G. Fritsch, 'Portraitcharaktere der altägyptischen Denkmäler', *Zeitschrift für Ethnologie*, 15 (1883), 183–189.

26   It is today part of the Archive of the Society for Anthropology, housed in Charlottenburg, Berlin. For more detailed discussion of this Album see Lewerentz, 'Der Mediziner Gustav Fritsch als Fotograf'.

27   C. Anderson, *Legible Bodies: Race, Criminality and Colonialism in South Asia* (Oxford and New York, 2004), 198–200.

28   G. Fritsch, 'Beiträge zur Kenntnis unserer Körperform', *Zeitchrift für Ethnologie*, 26 (1894), 25.

29   G. Fritsch, *Die Gestalt des Menschen* (Stuttgart, 1899), 91.

30   For reproductions of many of these plates, see Annette Lewerentz's essay in this volume.

31   Cited by Anne Lewerentz in this volume.

32   See E. Edwards, *Raw Histories: Photographs, Anthropology and Museums* (Oxford, 2001).

Part One

Emulsions, memories and histories

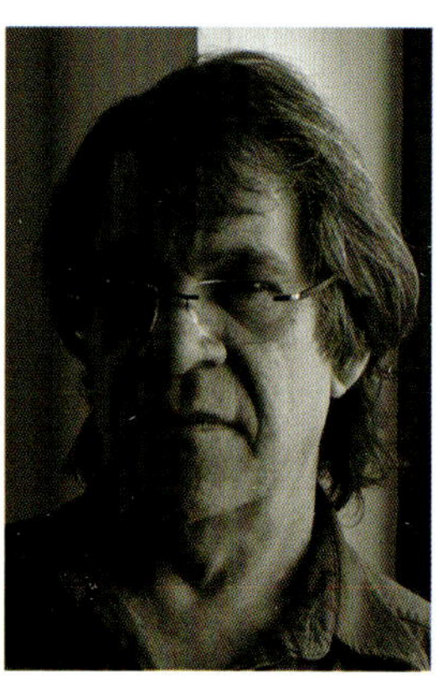

Keith Dietrich

Gustav Fritsch's contribution to southern African travel and anthropological illustration was unique. His detailed photographic records of people and landscapes he encountered on his travels were both original and pioneering. Until the latter part of the nineteenth century, photographs had played a minor role in travel and anthropological illustration. Earlier traveller-ethnographers, such as Peter Kolb, Anders Sparrman, François le Vaillant, Samuel Daniell, William Burchell, George French Angas and Thomas Baines, relied on second- or first-hand field sketches as source material for their studies and book illustrations. Their field observations were generally first captured on paper in pencil and wash, water-based paints and ink wash drawings, which were then later worked up into illustrations that appeared in popular and scientific literature.

The technological shortcomings in the printing process of the time as regards the reproduction of photographs were not a serious impediment to Fritsch's exclusive reliance on photographic means of recording. The wood engravings and etchings illustrating his books are all closely and accurately based on the photographs he took on his travels. His visual material is not mainly of aesthetic interest, as are the illustrations of Daniell and Angas, or simply sketches to enliven or enhance his text, as are the vignettes of Burchell and Baines, but forms a fundamental and integral part of his ethnological observations to which he constantly refers in *Die Eingeborenen* and its accompanying *Atlas*. Having made a comprehensive study of travel and scientific literature regarding South Africa before his journey through the country, Fritsch was keenly aware of the problems around the visual material illustrating Africans produced in Europe by draughtsmen and engravers. In *Die Eingeborenen*, he constantly referred to misconceptions created by these illustrations, his main criticism being their lack of accuracy and scientific value.[1]

It was the status of his photographs as scientific data for his anthropological project of recording a way of life that was already fast disappearing that Fritsch was keen to assert. In his introduction to *Die Eingeborenen,* Fritsch drew attention to the continuing disintegration of the traditional life and customs of indigenous South Africans under the pressures of colonialism. This cultural demise lent increasing urgency to the need articulated by European ethnologists to obtain more extensive and accurate pictorial records of local people before they were swept away on the tide of acculturation. Accordingly, Fritsch stated in his book that the purpose of his work was to provide a factual physical and anthropological description of local people in order to conserve a record of their disappearing social life and thereby promote knowledge about the origin and development of humankind as a whole.[2] He acknowledged his fortunate position as an anthropologist who had the opportunity to get to know indigenous peoples in their 'original' state.

At the time that Fritsch undertook his journeys through the sub-continent, the region had passed through a period of fundamental social, political and cultural change, involving substantial migrations of populations, the dispossession of ancestral lands and the emergence of white-dominated colonial and republican states and capitalist markets. In just over fifty years the eastern Cape had endured eight frontier wars between the Xhosa and Dutch and British colonial governments. Likewise, the Orange Free State, northern Cape and Bechuanaland had experienced embittered struggles involving the Tlokwa, Sotho, Ndebele, Tswana, Korana, San, Griqua and Boer trekkers. As a result of such conflict and upheaval, the way of life of many indigenous communities was being irreversibly transformed, and the onslaught of colonialism was threatening to sweep away traditional forms of social organisation before they could be scientifically observed and recorded. Fritsch's role was thus urgent and pressing.

Given that Fritsch's *Drei Jahre* and *Die Eingeborenen* have not yet been translated from German, and that his collection of southern African photographs has not yet been published in full, the primary

Keith Dietrich studied design and fine art at Stellenbosch University and the National Higher Institute of Fine Arts in Antwerp, Belgium. He holds a DLitt et Phil in Art History from the University of South Africa (Unisa) and has worked at the University of Pretoria and Unisa. He is currently Chair of the Department of Visual Arts, Stellenbosch University, and his areas of research include painting, book art and cultural studies.

task of Part One is to present his photographs in a way that allows them to speak for themselves in respect of what Fritsch was seeing and recording as an anthropological traveller and photographer. Part One therefore closely follows Fritsch's travel narrative and, alongside the photographs, provides a contextualising description of both the places he visited and the people he photographed, together with a summary of the observations he made in his travel accounts. Seen against the background of Fritsch's concern with race studies which preoccupied his academic career, his photographs of individual people from southern Africa are highly ambiguous in meaning. I have consciously tried to avoid giving my own critical interpretations of his photographs and texts in order not to divert attention from their complexity.

The sequence of the photographs in Part One follows the steps of Fritsch's journey through southern Africa. Fritsch often stressed the difficulties he encountered in photographing people for the purposes of his study. As he ventured northwards on his second journey to Bechuanaland, he met with increasing problems. By the time he reached Shoshong he saw no reason to continue, as he found that people were becoming far too difficult to photograph. Given the photographic techniques used at the time and the organisational intricacies in setting up photographic shoots with the co-operation of his subjects, considerable skill was required to produce accurate and reliable images. Fritsch was also bent on securing accurate measurements of the faces of his subjects, for which he used callipers. In his *Atlas* Fritsch discussed the co-ordinates of his measurements and provided a table recording the measurements of the people he photographed.[3] He mentioned that some of his data had been lost and that many subjects did not allow him to measure them.[4] For both his photographic and mensural work, therefore, Fritsch had to rely on mediators (*Mittelpersonen*) – often white missionaries, magistrates or traders –who could communicate his instructions to his subjects. It is possibly for this reason that his portraits were taken around mission stations, villages and towns where mediators were available, or where his subjects understood Dutch or English.

With some exceptions, Fritsch followed a fairly exact procedure when taking his portraits, in order that the scale of the subjects' heads was more or less in proportion to each other and that any form of photographic distortion was minimised. The subjects were seated upright on chairs at a consistently fixed distance from the camera and each person was photographed in full frontal and side views against a light background, which framed the heads and torsos.[5] With the frontal portraits the eyes were fixed more or less on the lens and the faces positioned upright so that both ears were visible. With the side views the subjects' faces were again held in a vertical position with the lower jaw parallel to the ground. In both *Die Eingeborenen* and *Atlas*, Fritsch discussed the importance of having both front and profile views in order to obtain the 'correct' facial measurements. He commented that the differences in the noses from these views were so great that sometimes the two images could seem to be of different people.[6]

In a letter written to his mother from Cape Town on 1 February 1865, Fritsch mentioned having 'prepared a portrait album of 179 images, 52 stereoscopes[7] and 60 views'.[8] Nowhere does he give a detailed account of the photographic process he used. From 1851 the wet collodion plate was widely in use. It required that glass plates be photosensitised on site, exposed while still wet, and developed immediately thereafter. Fritsch mentioned that while in Cape Town he began testing a new method. 'I used these days to prepare myself for a new photographic process that I thought of utilising on my journeys through the country.' He noted that he had taken the opportunity of testing prepared dry plates on his visit to Camps Bay.[9] The success of these tests led him to use the process on his excursion to Robben Island and to take photographs on Table Mountain.[10] It is most likely that Fritsch used the faster wet collodion plates for his portraits and experimented with the dry-plate process for his landscape photographs.

Dry-plate techniques were still in their infancy at the time. Three dry-plate processes had been introduced by the early 1860s, namely the dry collodion, collodio-albumen and tannin processes, the last two proving to be the most successful. With the dry-plate process a number of plates could be prepared and kept for several days, though it remains unclear what dry-plate method Fritsch used. Compared to the wet collodion process, where the exposure time in good lighting conditions was roughly 20 seconds, the dry-plate method needed double or triple the exposure time. When taking photographs of Mfengu people in Port Elizabeth, for instance, Fritsch mentioned that the subjects had to sit still for 20 seconds,[11] and in his *Atlas* he wrote of his frustration when his subjects moved during the exposures and how he had to adjust the focus and take the exposures before the plates dried out. An illustration (Fig. 1) from his *Drei Jahre* depicts his photographic tent standing next to his oxwagon.[12] He mentioned his darkroom tent again in his account of photographing Mfengu people in Port Elizabeth and when capturing a waterfall on the Umgeni River. Wet-plate photography necessitated the use of a dark tent to process the negatives before and after exposure.[13]

Fritsch therefore had to transport not only his camera and tripod through the country, but also his darkroom tent and the highly combustible chemicals used for his glass negatives, which had to be prepared and developed in the field. The wet collodion process was very demanding and involved unpacking the equipment and erecting the portable darkroom tent. The glass plate that would form the negative was first polished, rinsed and buffed with a soft cloth, after which it was then coated with a thin film of collodion emulsion (comprising cellulose nitrate and a mixture of ether and alcohol).[14] Before the ether and alcohol evaporated from the collodion, the plate would be taken into the darkroom tent and dipped into a solution of silver nitrate, where it remained for at least four minutes, allowing the silver nitrate to bond with the collodion to make a photosensitive film. While the plate was in the silver nitrate, it is likely that Fritsch would have seated his subject and focused his camera in preparation for the photograph to be taken. When the plate was ready, it was carefully placed in a lightproof holder, and taken to the camera. The ground-glass plate would be removed from the back of the camera and replaced by the lightproof holder.

Fritsch must have used a folding wet-plate camera designed for the field, with a folding bed or base similar to studio cameras. The ground-glass viewing screens were generally square, and wet-plate lightproof holders had a trough on the bottom to catch the dripping silver nitrate. The holder could only be installed in one direction, and was designed to hold a plate either horizontally or vertically.[15] Wet-plate cameras could also hold dry plates, as the focal length for both plates was the same.

Before the exposure, the 'dark slide' would be removed from the plate holder, exposing the plate to the inside of the camera. The exposure was made by removing the lens cap and counting off the required time, depending on whether a wet plate or dry plate was used. In his *Atlas*, Fritsch mentioned that, because his subjects found it difficult to sit still, he used a 3-inch Dallmeyer portrait lens in order to capture them in shorter exposure times. After the exposure, the lens cap was replaced and the slide placed once again in the plate holder. The holder was then detached from the camera and taken into the darkroom tent, where the plate was removed and developed. Within a few seconds the image would be visible, as the areas exposed to light in the camera turned to metallic silver. When the developing was complete, the developer was removed by washing the plate in clean water.[16] The developed plate would be taken from the darkroom and placed into a tray of sodium hyposulphate to remove the unused silver halides and then washed in fresh water, after which it was dried and sealed with a protective varnish.

As Fritsch mentioned giving one of his sitters a print of his portrait, it is likely that he made prints of his portraits in the field. Albumen-coated paper was the common printing paper of the time. This process involved coating paper with an emulsion of egg white (albumen) and table salt (sodium chloride), which sealed the paper, creating a slightly glossy surface. The paper was then dipped in a solution of silver nitrate and water, which sensitised the surface to light, after which it was dried in total darkness.[17] A contact print would be made with the glass negative by exposing the paper in direct sunlight until the image achieved the desired tonal range, after which the print would be fixed and toned with gold chloride to improve the print and stabilise it against fading.[18] Fritsch's portraits were printed in the *carte de visite* format introduced in 1854, shortly after the invention of the collodion wet plate (measuring roughly 6.35 x 8.89 cm, mounted on a card roughly 6.75 x 10.16 cm). His larger group and landscape photographs were made on Cabinet cards[19] (measuring 10.6 x 13.97 cm, mounted on a card measuring 10.8 x 16.51 cm).

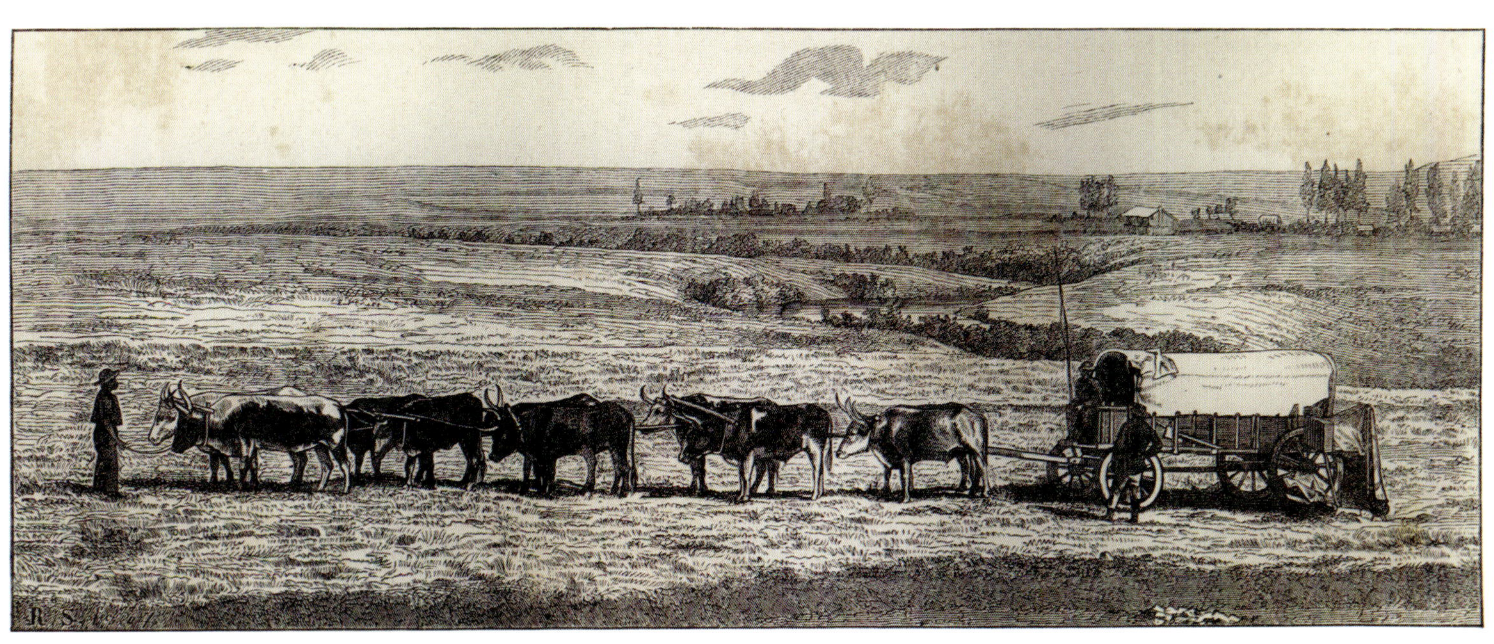

Fig. 1 ▲

Afrikanischer Ochsenwagen, daneben das photographische Zelt. Obere Lauf des Umgeni dicht vor dem Falle.

African oxwagon, nearby which is the photographic tent. Upper reaches of the Umgeni River close to the falls. (*Drei Jahre*, 165)

While in Cape Town, Fritsch obtained permission from the Colonial Office to undertake an excursion to Robben Island. He visited the Island on Friday, 4 November 1863. At the time the Island was used as a gaol for military and political prisoners and common criminals,[20] as well as an asylum for lepers and 'lunatics'. A group of Xhosa chiefs were among the most famous of its political prisoners.

The Ndlambe chief Siyolo had been sent to the Island with his wife in 1855 after having been captured during the frontier war known as the War of Mlanjeni (1850–3). Here he was to remain for close on 17 years. In 1858 he was joined by other chiefs imprisoned after the Cattle Killings of 1856–7. By 1859 eight Xhosa chiefs were living at the inlet to the north of the Island town, known as Murray's Bay, including the Rharhabe chief Maqoma, the greatest Xhosa military commander of the century, and his wife Katyi; his brother Xhoxho, and Dilima, son of Phatho of the Gqunukhwebe. In 1862 the minor chief Stokwe, Phatho's brother-in-law, who had in the interim been imprisoned in Cape Town, joined them. Shortly after Fritsch's visit to the Island, Dilima was released, but it was only in 1869 that Maqoma, Siyolo and Xhoxho secured their freedom and were allowed to return home. After an unsuccessful attempt to reoccupy his old land, Maqoma was sent back in 1871 to the Island, where he died a few years later in the pauper ward.[21]

In his travelogue Fritsch described how the chiefs at Murray's Bay lived in huts similar to those found in Xhosaland. These were covered by tarpaulins and the prisoners slept on mattresses on the ground.[22] Fritsch took photographs of Maqoma, Xhoxho, Siyolo, Stokwe and Dilima (see Figs. 2–11),[23] noting in his book that 'in return for some tobacco and one shilling per head, they readily allowed themselves to grant me their worthy presence for a while'.[24] Fritsch related how he prepared to take the portraits, though 'not without encountering some difficulties, as sitting still by no means seemed necessary to them'. While being photographed, Maqoma, for example, 'quite cheerfully rubbed his nose ... Some of the pictures therefore left much to be desired ...'[25]

As a physician, Fritsch also took particular interest in the general infirmary and was accompanied on a tour of the hospital by Dr William Edmunds, who had been appointed as the Surgeon-Superintendent in 1862. Fritsch noted that more than a hundred patients were kept there, including people suffering from eye diseases, arthritis and leprosy, as well as a group of 'lunatics'. Fritsch recorded that he had never seen such sick people in his life. It appeared to him that anyone who had a skin disease was labelled a leper.[26] Although he does not mention taking portraits of patients, it is fair to assume that his photograph of a leper (Fig. 12) was taken on Robben Island.

Magoma als Gefangener, Ngqika-Häuptling, Robben-Island, Tafel Bay.

Maqoma, Ngqika chief, Robben Island, Table Bay.
(EM-SMB/32/915-916)

Xoxo als Gefangener, Ngqika-Häuptling, Robben-Island, Tafel Bay.

Xhoxho, Ngqika chief, Robben Island, Table Bay.
(EM-SMB/32/918-917)

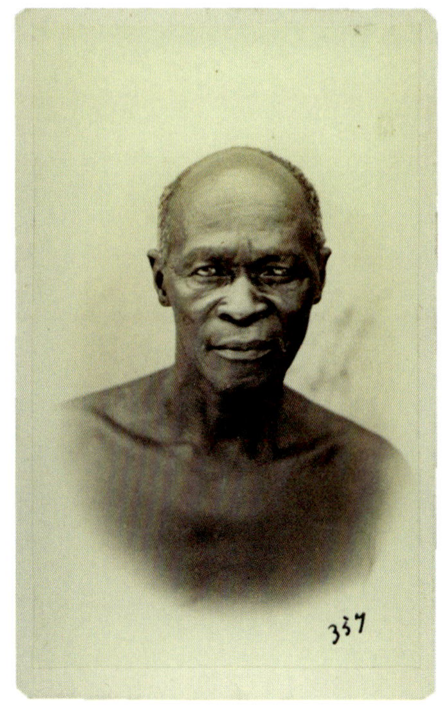

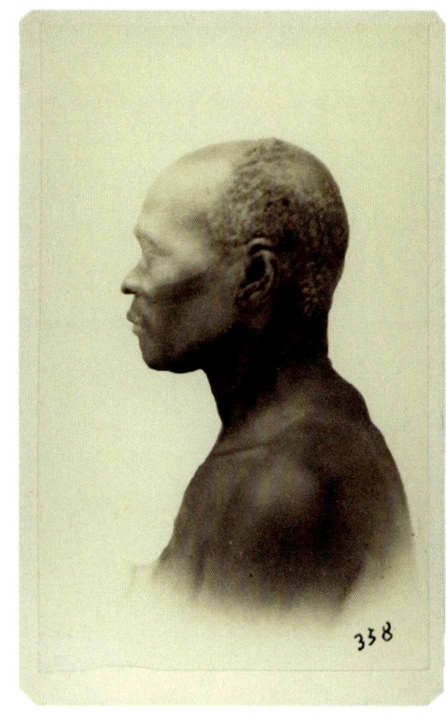

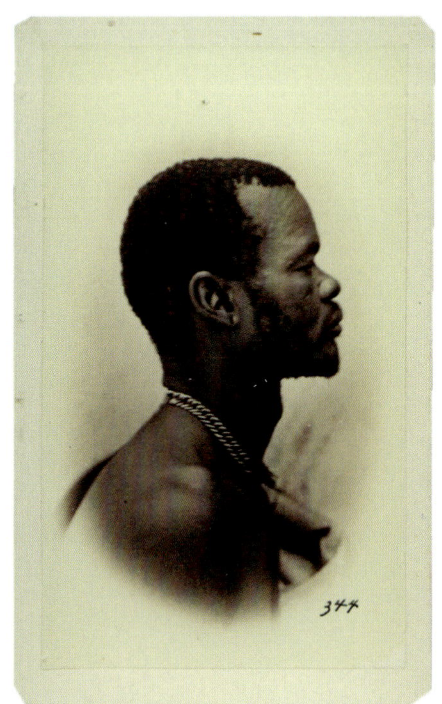

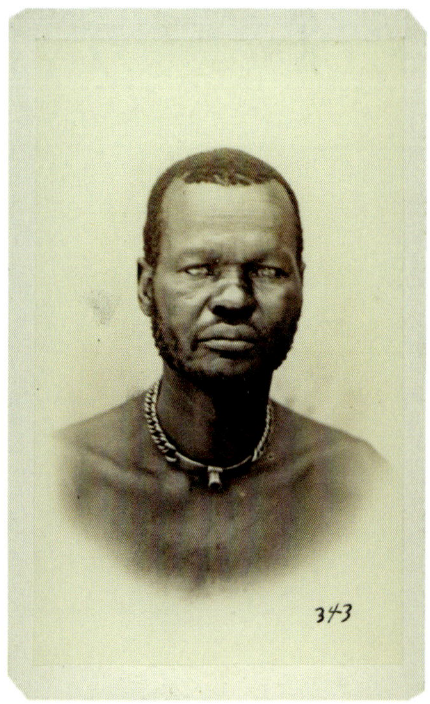

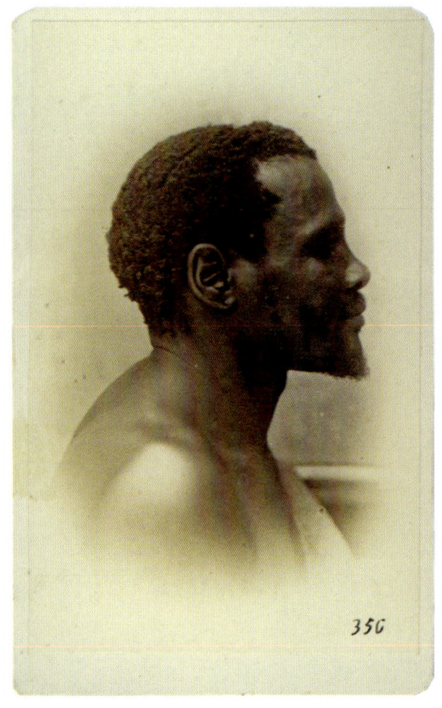

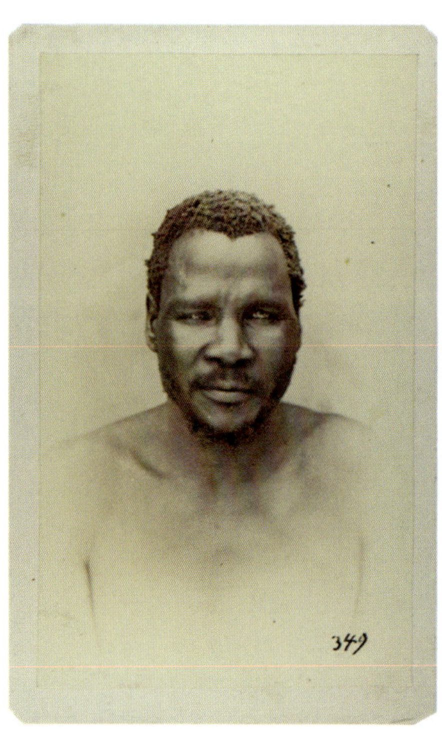

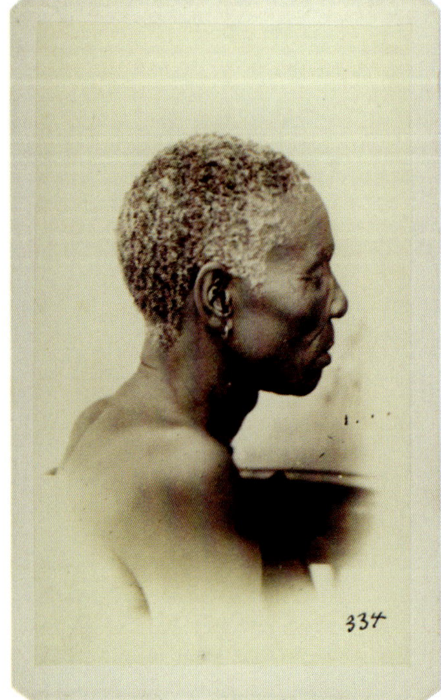

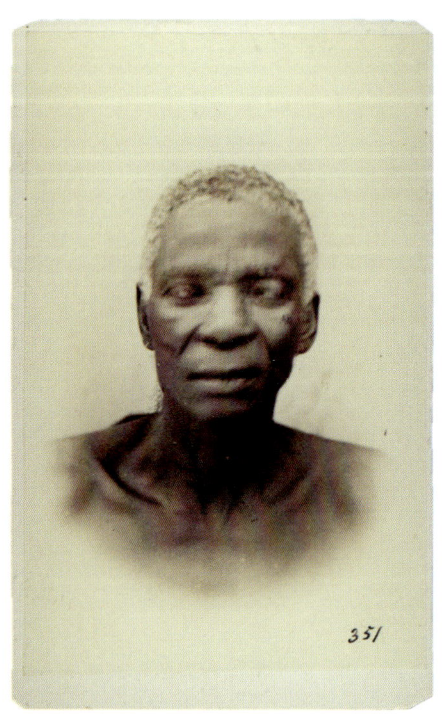

Seyolo als Gefangener, Ngqika-Häuptling, Robben-Island, Tafel Bay.

Siyolo, Ndlambe chief,
Robben Island, Table Bay.
(EM-SMB/32/922-921)

Stokwe als Gefangener, Ngqika-Häuptling, Robben-Island, Tafel Bay.

Stokwe, Mbalu chief,
Robben Island, Table Bay.
(EM-SMB/32/924-923)

◀ *Figs. 6-7*

◀ *Figs. 8-9*

Figs. 10-11 ▶

Dilima als Gefangener, Ngqika-Häuptling,
Robben-Island, Tafel Bay.

Dilima, Gqunukhwebe chief,
Robben Island, Table Bay.
(EM-SMB/32/926-925)

Leper, Robben Island, Table Bay.
(EM-SMB/32/960)

Fig. 12 ▶

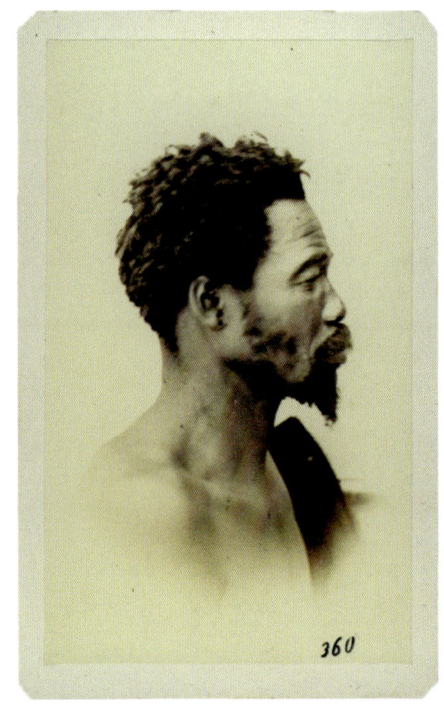

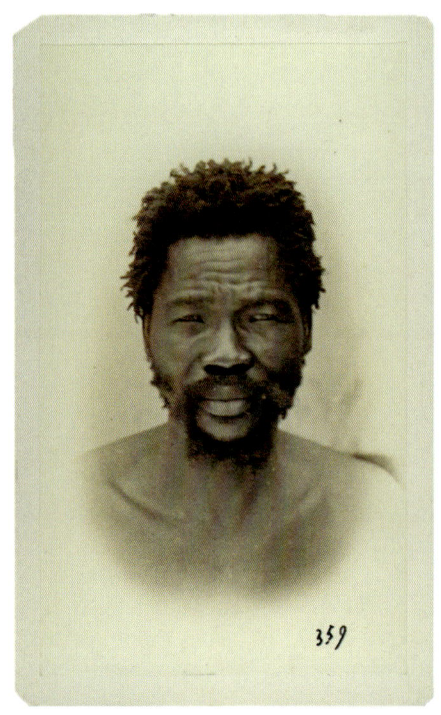

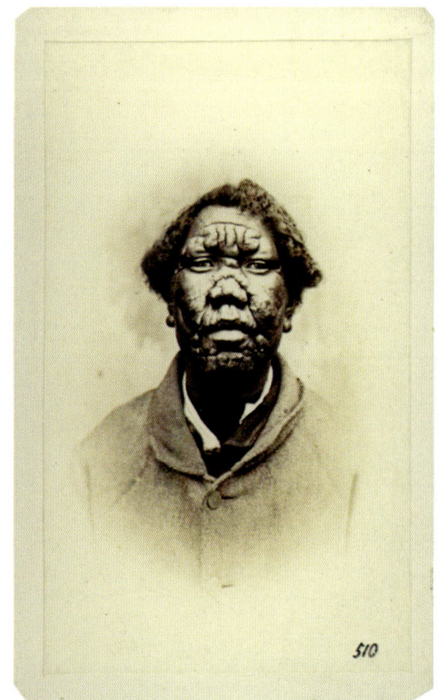

Ten days later, on 24 November, Fritsch departed from Cape Town for the eastern Cape in a horse-drawn cart. He took with him a passenger who needed a lift to Port Elizabeth, and they travelled via Swellendam, Mossel Bay, George, the Langkloof and Humansdorp, arriving in Port Elizabeth (Algoa Bay) on Sunday, 3 January 1864. He described Algoa Bay as a windy and desolate area, with few trees and many sand dunes that 'seem like enormous stretches of snow'.[27] First established in the 1820s, the town had expanded into a significant commercial and trading centre with a flourishing economy, the staple exports being wool, ivory, leather and ostrich feathers. The inhabitants were a diverse community including European settlers and Mfengu, who worked at the docks.

Fritsch visited the large Mfengu settlement (or 'location') on the outskirts of the town with a view to taking photographs, though his attempt to obtain material for his anthropological studies was thwarted: 'I took my apparatus out and attempted to approach them through the minister of religion who had been appointed for them. However, the parson did not want to do anything for me; the natives showed on the one hand a great fear for the mysterious apparatus, and on the other hand were brazen enough to want 5 shillings to sit still for 20 seconds.' Fritsch mentioned that he was surrounded by an inquisitive crowd who became bothersome when they started to touch and then broke some of his glass plates.[28] 'As I was trying to catch the unruly ones with candid shots [*Augenblicksbilder*], my old friend the southeaster came up and collapsed my tent so that I was forced to pack up and to leave without having achieved anything.'

While in Port Elizabeth Fritsch approached the local 'sheriff', who helped him find two 'authentic' Khoikhoi whom he wished to photograph. Yet even the influence of the official was not enough to allay what Fritsch described as their superstitious fears of the camera. Fritsch wrote that he was unlucky with his anthropological studies in Port Elizabeth, though he did take portraits of two men, one of whom he identified in his *Atlas* as a Sotho called George (Figs. 13–14), who had grown up in the Colony, and the other called Bajadur, who is identified in the Dammann *Album* as a Mfengu servant (*Diener*) (Figs. 15–16).[29] Given the difficulty he met with in photographing people, especially without the help of a mediator, it is likely that both these two men, being neatly dressed in European clothes, worked for whites and would have understood enough Dutch or English for Fritsch to communicate with them.

In Port Elizabeth Fritsch took the opportunity to walk along the beaches and explore the dunes, where he found interesting specimens of shells, birds and snakes for his zoological studies. On the morning of 19 January, he departed from Port Elizabeth for King William's Town, the chief town of British Kaffraria. En route, he was delayed for two days at Grahamstown while having repairs done to his cart. He finally left for King William's Town on Saturday, 23 January.

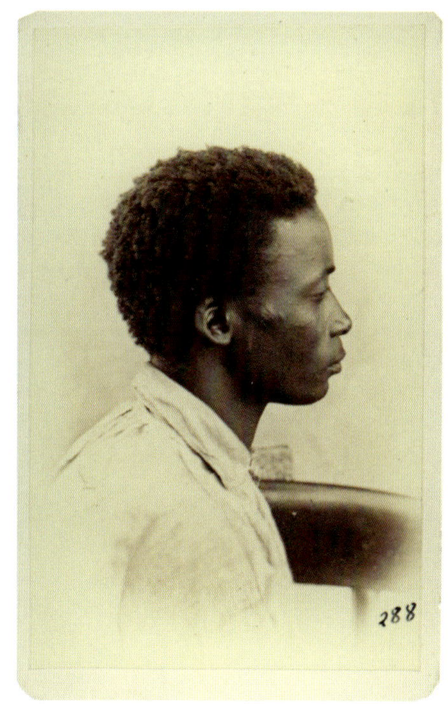

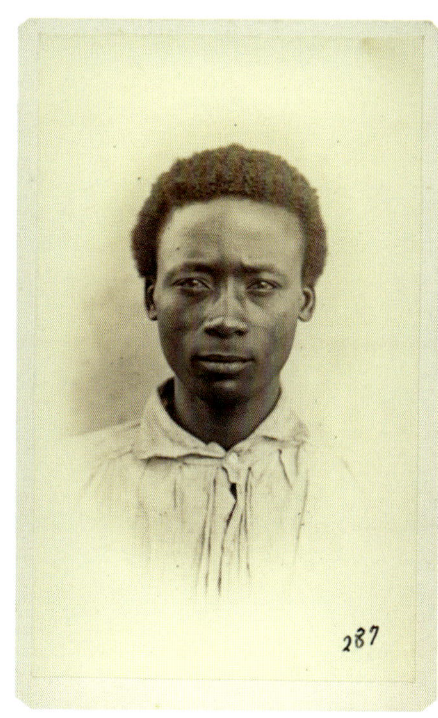

Figs. 13-14 ▶

Georg, Ba-suto, Port Elisabeth, östl. Colonie.

George, Sotho, Port Elizabeth, eastern Cape.
(EM-SMB/32/950-949)

Bajadur (Diener), Fengu, Port-Elisabeth, British Caffraria.

Bajadur (servant), Mfengu, Port Elizabeth, eastern Cape.
(EM-SMB/32/954-953)

Figs. 15-16 ▶

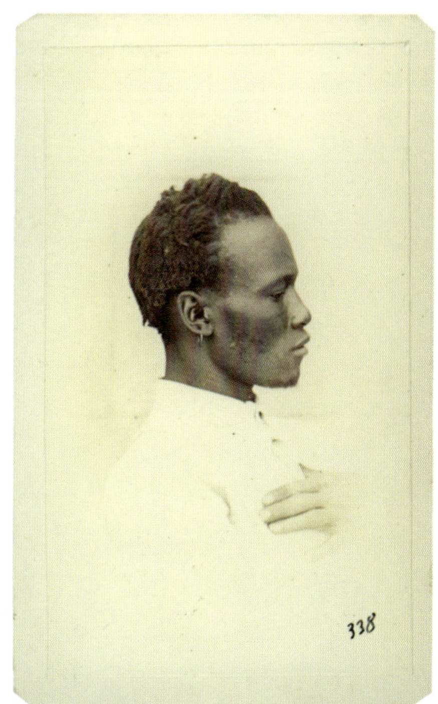

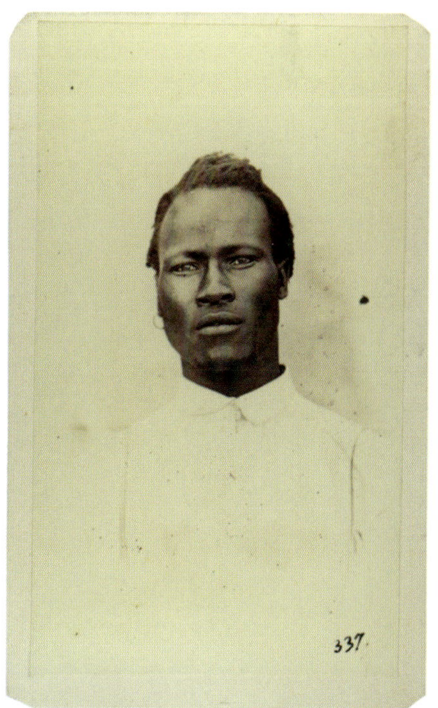

Fritsch left King William's Town for Queenstown on 26 January in heavy rain. On the way he stopped over at the Bethel mission station at Döhne, founded in 1837 by Pastor Jacob Ludwig Döhne of the Berlin Missionary Society.[30] The village of Stutterheim had been established twenty years later alongside the mission station by Baron von Stutterheim, leader of a party of German immigrants to the area. Shortly after his arrival at the hotel (*Trinkstube*) in Stutterheim, Fritsch was introduced to Sandile, the paramount chief of the Rharhabe, by the barman at the hotel.[31] Sandile, who lived to see the political and cultural integrity of his people collapse under the onslaught of colonialism, himself had 'run aground on the rocks'.[32] References to Sandile's drinking habits, common in colonial writings about him and several other chiefs at the time, seem to bear out this sense of disintegration. In his travel account Fritsch described Sandile as a tall, haggard figure, remarking too on the appearance of Sandile and his followers as 'wild' and half-naked, covered in their 'national dress', their *karosses*.

It was after five in the afternoon, and Fritsch decided to take the opportunity to photograph Sandile (Figs. 17–18), who wanted two litres of brandy for the honour. After further negotiations he agreed to accept just one bottle. As it was raining, Fritsch photographed Sandile through a door of the hotel, while Sandile sat indifferently on a chair outside. The event drew the attention of a crowd of curious onlookers. Fritsch also took a portrait of Sandile's first councillor, Somi (Figs. 19–20). In his account of the event, Fritsch mentions Somi's thick ivory armband, worn as a token of his rank. Fritsch was amused by the joyful astonishment and laughter of the crowd when they saw the image of Somi on the glass plate. He wrote: 'never will I forget ... the slap of admiration on the shoulder with which His Majesty Sandile honoured me' after seeing Somi's image. Fritsch found the responses of these people very different from those he had previously encountered in the eastern Cape. It should be borne in mind that Sandile had already been exposed to the convention of portraiture. As with Maqoma and Siyolo, his portrait had been painted on a number of occasions by Frederick Timpson I'Ons while he was in detention.

Sandile, son and successor of Ngqika, was still a minor when his father died in 1829. His half-brother Maqoma, whom Fritsch photographed on Robben Island, ruled over the Rharhabe until Sandile came of age in 1842. Increasing restrictions on land and a severe drought in the eastern Cape led to mounting tensions, which erupted in 1846 in the seventh frontier war, the War of the Axe, between the Xhosa and British, in which both sides suffered serious casualties. Sandile proved to be a capable leader, keeping the British at bay and earning the respect of local leaders.[33] The British finally resorted to a war of attrition, destroying villages and crops, and Sandile was eventually forced to the negotiating table where he signed an oath of allegiance to Britain and was imprisoned for a time. His continuing opposition led him to participate in the War of Mlanjeni and take the side of the 'believers' in the millenarian Cattle Killings.[34] Fritsch noted that at the time of his visit to Stutterheim, Sandile was still feared by the British and, in an attempt to 'render him harmless', was paid a daily salary of 10 shillings to 'grant him the possibility to ruin himself by means of brandy'. For this sum, he remarked, they 'so to speak' appointed him as 'chief of police' over the nearby districts, where he had to keep peace in order that 'the old divide and rule of the Romans was also applied here'.[35]

The following day, 27 January, Fritsch took portraits of four other people: a man whose name is recorded in his *Atlas* as Ukaas (Figs. 21–22), two unidentified Mfengu transport-riders dressed in European clothing (Figs. 23–26), and a 'Bastaard' (creole) transport-rider called Nelleka (Figs. 27–28).[36] Given their dress and occupations, it is likely that these transport-riders spoke some English or Dutch and that Fritsch would have been able to communicate directly with them, without the help of a mediator. Fritsch remarked that some of these negatives were damaged by rainwater, which might account for the mark on the portrait in Fig. 25.[37] In *Die Eingeborenen* he also included a wood engraving of a naked Mfengu woman whom he photographed at Döhne (see Fig. 237), ascribing her healthy condition to the fact of her working for an English family in Stutterheim.[38]

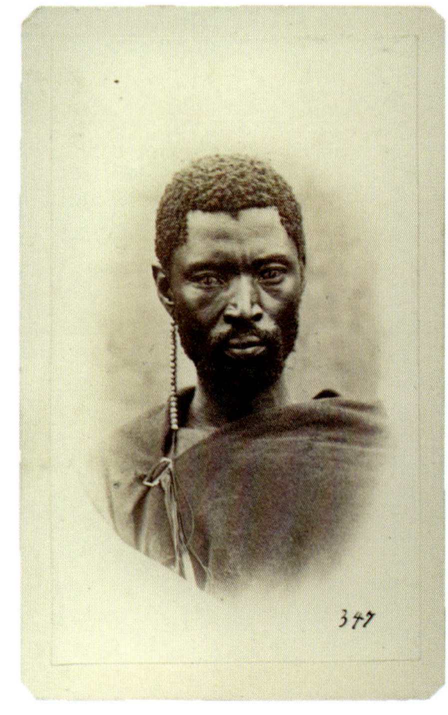
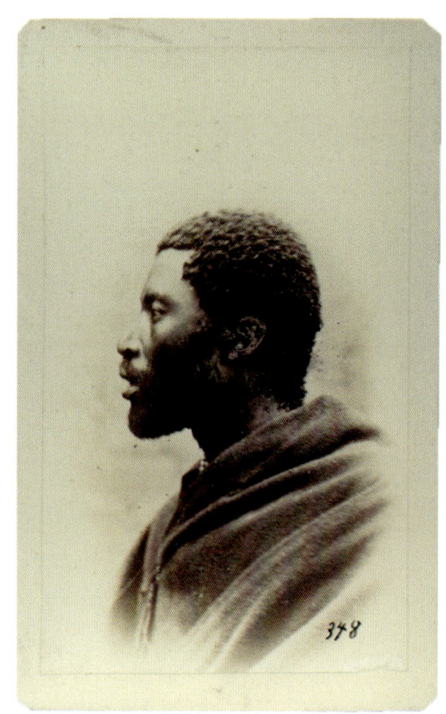

Figs. 17-18 ▶

Sandili, Ngqika-Häuptling, Duhne, British Kaffraria.

Sandile, senior Ngqika chief,
Döhne, British Kaffraria.
(EM-SMB/32/913-914)

Somi, Mponda, erste Rathgeber d. Sandili, Duhne, British Caffraria.

Somi, first councillor of Sandile. Döhne, British Kaffraria.
(EM-SMB/32/889-890)

Figs. 19-20 ▶

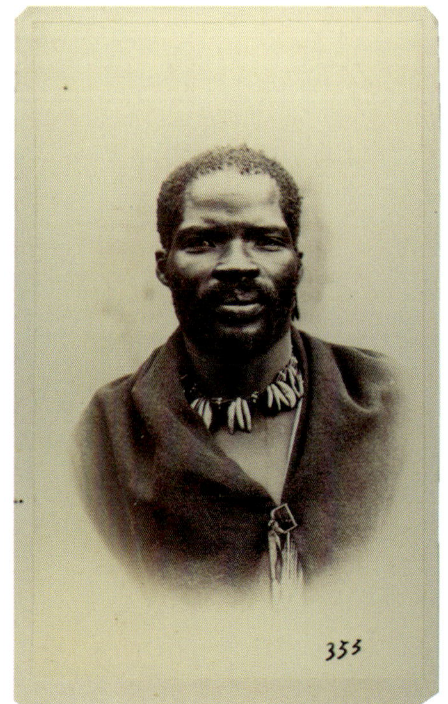
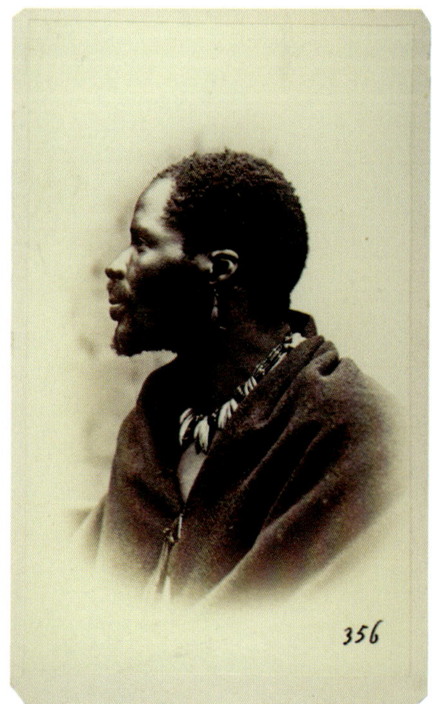

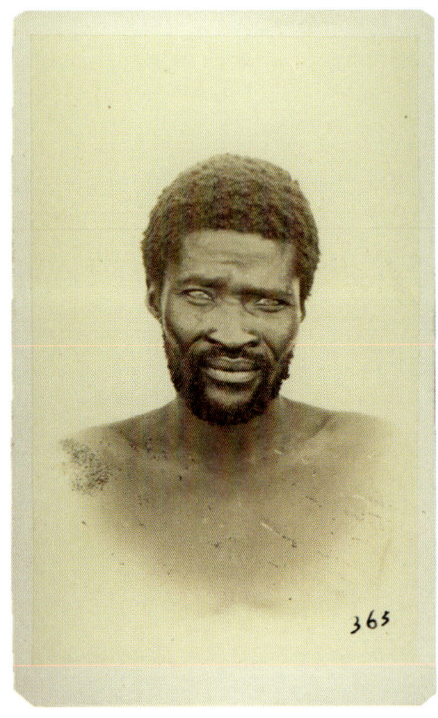 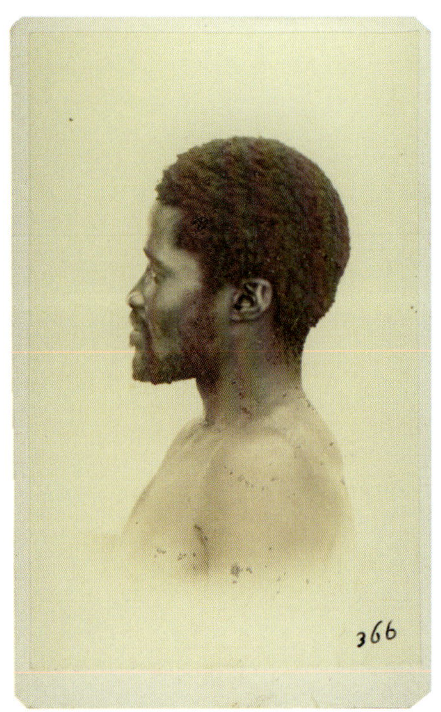

◀ *Figs. 21-22*

U'kaas, Tembu, Duhne, British Kaffraria.

U'kaas, Thembu, Döhne, British Kaffraria.
(EM-SMB/32/891-892)

(Transport-rider), Fengu, Duhne, British Caffraria.

Mfengu transport-rider, Döhne, British Kaffraria.
(EM-SMB/32/939-940)

◀ *Figs. 23-24*

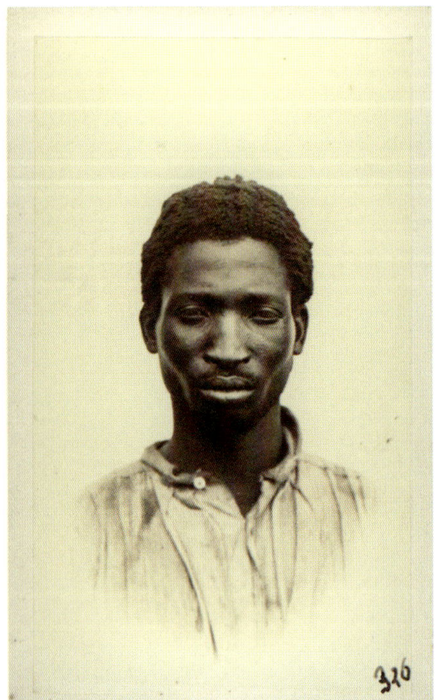

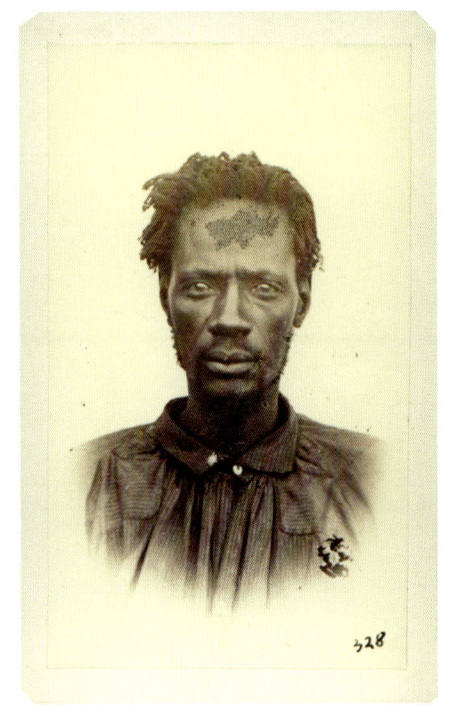
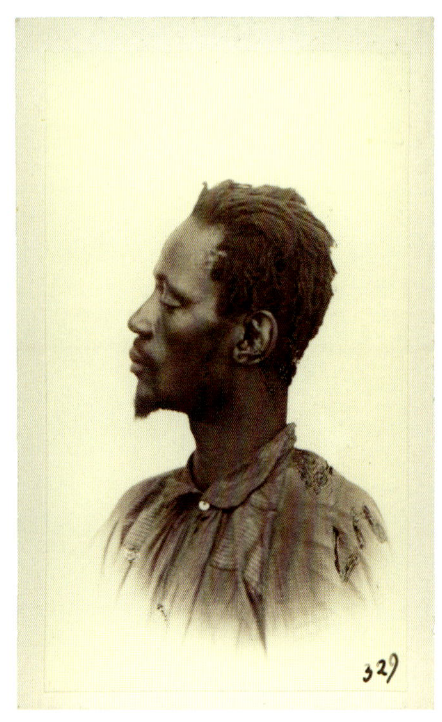

Figs. 25-26 ▶

(Transport-rider), Fengu, Duhne, British Kaffraria.

Mfengu transport-rider, Döhne, British Kaffraria.
(EM-SMB/32/933-934)

Nelleka, (Transport-rider), Duhne, British Caffraria.

Nelleka, transport-rider, Döhne, British Kaffraria.
(EM-SMB/32/1037-1033)

Figs. 27-28 ▶

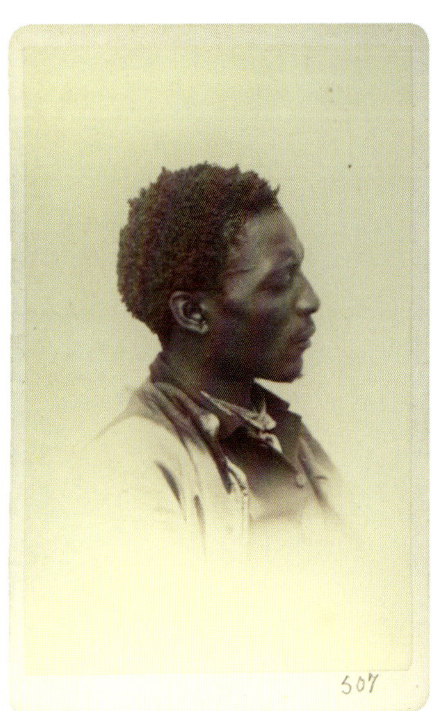

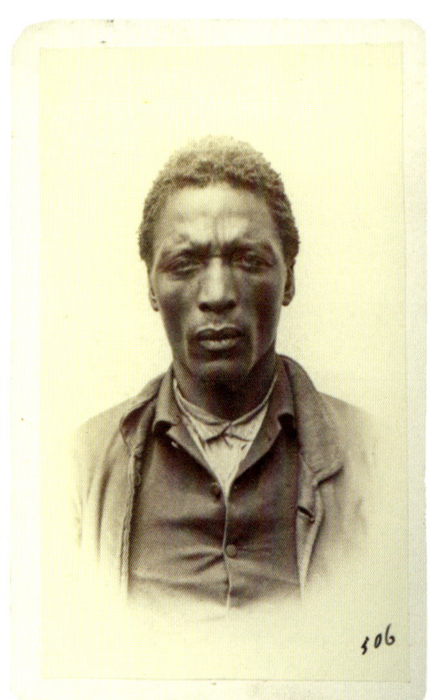

Windvogelberg (Cathcart): 27 January 1864

Fritsch arrived in high-lying Windvogelberg (modern-day Cathcart) in the pouring rain in the afternoon of 27 January. As he entered the town a group of Xhosa men approached on horseback. He was informed that it was Anta (half-brother of Sandile) and his followers. Fritsch had heard much of Anta – a British official called him 'a haughty man [with] a good mind and [a] noble appearance'[39] – and was impressed by his size, writing that he was over 1.8 metres tall with broad shoulders. Fritsch decided to stay over for a day at Windvogelberg to make Anta's acquaintance. The magistrate, Hugh Thompson, was fluent in Xhosa and facilitated Fritsch's request to meet Anta at the inn the following morning. Anta accepted and arrived with his first councillor, Sazini. Following their agreement on a bottle of brandy, Anta undertook to sit for the photograph (Figs. 30–31). Fritsch was struck by Anta's resemblance to his half-brother Xhoxho, whom Fritsch had met and photographed on Robben Island.

Exceptionally impressed with Sazini (Figs. 32–33), Fritsch described him as a 'beautiful example of a man with a well-built physique'; his facial features as 'regular and noble, his hands small, with long, tapering fingers; a genuine aristocratic type who wore his ivory arm-band and leopard-tooth necklace with pride'. It was perhaps Sazini he had in mind when describing the facial features of the Xhosa in *Die Eingeborenen*, where he wrote that one aspect of the 'A-Bantu' physique that could be described as noble (*edel*) was the fine and slender shape of the hands, which conformed to 'what we [Europeans] would call the aristocratic type'.[40]

Fritsch took two other portraits in Windvogelberg. These he recorded in his *Atlas* as those of a Thembu man called Isangani (Figs. 34–35) and a Xhosa man named Ngonde (Figs. 36–37).[41] Besides these portraits, he also photographed Anta and his followers on horseback outside the Windvogelberg hotel (Fig. 29). This image is unique, both as a technical photographic achievement (one would have expected a considerably blurred photograph from a 20-second exposure involving so many horses) and as a rare historical document.

Before leaving for Queenstown, Fritsch undertook an excursion to study San rock art in the vicinity of Windvogelberg. Fritsch was astounded by the paintings, describing them in considerable detail in his travel account. He noted in particular that some depicting armed European soldiers and horses had been recently executed, explaining how they had been painted using four colours, namely black, white, ochre and red. In recognition of the artistic achievements of San people, Fritsch dedicated a section of *Die Eingeborenen* to reproductions of their rock paintings,[42] and later published an article on 'Rock paintings near !Ameib in Damaraland' in the *Cape Monthly Magazine* of 1879.

Fig. 29 ▶

*Hanta und seine Gevolge vor den Gasthause
Windvogelberg.*

Anta and his followers outside the inn, Windvogelberg,
British Kaffraria.
(EM-SMB/32/1004)

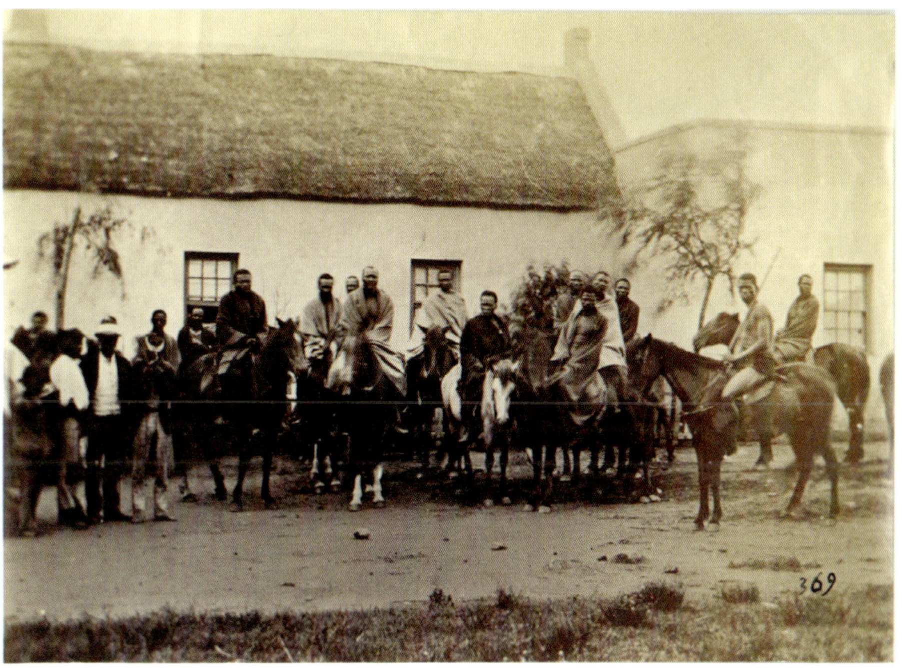

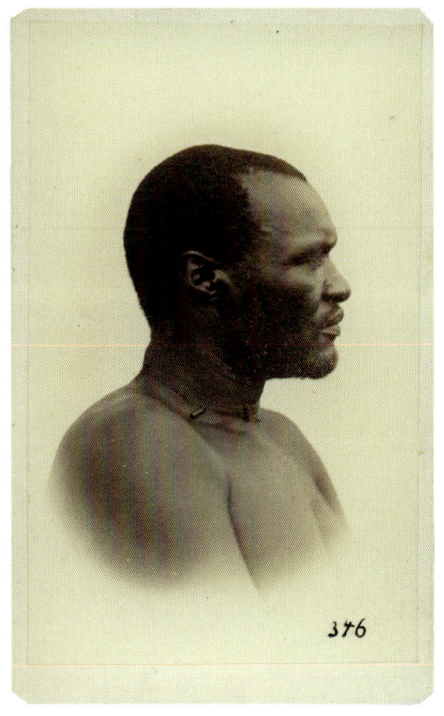

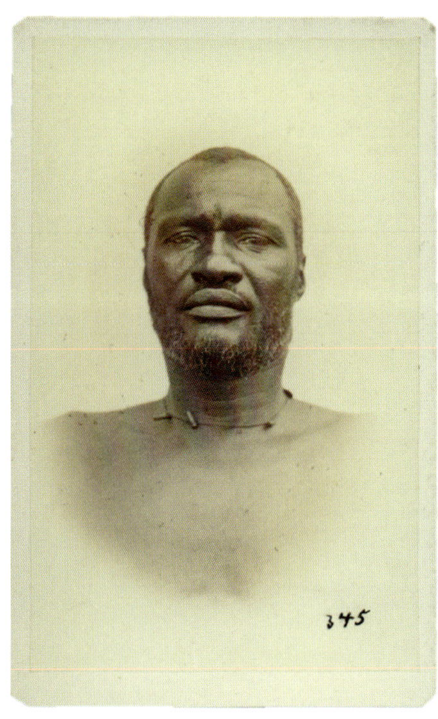

◀ *Figs. 30-31*

Hanta, Ngqika-Häuptling, Windvogelberg, British Kaffraria.

Anta, Ngqika chief, Windvogelberg,
British Kaffraria
(EM-SMB/32/920-919)

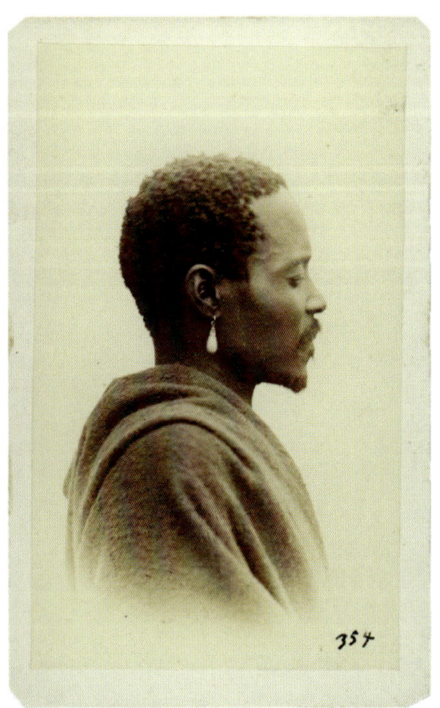

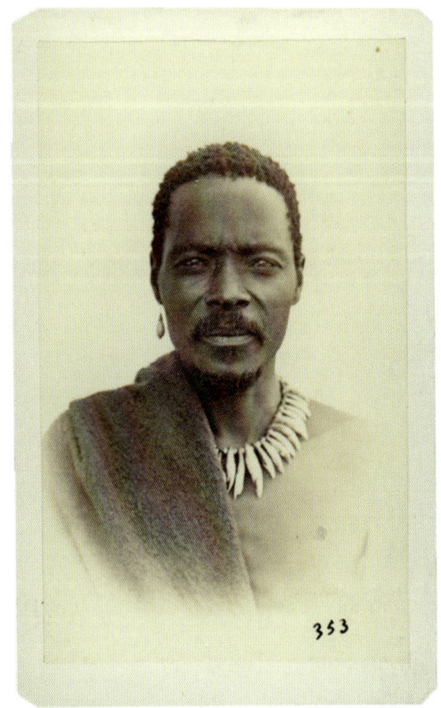

*Sazini, Mbalu, erste Rathgeber d. Hanta,
Windvogelberg, British Caffraria.*

Sazini, first councillor of Anta, Mbalu,
Windvogelberg, British Kaffraria.
(EM-SMB/32/928-927)

◀ *Figs. 32-33*

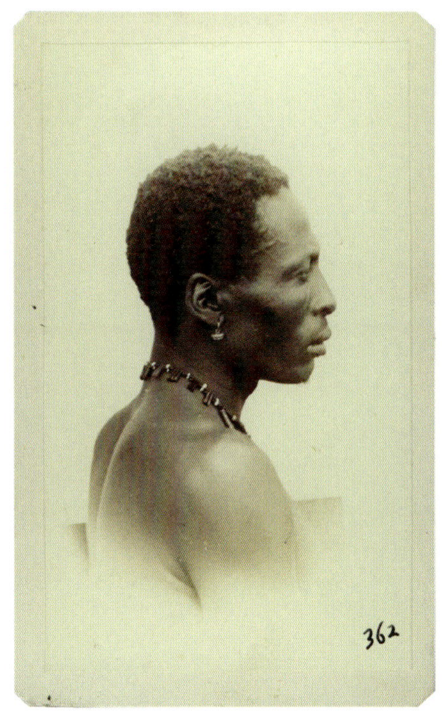
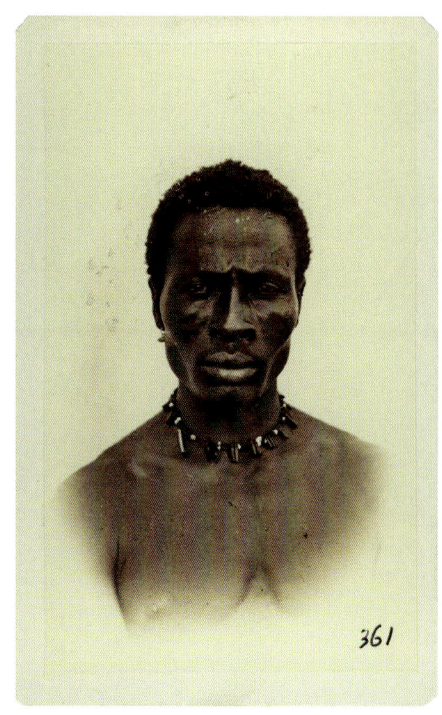

Figs. 34-35 ▶

Isangani, abaTembu, Windvogelberg, östliche Colonie.

Isangani, Thembu, Windvogelberg,
British Kaffraria.
(EM-SMB/32/894-893)

*Ngonde, Ama-xoxa, Windvogelberg,
British Kaffraria.*

Ngonde, Xhosa, Windvogelberg,
British Kaffraria.
(EM-SMB/32/896-895)

Figs. 36-37 ▶

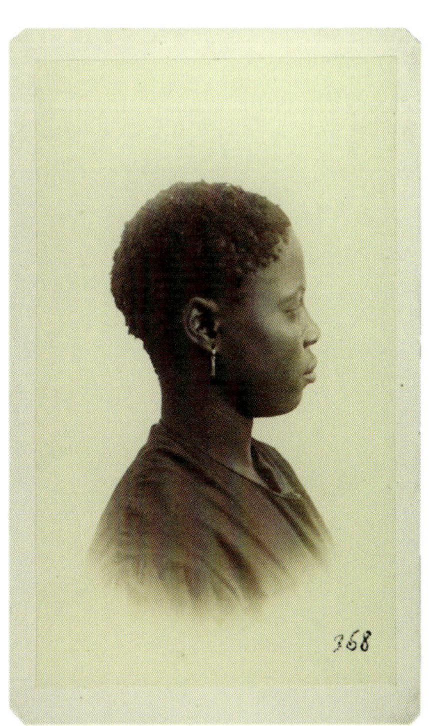

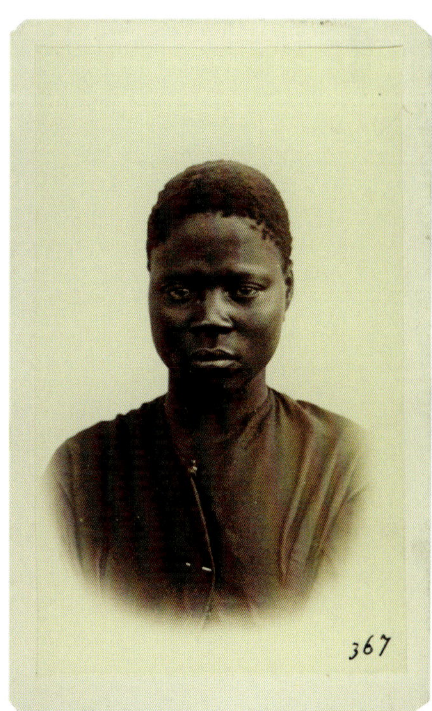

Having rested his horses for a day in Queenstown, Fritsch departed on 1 February for the Shiloh mission station, which he reached that afternoon. Shiloh had been founded in 1828 by the Moravian Missionary Society on the Klipplaat River near Queenstown, to evangelise among the Thembu. On the evening of his arrival Fritsch attended a religious service held for the community by a Sotho preacher, Johannes Nakin (or Nakeng) (Figs. 38–39), who also taught at the mission. He recalled that Nakin, who spoke in his mother tongue, made a great impact on his audience through the passionate way in which he preached.[43]

Nakin's parents had settled in Shiloh in 1828 after having fled from the Free State during the turmoil known as the Mfecane. His mother was the first person to be baptised at Shiloh. Johannes Nakin was born at Shiloh in 1832 and trained as a teacher at Genadendal, the first and largest Moravian mission situated near Caledon in the western Cape, between 1846 and 1853.[44] He was still living at Genadendal when Shiloh suffered considerable damage during the War of Mlanjeni. In 1847 the Governor of the Cape, Sir Harry Smith, had extended the border of the colony to the Keiskamma and Klipplaat rivers, and in 1851, when war broke out, Shiloh became caught between the opposing forces. The missionaries under Sebastian Gysin fled, accompanied by loyal Mfengu and Khoikhoi congregants, and the station was attacked from both sides.[45] On returning to Shiloh after the war, Nakin married a Khoikhoi woman, Emma Stompjes, in 1854.

She was described by Gysin as 'the fairest girl in Shiloh, and though much admired by her own countrymen, and even by Englishmen, has always maintained an unblemished character'.[46]

Emma was the daughter of Carl and Wilhelmine Stompjes. Fritsch photographed Carl (Figs. 40–41), whom he described as 'the oldest pupil [*Schüler*] at the mission'. Carl's wife, Wilhelmine, was a Xhosa woman who played a significant role as an interpreter and facilitator between the Moravian missionaries and the Xhosa and Khoikhoi communities at Shiloh. In the early 1800s she had found her way from the eastern Cape to Genadendal, where she was baptised and received her Christian name.[47] In 1818 she joined the party of Johann Heinrich Schmidt to establish a mission station, Enon, at Witte River in the Uitenhage district,[48] and again in 1828 she accompanied a party under Johannes Lemmerz and Johan Friedrich Hoffmann to found Shiloh.[49] Her son-in-law Johannes Nakin was ordained as a missionary in 1870, and in 1884, the year after Emma Nakin's death, he married Maria Stompjes.[50]

Besides the portraits of Johannes Nakin and Carl Stompjes, Fritsch also took photographs of six other pupils at the mission whose names he recorded in his *Atlas* as A. Minell (Figs. 42–43) and Rosalie Schlinger, two Khoikhoi women (Figs. 44–45), Xibene, a Mfengu man (Figs. 46-47), Mani, a Xhosa man (Figs. 48–49), and Kwadana, a Thembu (Figs. 50–51).[51]

*Nankin (Lehrar an der Missionsschuler), Ba-sotu,
Siloh, östliche Colonie.*

Johannes Nakin, Sotho, teacher at the mission school,
Shiloh, eastern Cape.
(EM-SMB/32/946-945)

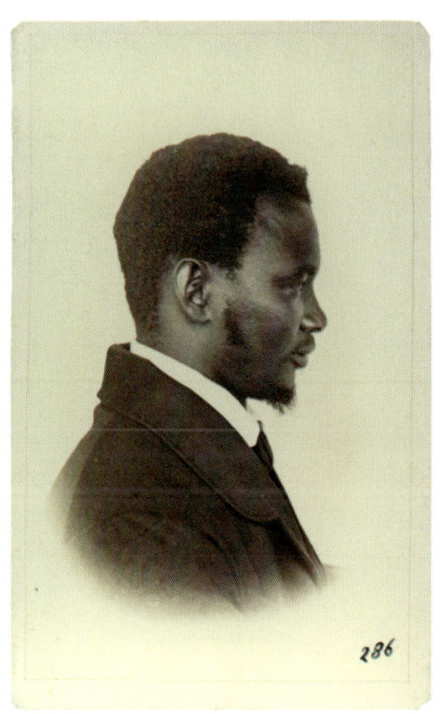

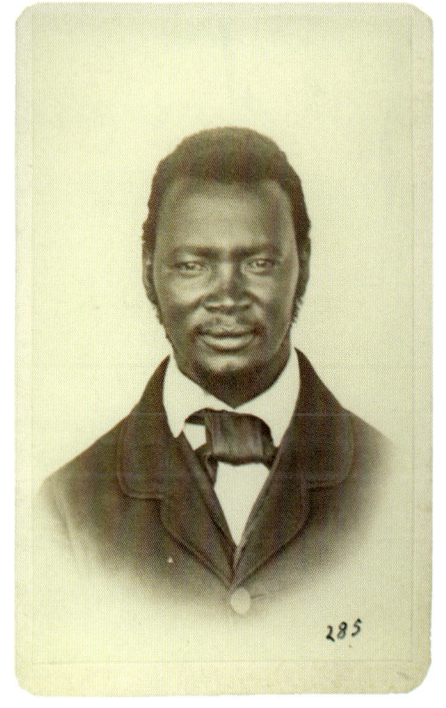

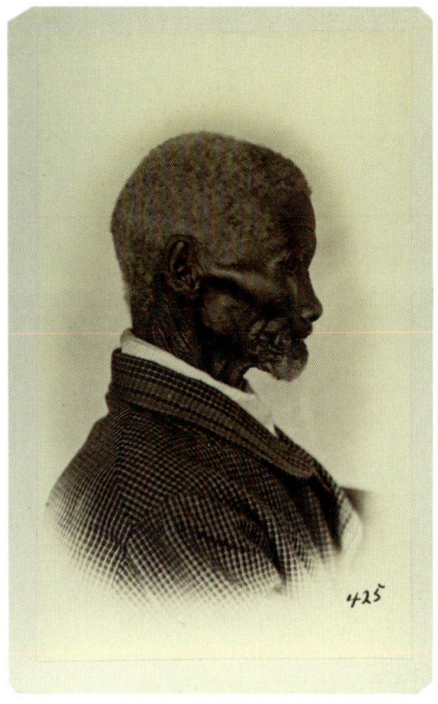 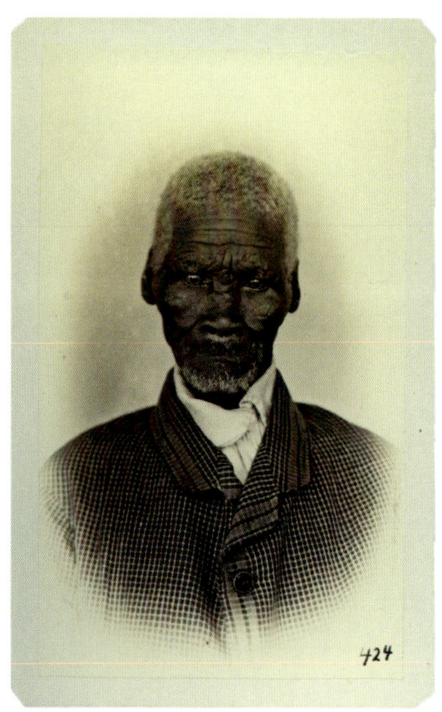

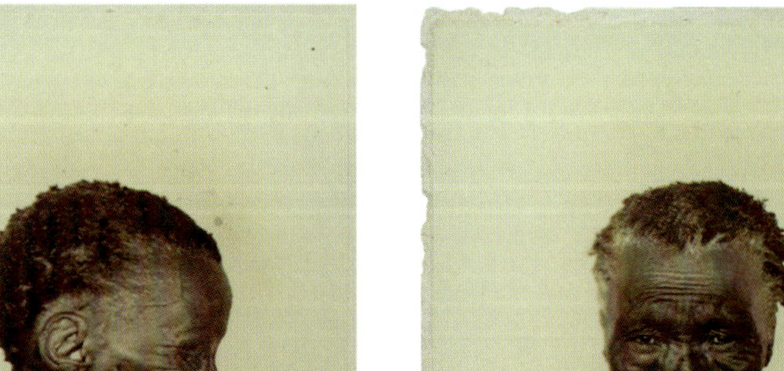

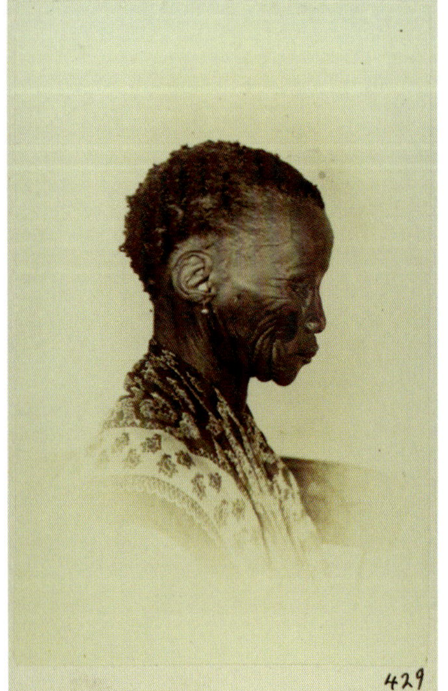 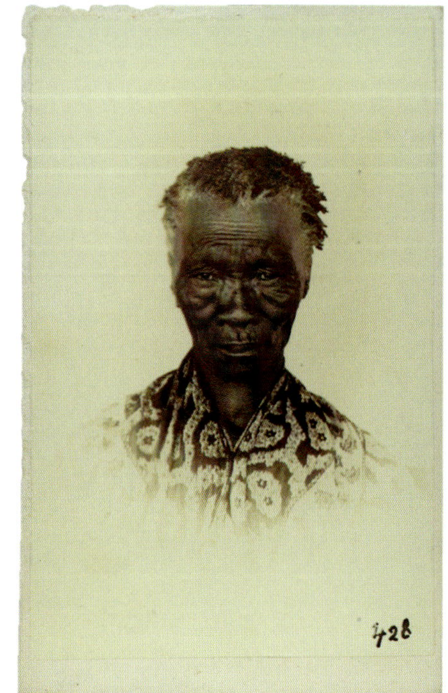

◀ *Figs. 40-41*

Karl Stompjes (ältester Schüler der Mission), Hottentot, Siloh, östliche Colonie.

Carl Stompjes, Khoikhoi, oldest pupil at the mission, Shiloh, eastern Cape.
(EM-SMB/32/747-746)

A. Minell (Missionsschülerin), Hottentotin, Siloh, östliche Colonie.

A Minell, Khoikhoi, pupil at the mission, Shiloh, eastern Cape.
(EM-SMB/32/749-748)

◀ *Figs. 42-43*

*Rosalie Schlinger (Missionsschülerin), Hottentotin,
Siloh, östliche Colonie.*

Rosalie Schlinger, Khoikhoi, pupil at the mission, Shiloh,
eastern Cape.
(EM-SMB/32/751-750)

*Xibene (Missionschüler), Fengu, Siloh,
British Kaffraria.*

Xibene, Mfengu, pupil at the mission,
Shiloh, eastern Cape.
(EM-SMB/32/930-929)

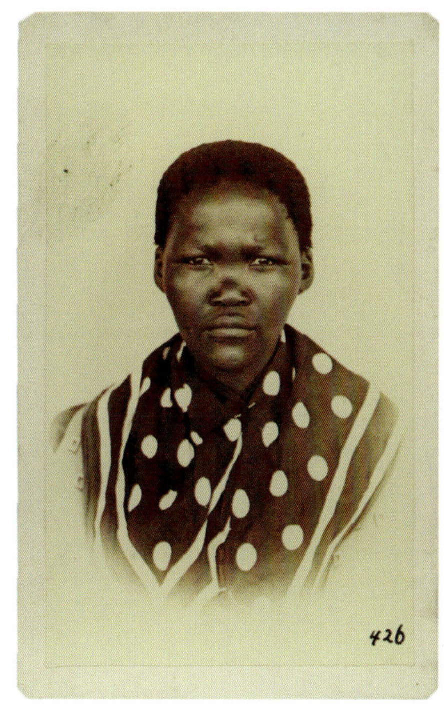

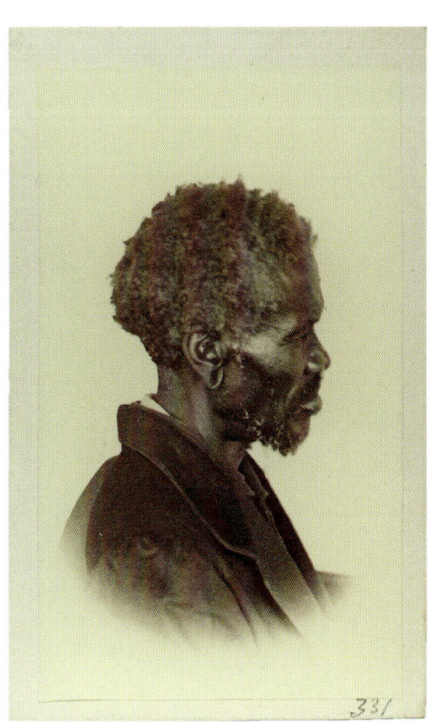

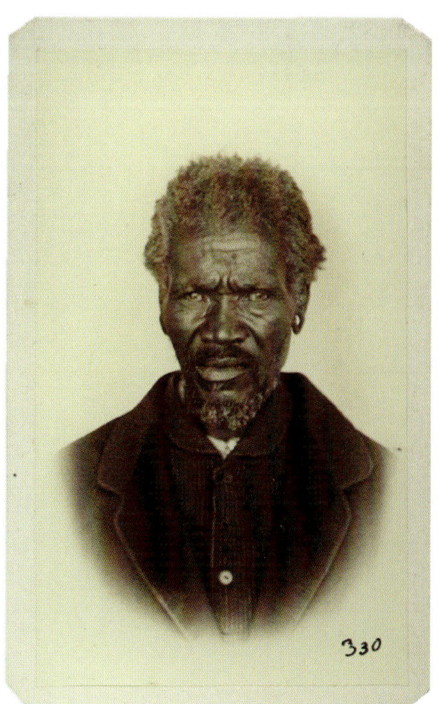

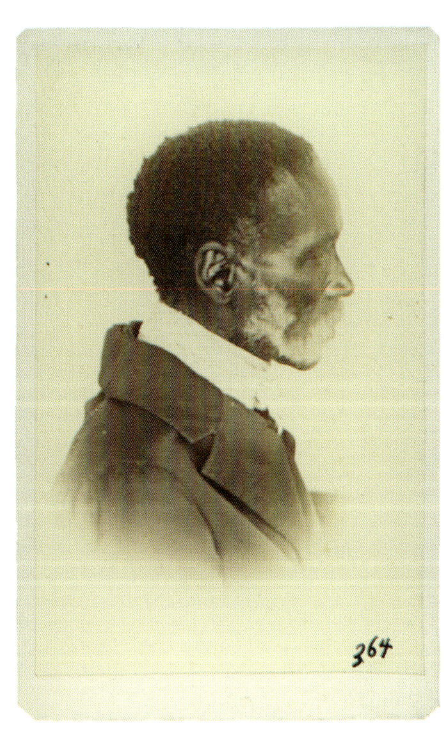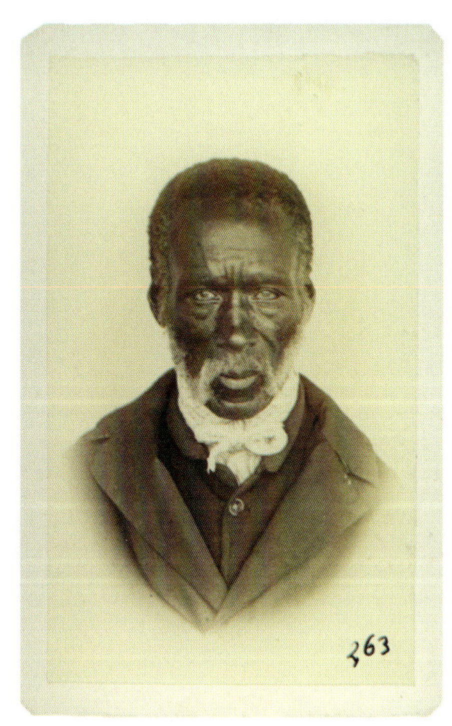

Figs. 48-49

*Mani (Missionsschüler), amaXosa,
Siloh, östliche Colonie.*

Mani, Xhosa, pupil at the mission,
Shiloh, eastern Cape.
(EM-SMB/32/936-935)

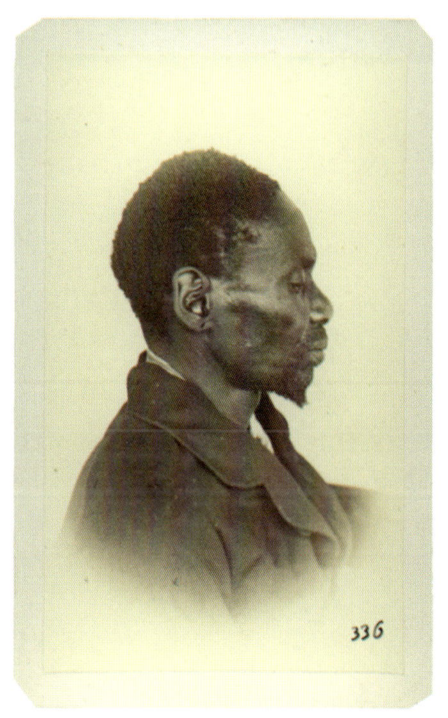

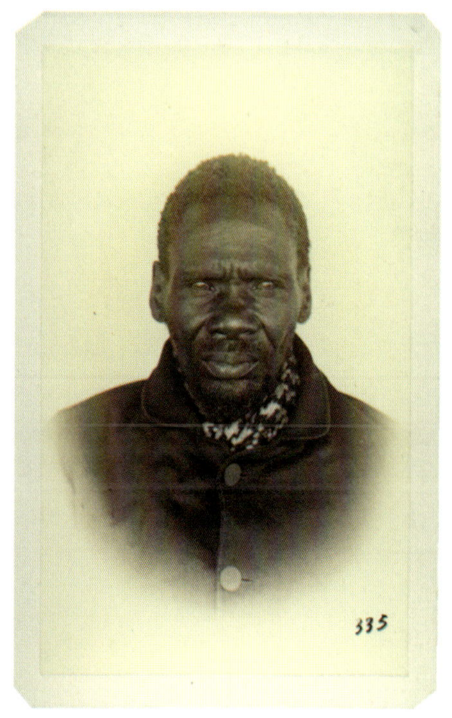

Figs. 50-51 ▶

*Kwadana (Missionsschüler), Tembu/Tambuki,
Siloh, östliche Colonie.*

Kwadana, Thembu, pupil at the mission,
Shiloh, eastern Cape.
(EM-SMB/32/932-931

Fritsch left Shiloh for Colesberg on Wednesday, 3 February. After having endured exceptionally rainy weather and poor roads between Lesseyton, Burghersdorp and Colesberg, he arrived at his destination on the afternoon of 7 February. He decided to stay in Colesberg for two days to rest his horses. The town lay close to the Gariep (Orange) River on one of the most well-travelled routes to the interior of the country used by traders, hunters and explorers. Formerly known as Toverberg (Toverberg, or Coleskop, is a prominent hill and landmark near the town), it was founded in 1830 on the site of the abandoned mission station Toverberg or Gracehill, established by the London Missionary Society in 1814, and was named after Sir Lowry Cole, then Governor of the Cape Colony.[52]

While in Colesberg, Fritsch stayed in his cart as the hotel was infested with insects.[53] Owing to heavy rains he was compelled to remain in the area for 14 days until the Gariep subsided enough to enable him to cross to Philippolis. He used his time exploring the botanical and zoological features of the area. Describing the small settlements or neighbourhoods of local people dotted around the town, he noted in particular the light from their fires during the evenings and the sounds of singing and dancing.[54] During his stay in Colesberg, Fritsch took the opportunity to photograph individuals from diverse groups of Khoikhoi, San, Sotho and Tlokwa (known then as Mantatees). These included a San man named George (Figs. 52–53), the Sotho leader Stoffel (Figs. 54–55), two Tlokwa men, Willem and Jani (Figs. 56–59), and an unidentified Khoikhoi man (Figs. 60–61).[55]

Fritsch was very eager to photograph 'authentic Bushmen', as the /Xam of the Cape and southern Transgariep regions were widely recognised, by Dr Wilhelm Bleek and others, as being on the verge of extinction or absorption within colonial society as 'coloured' servants and herdsmen. He described photographing an old beggar named Job (Figs. 62–63), who had lived at the mission station,[56] and commented that Job appeared to show no interest in the photographic process. Fritsch took a second, full-length photograph of Job, but this time naked (see Fig. 238). This image was reproduced as a wood engraving in *Die Eingeborenen*, where it is discussed in the context of anatomical features related to diet.[57]

In his book *Drei Jahre*, Fritsch wrote at length on the extermination of the San people in South Africa. He discussed how, because of the depletion of game, which had been hunted out by the colonists, the San had resorted to cattle theft. This, in turn, had led to extensive hunting raids on the San by colonist commandos authorised by the landdrosts or local magistrates. Fritsch likened these raids to animal hunts in Europe. Afterwards, he wrote, the landdrosts would note with satisfaction the number of people who had been 'executed without mercy'.[58]

Figs. 52-53 ▶

Georg, Buschmann, Kolesberg, östliche Colonie.

George, San, Colesberg, eastern Cape.
(EM-SMB/32/687-28/688).

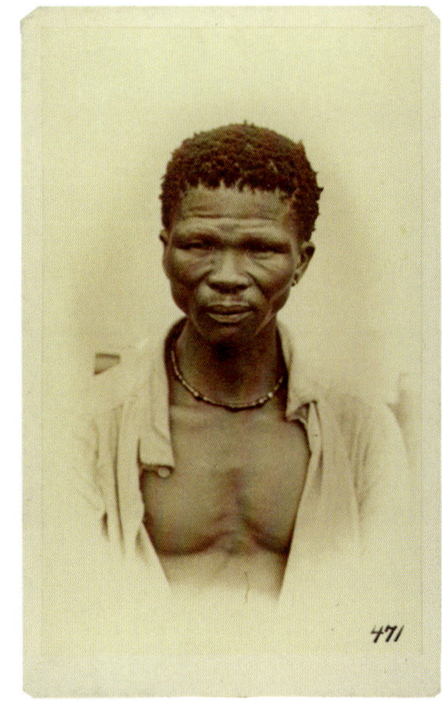
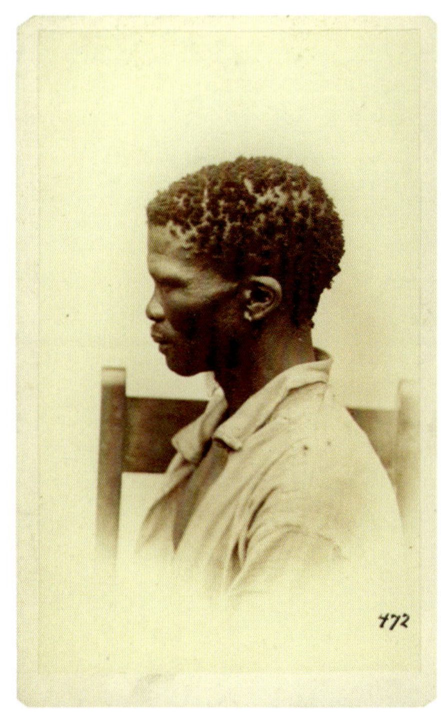

Stoffel, Ba-suto, Colesberg, östliche Colonie.

Stoffel, Sotho, Colesberg, eastern Cape.
(EM-SMB/32/947-948).

Figs. 54-55 ▶

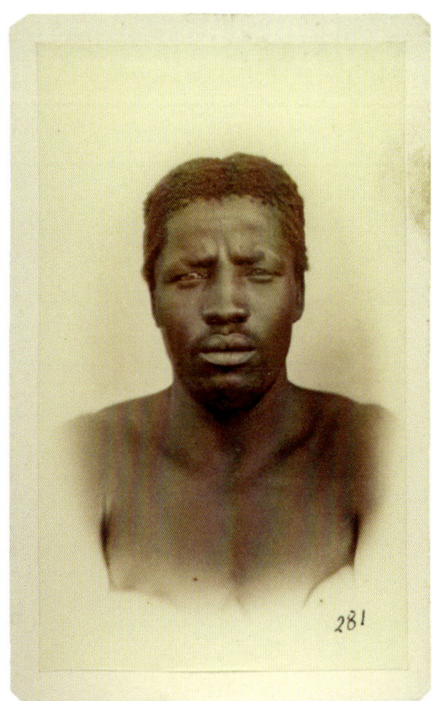
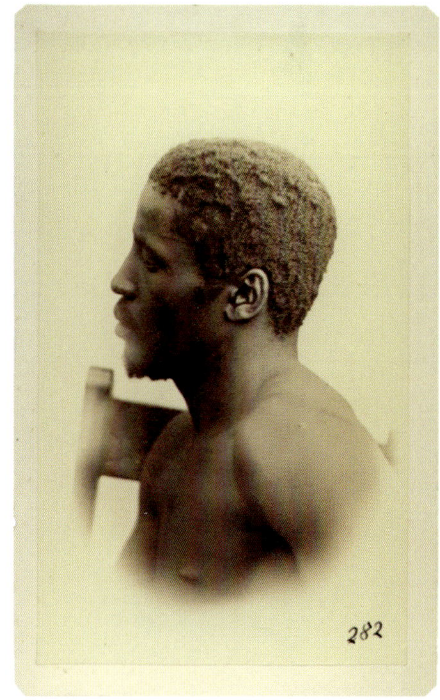

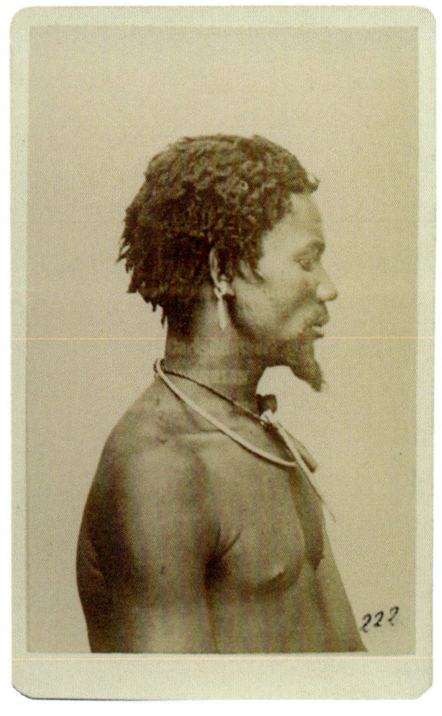

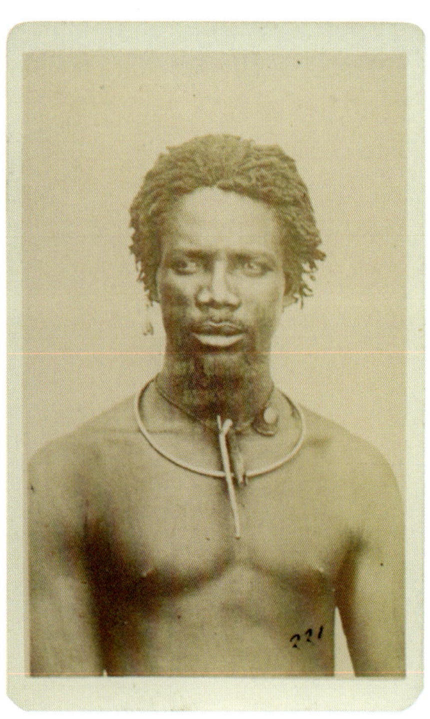

Wilhelm, *Bamantatisi*, Colesberg, östliche Colonie.

Willem, Tlokwa, Colesberg, eastern Cape.
(EM-SMB/32/863-862)

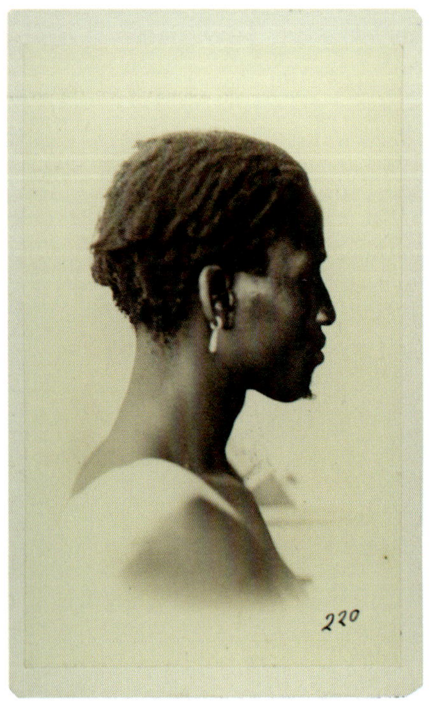

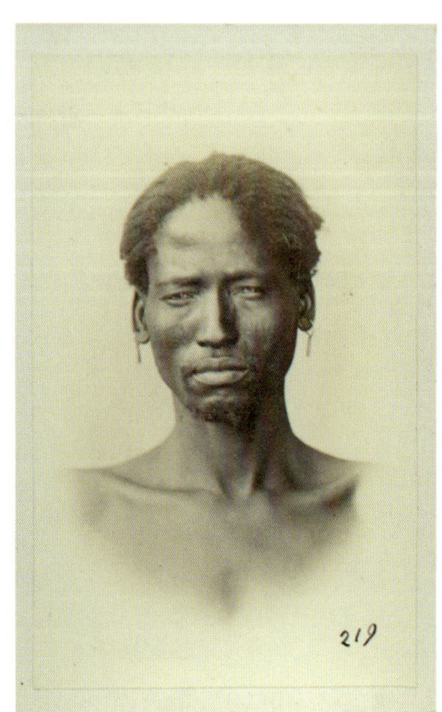

Jani, Mantati, Colesberg, östliche Colonie.

Jani, Tlokwa, Colesberg, eastern Cape.
(EM-SMB/32/861-860)

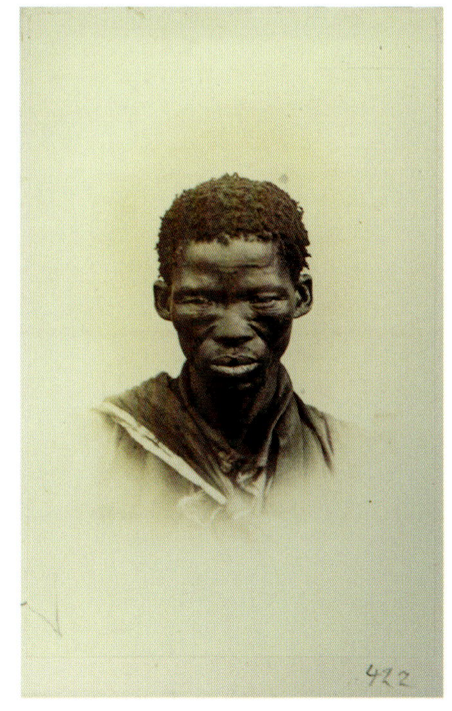
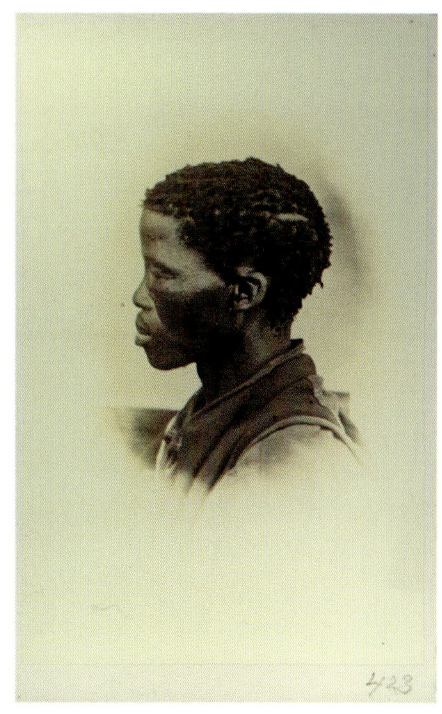

Figs. 60-61 ▶

Hottentott, Kolesberg, östliche Colonie.

Khoikhoi, Colesberg, eastern Cape.
(EM-SMB/32/744-745)

*Job, Buschmann, (Missionsschüler), Kolesberg,
östliche Colonie.*

Job, San, pupil at the mission, Colesberg, eastern Cape.
(EM-SMB/28/690-689)

Figs. 62-63 ▶

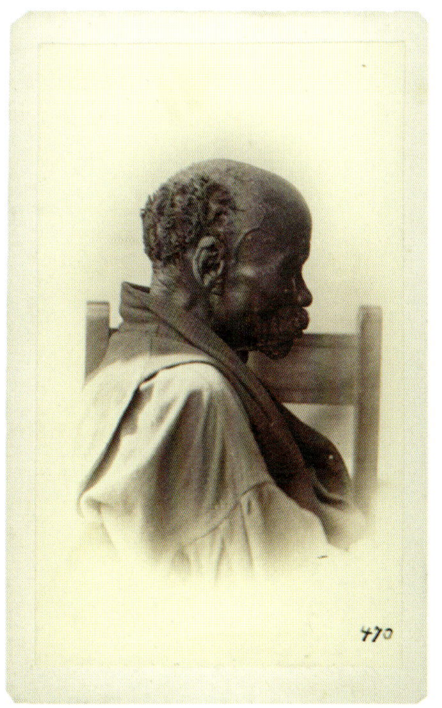
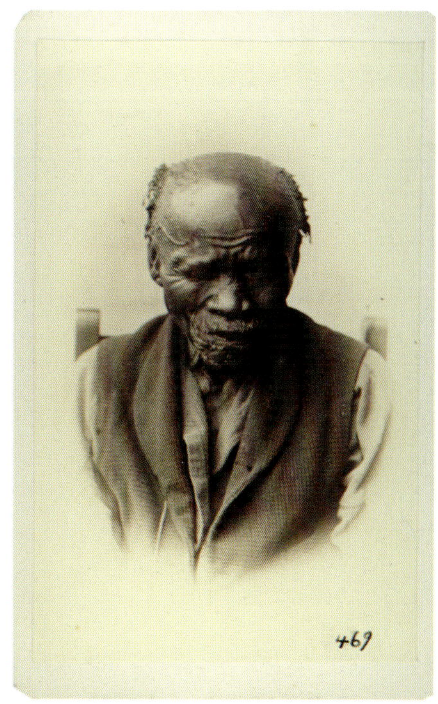

When he arrived at the pontoon on the Gariep, on Wednesday, 17 February, Fritsch found a crowd of carts and wagons waiting to cross the river. As a result of this congestion he was told that he would only be able to make the crossing that evening. A farmer agreed to let Fritsch join him for an additional fee, but he found an even earlier opportunity to cross with a wagon and livestock and sent his assistant Jacob to negotiate their passage.[59] This is the first time that he made any reference to a travelling assistant.

Having got to the other side, Fritsch set out for Bloemfontein, stopping over at Philippolis, the former residence of the Griqua captain Adam Kok, and at Boomplaats. He arrived at the Riet River on the morning of 24 February. Here he met a group of travellers stranded on the bank of the river waiting for the water to subside. By this time his provisions had run out and all he could obtain from another party were some rusks. He sent Jacob to a nearby farm to buy bread, but this also proved unsuccessful. Eventually a group of black men arrived on horseback and offered to take a letter to the mission station at Bethany, requesting bread. The missionary at Bethany, Carl Friedrich Wuras, came to Fritsch's aid and helped him cross the Riet the next morning.[60] Wuras had been sent to South Africa by the Berlin Missionary Society and established the station at Bethany in 1834 among the Korana in the Orange River Sovereignty. He invited Fritsch to visit Bethany, where Fritsch stayed with the missionary Meiffert, who helped him with his photography.[61]

Here Fritsch entered a region that had been ravaged by conflicts involving at various times Ndebele, Tlokwa, Sotho, Korana, Griqua, Boers and British settlers. The Korana were descendants of the Cape Peninsular group of Khoikhoi called Gorachoqua under the leadership of !Kora.[62] After the Dutch settled at the Cape in 1652, they retreated inland towards the end of the seventeenth century, crossing the Gariep and then moving on to the present-day districts of Boshof and Bethany. In the mid-1840s the Korana captain Goliath Yzerbek and most of his followers left Bethany to join another Korana segment, after which the mission station gradually became populated by Tswana.[63]

Fritsch recorded photographing seven people at Bethany, namely a San man with the name of Danster (a pupil at the mission school) (Figs. 64–5), two Korana men, Jochem and Gaar (Figs. 66-69), the Rolong man, Mokaue (who, Fritsch noted in his *Atlas*, had a deep scar on his neck from an assegai stab by an Ndebele) (Figs. 70-71), Mangue, a Gamalete man originally from the Ramotswa area in Bechuanaland (Figs. 72–73), a San man named Rooiman (Figs. 74–75), of whom Fritsch also took a full-length photograph (Fig. 76), and a Rolong woman named Linti (Figs. 77–78).[64]

Figs. 64-65 ▶

Danster, Buschmann, Bethanien, Oranje-Frystaat.

Danster, San, Bethany, Orange Free State.
(EM-SMB/15/P436-437)

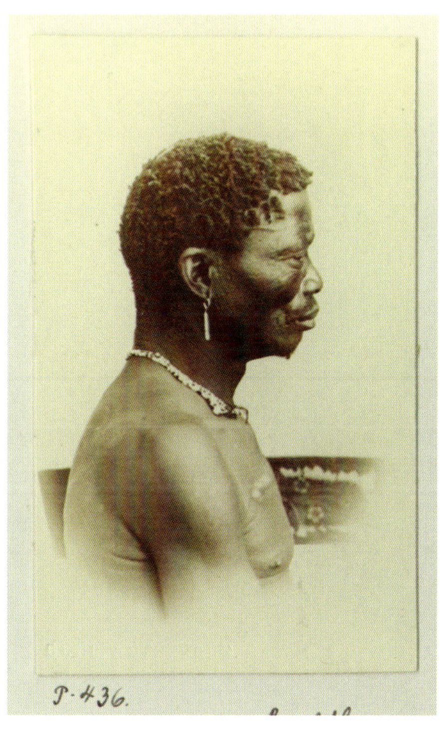

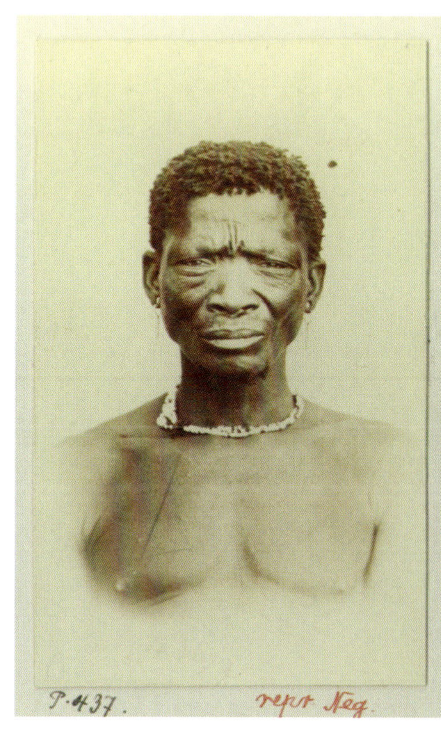

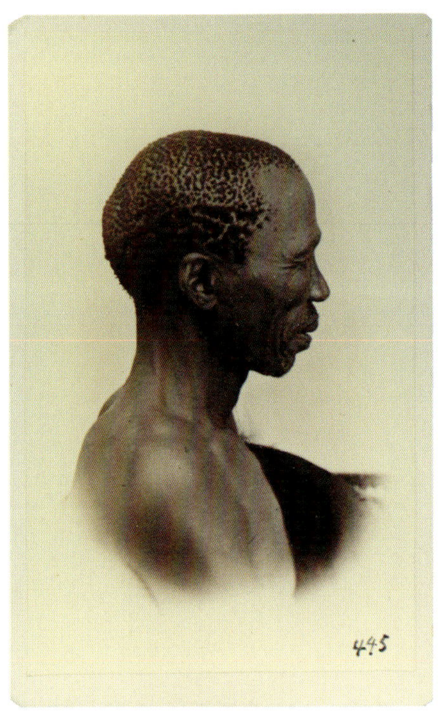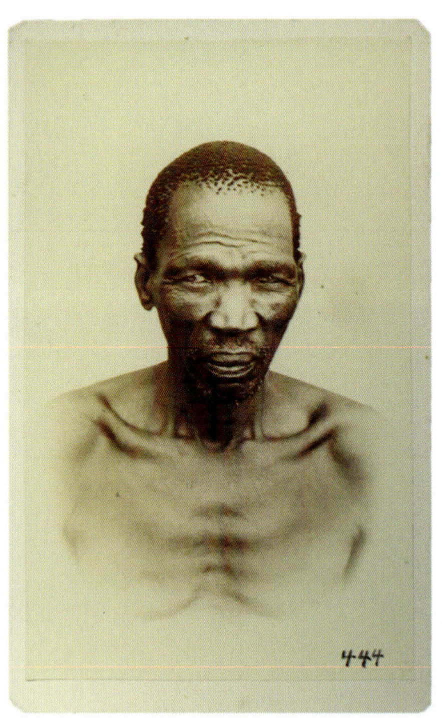

◀ *Figs. 66-67*

Jochem, Korana, Bethanien, Oranje-Frystaat.

Jochem, Korana, Bethany, Orange Free State.
(EM-SMB/32/761-760)

Gaar, Korana, Bethanien, Oranje-Frystaat.

Gaar, Korana, Bethany, Orange Free State.
(EM-SMB/32/763-762)

◀ *Figs. 68-69*

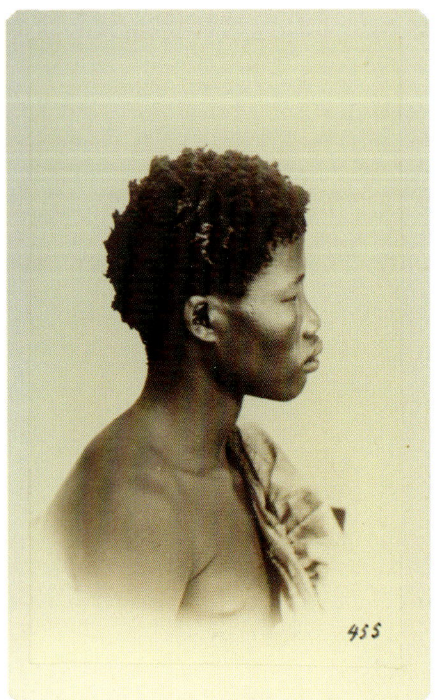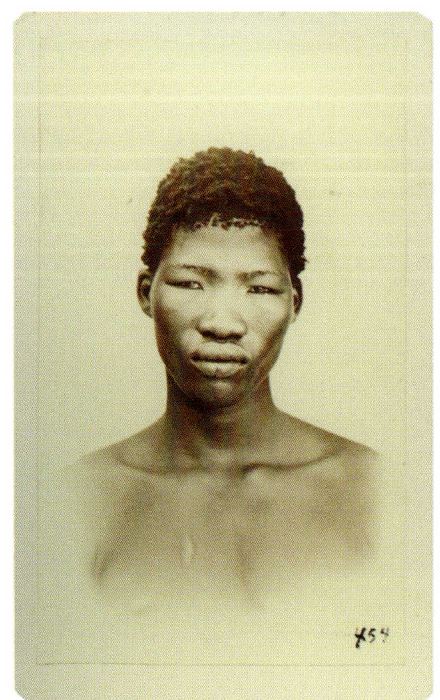

Mokaue, Ba-rolong, Bethanien, Oranje-Frystaat.

Mokane/Mokaue, Rolong, Bethany, Orange Free State.
(EM-SMB/32/827-826)

Mangue, Ga-malete, Bethanien, Oranje-Frystaat.

Mangue, Gamalete, Bethany, Orange Free State.
(EM-SMB/32/829-828)

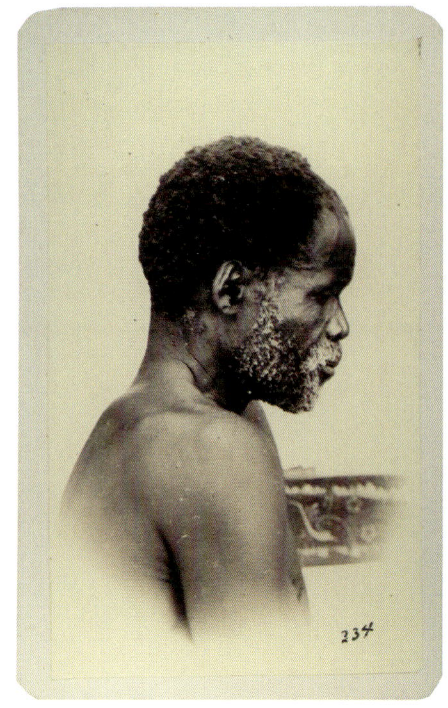
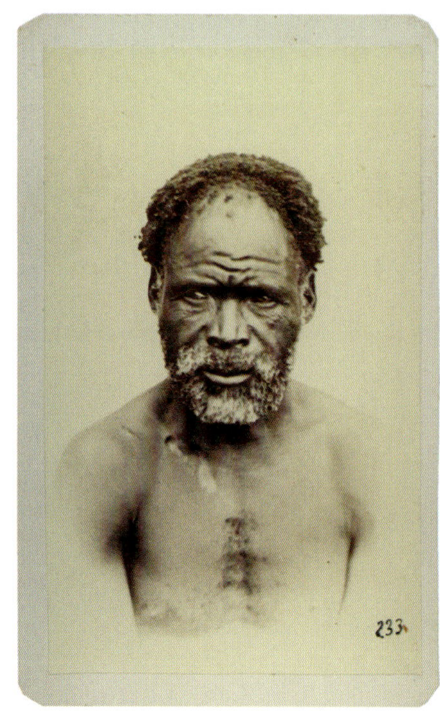
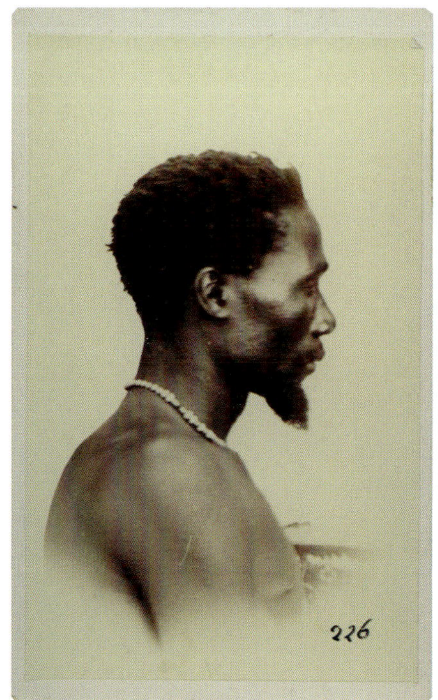
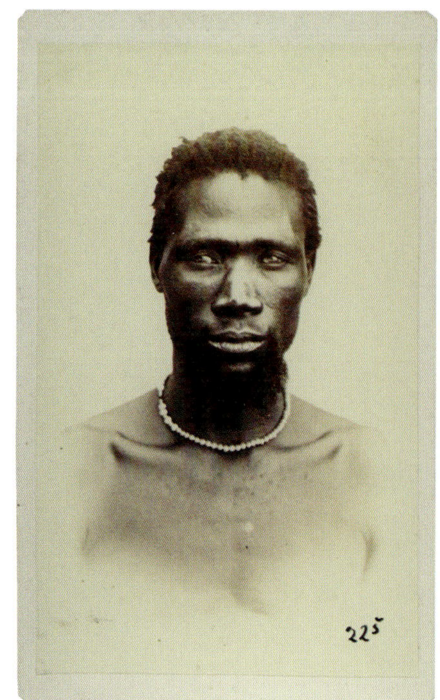

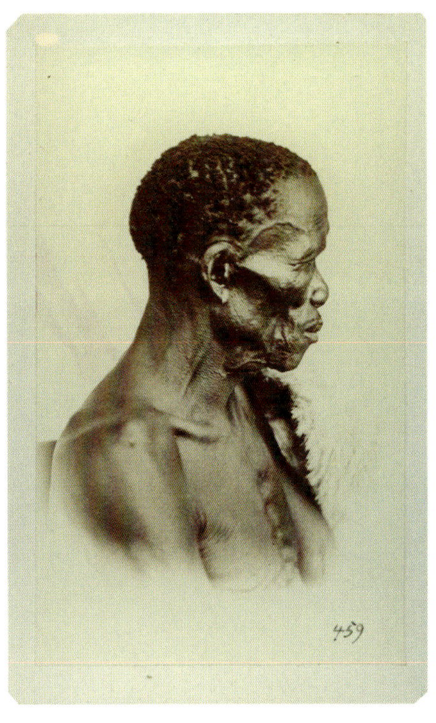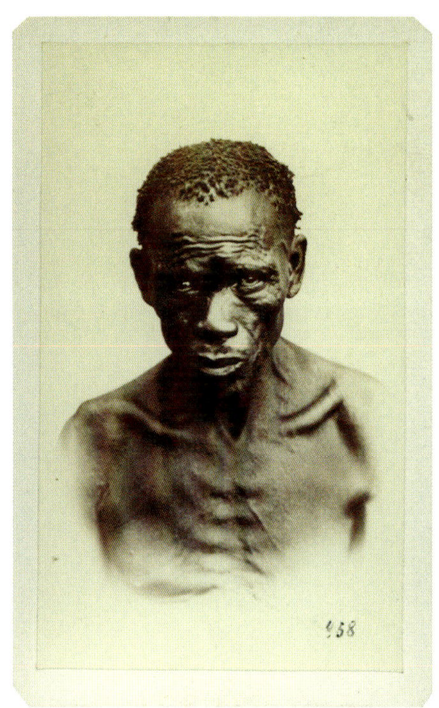

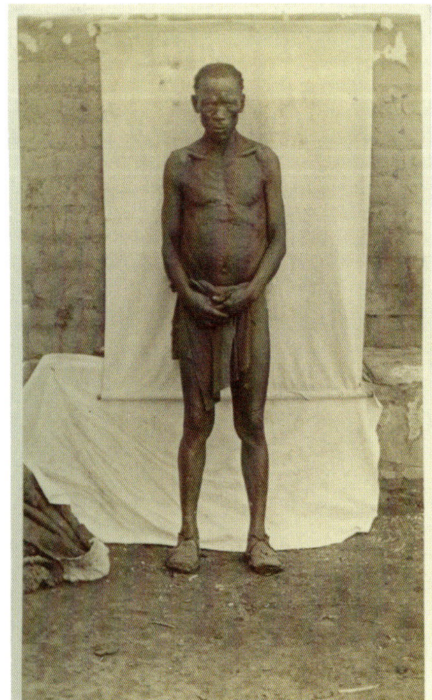

◀ *Figs. 74-75*

Rooiman, Buschmann, Bethanien, Oranje-Frystaat.

Rooiman, San, Bethany, Orange Free State.
(EM-SMB/28/682-681)

Buschmann, Bethanien, Oranje-Frystaat.

Rooiman, San, Bethany, Orange Free State.
(EM-SMB/32/712)

◀ *Fig. 76*

Figs. 77-78 ▶

Linti, Ba-rolong, Bethanien, Oranje-Frystaat.

Linti, Rolong, Bethany, Orange Free State.
(EM-SMB/32/853-852)

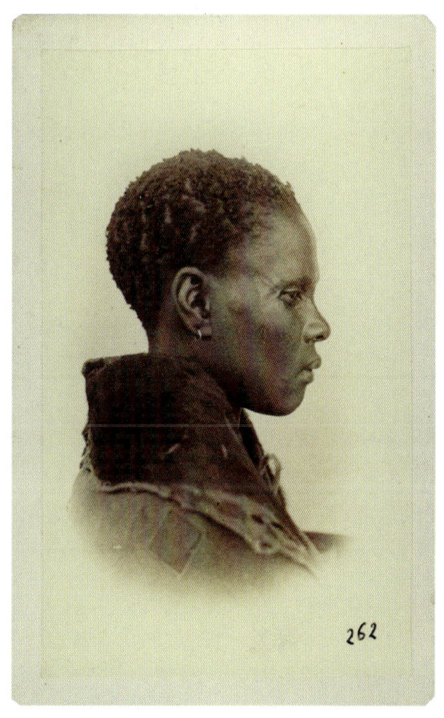

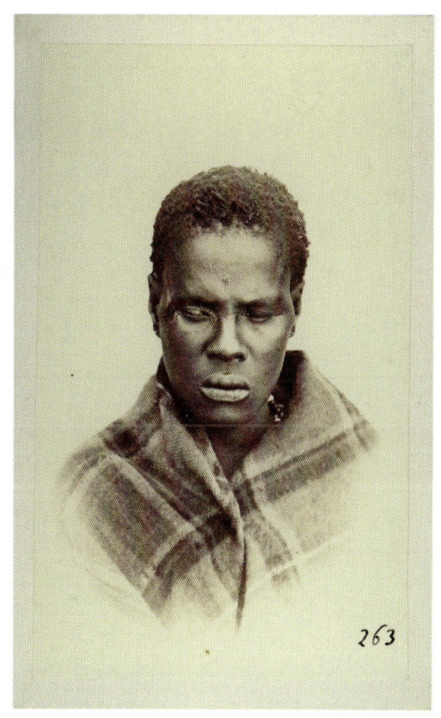

Leaving Bethany on the morning of Saturday, 27 February, Fritsch arrived in Bloemfontein that evening. His equipment had been damaged by water while crossing the Riet River and he needed time to restore it. He stayed in Bloemfontein for five months, residing with the German district surgeon and former mayor of the town, Dr C.J.B. Krause, and his wife, Frederika.[65]

Fritsch did not seem to take much interest in Bloemfontein, describing it as a lawless society. He related how the Boers feared the indigenous people of the region and wanted little to do with them, and how it was seen as a scandal for a white person even to shake hands with a black person. In his travel account he said that the Boers did not regard black people as humans, the speaker of the Volksraad referring to them as 'scoundrels' (*schepsels*). Blacks living within the Boer republic of the Orange Free State were not permitted to own land and could not vote or carry firearms. According to Fritsch, they were poor and very few worked for whites of their own free will. He described how men lived in locations on the outskirts of the towns or worked on the farms, saving money to return home and purchase livestock for their *lobola* or brideprice.[66]

Fritsch photographed six people from Bloemfontein, namely a Mfengu woman, Sarah (recorded as 'the beautiful Sarah, servant of a trader in Bloemfontein') (Figs. 79–80), a Mfengu man called Piet (Figs. 81–82), three Maaue (or Maauwa) men, January, Mazuan and Mawiledm (Figs. 83–88), a Sotho man with the name of Ziwa (Figs. 89–90), and an unidentified San woman (Figs. 91–92).[67] In *Die Eingeborenen*, Fritsch noted that the name 'Maaue' was used to refer to dispersed or wandering groups of Sotho who roamed the Free State, and he described them as having similar features to people from the east bank of the Limpopo River. It is most likely that they were Mahowa, who were related to the Pedi.

Fritsch was eager to meet Moshoeshoe, the renowned king of the Sotho, but was unable to travel to his headquarters at Thaba Bosiu on account of inadequate transport and mounting tensions between the Boer Republic and the Sotho kingdom.[68] While in Bloemfontein he used the opportunity to explore the vicinity of the town to pursue his botanical and zoological interests. He also joined a hunting party on an expedition to the Modder River.[69]

'Die schöne Sarah', dienstmädchen eine Kaufmanns, Fengu, Bloemfontein, Oranje-Frystaat.

'The beautiful Sarah', Mfengu servant of a merchant, Bloemfontein, Orange Free State.
EM-SMB/32/944-943)

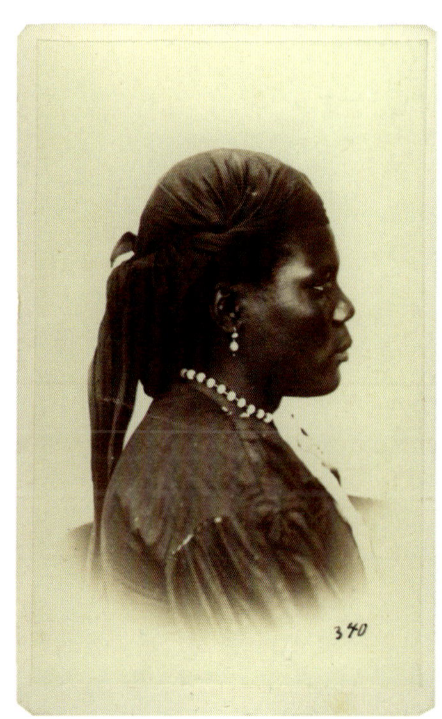
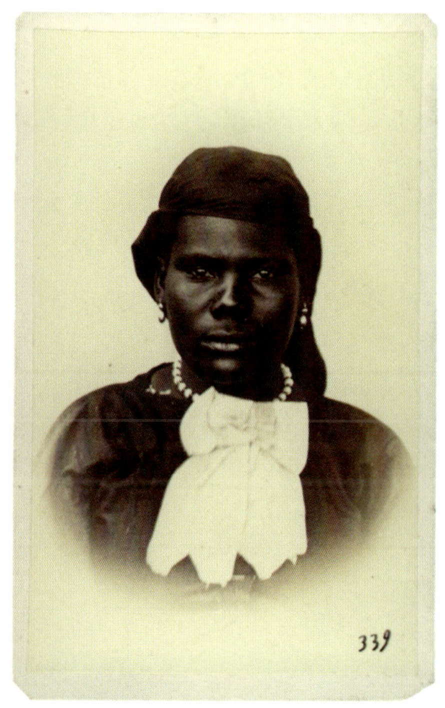

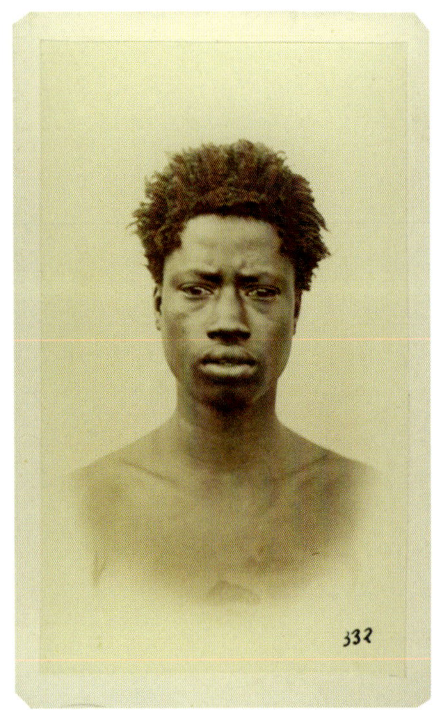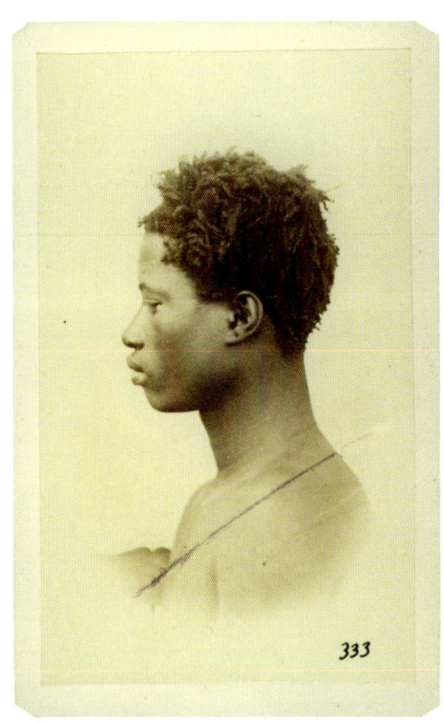

Figs. 81-82

Piet, Fengu (Fingoe), Bloemfontein, Oranje-Frystaat.

Piet, Mfengu, Bloemfontein, Orange Free State.
(EM-SMB/32/937-938)

Mawiledm, Maaue, Bloemfontein, Oranje-Frystaat.

Mawiledm, Maauwa, Bloemfontein, Orange Free State.
(EM-SMB/32/859-858)

Figs. 83-84

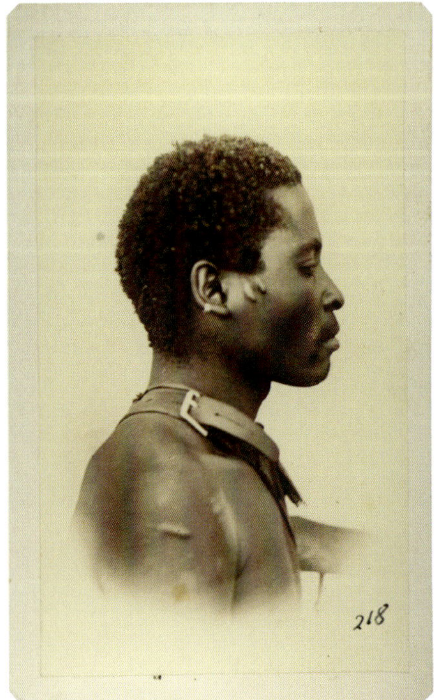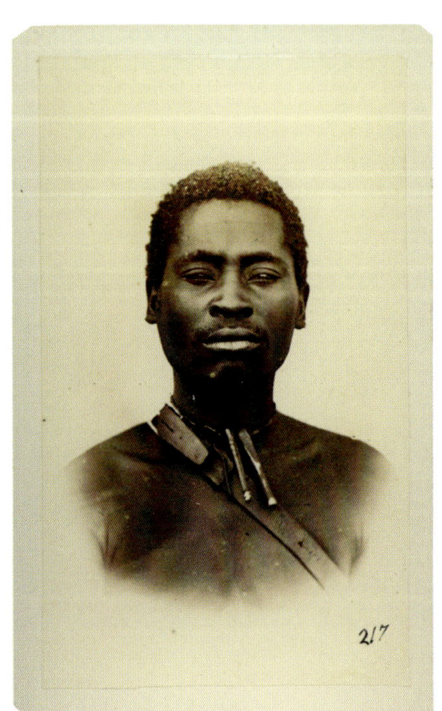

Figs. 85-86 ▶

Mazuan, Maaue, Bloemfontein, Oranje-Frystaat.

Mazuan, Maauwa, Bloemfontein, Orange Free State.
(EM-SMB/32/856-857)

Januarius, Maaue, Bloemfontein, Oranje-Frystaat.

January, Maauwa, Bloemfontein, Orange Free State.
(EM-SMB/32/869-868)

Figs. 87-88 ▶

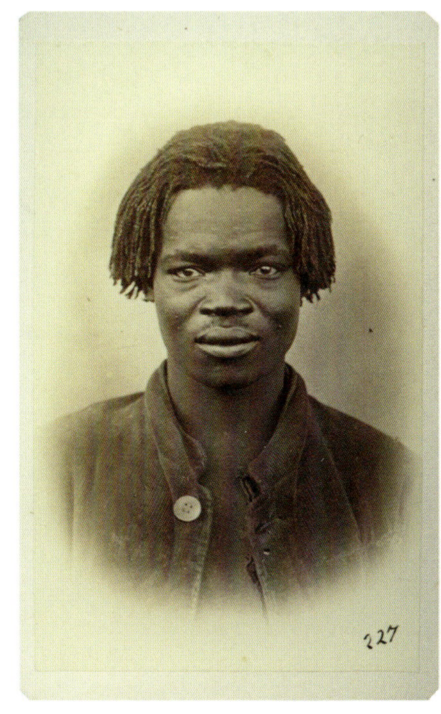
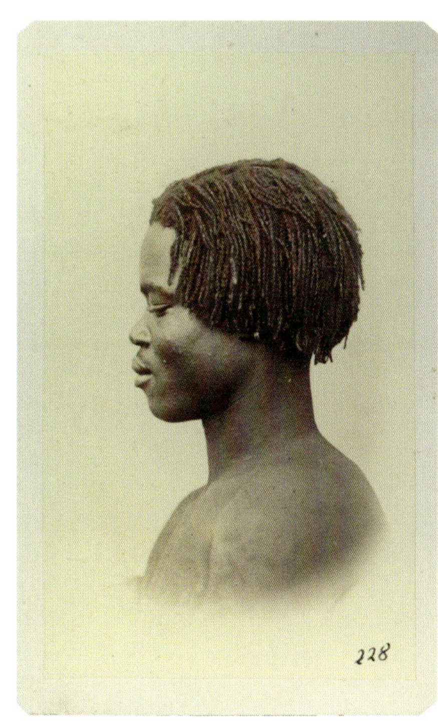
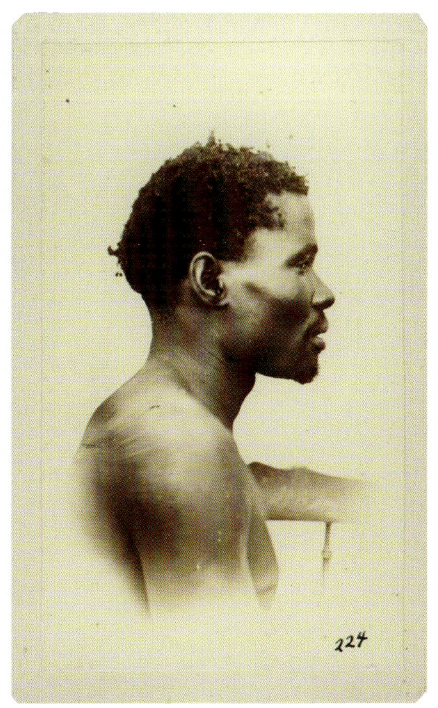
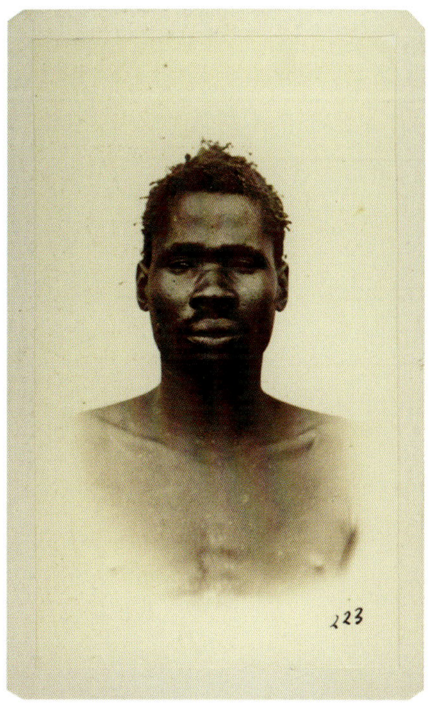

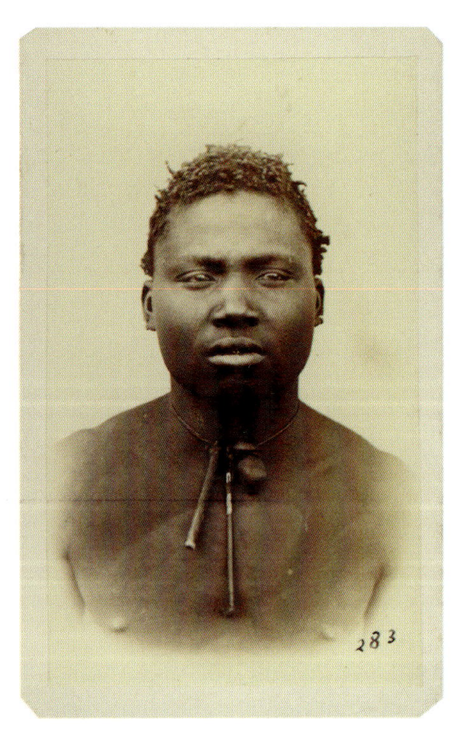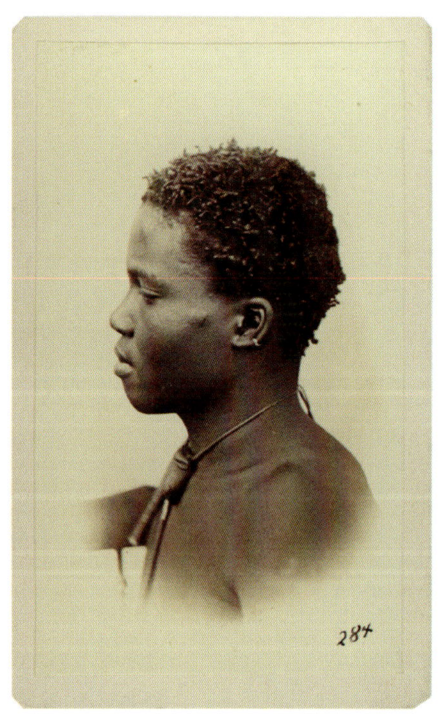

◀ *Figs. 89-90*

Ziwa, Ba-suto, Bloemfontein, Oranje-Frystaat.

Ziwa, Sotho, Bloemfontein, Orange Free State.
(EM-SMB/32/870-871)

Figs. 91-92 ▶

Buschmännin, Bloemfontein, Oranje-Frystaat.

San, Bloemfontein, Orange Free State.
(EM-SMB/32/700-699)

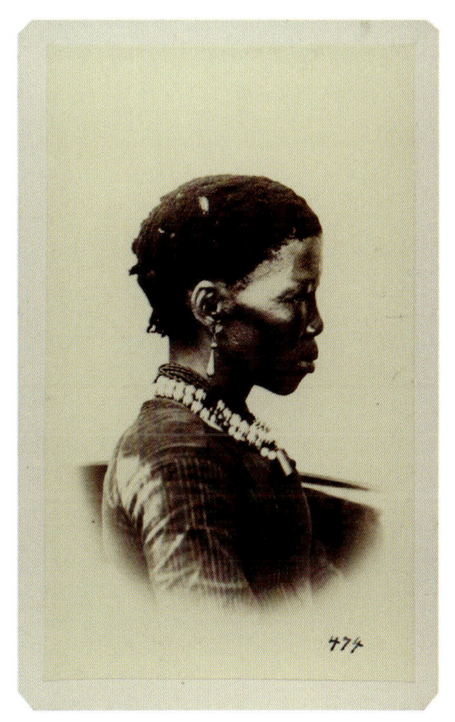

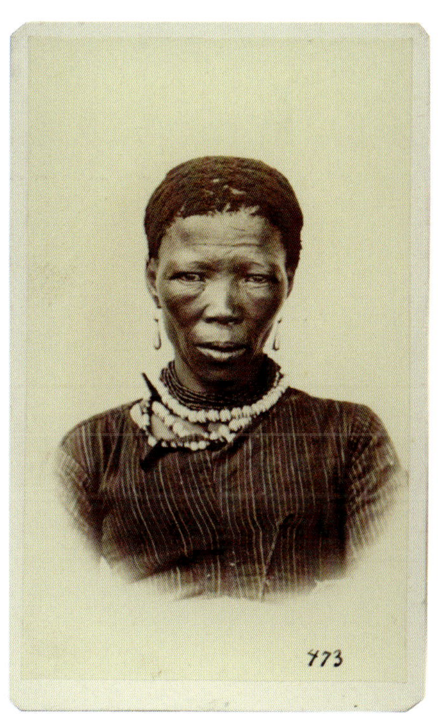

Having heard of the site of a massacre of San and Korana that had taken place in the vicinity of Boshof in 1858, Fritsch left the hunting party and crossed the Modder River with a view to studying the remains of skulls and bones at Prisonierskoppie. On Tuesday, 24 March he visited the site with a man from Boshof who was acquainted with the area.[70]

By the late 1840s relations between the Korana, San, Taung, Tlokwa and Sotho, and the white trekkers in the region had become increasingly strained. In 1858 matters came to a head when the Orange Free State became engaged in war with the Sotho. The San captain Kausob, with the help of around 300 men who included the Korana captain Goliath Yzerbek, launched attacks against white farmers, killing some Boers and raiding cattle from their farms.[71] A commando of Boers and Mfengu under Field Commandant Hendrik Venter forced Kausob's followers to surrender, after a battle in which Kausob and 129 of his followers were killed. Forty-three of the men captured were placed under Mfengu guards and sent to Bloemfontein to be tried. Outside Boshof, however, a commando of Boers attacked and murdered all the prisoners, and the place became known as 'Prisonierskoppie'.[72]

When Fritsch arrived at the site, he found the remains of the murdered prisoners, coming across mainly spinal and pelvic bones and pieces of skulls. He took two pelvic bones and three lower jaw-bones, and later obtained four skulls in Boshof.[73] While in Boshof Fritsch took portraits of the Korana captain Zwart Jaan and his father, Gerrit (Figs. 94–97), as well as four other Korana men, namely David, Klaas, Boos and Piet (Figs. 98–105).[74] It is evident from these portraits as reproduced in the Dammann *Album* that Gerrit, David, Klaas, Boos and Piet were asked to remove their shirts for the photographs. Fritsch also took a larger-format cabinet card photograph of a group of Korana men sitting outside a store in Boshof (Fig. 93); some appear to be the same people who sat for his portraits. Zwart Jaan's father, Gerrit, and Klaas sit next to each other on the stack of timber to the right in the back row, and Boos and David sit on the left-hand side. Piet sits in the front row, second from the left.

Commenting on the Korana subjects in *Die Eingeborenen*, Fritsch observed that this group exhibited variations in physical appearance that could be attributed to the influence of both the San and black people. According to him, the shorter stature of some Korana was evidence of San blood lines, while those with a darker skin tone and taller stature showed the influence of intermarriage with black people. He described Zwart Jaan as representing the latter type.[75] A full-length photograph of a 35-year-old naked Khoikhoi ('Gonaqua') woman from Boshof reproduced in the Carl Dammann *Album* (see Fig. 239) was also credited to Fritsch. This image is reproduced as a wood engraving in *Die Eingeborenen*.[76]

Fig. 93 ▶

Korana bei Boshof.

Korana from Boshof, Orange Free State.
(EM-SMB/32/736)

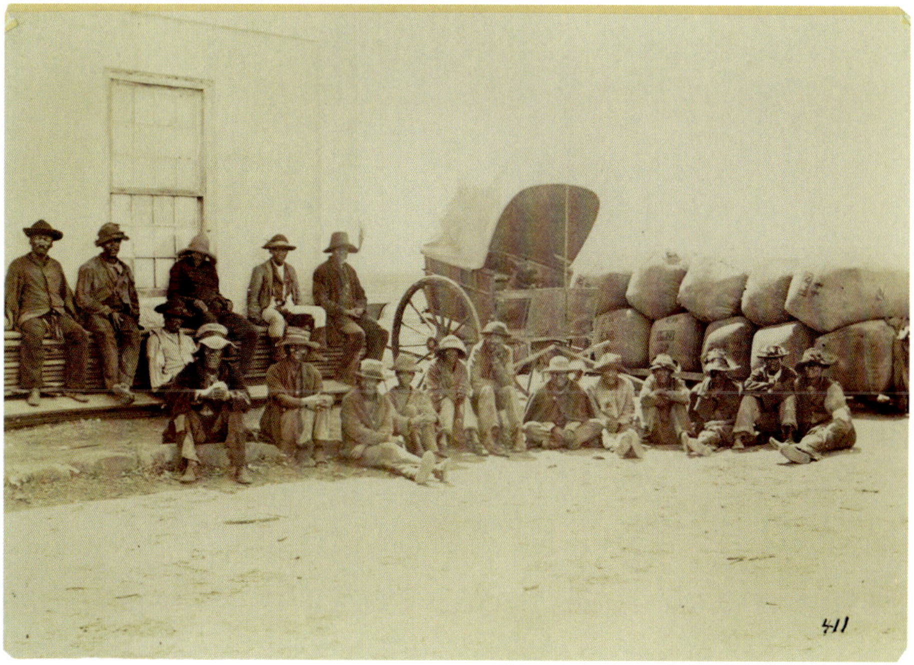

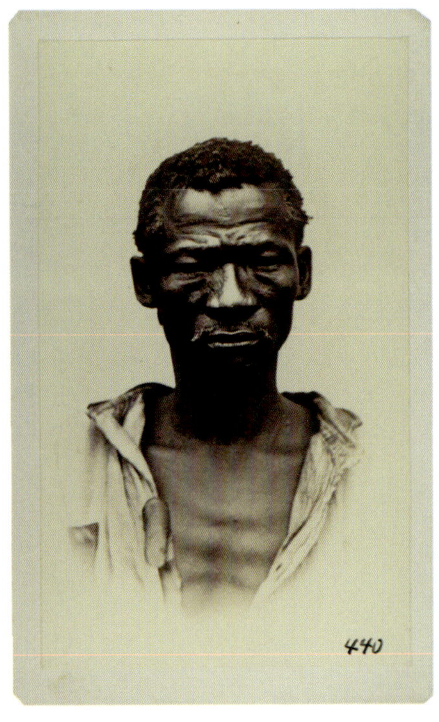
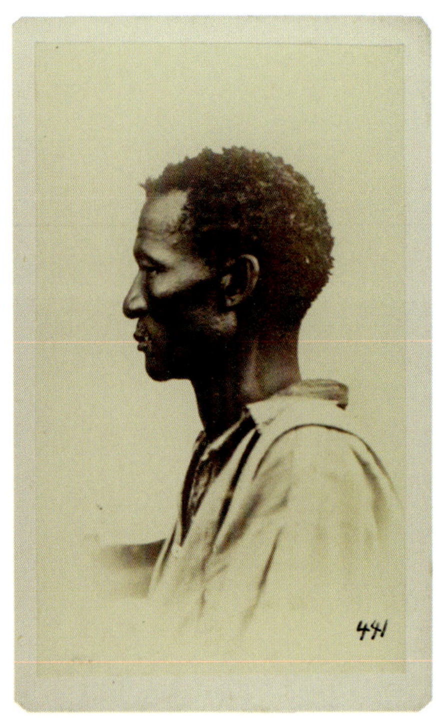

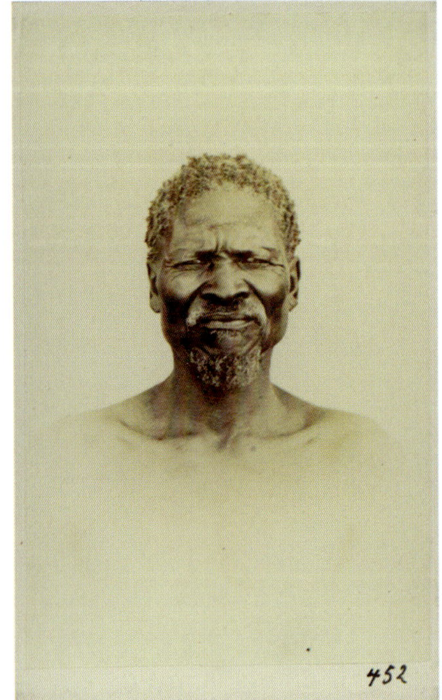
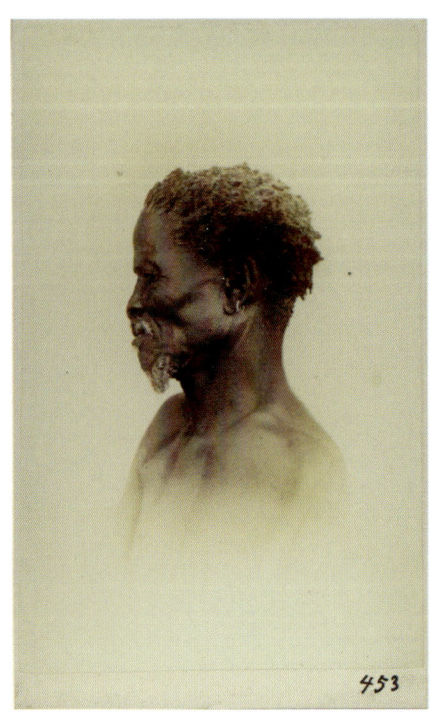

◀ *Figs. 94-95*

Zwart Jaan (Häuptling), Korana, Boshof, Oranje-Frystaat.

Zwart Jaan, Korana captain, Boshof, Orange Free State. (EM-SMB/32/774-775)

Gerrit, Vater des Zwart Jaan, Korana, Boshof, Oranje-Frystaat.

Gerrit, father of Zwart Jaan, Korana, Boshof, Orange Free State. (EM-SMB/32/766-767)

◀ *Figs. 96-97*

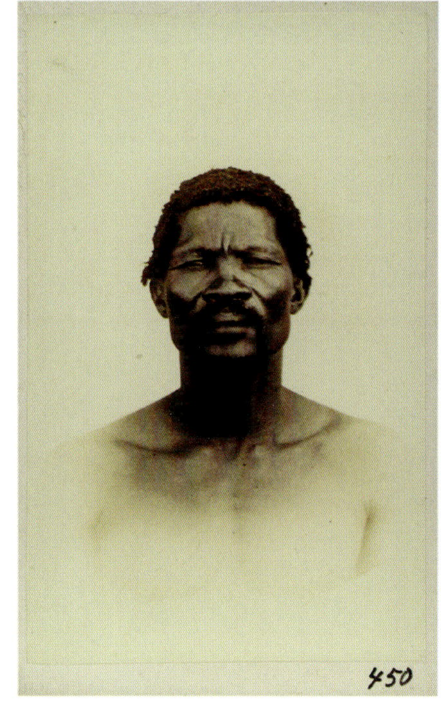
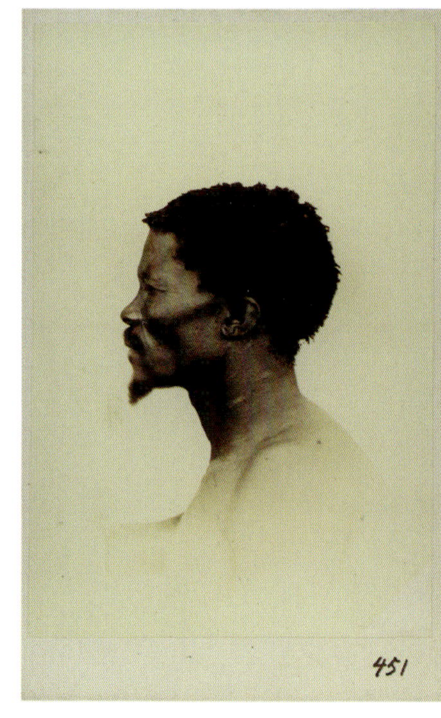

Figs. 98-99 ▶

David, Korana,
Boshof, Oranje-Frystaat.

David, Korana,
Boshof, Orange Free State.
(EM-SMB/32/764-765)

Klaas, Korana,
Boshof, Oranje-Frystaat.

Klaas, Korana,
Boshof, Orange Free State.
(EM-SMB/32/772-773)

Figs. 100-101 ▶

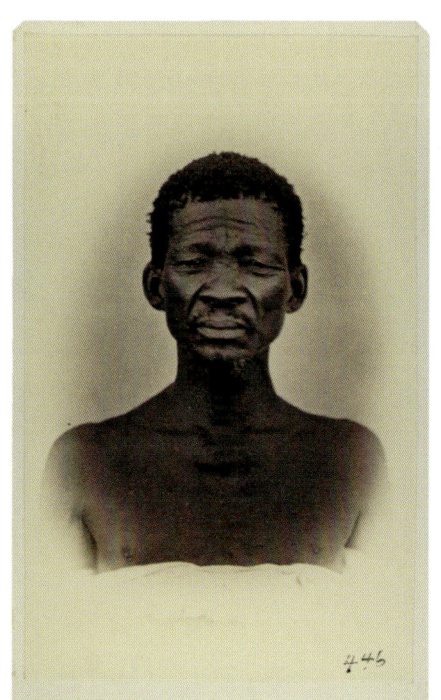

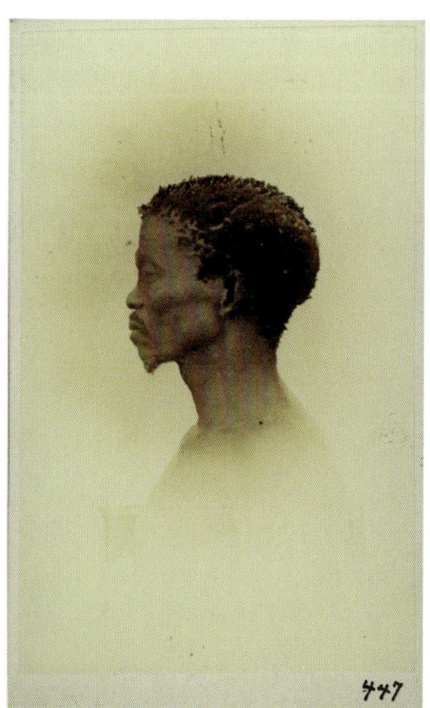

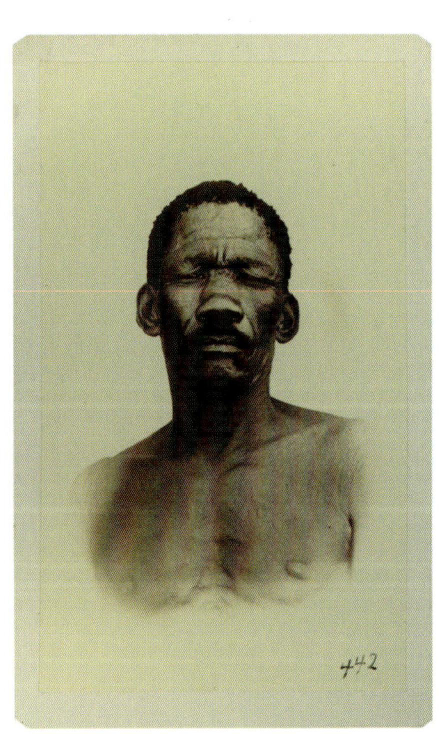
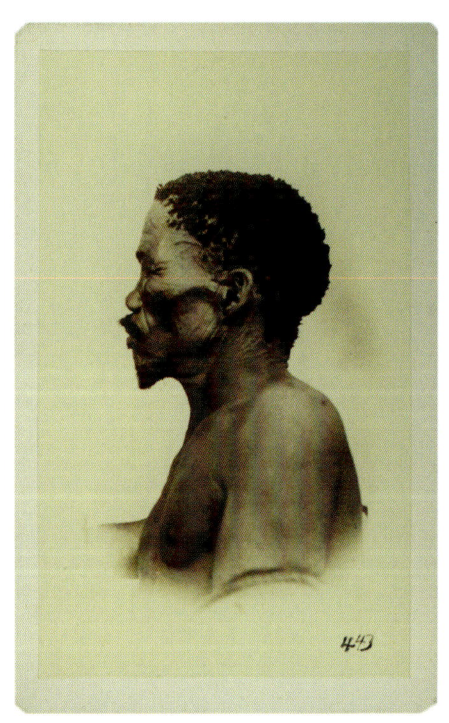

◀ *Figs. 102-103*

Boos, Korana, Boshof, Oranje-Frystaat.

Boos, Korana, Boshof, Orange Free State.
(EM-SMB/32/768-769)

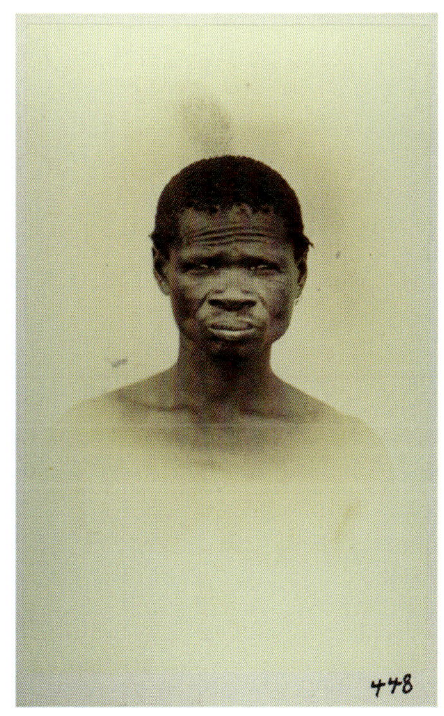

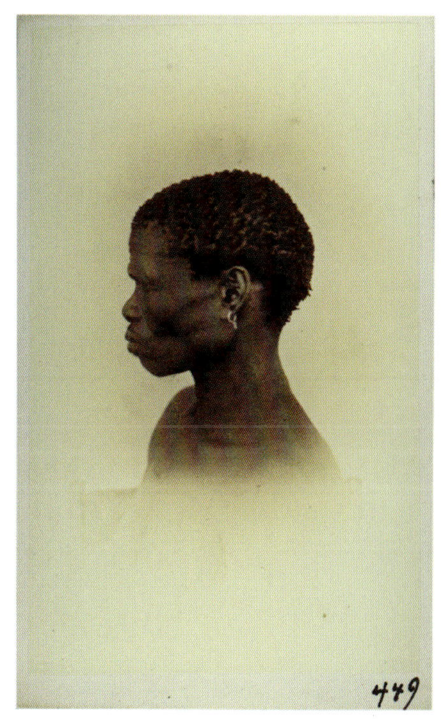

Figs. 104-105 ▶

Piet, Korana, Boshof, Oranje-Frystaat.

Piet, Korana, Boshof, Orange Free State.
(EM-SMB/32/770-771)

Bainsvlei (Guaggafontein/Bain's Farm): 8 April 1864

Fritsch arrived back in Bloemfontein on 28 March. There he met Andrew Hudson Bain, a Scotsman who owned a farm between Bloemfontein and Kimberley, which he had purchased in 1849. It is known today as Bainsvlei. Fritsch accepted Bain's invitation to visit his farm and travelled there on Friday, 8 April.[77]

Fritsch was fascinated by Bain's collection of curiosities, which included stuffed heads of lions, hyenas and antelope mounted on the walls, bottles of preserved lizards and snakes placed on a shelf above the hearth, and an array of weapons and other cultural items hanging from the walls such as San bows and arrows, assegais, kieries and calabashes used as drinking vessels. Fritsch also mentioned garments mounted on leather mannequins and a glass cabinet containing human skulls.[78] Outside, Bain had erected enclosures containing quaggas, antelope and birds, and there were ostriches roaming around the garden.

The main object of Fritsch's visit was a small community of San who lived on Bain's farm and were in his employ. In his book he commented that, while photographing the San, some could not sit still, having smoked too much *dagga*. He noted that it appeared to be a practice among farmers to plant *dagga* for their workers in order to retain them. In his *Atlas* he recorded the names of the people he photographed at Bainsvlei (see Figs. 106–120), namely Ou Kaati, Rose, Carlo, Sanna, Kaati (of whom Fritsch also took a full-length photograph (Fig. 116)), Danster and Bosseck.[79] Fritsch mentioned that the wrinkled skin characteristic of San people was already apparent in Carlo, the 13-year-old son of Sanna.[80] He also reported having heard a story of how Carlo managed to tackle and kill a hyena unarmed.

Fritsch mentioned in his travel account the famous occasion of a few years previously when Andrew Bain invited Prince Alfred, the second son of Queen Victoria who was on a tour of South Africa, to one of the biggest hunts ever staged in the subcontinent. This had taken place on his farm in 1860. At this spectacular event, 20,000 to 30,000 head of game were surrounded and herded by hundreds of Rolong servants towards the royal party. Prince Alfred and his friends shot 1000 head while another 5000 head were killed by the Rolong servants.[81]

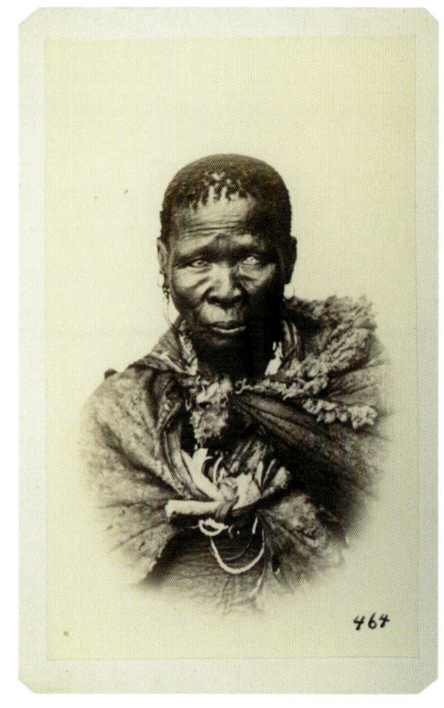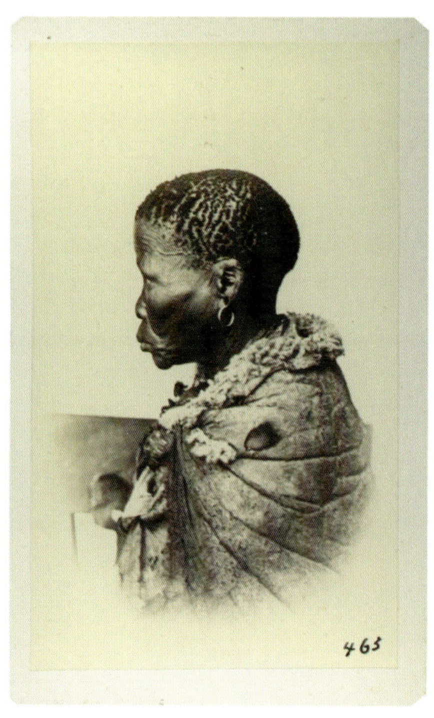

Figs. 106-107 ▶

Oú Kaati, Buschmännin, Guaggafontein,
Oranje-Frystaat.

Ou Kaati, San, Bainsvlei, Orange Free State.
(EM-SMB/32/695-696)

Rose, Buschmännin, Guaggafontein, Oranje-Frystaat.

Rose, San, Bainsvlei, Orange Free State.
(EM-SMB/32/698-697)

Figs. 108-109 ▶

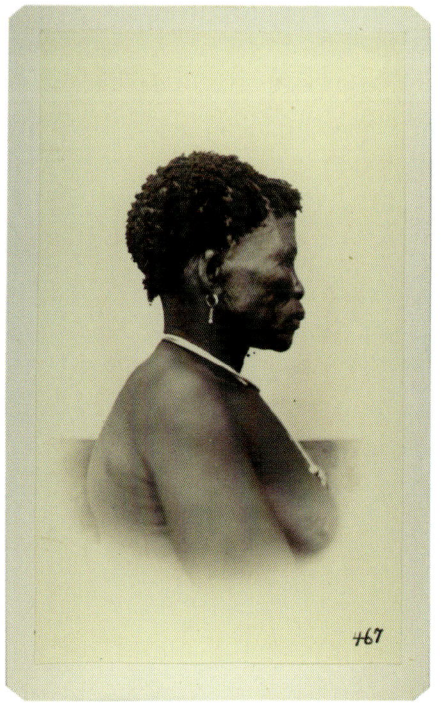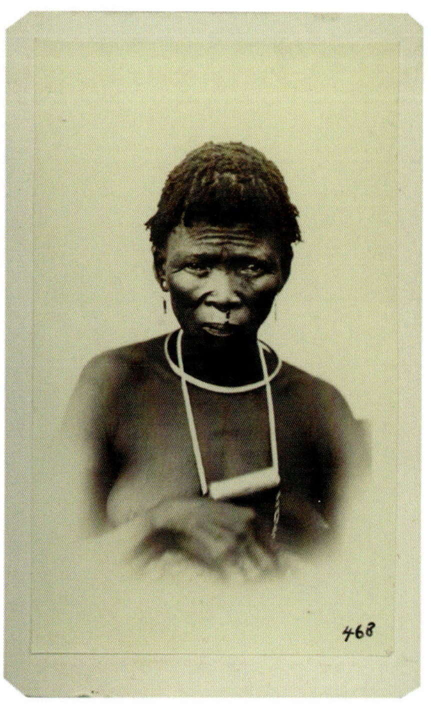

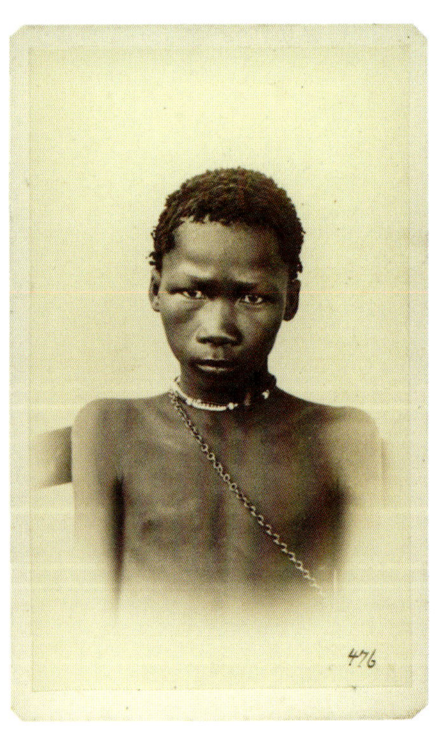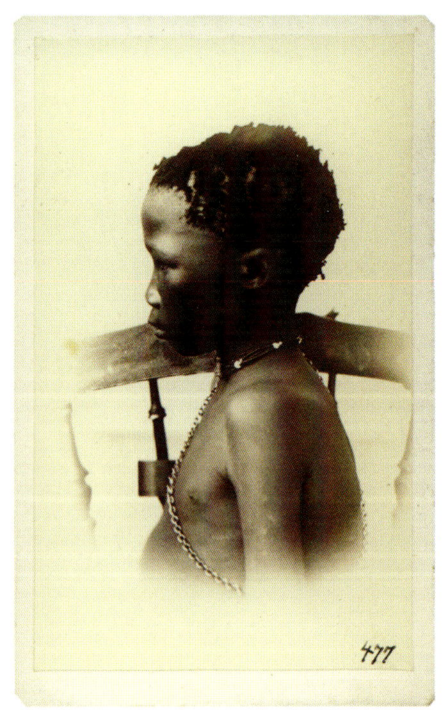

◀ *Figs. 110-111*

Carlo, Buschmannanna, Buschmännin, Guaggafontein,
Oranje-Frystaat..

Carlo, San, Bainsvlei, Orange Free State.
(EM-SMB/28/685-686)

Figs. 112-113 ▶

*Sanna, Buschmännin, Guaggafontein,
Oranje-Frystaat.*

Sanna, San, Bainsvlei, Orange Free State.
(EM-SMB/32/703-704)

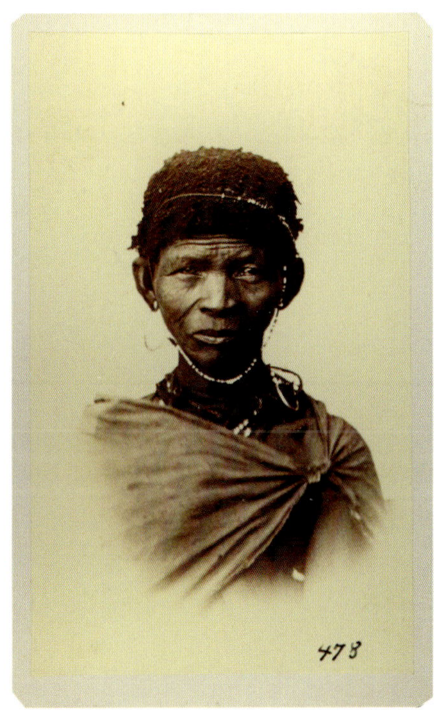 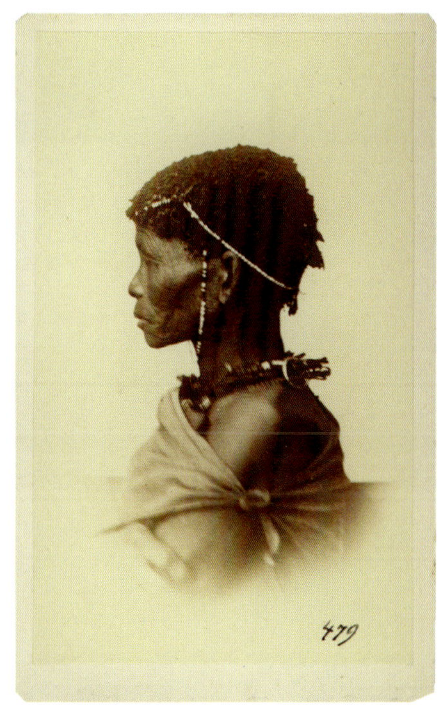

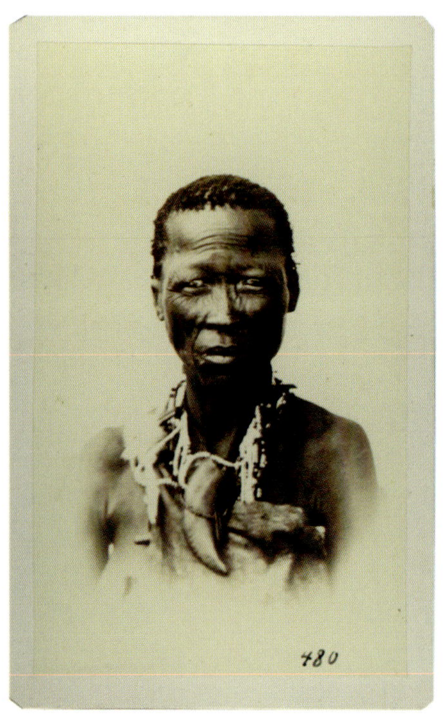
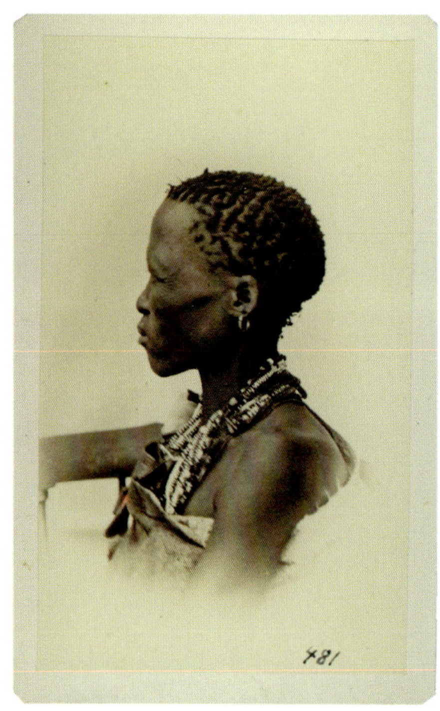

Figs. 114-115

*Kaati, Buschmännin, Guaggafontein,
Oranje-Frystaat.*

Kaati, San, Bainsvlei, Orange Free State.
(EM-SMB/32/705-706)

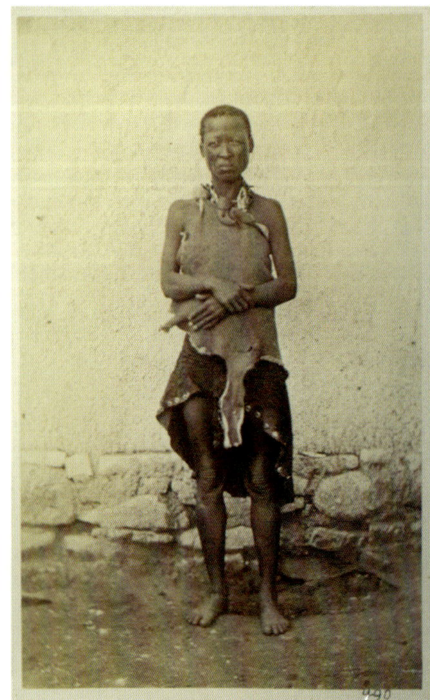

*Buschmännin, Bloemfontein,
Oranje-Frystaat.*

Kaati, San, Bainsvlei, Orange Free State.
(EM-SMB/32/711)

Fig. 116

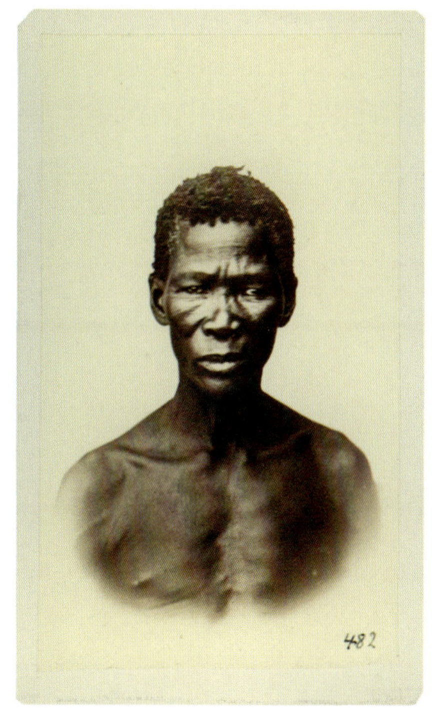

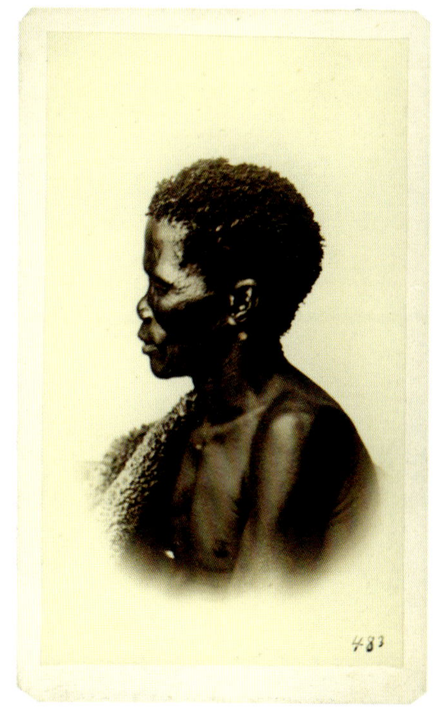

Figs. 117-118 ▶

*Danster, Buschmann, Guaggafontein,
Oranje-Frystaat.*

Danster, San, Bainsvlei, Orange Free State.
(EM-SMB/28/691-692)

*Bosseck, Buschmann, Guaggafontein,
Oranje-Frystaat.*

Bosseck, San, Bainsvlei, Orange Free State.
(EM-SMB/28/683-684)

Figs. 119-120 ▶

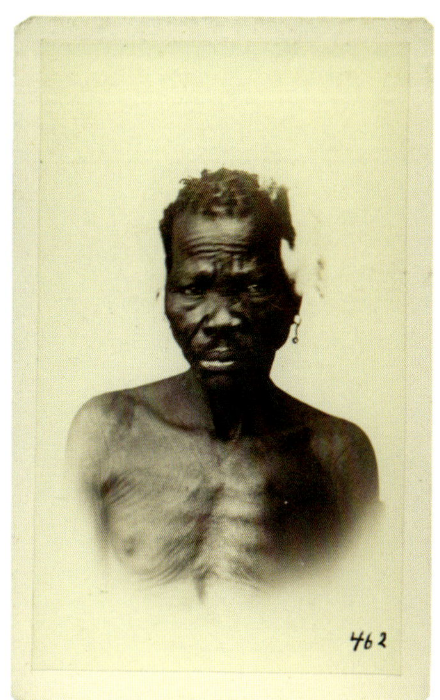

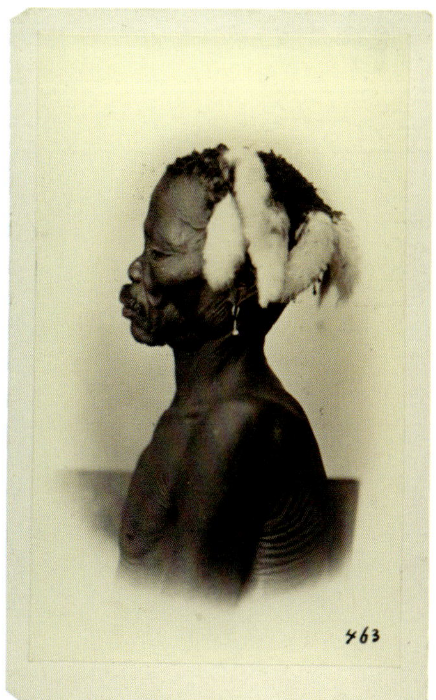

Harrismith: 24 August 1864

Fritsch bade farewell to his Bloemfontein hosts on 23 July. Dr Krause took him some distance from the town, where he exchanged his cart for a passage on an oxwagon. Describing the wagon as heavy and clumsy compared to his horse-drawn cart, Fritsch walked most of the way on their month-long journey to Harrismith in the eastern Free State, arriving there on 24 August.[82] He described the population of the town as poor and dependent on the surrounding farms for supplies, especially milk and meat. Despite the shortage of provisions, the Dutch couple with whom he boarded provided him with ample food.[83]

Fritsch rented an oxwagon from his host, and while waiting for the wagon to arrive, he used the opportunity for work on his photographic project. It was during his visit to Harrismith that Fritsch first photographed 'coloured' (*farbige*) people 'who described themselves as "Griqua"'. These were presumably Mickie and Piet Nero (Figs. 121–124), whose portraits were reproduced in the *Atlas* and the Dammann *Album*. Although they referred to themselves as Griqua, Fritsch was of the opinion that they lacked sufficient 'white blood lines', having very 'short and woolly hair'.[84] He also mentioned photographing several Zulu and Tlokwa ('Mantatees'), whom he recorded in his *Atlas* as Booi, Umsugune and Louis (Figs. 125–130), and Jaantje and Malao (Figs. 131–134), respectively. In his *Atlas* he also noted that Booi had a 'large and well-structured body'.[85]

Fritsch described these people as being 'pure' in terms of their ethnic origins, even though they mostly dressed in European clothes.[86] This was also the case with a young man whom he photographed smoking *dagga* with a companion. Fritsch was particularly fascinated by the incident and noted how they smoked *dagga* from a wonderfully constructed pipe partly filled with water. He described them passing the pipe around, giving each other the opportunity to puff on it, blowing smoke in different ways and fantasising about the images they saw in the clouds of smoke.[87]

Figs. 121-122 ▶

Mickie, Hottentottin, Harrismith, Oranje-Frystaat.

Mickie, (Gona) Khoikhoi, Harrismith, Orange Free State.
(EM-SMB/32/753-752)

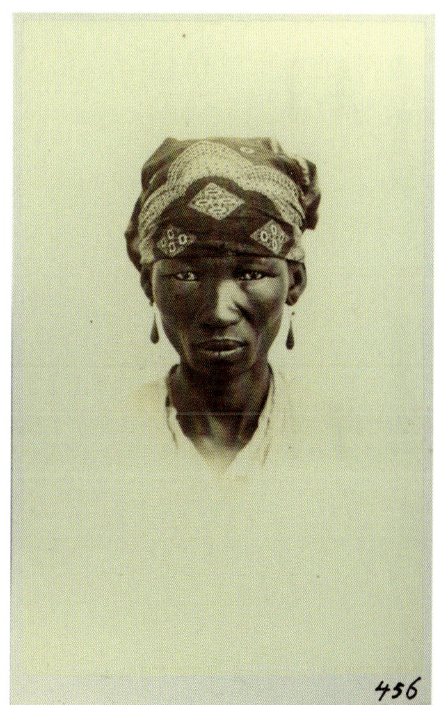

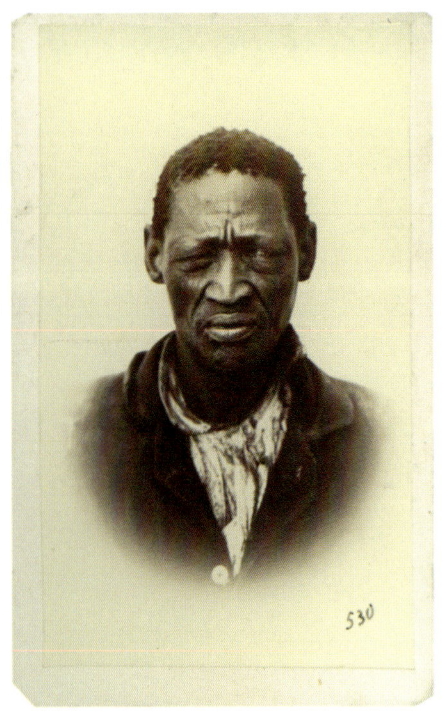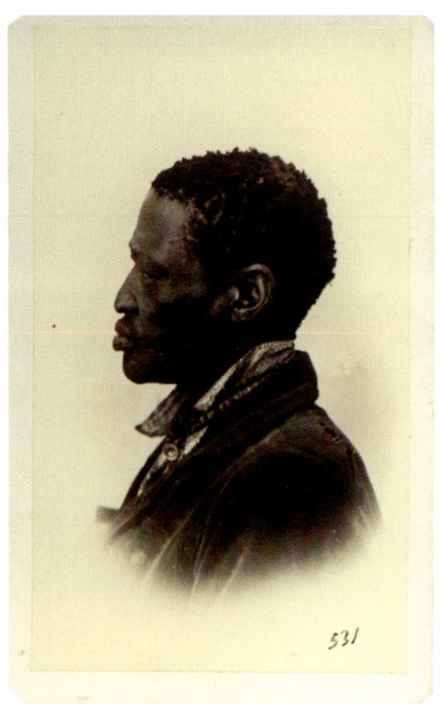

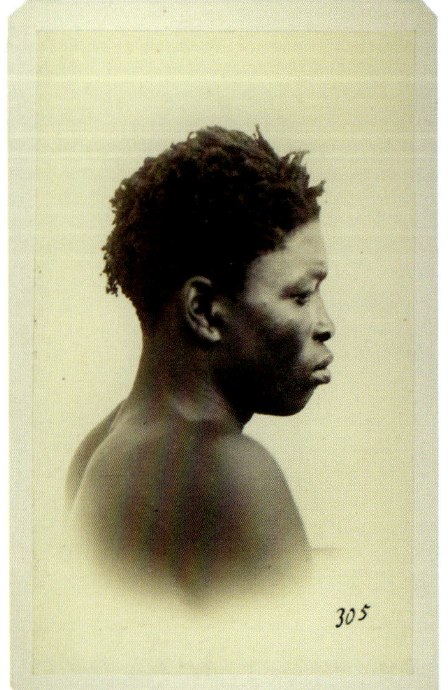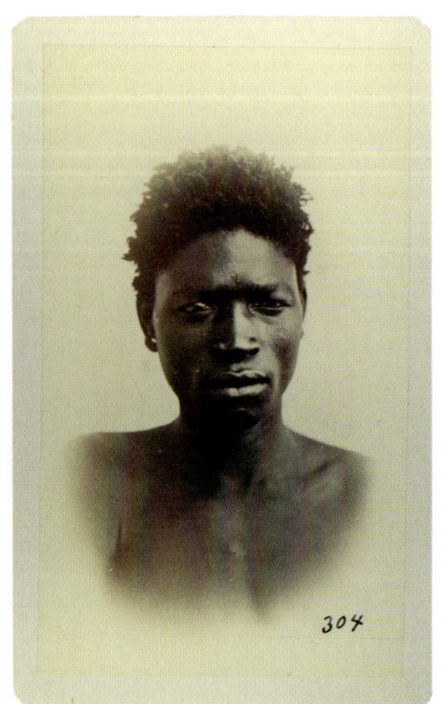

◀ *Figs. 123-124*

Piet Nero, Griqua, Harrismith, Oranje-Frystaat.

Piet Nero, Griqua, Harrismith, Orange Free State.
(EM-SMB/32/1051-1052)

Booi, Ama-zulu, Harrismith, Oranje-Frystaat.

Booi, Zulu, Harrismith, Orange Free State.
(EM-SMB/32/906-905)

◀ *Figs. 125-126*

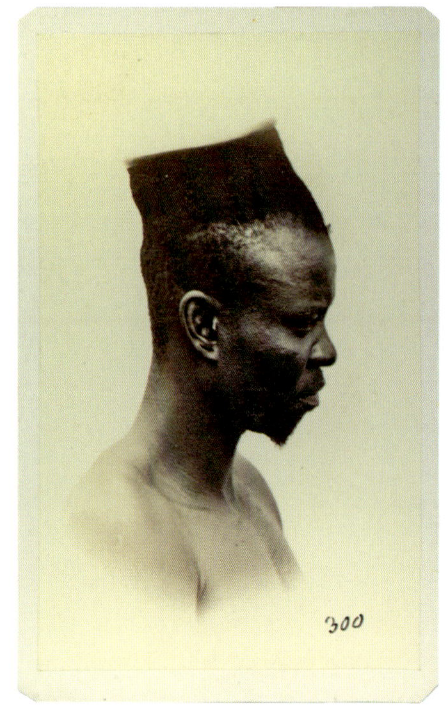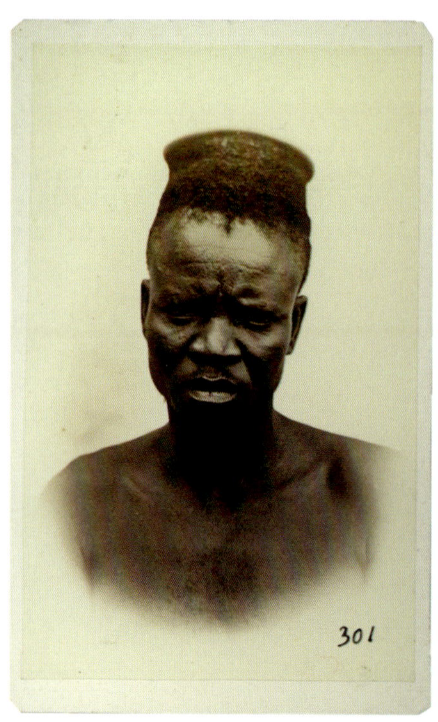

Figs. 127-128 ▶

U'msungune, Ama-zulu, Harrismith, Oranje-Frystaat.

Umsungune, Zulu, Harrismith, Orange Free State.
(EM-SMB/32/898-897)

Louis, Ama-zulu, Harrismith, Oranje-Frystaat.

Louis, Zulu, Harrismith, Orange Free State.
(EM-SMB/32/908-907)

Figs. 129-130 ▶

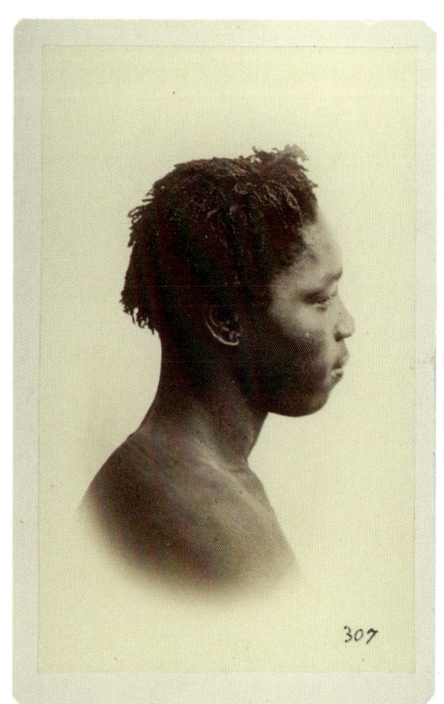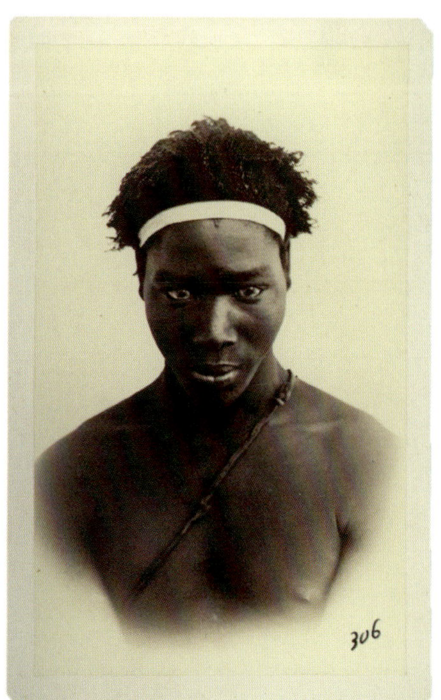

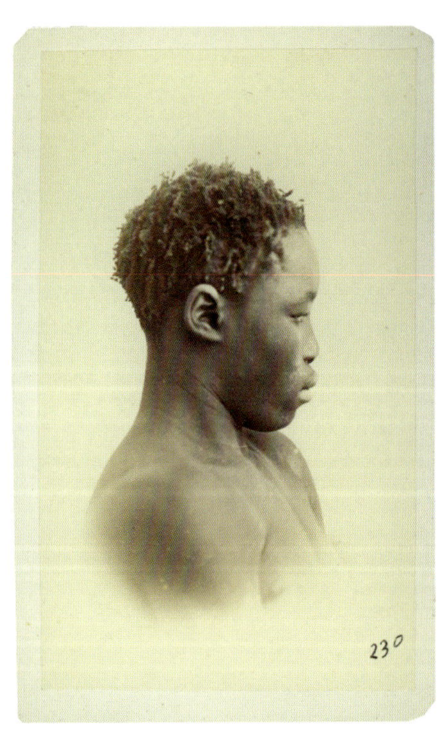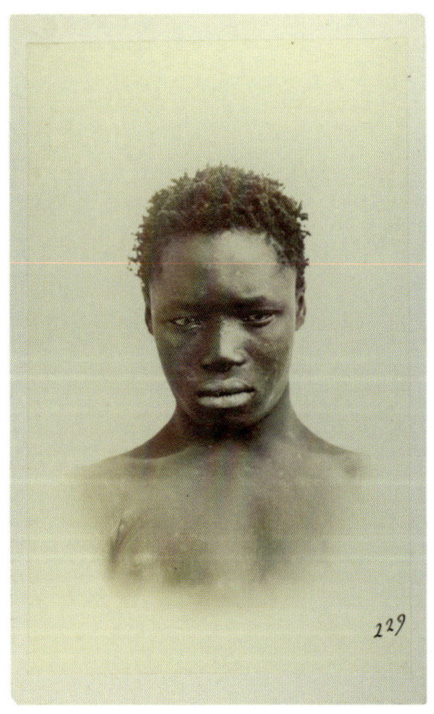

◀ *Figs. 131-132*

Jaantje, Mantatisi, Harrismith, Oranje-Frystaat.

Jaantje, Tlokwa, Harrismith,
Orange Free State.
(EM-SMB/32/865-864)

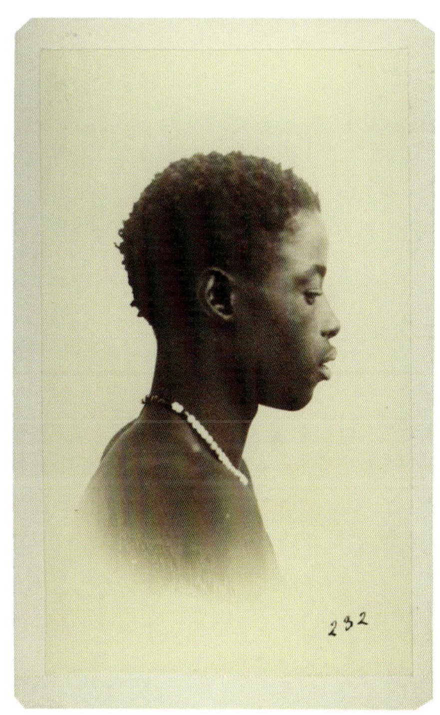

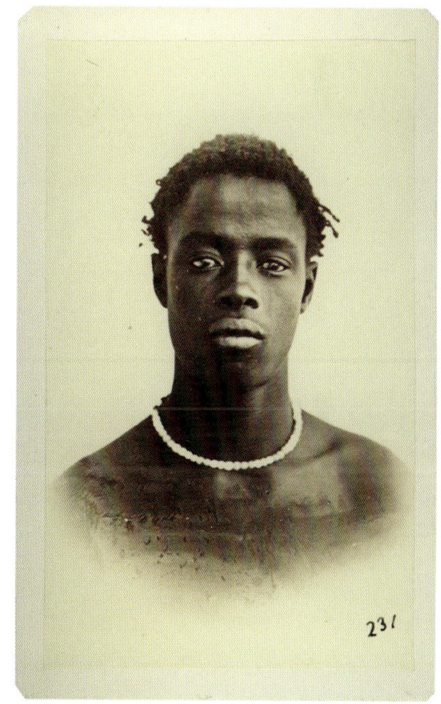

Figs. 133-134 ▶

Malao, Mantatisi, Harrismith, Oranje-Frystaat.

Malao, Tlokwa, Harrismith,
Orange Free State.
(EM-SMB/32/867-866)

Fritsch stayed in Harrismith for almost a month, departing for Durban on Tuesday, 13 September. He crossed the Tugela, Bushmans and Mooi rivers, and stopped to photograph the magnificent view of the Umgeni River plunging into a deep gorge. Setting up his photographic tent, he proceeded to capture the scene. Then, while he was still packing his equipment, a fire, driven by the wind, swept across the veld. Although he was safely encamped on an open stretch of gravel, the draught of the fire uprooted his photographic tent and caused considerable damage to his photographic equipment, with bottles of chemicals, glass containers, finished negatives and glass plates being dashed to pieces. He worked throughout the night to restore his equipment and was bitterly disappointed that he had lost many of his negatives.[88]

Fritsch stopped over in Pietermaritzburg, the capital of the Colony of Natal, where he wanted to photograph Zulu people, whom he described as particularly well developed, compared to the Xhosa he had encountered: 'Among the great number of Zulus who enliven the streets of Maritzburg I saw many splendid specimens whom I would have liked to have included in my picture gallery.' But owing to his inability to find a suitable translator and intermediary, he was not able to photograph them.[89]

On his arrival in Durban on Thursday, 6 October, Fritsch was obliged to surrender his three rifles as the colonial government in Natal had instituted a clampdown on the possession of firearms. This offended him and led him to arrange an early departure.[90] Fritsch does not mention the people he photographed in Durban in his travel narrative, though in *Die Eingeborenen* he goes to some length in describing the hairstyles of the Zulu men he photographed there. 'A national peculiarity which strikes one when viewing the portraits is the artistically formed hairstyles, the bizarre form of which contributes much to the wild expressions of the faces.'[91] Referring to the figures in his *Atlas*, Fritsch described how with young men the hair hung wildly around their heads in thin matted strings, as with the young Tsonga man, Umgumele (Figs. 137–138).[92] In the case of Undewel (Figs. 135–136),[93] the hair was dressed in a particular way by matting and mixing gum into the hair to form a 'cap' (*Kappe*). In other subjects, such as Ungeke (Figs. 141–142),[94] combs were inserted into the hair so that the long matted strings stood upright and formed a type of 'halo' framing the head. Fritsch wrote that these marvellous hairstyles were the product of caprice and the individual taste of these Zulu 'dandies', and their creation took much patience, considerable effort being required to achieve these effects. These styles, he noted, were only indulged in 'as long as the boys cannot be called warriors'.[95]

With mature men, such as Utambosa (Figs. 139–140),[96] the 'national hairstyle' took the form of a crown built up on the top of their heads, the rest of the hair being cut short. Referring to the wood engraving in *Die Eingeborenen* (reproduced from the photograph in Fig. 241), Fritsch remarked that this hair styling took much time and effort to maintain, and that the hair had to be kept smooth with an ivory skewer.[97] In the *Atlas*, Fritsch mentioned that Utambosa had a snuff spoon stuck into his hair. In addition to these Zulu men, Fritsch photographed three indentured Indian labourers from Madras, including Wenketazami and Coota (Figs. 143–145).[98]

During his month-long stay in Durban, Fritsch focused predominantly on his botanical and zoological interests in the area surrounding the town. He was invited to visit the farm of Joachim Friedrich Kahts, a German shipping agent and real estate broker from Hamburg. Here he had an opportunity to excavate a grave at a deserted homestead in Umhlanga, with a view to learning how the Zulu buried their dead.[99] On Monday, 5 November he boarded the RMS *Dane* for Cape Town.

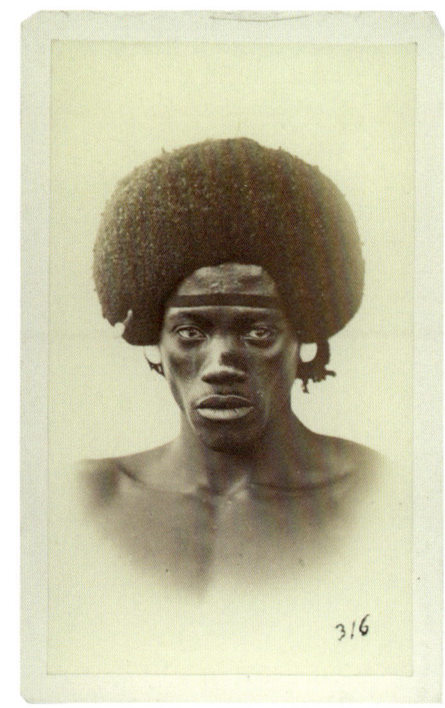
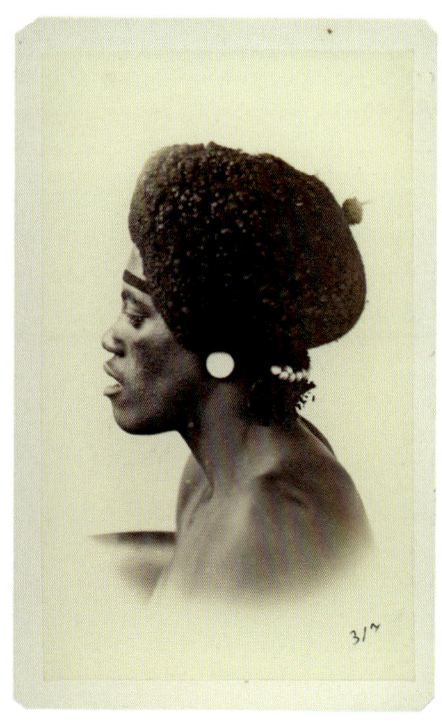

Figs. 135-136 ▶

U'ndéwel, Ama-zulu, Durban, Natal.

Undewel, Zulu, Durban, Natal.
(EM-SMB/32/903-904)

U'mguméle, Tonga, L'urban [sic]*, Natal.*

Umgumele, Tsonga, Durban, Natal.
(EM-SMB/32/909-910)

Figs. 137-138 ▶

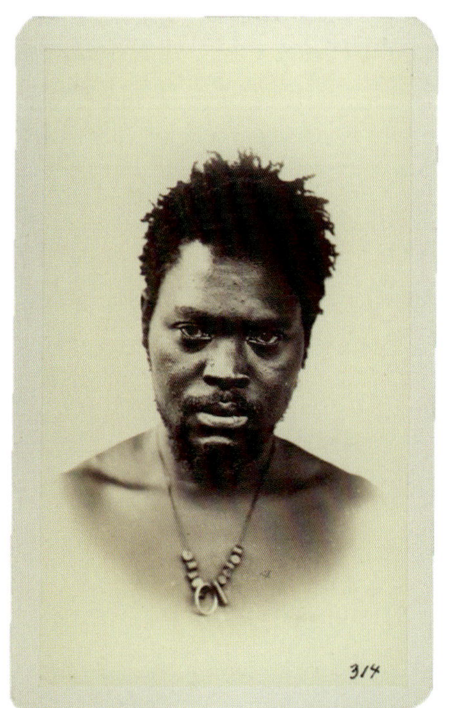

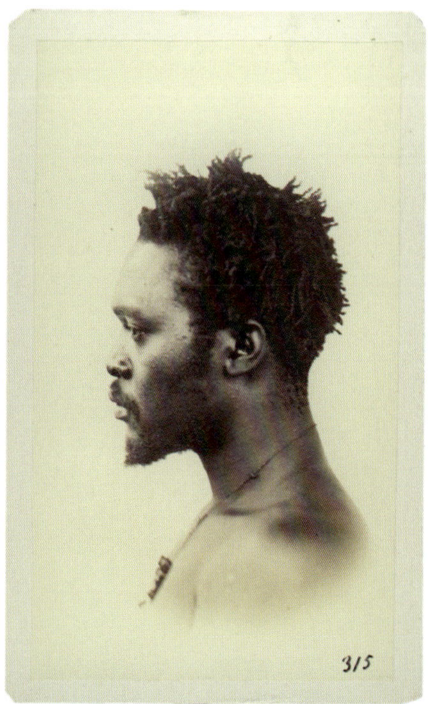

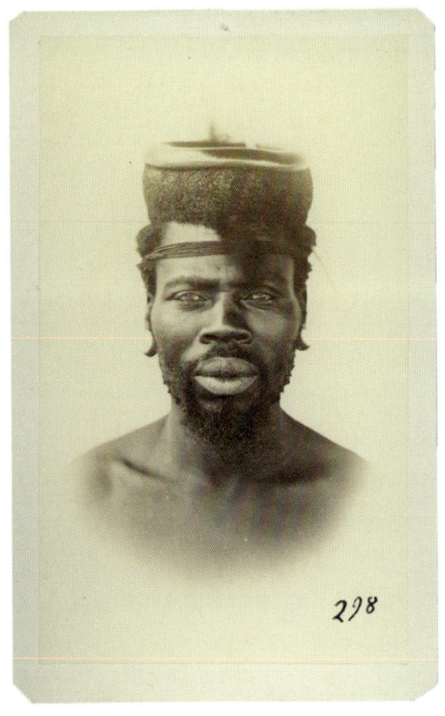

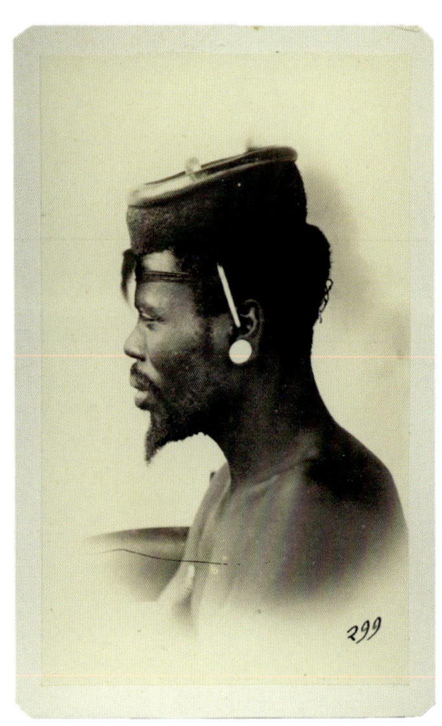

◀ *Figs. 139-140*

U'tambosa, Ama-zulu, Durban, Natal.

Utambosa, Zulu, Durban, Natal.
(EM-SMB/32/899-900)

U'ngéke, Ama-zulu, Durban, Natal.

Ungeke, Zulu, Durban, Natal.
(EM-SMB/32/901-902)

◀ *Figs. 141-142*

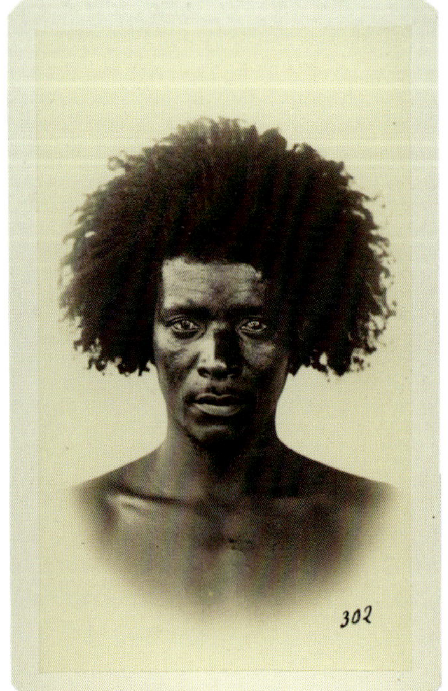

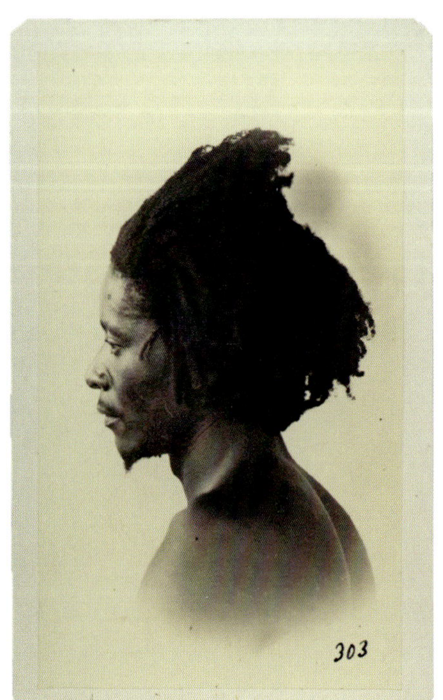

Figs. 143-144 ▶

Indian Coolie, Madras, D'Urban.

Indian (from Madras), Durban, Natal.
(SANL/INIL/14200)

Wenketazami, Indian Coolie, Madras, D'Urban.

Wenketazami, Indian (from Madras), Durban, Natal.
(SANL/INIL/14201)

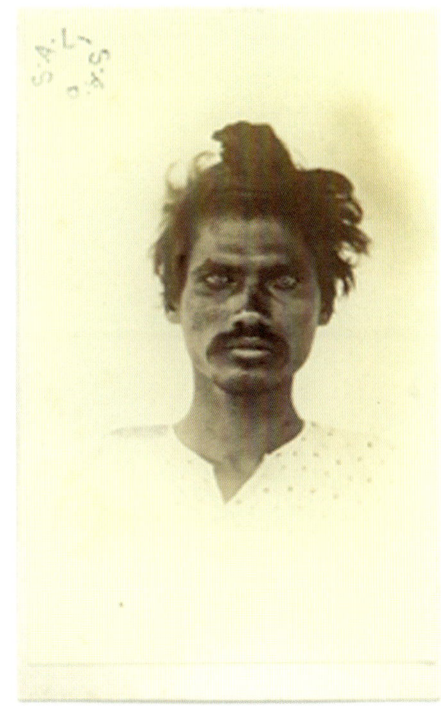

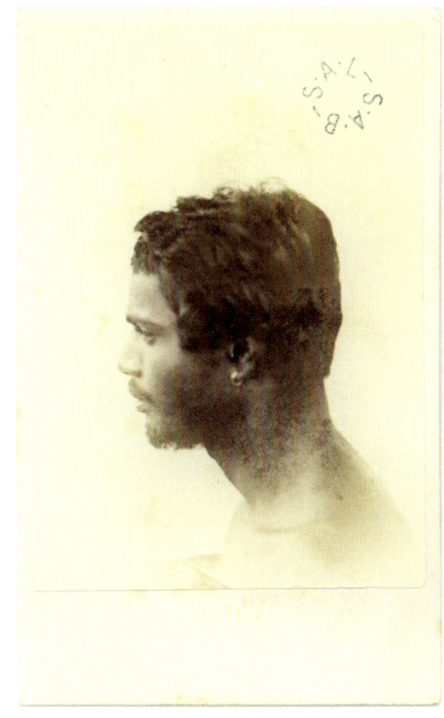

Coota, Indian Coolie, Madras, D'Urban.

Coota, Indian (from Madras), Durban, Natal.
(SANL/INIL/14202)

Fig. 145 ▶

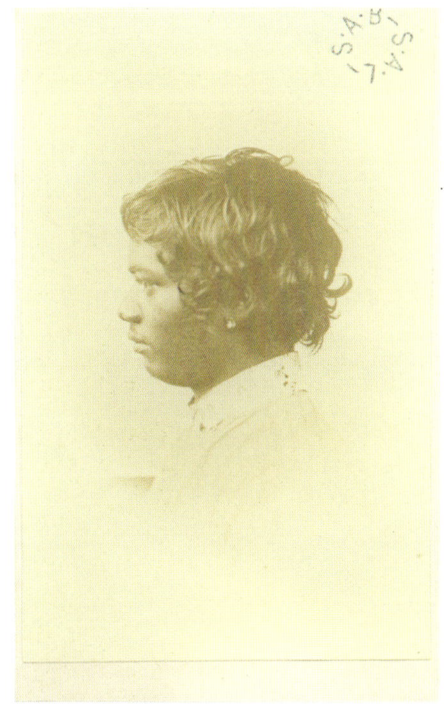

Setting out on his second journey to the north four and a half months later, Fritsch boarded the *Saxon* on 17 March 1865, and sailed from Cape Town to Port Elizabeth. He first travelled to Grahamstown to collect the oxwagon that he had sent ahead, and then went on to Cradock and Colesberg, en route to Griquastad. Arriving at the Gariep on 9 June, he experienced yet another eventful river crossing. He encountered a group of Tswana men crossing the river in a boat. They approached him for '*lekkere warm water*' (alcohol). Having negotiated a bottle of gin and payment for assisting him, they disassembled his wagon, transported it across the river, and reassembled it on the right bank. Fritsch commented favourably on the physique of these Tswana men, who swam across the river while ferrying his belongings. The following day he continued his journey to Griquastad.[100]

Griquastad had been established around the LMS mission station of Klaarwater founded by William Anderson and Cornelius Kramer in 1802. On his visit to Klaarwater in 1813, the Revd John Campbell persuaded the community, comprising Korana, San, Bergenaars, Tlhaping, 'Bastaards' (creole people), Oorlam (formerly bandit groups of colonial fugitives) and trekboers, to adopt the collective designation of Griqua, and change the name Klaarwater to Griquastad, or Griqua Town.[101] By 1822 Griqua communities stretched along the course of the Gariep River from Griquastad to Philippolis and inland towards Kuruman. The captaincies included Griquastad (headed by Andries Waterboer), Campbell (the residence of Cornelius Kok), Daniel's Kuil (where Barend Barends held sway), Boetsap and Philippolis (the town of Adam Kok).[102] The first two decades of the Griqua nation were dominated by rivalries over leadership, family and mission loyalties, grazing land, water and hunting, as well as hostilities with other groups who had moved into the area. Notwithstanding their alliances with the Griqua, Britain abandoned them by handing over the sovereignty of the Orange Free State to the Republican Boers in 1854 and annexing Griqualand West in 1871 after the discovery of diamonds.

The subjugation of the once independent Griqua is evident in Fritsch's description of his arrival at the desolate residence of Andries Waterboer at Griquastad on 13 June 1864. He described Waterboer as an intelligent and well-educated man, though Waterboer resisted Fritsch's offer to take his portrait. Fritsch attributed this to Waterboer's suspicion of Europeans in general, but more specifically to his dislike of having his face captured in a photograph. There are no records of Griqua people that Fritsch might have photographed while in Griquastad, though he did photograph four Tswana men there, who are recorded in his *Atlas* and the Dammann *Album*, namely Lerumo and Mossao (two Kgatla men) (Figs. 146–149), Hendrik (of the Ngwaketse) (Figs. 150–151) and April ('Babidiji', perhaps Bididi, who were attached to Mokgatle's Fokeng in the Rustenburg district) (Figs. 152–153).[103]

While in Griquastad, Fritsch performed surgery on a woman who had developed a fatty growth. Her wound healed within three days. This incident earned him the reputation of being a learned doctor. Throughout his travels, Fritsch was constantly beset by people wanting medical treatment, and after his crossing of the Gariep River, news of his medical status appears to have gone ahead of him.[104]

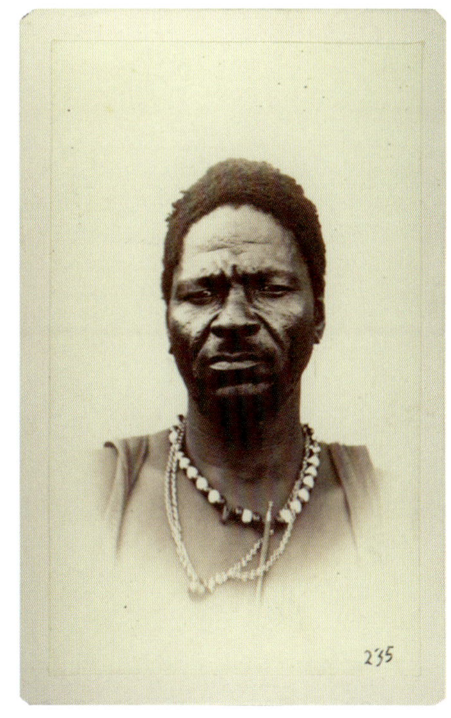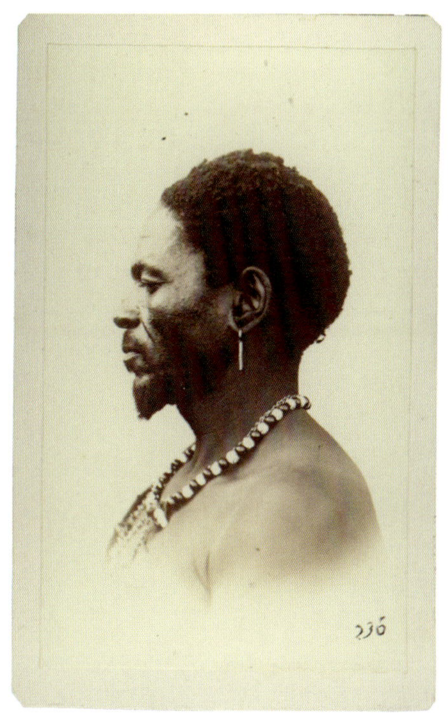

Lerumo, Ba-khatla, Griqua-Stad.

Lerumo, Kgatla, Griquastad.
(EM-SMB/32/834-835)

Mossao, Ba-khatla, Griqua-Stad.

Mossao, Kgatla, Griquastad.
(EM-SMB/32/838-839)

Figs. 148-149 ▶

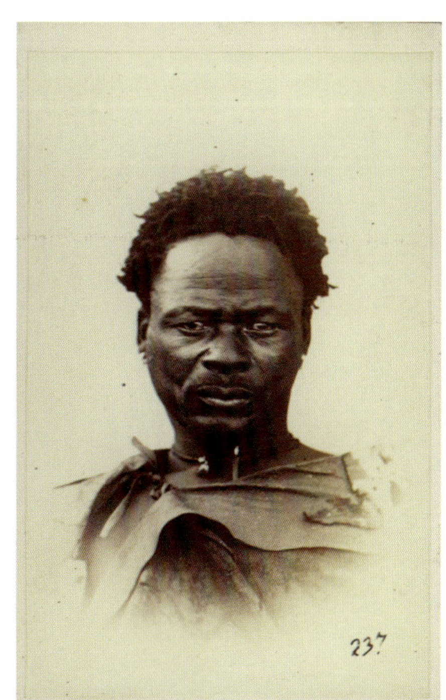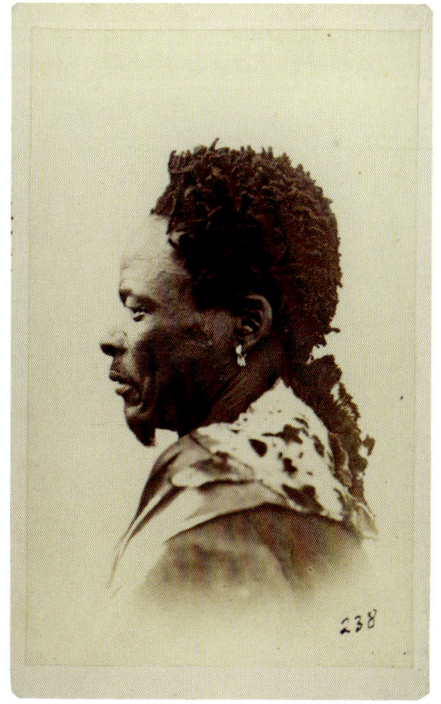

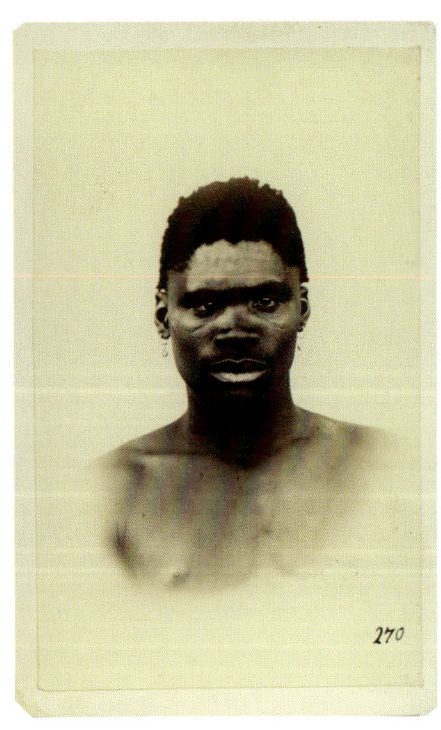 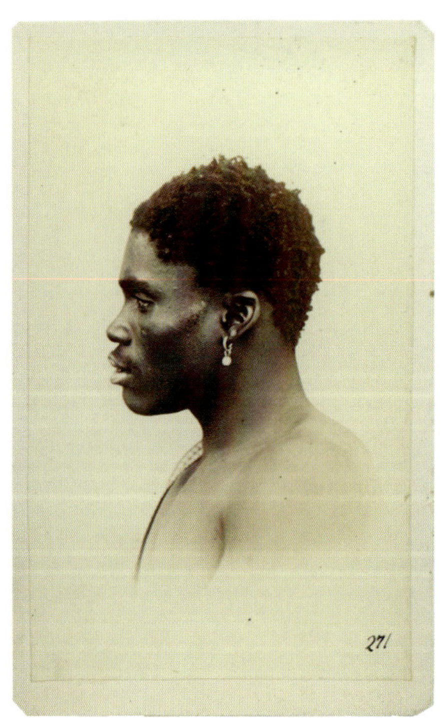

◀ *Figs. 150-151*

Hendrik, Bawanketsi, Griqua-Stad.

Hendrik, Ngwaketse, Griquastad.
(EM-SMB/32/830-831)

April, Ba-bidiji, Griqua-Stad.

April, Bididi, Griquastad.
(EM-SMB/32/819-823)

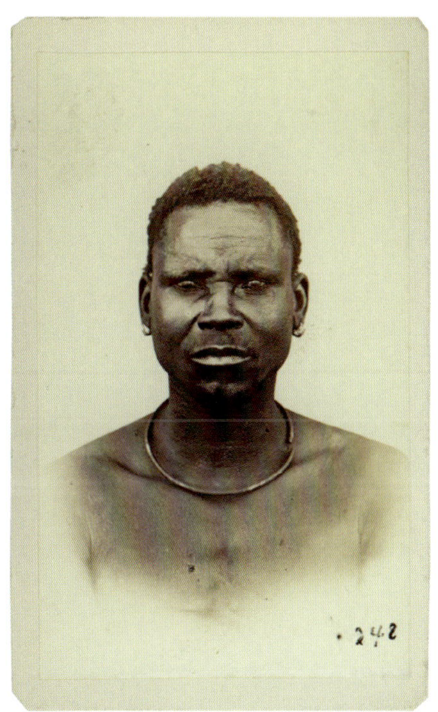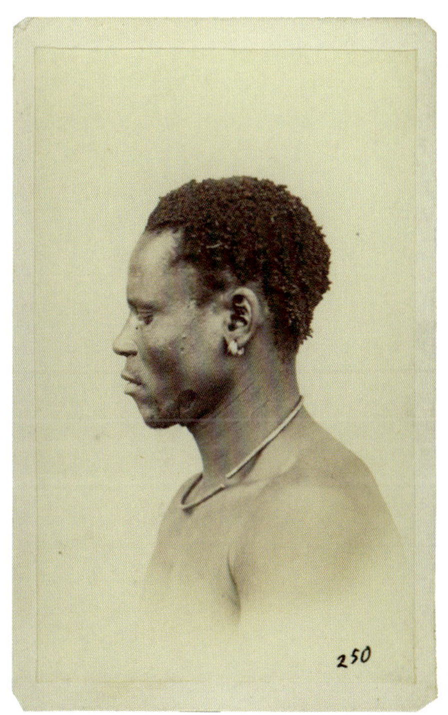

Having procured a new span of oxen, Fritsch set out from Griquastad on 24 June, travelling via Blinkklip (Postmasburg) to Kuruman. After a fairly harrowing journey characterised by a lack of water, he arrived at Kuruman on 31 June.[105] Fritsch described Kuruman as a beautiful oasis in the Kalahari desert. He commented on the gardens and orange trees, the glimmering saltpans and magnificent sunsets.[106] From the beginning of the nineteenth century, the area around Kuruman had captured the imagination of travellers and administrators, particularly Dithakong, the southernmost Tlhaping town to the northwest of Kuruman, known on maps of the time as Lattakoo, Lithakun or Takoon.[107] In 1820 the great Scottish missionary Robert Moffat arrived in South Africa and, after having gained permission from the Tlhaping chief Mothibi at Dithakong, established a mission station at Kuruman, which was to play a key role in missionary enterprise and colonial expansion in southern Africa. It was also to act as the northernmost springboard for further expeditions into the interior of southern Africa, such as those of David Livingstone.

Fritsch commented in detail on the indigenous architecture in Kuruman, noting that people were beginning to replace their traditional cone on cylinder dwellings with rectangular and square-plan buildings. He remarked that they did not have an eye for rectilinear construction, as walls would often break into curves. He described how the locals would congregate around the fires in their courtyards outside, smoking their pipes and exchanging news.[108] Robert Moffat (Fig. 154), a large man with a great beard, then in his sixties, assisted Fritsch with his photography. Fritsch commented that photographing people was becoming increasingly difficult. He had to work outdoors and the weather was always interfering with his ability to obtain good images. Four portraits from Kuruman are recorded in Fritsch's *Atlas* and the Dammann *Album*, namely the Rolong women Malitabe and Cuenyone (Figs. 155–158), the Tlhaping man Cuenyone (he records both as having the same name), and the Ratlou man Motlomeri (Figs. 159–162).[109] The National Library of South Africa (Cape Town campus) also has a Fritsch portrait of Robert Moffat himself in its Grey Ethnological Album.

According to Fritsch, it was a rule at Kuruman for travellers to receive medical help and sufficient provisions for their ongoing journeys. He himself was provided with a generous supply of food that lasted from his departure on 13 July until he reached Ntsweng. Moffat also gave him some books with inscribed dedications which Fritsch regarded as valuable memorabilia.[110]

The missionary Revd Robert Moffat, Kuruman,
Bechuanaland.
(SANL/INIL/14196)

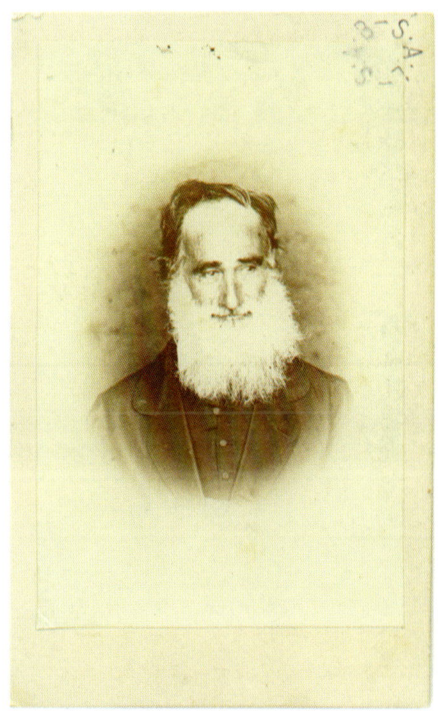

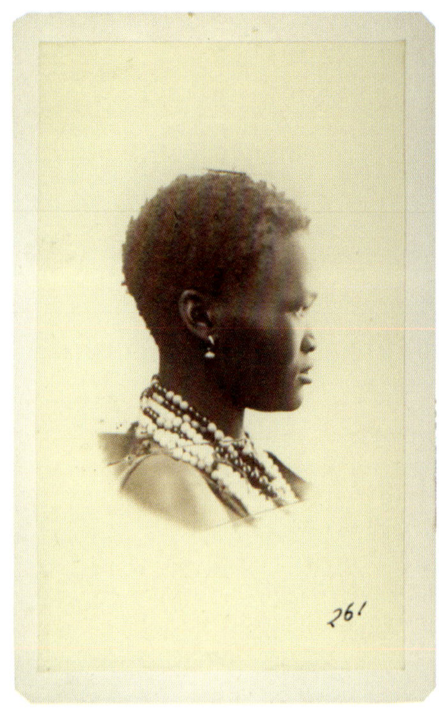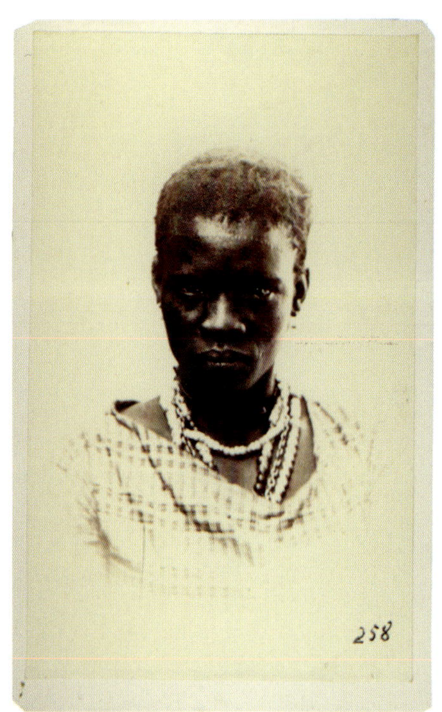

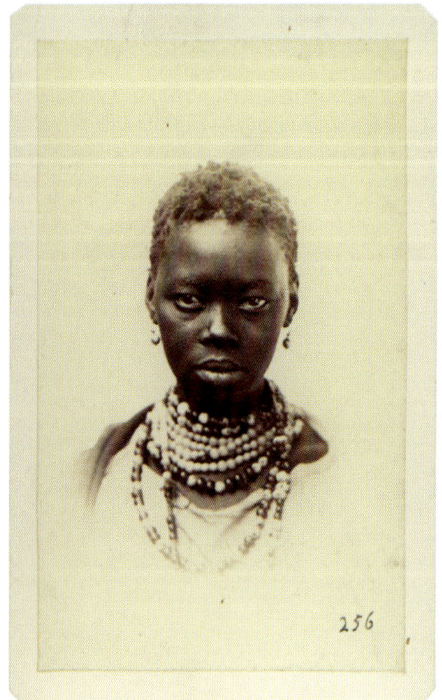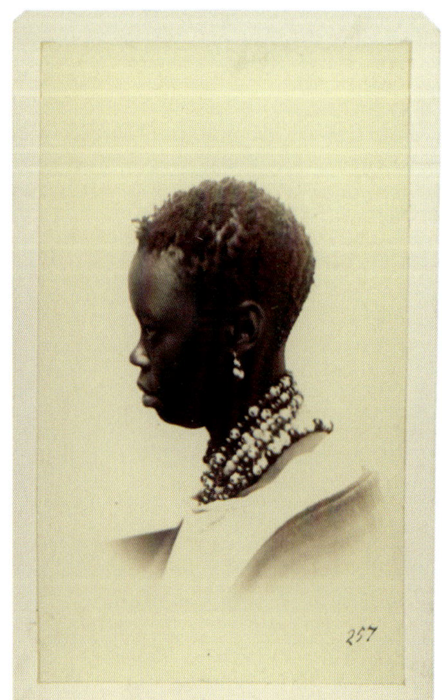

◀ *Figs. 155-156*

Malitabe, Morolong, Kuruman.

Malitabe, Rolong, Kuruman, Bechuanaland.
(EM-SMB/32/849-850)

Cuenyone, Ba-rolong, Kuruman, Be-chuanaland.

Cuenyone, Rolong, Kuruman, Bechuanaland.
(EM-SMB/32/846-847)

◀ *Figs. 157-158*

Cuenyone, Ba-tlapi, Be-chuanaland, Kuruman.

Cuenyone, Tlhaping, Kuruman, Bechuanaland.
(EM-SMB/32/833-832)

Motlomeri, Ba-tlaru, Kuruman, Be-chuanaland.

Motlomeri, Ratlou, Kuruman, Bechuanaland.
(EM-SMB/32/854-855)

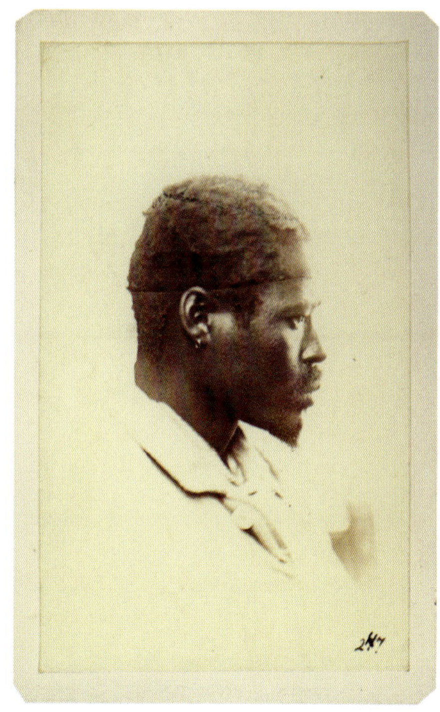

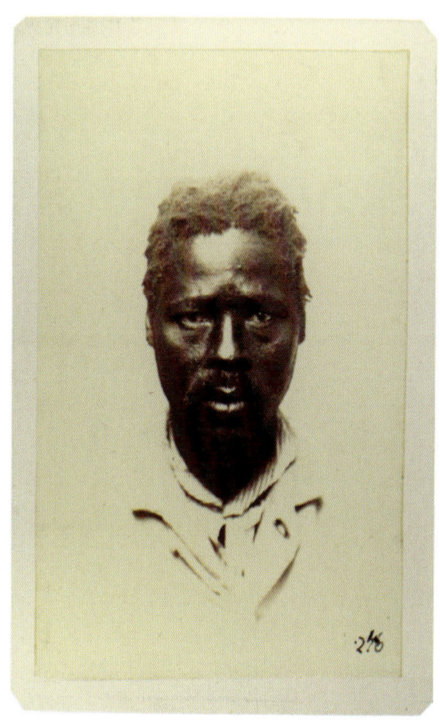

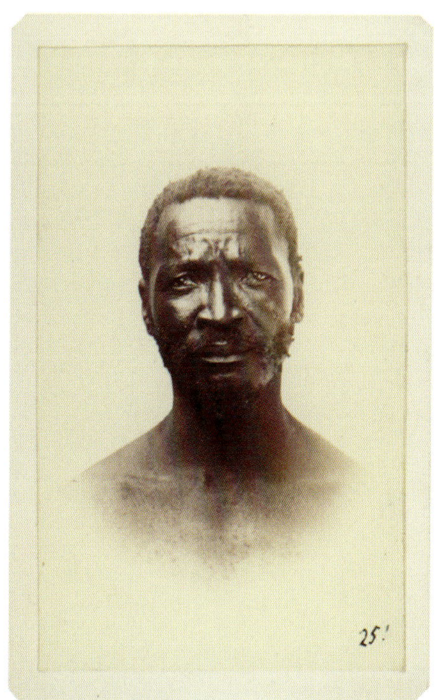

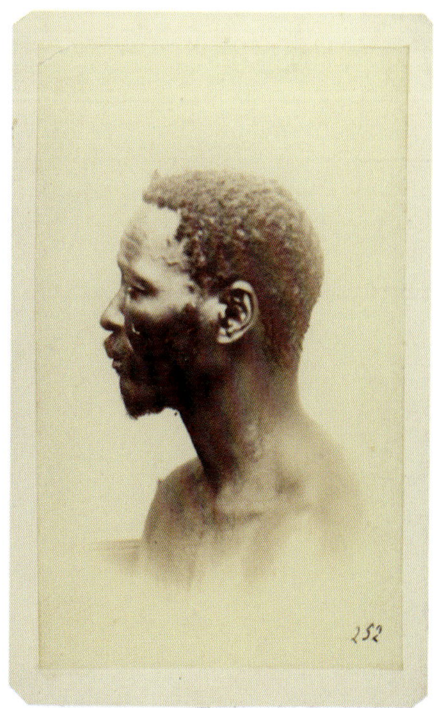

On 2 August Fritsch arrived in the Ngwaketse town of Kanye, founded by Makaba in the late eighteenth century. The town was situated in the hills that today define Botswana's southeastern border with South Africa. Until the Ndebele invasion of 1832, the Ngwaketse were the most powerful Tswana *merafe* ('tribe'). It was Gaseitsiwe who brought them together again in the 1830s, restoring them to their former standing.[111]

The morning after his arrival, Fritsch wandered along the narrow lanes through the village, and was struck by the friendliness of the people and charmed by the manner in which they greeted a stranger. He found his way to the *kgotla* (the ruler's courtyard) where he approached Gaseitsiwe (Figs. 164–165), who was surrounded by some of his followers. Close to Gaseitsiwe, to his right, sat his brother (possibly Segotshane) and brother-in-law, while three of his wives sat to his left. Fritsch sat down opposite Gaseitsiwe and handed him a letter from Robert Moffat. He was amused by the manner in which Gaseitsiwe and his people dressed. He described Gaseitsiwe as wearing a nightcap, nightgown (*negligée*), bed socks and printed cotton quilt draped over his shoulders, which, Fritsch wrote, he wore throughout the day. Gaseitsiwe and his followers were at first wary of Fritsch, suspecting him to be an emissary of the Boers, whom they mistrusted after the Transvalers took to war in the 1850s to subject the Tswana chiefdoms to their west.[112]

The following evening Gaseitsiwe visited Fritsch at his wagon, and in the course of the visit inspected his equipment. He was particularly inquisitive about Fritsch's firearms and photographic equipment. Once Gaseitsiwe was satisfied that he had seen everything, their relations eased. The next day, Fritsch went to the *kgotla* to photograph Gaseitsiwe and some of his people. He first had to demonstrate that the procedure was harmless before he was permitted to photograph Gaseitsiwe. The group photograph taken in the *kgotla* (Fig. 163) closely resembles Fritsch's description of his first audience with Gaseitsiwe when he arrived. He was also allowed to photograph Motuane (Figs. 166–167), Gaseitsiwe's favourite wife (*Lieblingsfrau*), whom he describes as having an 'intelligent and regal composure', and whose hair was plastered with specularite powder (*Eisenglimmer-Pomade*) which caused it to glimmer. In his *Atlas*, Fritsch also featured the portraits of Gaseitsiwe's unidentified brother-in-law and a man named Mori (Figs. 168–171), as well as that of a woman named Mantille (Figs. 172–173), describing her as a *Vaalpenz Dirne* (Bakgalagadi harlot) in the service of Gaseitsiwe. He noted that he was not permitted to photograph Mori's wife, whom he regarded as a fine instance of Tswana beauty.[113] His group photograph of Ngwaketse women and children (Fig. 174) is particularly interesting in that the people depicted are curiously watching themselves being photographed. Here the spectacle is not only the subjects, but also Fritsch behind his camera. There is a strong sense of looking and counter-looking, mediated by the camera.

Gaseitsiwe displayed a keen interest in Fritsch's medical skills, requesting him to pay a visit to a sick Tswana preacher who had been sent to the area by Moffat. On 5 August, accompanied by a guide, Fritsch visited the preacher at his village about three hours from Kanye. He had hoped to find skulls and bones in the vicinity, but acknowledged that the Tswana would never have allowed him access to such specimens, even had they been skulls of Tlokwa ('Mantatees') killed by the Tswana. Compelled to stay in Kanye for a little longer when he was unable to find servants who would travel with him, Fritsch finally departed on 16 August.

Fig. 163 ▶

Der Ba-wanketsi-Hauptling und seiner Gevolge in der Khotla von Khanije.

The Ngwaketse chief Gaseitsiwe and his followers in the *kgotla*, Kanye, Bechuanaland.
(EM-SMB/32/876)

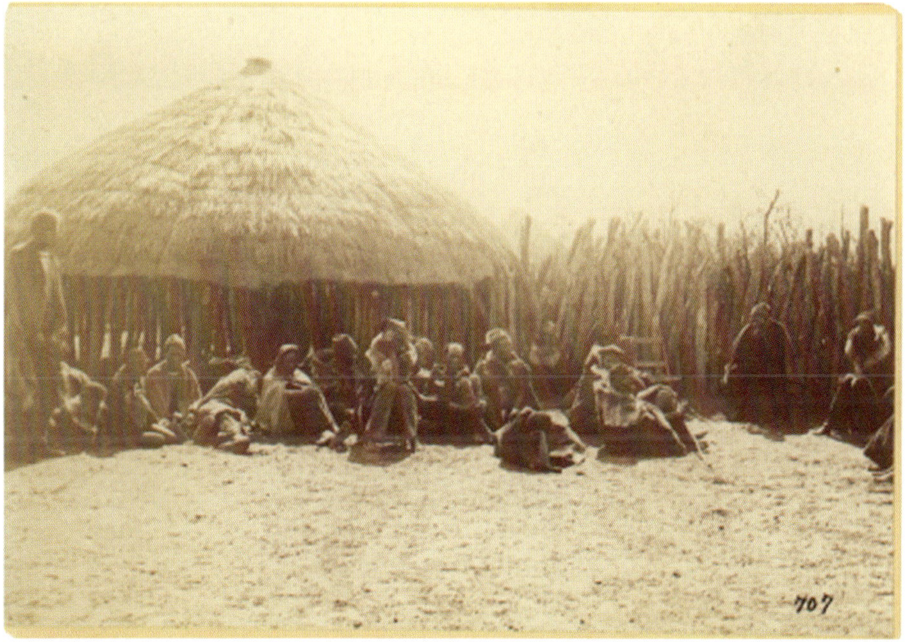

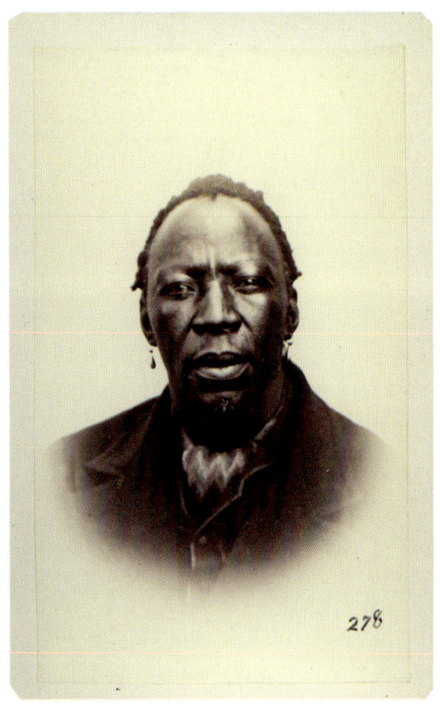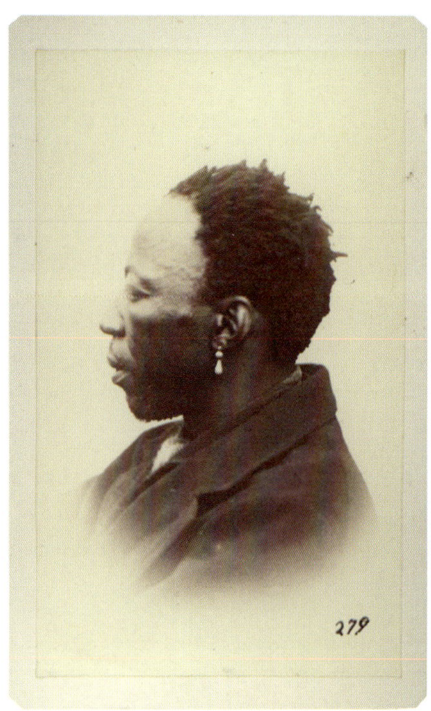

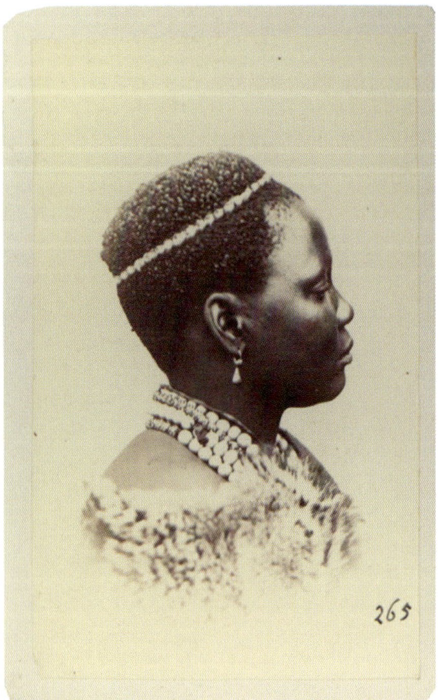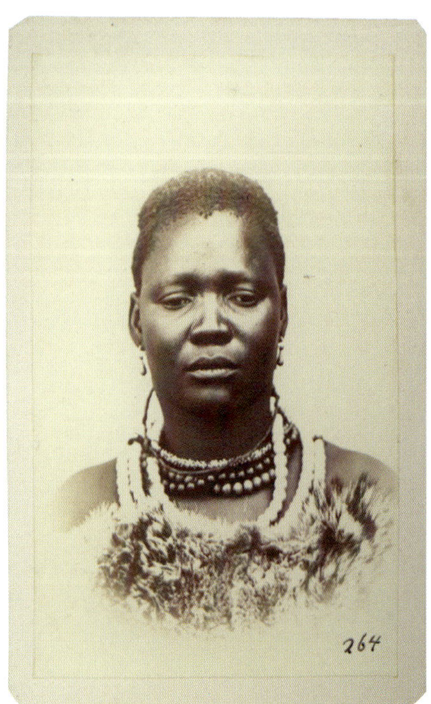

◀ *Figs. 164-165*

Gassisioe, Häuptling der Ba-wanketsi.

Gaseitsiwe, chief of the Ngwaketse, Kanye,
Bechuanaland.
(EM-SMB/32/809-813)

Motuane, Ba-wanketsi, Kanya.

Motuane (wife of Gaseitsiwe), Ngwaketse, Kanye,
Bechuanaland.
(EM-SMB/32/841-840)

◀ *Figs. 166-167*

Ba-wanketsi, Kanya.

Unidentified brother-in-law of Gaseitsiwe, Ngwaketse,
Kanye, Bechuanaland.
(EM-SMB/32/817-821)

Mori, Ba-wanketsi, Kanya.

Mori, Ngwanketse, Kanye,
Bechuanaland.
(EM-SMB/32/836-837)

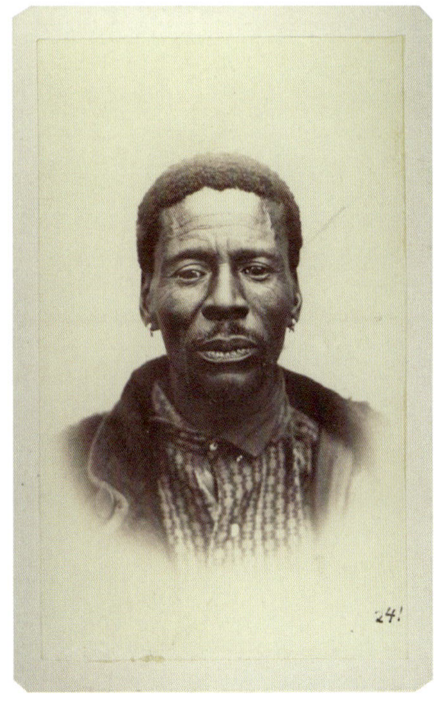

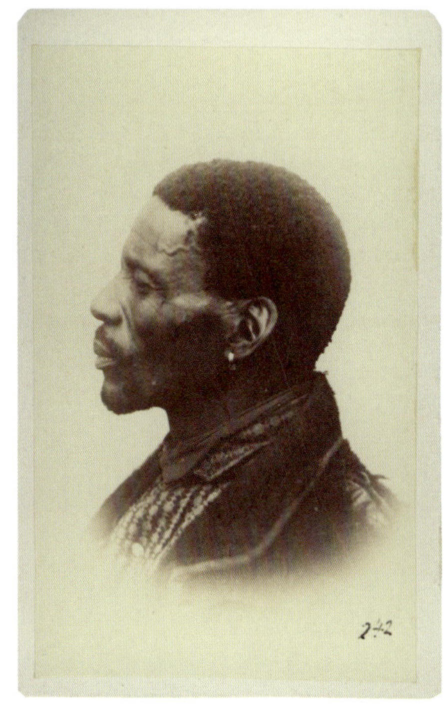

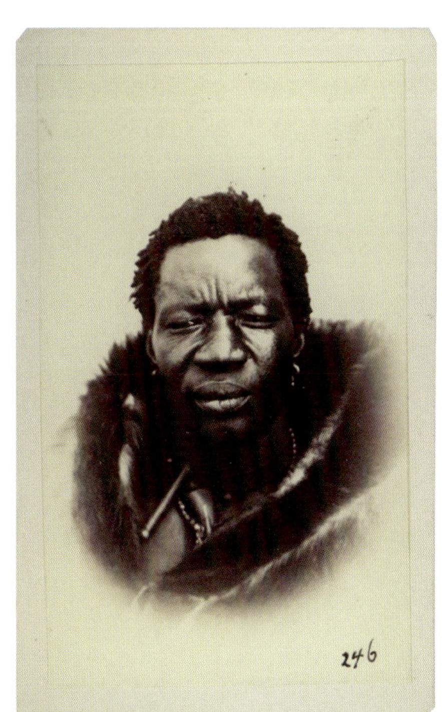

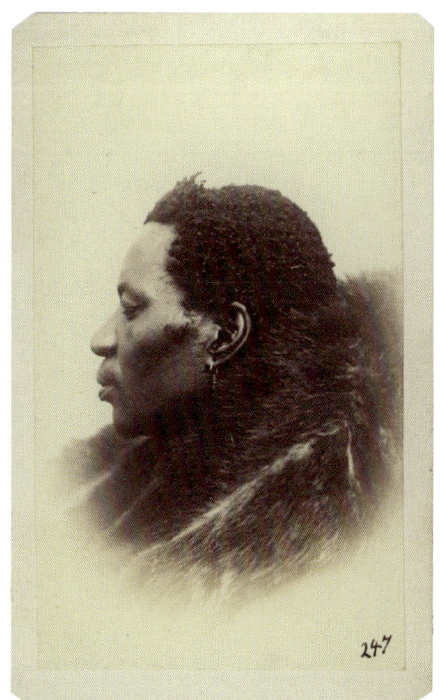

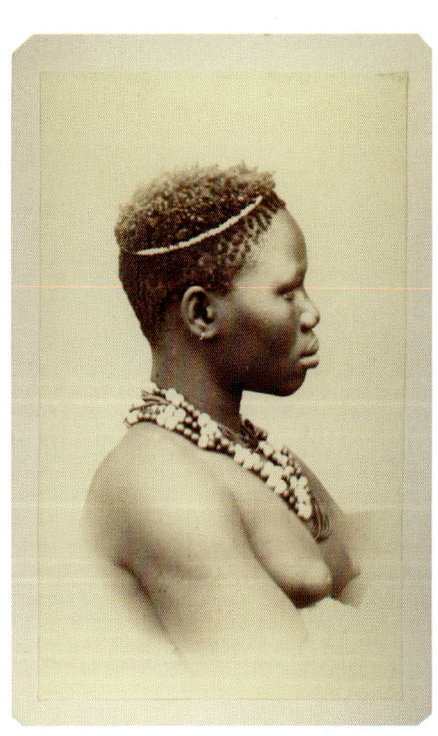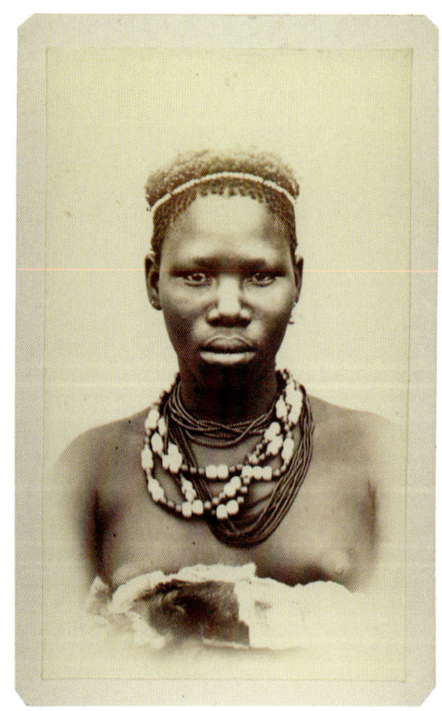

◀ *Figs. 172-173*

Mantille, Ba-wanketsi, Khanje, Be-chuanaland.

Mantille, Ngwaketse, Kanye,
Bechuanaland.
(EM-SMB/32/843-842)

Figs. 174 ▶

Frauen und Kinder der Ba-wanketsi.

Ngwaketse women and children,
Bechuanaland.
(EM-SMB/32/879)

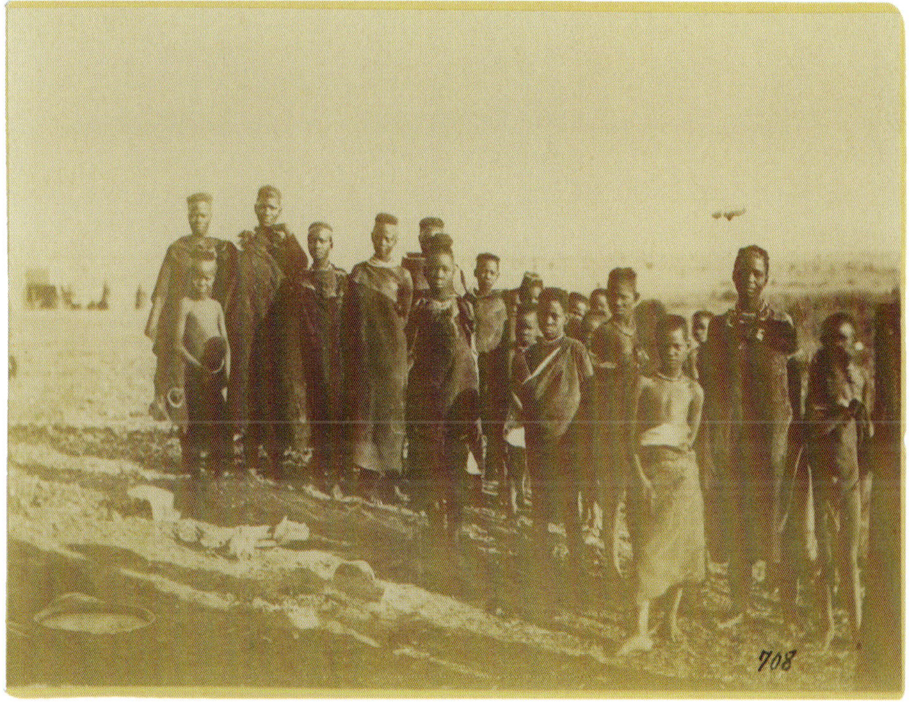

Moshupa: 16 August 1865

At sunset Fritsch arrived in Moshupa (or Mosopa), a village north of Kanye. At an audience with Mosielele, chief of the Mmanaana-Kgatla, Fritsch handed him a letter from Robert Moffat, which greatly impressed Mosielele as he saw himself as Moffat's friend and brother. Fritsch noted that Mosielele seemed to enjoy talking about his own strengths and virtues, and although Fritsch listened attentively, he doubted that Mosielele held very much power.[114] Mosielele and his people originated from an area near to Pretoria but fled after being threatened by the Transvalers, who wished to subject them to taxation and labour service, and sought protection from Sechele, the Kwena chief, at Dimawe. Although the Boers followed Mosielele to Dimawe and demanded that Sechele surrender Mosielele, Sechele stood his ground.[115] After this stand-off in 1852, Sechele settled the Mmanaana in the Moshupa valley because of its natural defences, fertile soil and ample water.[116]

Mosielele, like Gaseitsiwe, was especially interested in Fritsch's medical skills and requested that he help him with a stomach ailment, which Fritsch attributed to his fondness for beer. After his consultation, Mosielele inspected Fritsch's firearms and equipment, and was impressed with his powder horn, intimating that it would serve as an appropriate gift. Fritsch was intrigued by etiquette among the Tswana regarding the presentation of gifts, which, he noted, formed a kind of tax for crossing through their territories. It was important, he recorded, to remain diplomatic when negotiating and keep within specific boundaries. If a traveller offered a gift of his own accord, it was received gracefully, even though it might be small. However, if one transgressed protocol or left it up to the bargaining power of the *kgosi* (or chief), the traveller might be compelled to forfeit something of higher value.[117]

Fritsch intended to stay in Moshupa only for a day but was obliged to remain for longer as the water in the village was not clean enough for the photographic process and had to be filtered for a few days before he could use it for rinsing his negatives. Despite these efforts, he only took three photographs while there, two of Mosielele (Figs. 175–176) and one of Moshupa (Fig. 177). During his stay he explored the environs, paying particular attention to his botanical and zoological studies and observing the people, their religious practices, and particularly their fondness for European clothing.[118]

Figs. 175-176 ▶

Mosielélè, Häuptling der Ba-khatla

Mosielele, chief of the Mmanaana-Kgatla, Moshupa, Bechuanaland.
(EM-SMB/32/811-815)

Gamashopa, Stadt der Ba-khatla.

Moshupa, town of the Kgatla, Bechuanaland.
(EM-SMB/32/875)

Fig. 177 ▶

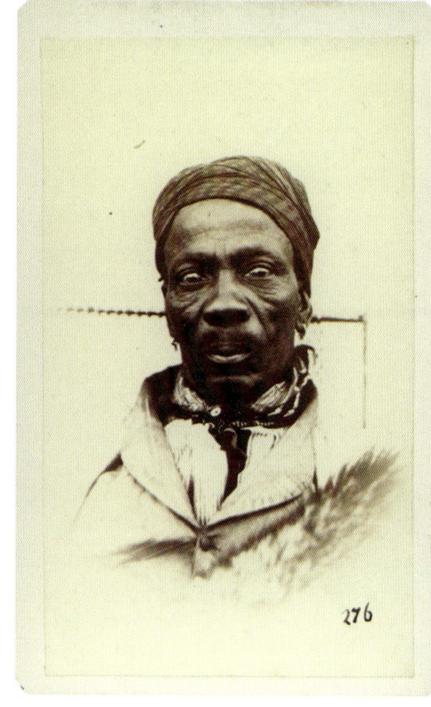
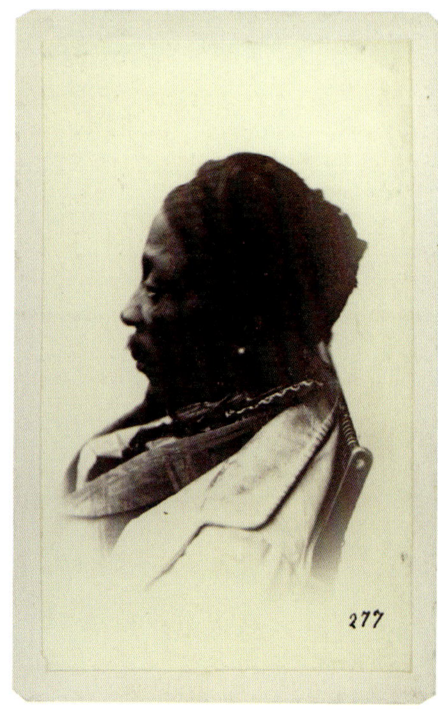

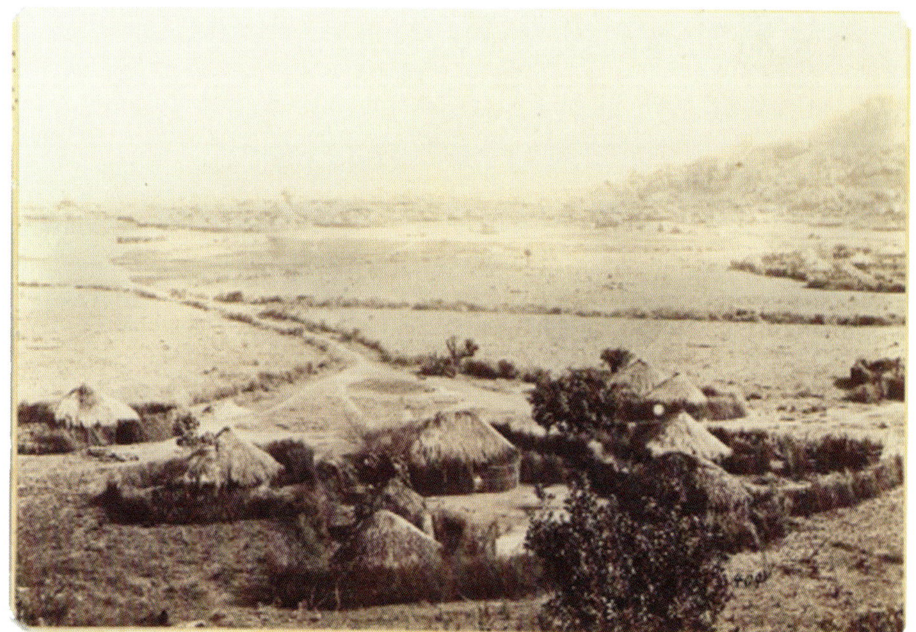

Fritsch departed from Moshupa on 20 August, outspanning over two nights before arriving on 23 August at Ntsweng (which Fritsch called Logageng) in the Molepolole area, where he met Sechele (Figs. 179–180) and the hunter and trader Joseph McCabe at the *kgotla*. Fritsch was impressed by Sechele and described him as an imposing figure who reminded him of Anta. Sechele was dressed in a suit, cravat and Panama hat, and, said Fritsch, 'played the role of a gentleman'. Sechele was excited by Fritsch's arrival and was particularly impressed by his medical knowledge.[119]

Sechele was one of the most extraordinary Tswana leaders of this period. When he came to power in 1831, the Kwena were split into three sections, which he reunited in 1853. He allied himself with British traders and missionaries and was himself baptised by David Livingstone in 1848. He also resisted the Boers, who tried to subject several Tswana communities (such as Mosielele's), and preserved 'a tenuous autonomy between the white farms [of the Transvaal] and the Kalahari desert'.[120] After surviving the attacks of the Transvalers at Dimawe, Sechele moved his people to Ntsweng (known today as Old Molepolole) in 1863. During the 1880s he and other Tswana chiefs accepted British overrule. Sechele had three sons, Kgari, Sebele and Tumagole. Sebele (Figs. 181–182) was a well-educated man. He and two of his sisters were sent by their father to be educated at Kuruman.[121] When Sechele died in 1892, a succession dispute ensued between Sebele and Kgari, and Sebele managed to drive Kgari and his

people away from Ntsweng.[122] During Sebele's reign it seemed likely that the entire British Protectorate would be transferred to Rhodes's British South Africa Company, a prospect that alarmed the Tswana chiefs, who had learned of the Company's crushing of the Ndebele in what became Rhodesia. Sebele resisted the transfer and travelled to London with the Ngwaketse and Ngwato chiefs to oppose the plan. Their request that they should stay under direct British control was granted.[123]

Sechele was happy to be photographed and dressed himself for the occasion in a black 'dress' with a colourful silk cravat, 'fez', 'mackintosh' and riding boots, which, Fritsch noted, he wore on Sundays when he preached. Fritsch gave Sechele an albumen print of his portrait that included the fez, though the photograph used for his book excluded this. Fritsch also recalled that Sechele was very disappointed that the photograph did not include his boots. Apart from his descriptions of photographing Sechele, Fritsch said nothing of the other six photographs he took in Ntsweng. These include the portraits of Sechele's son Sebele, the hunter Mozissi, the 12-year-old girl Mampok, Mzilikazi's son Mapotla, who was living in Ntsweng in exile after he had fled from his father, the Ndebele woman Umbumbulu, and the Griqua man Piet.[124] In his *Atlas* Fritsch remarked that Mozissi had stuffed his hat with black ostrich feathers, which he said 'imitated European hair'.[125]

Morauxomo (Logageng), Stadt der Ba-kuéna.

Ntsweng, town of the Kwena,
Bechuanaland.
(EM-SMB/32/880)

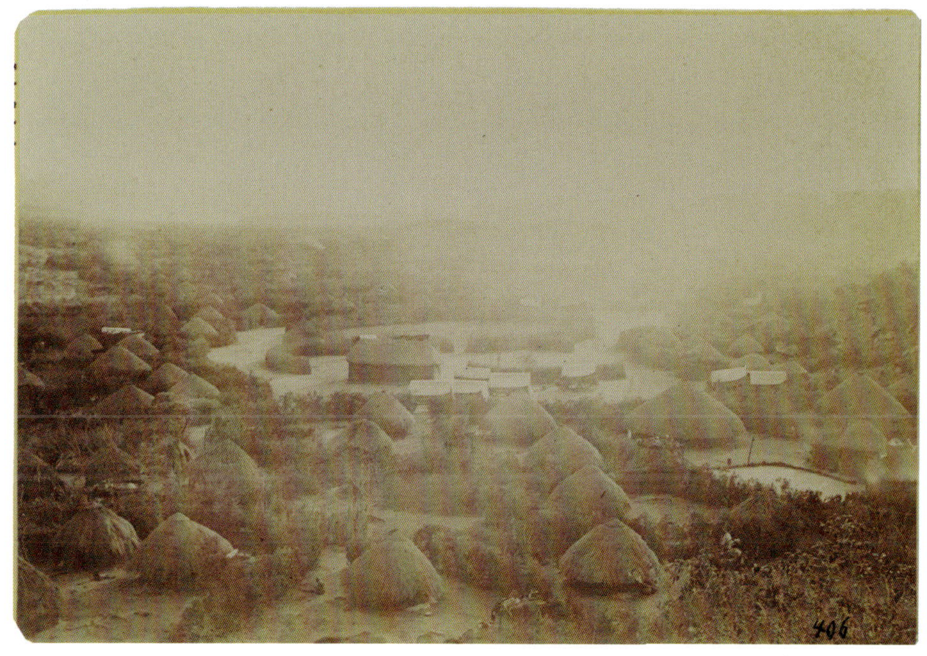

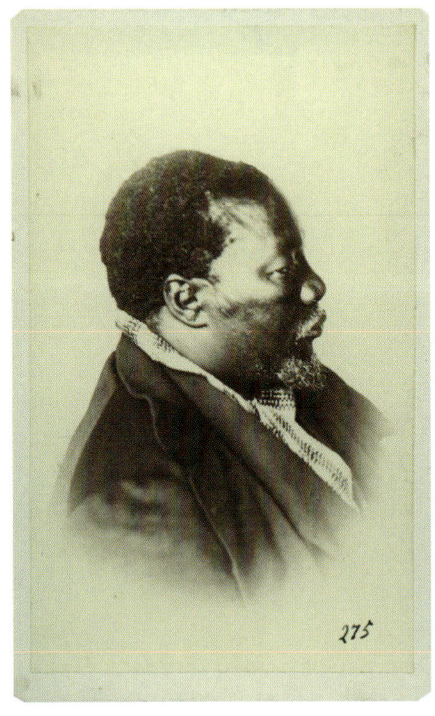
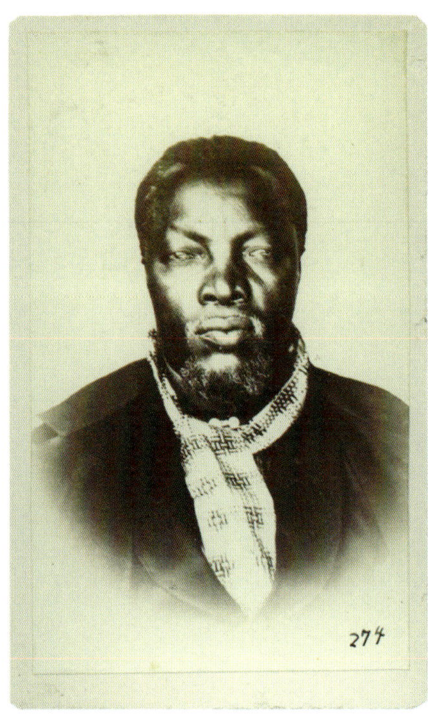

◀ *Figs. 179-180*

Sechèli, Häuptling der Ba-kuéna

Sechele, chief of the Kwena, Ntsweng, Bechuanaland.
(EM-SMB/32/814-810)

Sebele, son of Sechele,
Ntsweng, Bechuanaland.
(EM-SMB/32/816-820)

◀ *Figs. 181-182*

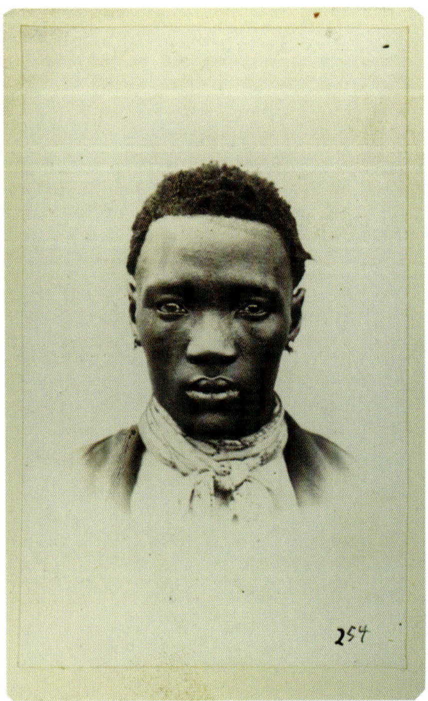
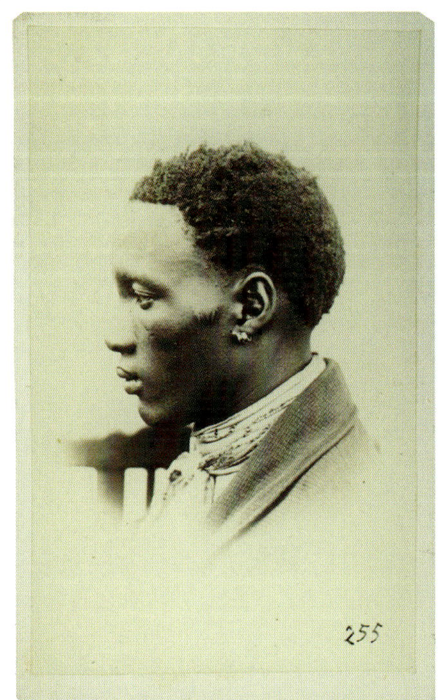

Figs. 183-184 ▶

Mozissi, Ba-kuéna, Logageng.

Mozissi, Kwena, Ntsweng, Bechuanaland.
(EM-SMB/32/824-825)

Mampok, Ba-kuéna, Logageng, Be-chuanaland.

Mampok, Kwena, Ntsweng, Bechuanaland.
(EM-SMB/32/844-845)

Figs. 185-186 ▶

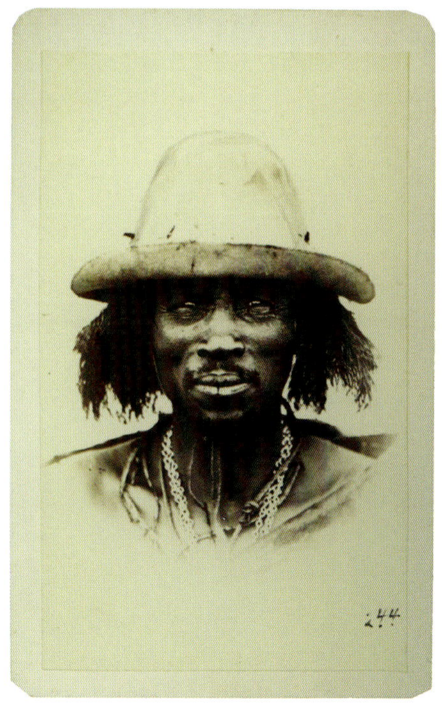

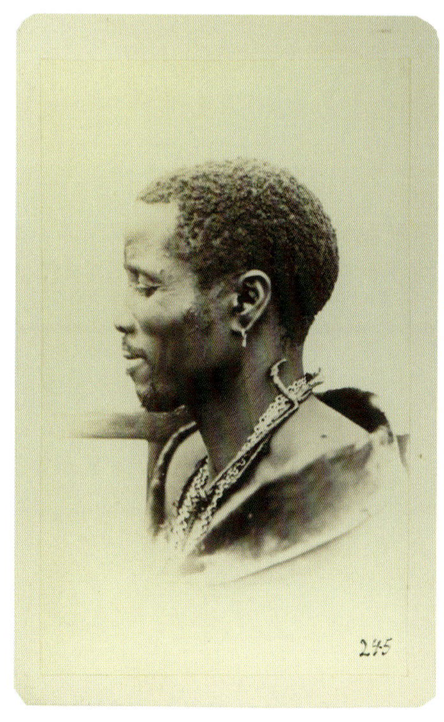

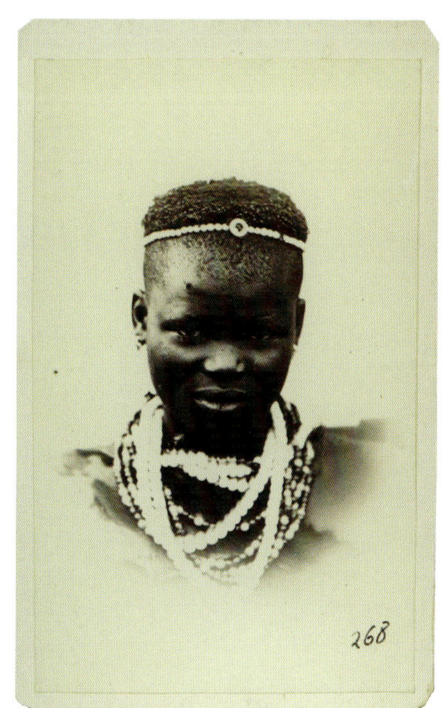

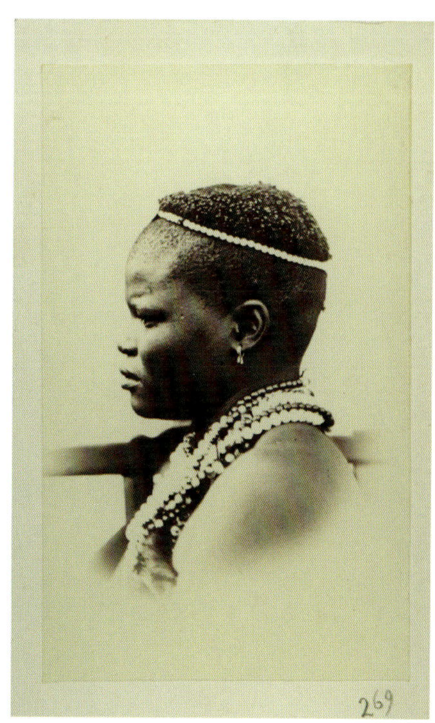

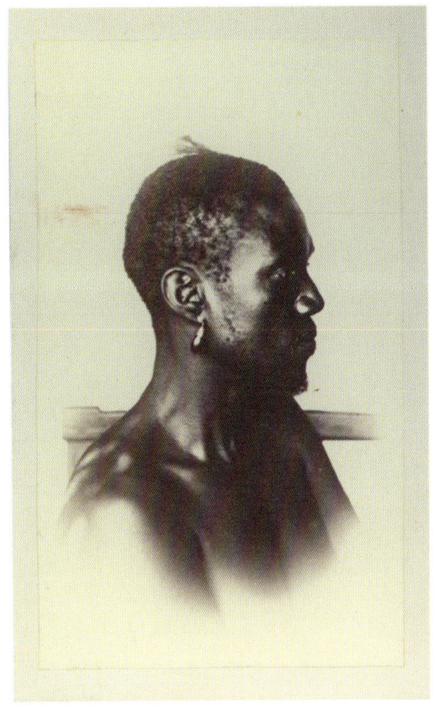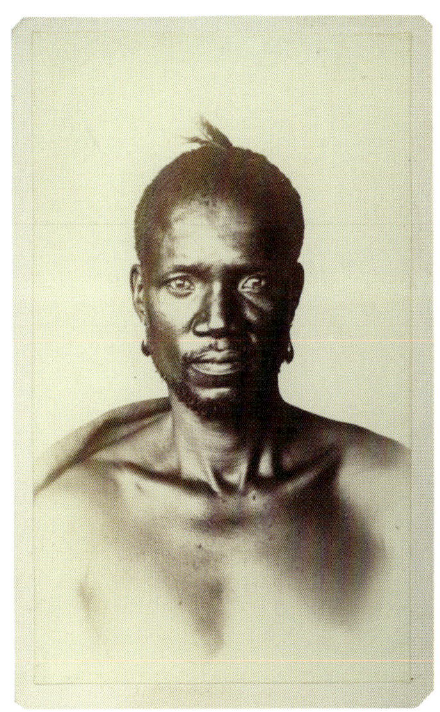

◀ Figs. 187-188

U'mpotla, Sohn des Umselekazi, Matabele, Logageng, Ba-kuéna Gebiet.

Mapotla, son of Mzilikazi, Ndebele, Ntsweng, Bechuanaland.
(EM-SMB/32/882-881)

U'mbumbulu, Logageng, Ba-kuéna Gebiet.

Umbumbulu, Ndebele, Ntsweng, Bechuanaland.
(EM-SMB/32/888-887)

◀ Figs. 189-190

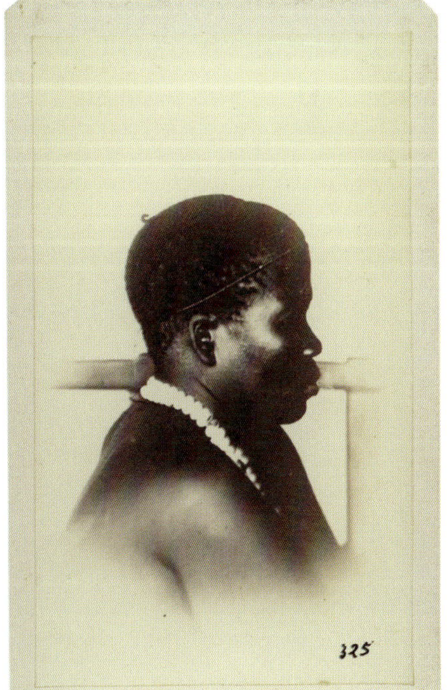

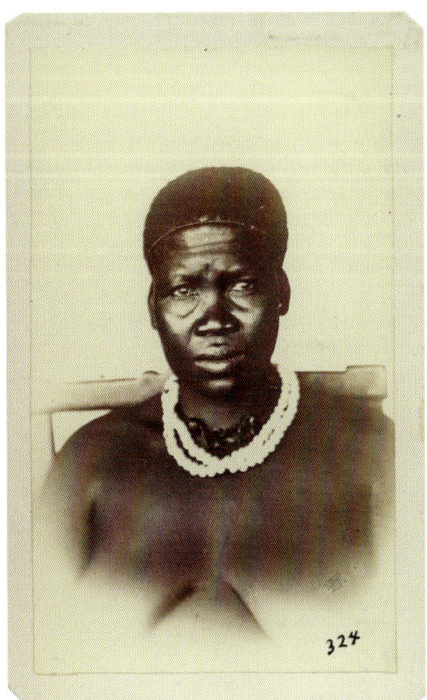

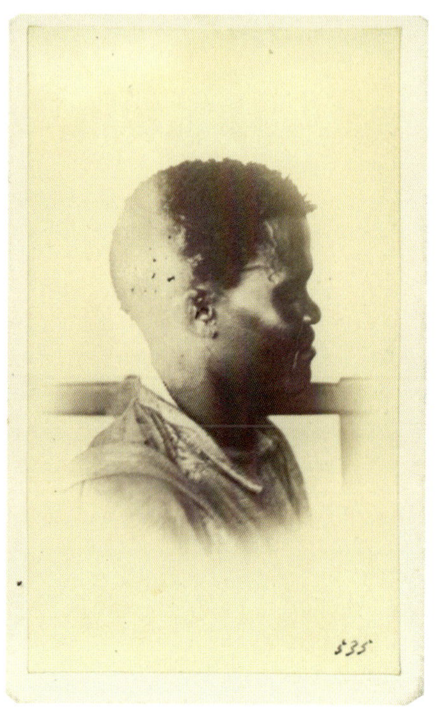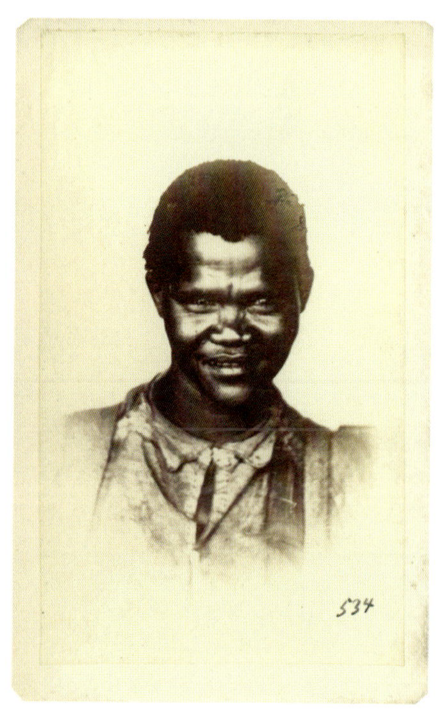

Figs. 191-192 ▶

Piet, Griqua, Logageng Baruba.

Piet, Griqua, Ntsweng, Bechuanaland.
(EM-SMB/32/1056-1055)

Fritsch's arrival initially created some tension among the white traders there as they did not like competition, but this was eased when they realised his visit was of a scientific nature. The number of traders is evident in Fritsch's photograph of Ntsweng (Fig. 178), where at least eleven wagons are parked around the centre of the town dominated by Sechele's rectangular house. As Fritsch's wagon stood close to Joseph McCabe's dwelling, he was afforded the opportunity to observe the trading that took place there. In his travel account he mentioned an occasion, of which there are two photographs (Figs. 193–194), when women and children brought water that they had carried for some distance in calabashes and earthenware receptacles, which they traded mainly for beads. Other produce included bundles of firewood, wooden bowls filled with wild fruits, roasted locusts, groundnuts, maize and sorghum, and milk. The milk was boiled in huge 'tea pots' to prevent it from souring, bringing with it an infestation of flies that were removed from the milk by hand. Fritsch described the excited mingling of the people and their chattering and shouting, barking dogs fighting over old bones, and ostriches picking up anything they could find from the ground. While the cacophony disturbed him, it did not at first appear to have any effect on McCabe, who remained calm all the while, consuming roasted locusts. Finally McCabe lost his patience and chased the crowd away.[126]

Once the area had been cleared, McCabe returned to his hut to await Sechele's brother Kgosidintsi and his associates, who had made an appointment to trade for firearms. The meeting began with an introductory conversation about the state of people's health and news of the day before settling down to business. Kgosidintsi checked the rifles, while karosses were unrolled, revealing ostrich feathers. The trading value of the feathers varied between 30 pieces of white feathers and one to two pounds of black feathers for a rifle, and up to 100–150 pieces of white feathers for a better-quality firearm. As an experienced trader, McCabe weighed the feathers with his hands and ran his fingers through them to test their elasticity and softness. He wanted to see whether Kgosidintsi would offer more feathers or accept less valuable rifles, and after further bargaining, which involved more eye contact than verbal exchange, the deal was struck. Fritsch observed that only an experienced observer could understand the complexities of this cross-cultural negotiation.[127]

Fig. 193 ▶

Frauen und Kinder der Ba- kuéna, Victualien zum verkauf bringend.

Kwena women and children bringing produce to sell, Ntsweng. (The figure with the hat is Joseph McCabe.) (EM-SMB/32/872)

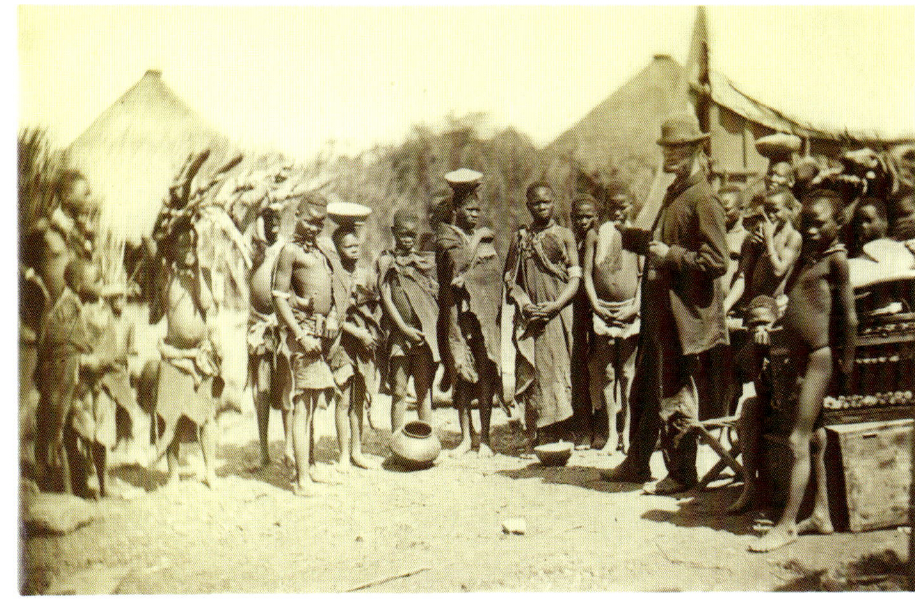

Kinder der Ba-kuéna zum Milchverkauf kommend.

Kwena children selling milk, Ntsweng, Bechuanaland. (EM-SMB/32/874)

Fig. 194 ▶

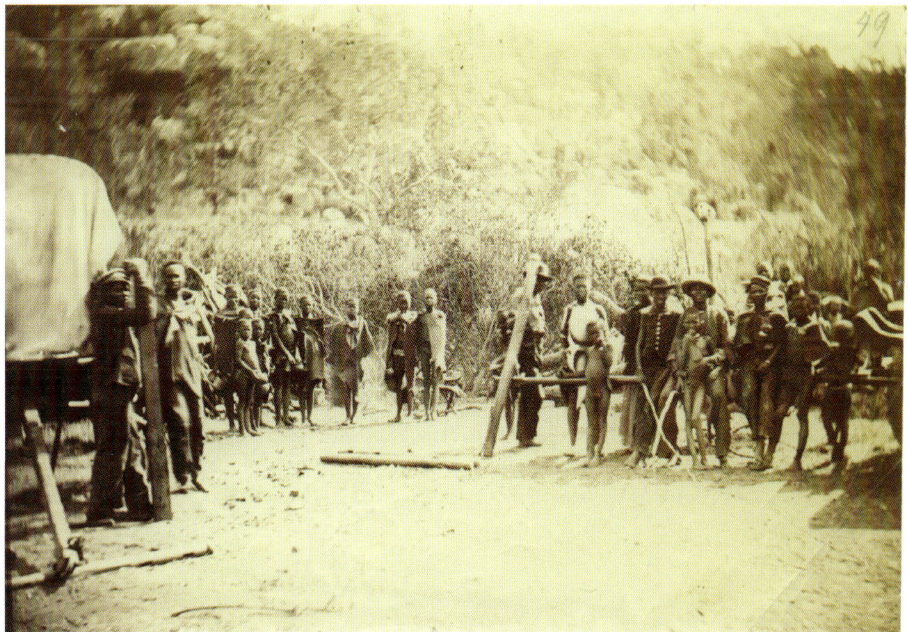

Fritsch took two other group photographs in Ntsweng, one of some Kwena men sewing karosses and another of women weaving an enclosure fence with branches (Figs. 195–196). Judging by the layout of the town in Fritsch's photograph (Fig. 178), with the hill in the background and the wagons and thatched roofs of the huts (see Figs. 195 and 196), it is likely that these, and the trading photographs, were taken in the vicinity of the two wagons parked at the right-hand side of his photograph of Ntsweng.

Fritsch did not like Ntsweng, finding it unhygienic, claustrophobic and infested with flies and other insects. He needed to get away into the open countryside. Being passionate about hunting, he arranged to go on a hunting expedition with McCabe's son in the vicinity of Kopong, to the north of Ntsweng, after which he would return to the Colony. They arrived back in Ntsweng on 15 September, by which time Fritsch had changed his plans for returning to the Cape.[128] Although he had originally planned to travel as far as Ntsweng, and then return to the Cape via the Transvaal and Free State, Fritsch decided to abandon this idea. Given that it was spring, it was too late in the year to venture through the strong summer thunderstorms and swollen rivers of the highveld. The political instability in these regions also made it insecure for travel. From the time the British had granted

independence to the Boer trekkers in the Transvaal in 1852, the region remained in an almost constant state of anarchy. Besides the wars waged by the Transvalers against the Tswana in 1852 and 1858, and against the Sotho chief Makapane in the northern Transvaal in 1854, the factional Boer polities were also in a state of conflict with one another. Although much of this strife had ended in 1864 with the unification of the Transvaal under President Marthinus Pretorius, Fritsch was concerned about Boer commandos in the Transvaal Republic who were sent out to apprehend and confiscate the wagons of travellers, even if they were foreigners. Travelling through the Orange Free State was even more unsafe, owing to the renewed war between the Republic and Moshoeshoe.[129]

Joseph McCabe had planned to send his son to Shoshong with two wagons and invited Fritsch to make use of one of them, an offer which Fritsch accepted. By going to the Ngwato capital, he could make up for not visiting the Transvaal, and at the same time concentrate his attention on looking for skulls, which he believed were abundant in the area. This arrangement also meant that he could rest his span of oxen in preparation for his return journey to Cape Town. On 26 September the party left Ntsweng, arriving in Shoshong on 2 October.[130]

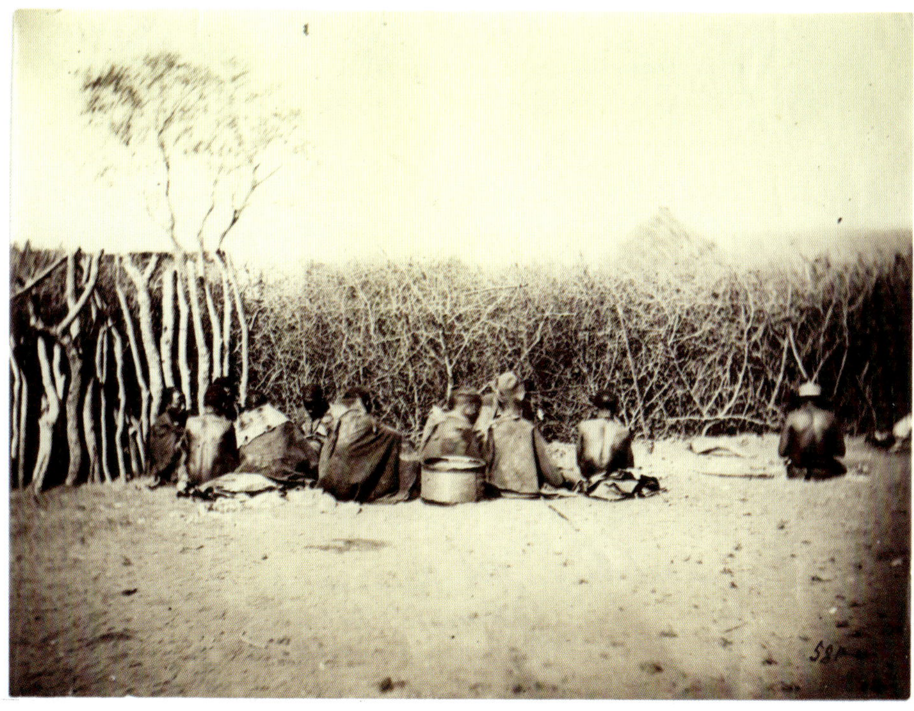

Männer, karosse nähend.

Kwena men sewing karosses, Ntsweng,
Bechuanaland.
(EM-SMB/32/873)

Frauen beim Zaunflechten.

Kwena women weaving an enclosure, Ntsweng,
Bechuanaland.
(EM-SMB/32/878)

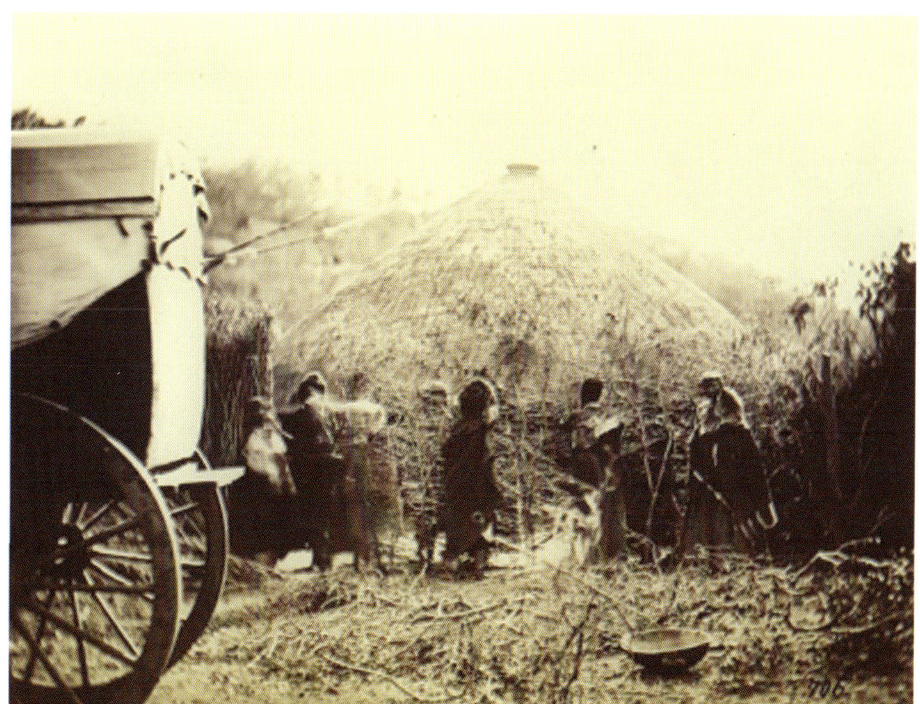

In the 1850s, Sekgoma I established Shoshong as the capital of the Ngwato, the site being easily defensible against the Ndebele army. Shoshong developed into an important crossroad for trade routes from the south to Lake Ngami in the west and to Matabeleland in the northeast. Heinrich C. Schulenburg of the Hermannsburg Lutheran Missionary Society founded a station there in 1860, and after his withdrawal John Mackenzie, the last great Scottish missionary to the Tswana, reinstituted the station under the auspices of the London Missionary Society in 1862. By the time of Fritsch's visit the missionaries Roger Price and John Mackenzie were conducting three schools in a town whose inhabitants numbered thirty thousand people.[131]

On their arrival, Fritsch accompanied McCabe to visit Sekgoma, who was sitting with his councillors under a mimosa tree. He was introduced as McCabe's companion, but having heard about Sekgoma, Fritsch kept himself in the background. Fritsch described Sekgoma as a 'sly, cunning and despotic character'. In his outward appearance, Fritsch wrote, he was unprepossessing and no different from his common subjects. Sekgoma appeared to be restraining himself and, when anyone looked at him, he would reel back with his one squint eye half closed. Fritsch thought that Sekgoma had once been a very different person: he had restored the integrity and increased the size of the Ngwato chiefdom and established its independence from the Ndebele. Fritsch ascribed his change of character to the onset of dementia and Sekgoma's fear of growing opposition to his leadership.[132]

Khama (Kgama) (Figs. 197–198) and his brother Kgamane were not present at Fritsch's first audience with their father, Sekgoma.[133] Unlike his traditionalist parent, Khama had joined Schulenburg's church even though his father objected to the practices of Christianity. At the age of 25 Khama converted to Christianity and was baptised in 1860. He received military acclaim when he wounded Lobengula of the Ndebele in 1863, and between 1865 and 1866 he revolted against his father and led the youth at Shoshong to adopt Christianity, a situation that gave rise to internecine strife among the Ngwato.[134] Like Mackenzie and others, Fritsch set Khama up against Sekgoma as the Christian versus the villain. Perhaps Fritsch might have been correct in ascribing Sekgoma's bitterness to the onset of dementia. Sekgoma had originally invited the missionaries to Shoshong for the purpose of educating Khama, and given Sekgoma's powerful traditionalist beliefs, he was mortified when his sons rejected Tswana customs by refusing to undergo *bogwera* (initiation).[135] The rift between the traditionalist Sekgoma and his Christian sons instigated one of the most unfortunate conflicts between Christianity and traditional religion in Tswana history,[136] and the year after Fritsch's visit, Khama and Kgamane, with the help of Sechele, drove Sekgoma from Shoshong and brought back Macheng as paramount chief of the Ngwato. A decade later, Macheng was overthrown by Khama, and Khama (known afterwards as Khama III or Khama the Great) ruled over the Ngwato for the next forty years, widely acclaimed as the model christianised African chief.[137]

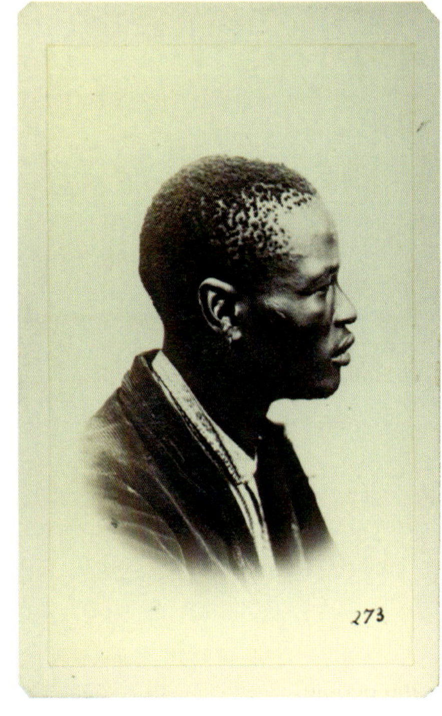
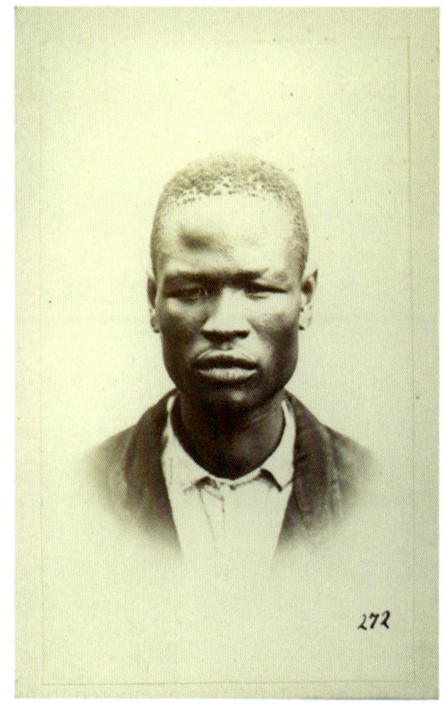

Figs. 197-198 ▶

Khaama, Thronfolger der Ba-mangwato.

Khama, successor to the Ngwato chief, Shoshong,
Bechuanaland.
(EM-SMB/32/812-808)

Mocotcane, Matabele, Shoshong, Ba-mangwato Gebiet.

Mocotcane, Ndebele, Shoshong,
Bechuanaland.
(EM-SMB/32/884-883)

Figs. 199-200 ▶

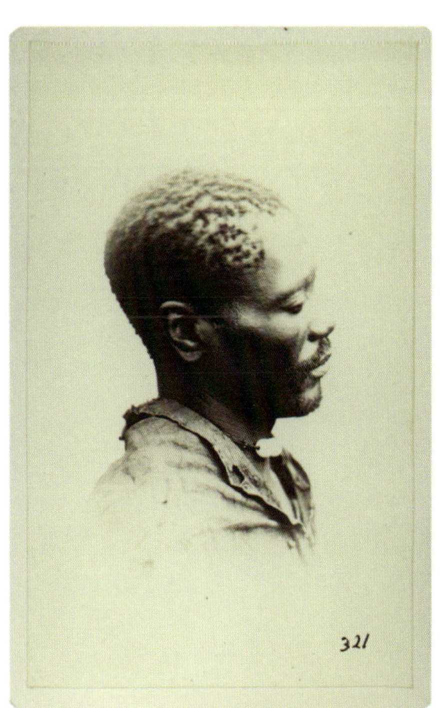

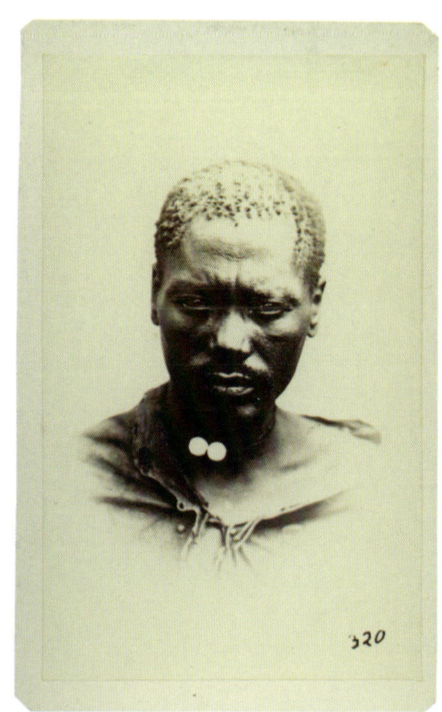

Fritsch remarked that he felt at ease in the presence of Khama, a degree of ease he had not yet experienced in the company of black people. This, he claimed, made him realise that it was not the colour of their skin that prejudiced him against the 'Ethiopian race'. 'I am glad', wrote Fritsch, 'by my acquaintance with Khama, to have the opportunity of mentioning a black man whom I would under no circumstances be ashamed to call my friend. The simple, modest, and at the same time noble deportment of the son of a chief awoke a delightful feeling.'[138]

Sekgoma was a skilled *ngaka* (herbalist) and celebrated rain-maker.[139] Once Fritsch's medical background became known, the *kgosi* behaved indifferently towards him. He was weary of Fritsch and would not look him in the eyes. Fritsch's photographic equipment added to Sekgoma's fears, as many believed Fritsch to be a magician. Fritsch was especially anxious to conceal the fact that his primary reason for visiting Shoshong was to locate human skeletons, of which he believed there were a number in the vicinity because of a smallpox epidemic that had struck the area between 1862 and 1863, resulting in thousands of deaths. He persuaded Khama to show him where he could find skulls. Khama agreed but pleaded with Fritsch to let nobody else know about it. When they arrived at the site they found only crushed skulls, which Fritsch believed to have been smashed by passersby with stones.[140]

Fritsch took four photographs while in Shoshong. They include the portraits of Khama and the Ndebele men Mocotcane and Makuatse (Figs. 199–202), and a group photograph of Sekgoma, Khama, a hunter named Chapman, Joseph McCabe's son and other unidentified Tswana men and white traders (Fig. 203).[141] Fritsch made reference to this photograph in his travel account, writing that 'once I caught the old fox [Sekgoma] when I took a photograph of a group of traders, and without knowing what was going on he was drawn into the middle, but after he had seen how successful I was, no power in the world would have made him sit down again'.[142] Considering the deep animosity between Sekgoma and Khama, Fritsch's coup in managing to capture both in a single image is of historical significance. The hunter he referred to as Chapman was most likely Edward George Chapman, a trader from Kuruman and not the hunter, trader and photographer James Chapman, who had left Walvis Bay for Cape Town a year before. Fritsch remarked that Edward Chapman was one of the most daring lion hunters of the time and that he had come to the rescue of an English hunting party from Natal who were being terrorised by a lion on their return from Mzilikazi's country.[143]

Fritsch spent a happy time at Shoshong, where he was entertained by John Mackenzie, John Smith Moffat (son of Robert Moffat) and Roger Price, who helped him with his researches.[144] He saw no reason to venture further north as people were becoming more difficult to photograph. More importantly, his photographic equipment was in a state of disrepair and his stock of chemicals and materials was depleted. Furthermore, with the summer came the dangers of horse sickness and lung disease. On 19 October, Fritsch joined the party of John Moffat jnr, who was returning to Kuruman. From Kuruman,

Fritsch travelled to Hope Town, and from there he returned to Cape Town as a passenger on a cart.[145]

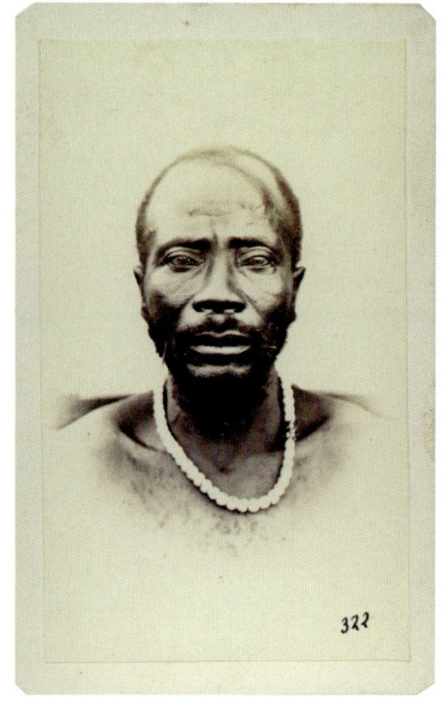 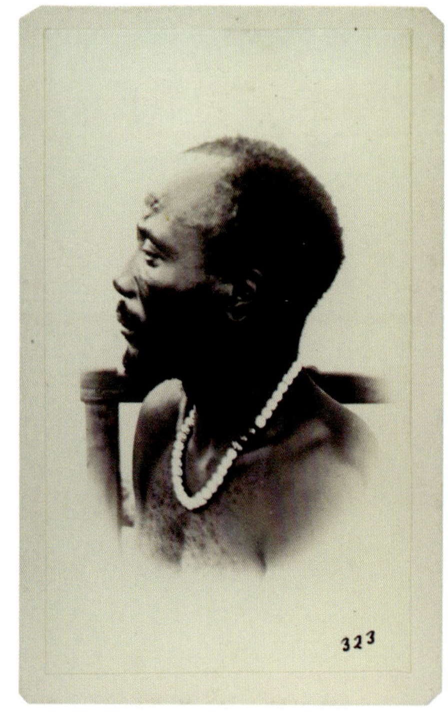

Figs. 201-202 ▶

Makuatse, Matabele, Shoshong, Ba-kuéna Gebiet.

Makuatse, Ndebele. Shoshong,
Bechuanaland.
(EM-SMB/32/885-886)

Standing in the centre (in traditional dress):
Sekgoma

Seated in the front (with hat and light suit):
McCabe jnr, son of Joseph McCabe.

Standing behind McCabe (wearing a hat):
Khama, son of Sekgoma.

Standing to the right of Khama (obscured):
the hunter Edward George Chapman.

Shoshong, Bechuanaland.
(EM-SMB/32/1212)

Fig. 203 ▶

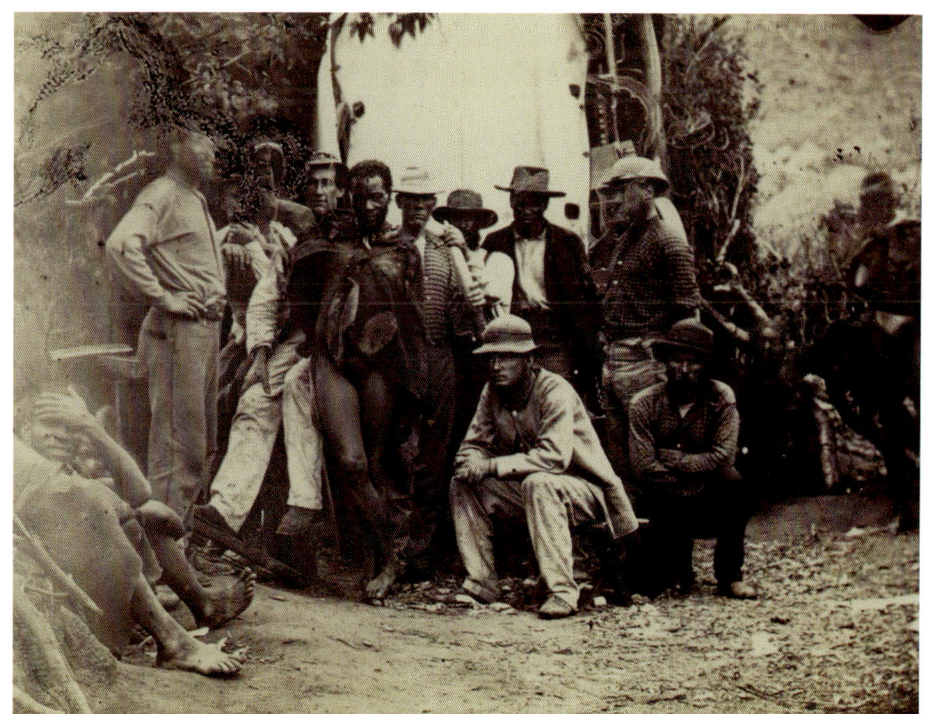

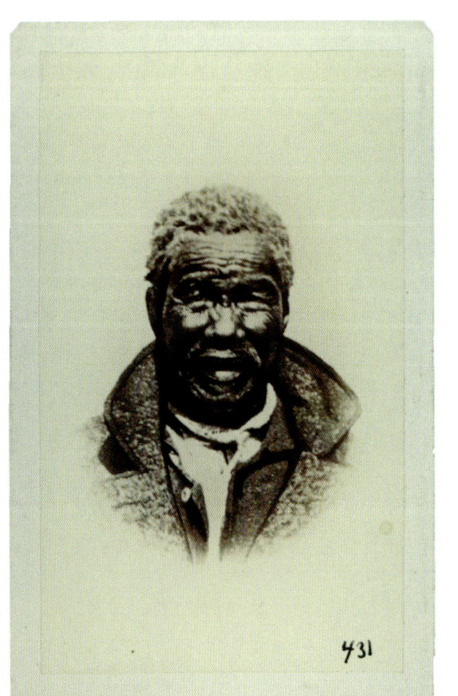

Fig. 204 ▼ (EM-SMB/32/756)

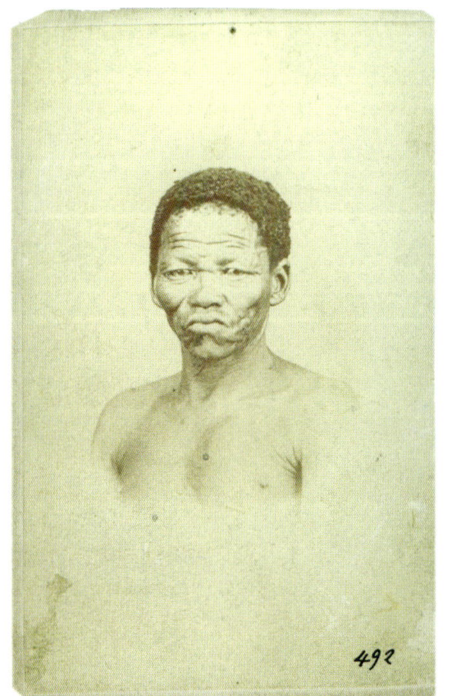

Buschmann der westlichen Colonie.

San from the western Cape.
(EM-SMB/2/694)

Fig. 205 ▼

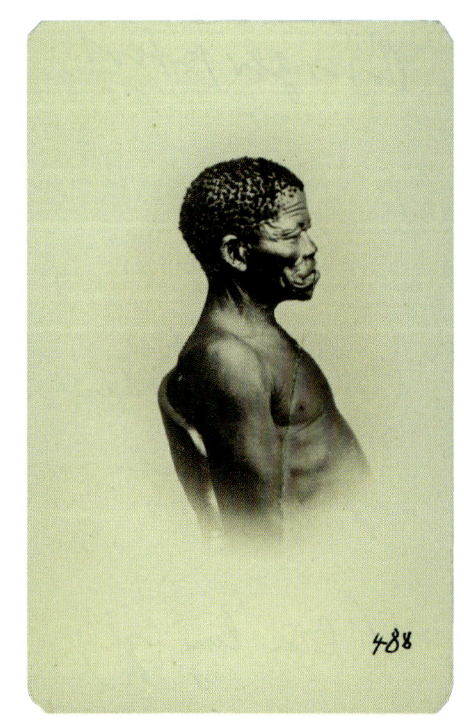

Buschmann der westlichen Colonie.

San from the western Cape.
(EM-SMB32/709)

Fig. 206 ▼

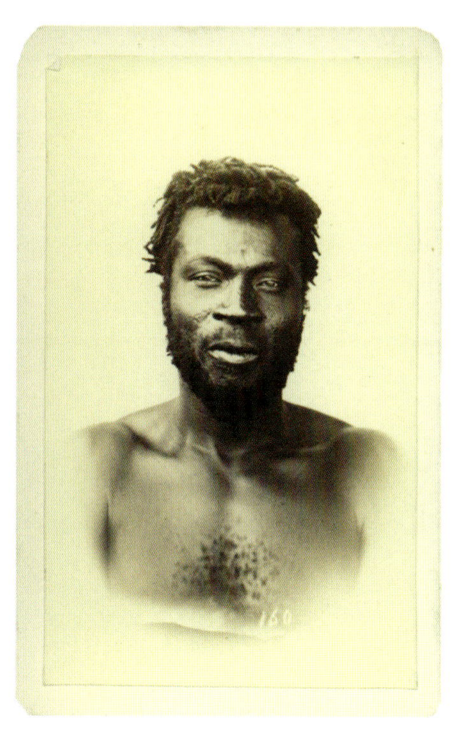

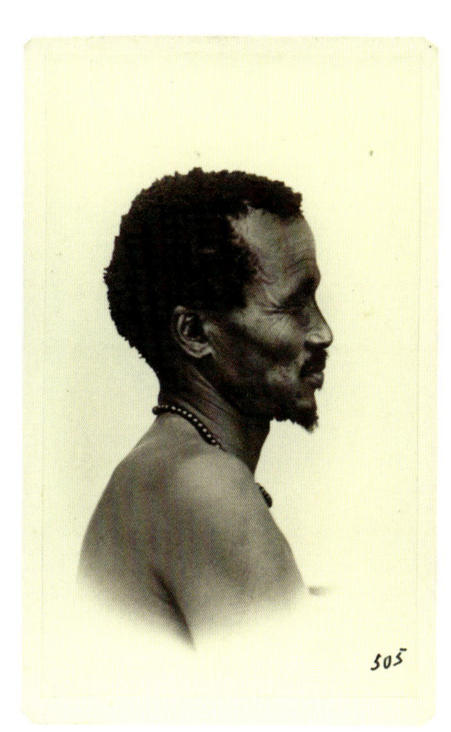

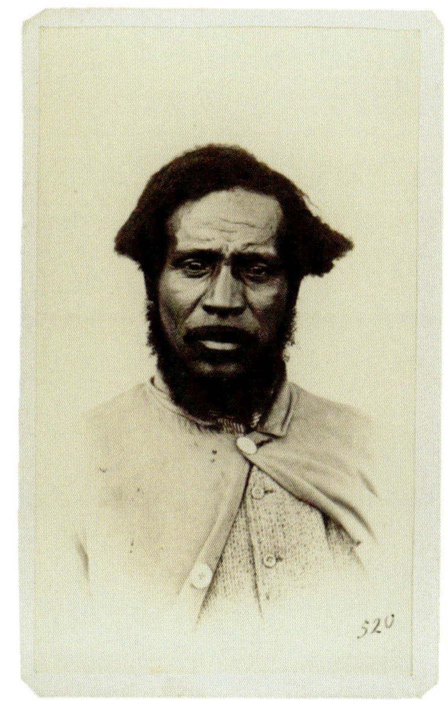

Figs. 207-208 ▲ ▼ (EM-SMB/32/951-952)   *Figs. 209-210* ▲ ▼ (EM-SMB/32/1039-1035)   *Figs. 211-212* ▲ ▼ (EM-SMB/32/1061-1062)

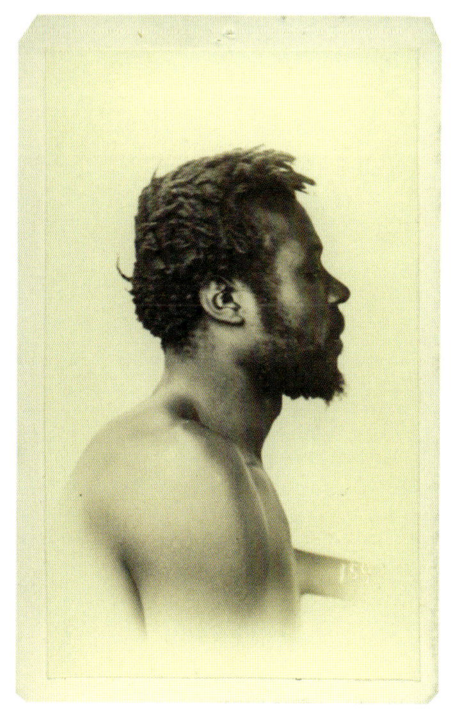

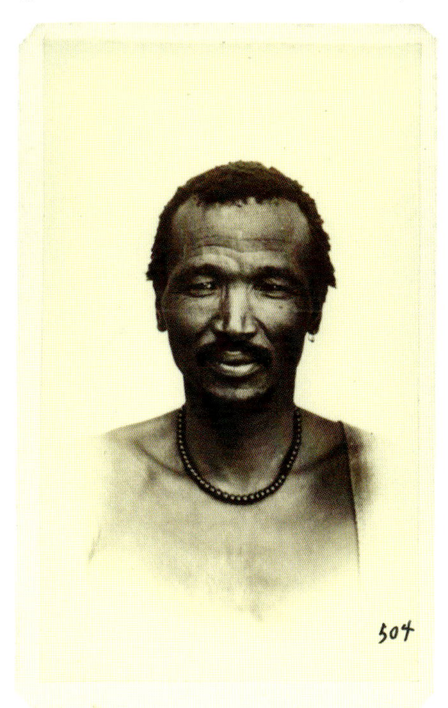

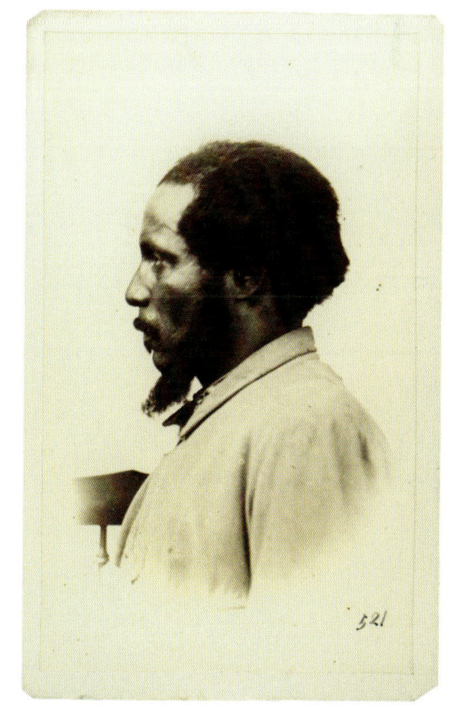

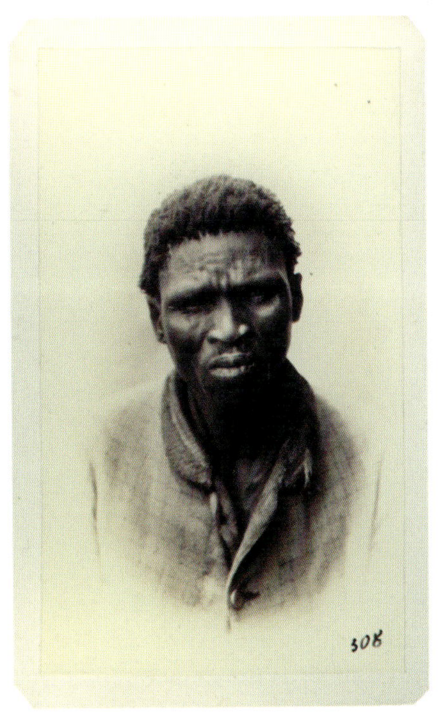

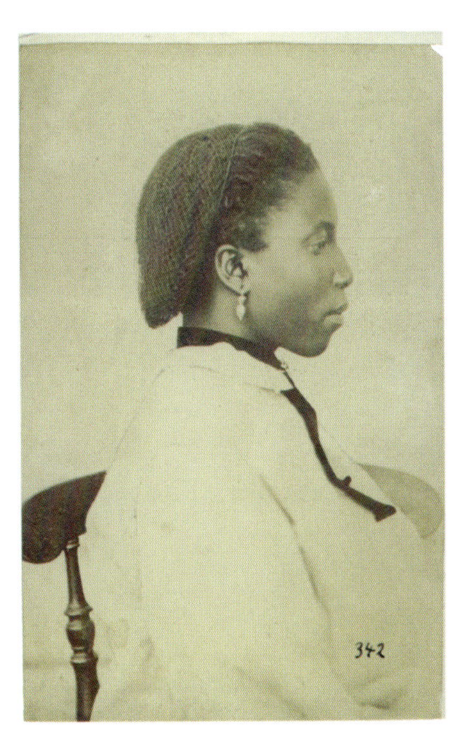

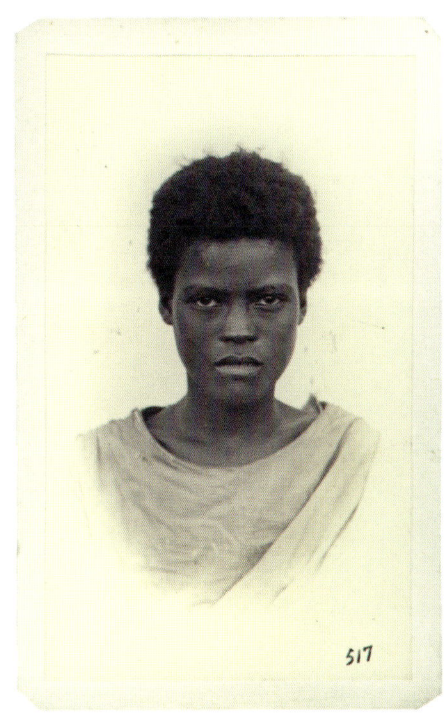

Figs. 213-214 ▲ ▼ (EM-SMB/32/1041-1045)   *Figs. 215-216* ▲ ▼ (EM-SMB/32/942-941)   *Figs. 217-218* ▲ ▼ (EM-SMB/321044-1048)

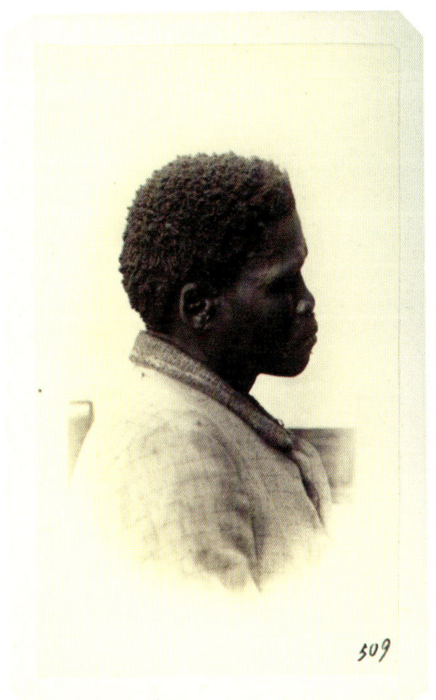

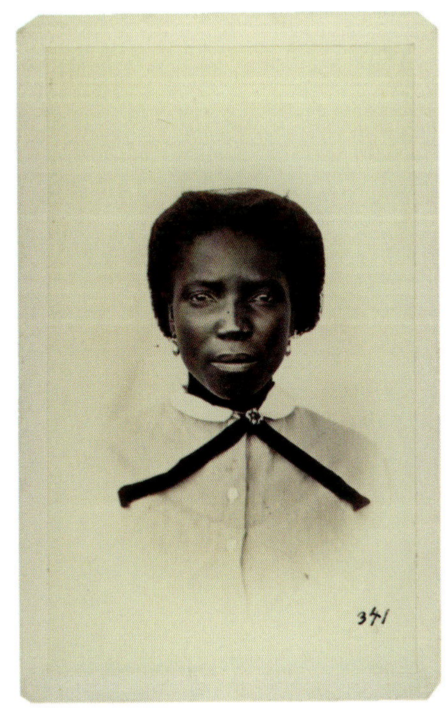

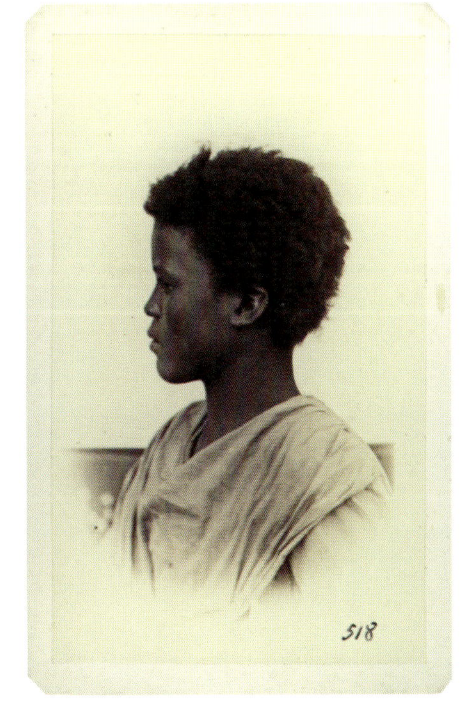

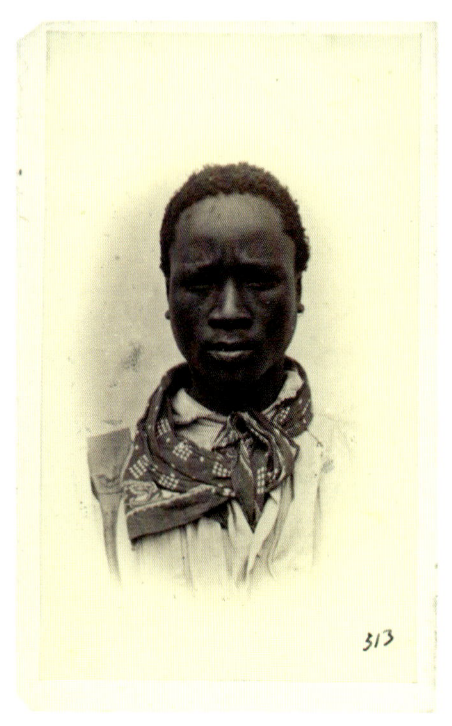

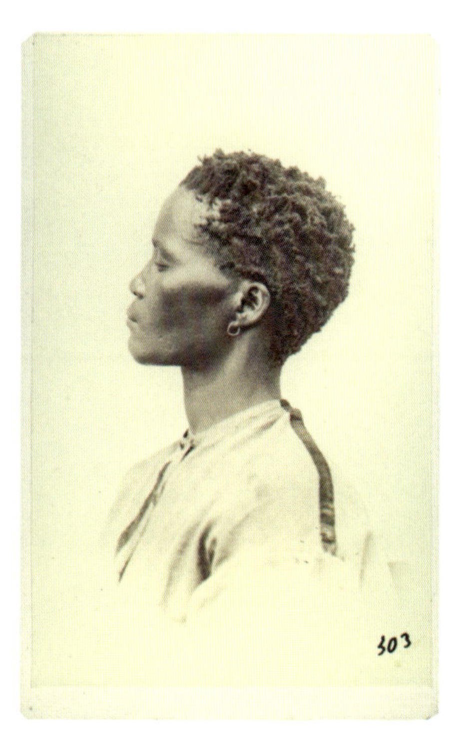

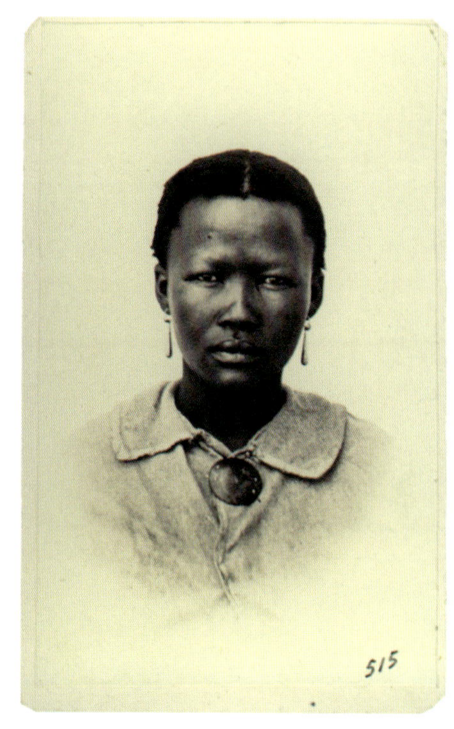

Figs. 219-220 ▲ ▼ (EM-SMB/32/1036-1040)   Figs. 221-222 ▲ ▼ (EM-SMB/32/1046-1042)   Figs. 223-224 ▲ ▼ (EM-SMB/321043-1047)

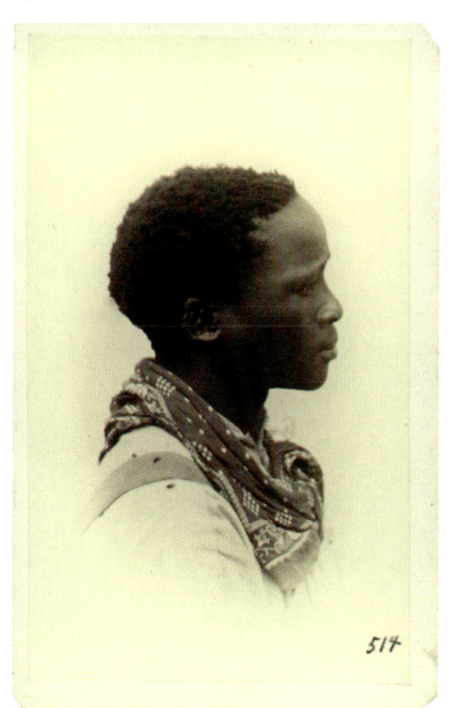

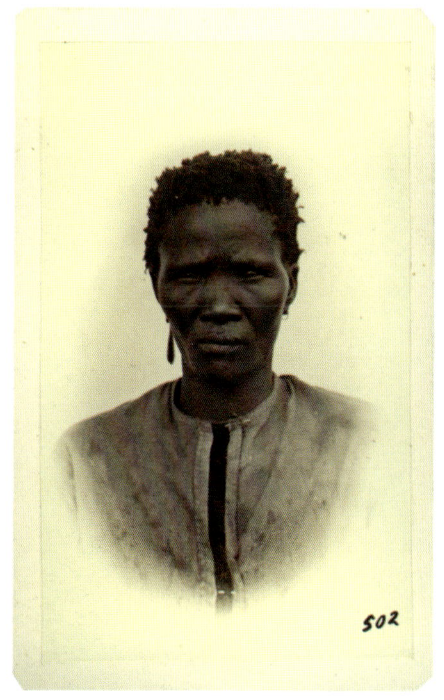

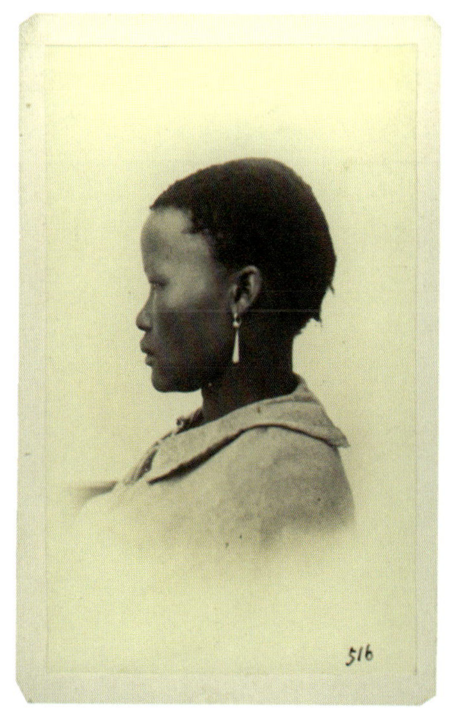

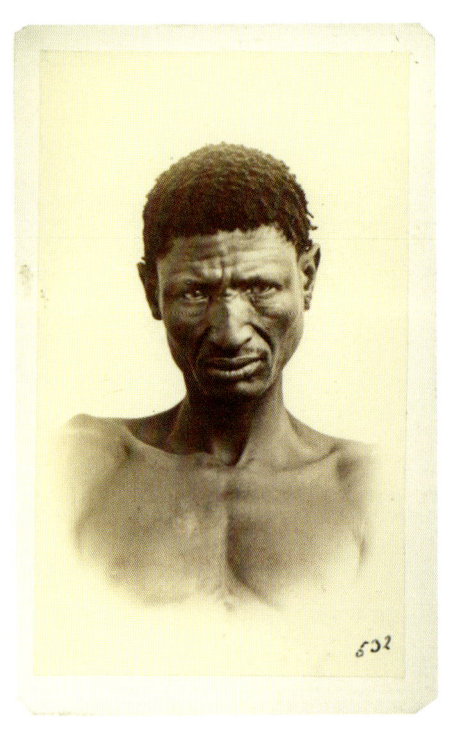

Figs. 225-226 ▲ ▼ (EM-SMB/32/1049-1050)

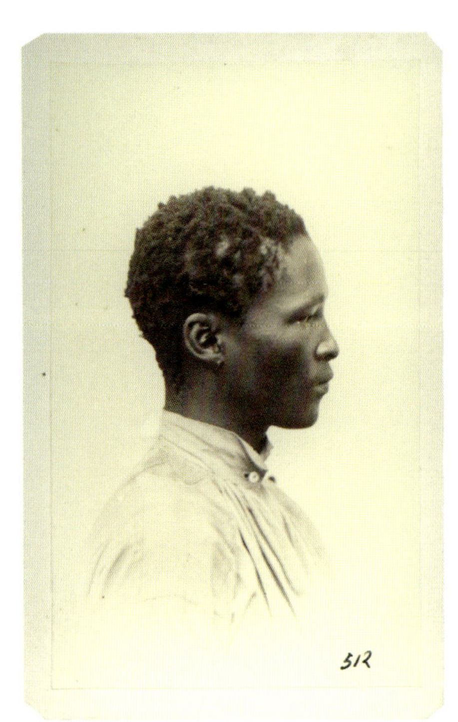

Figs. 227-228 ▲ ▼ (EM-SMB/32/1038-1034)

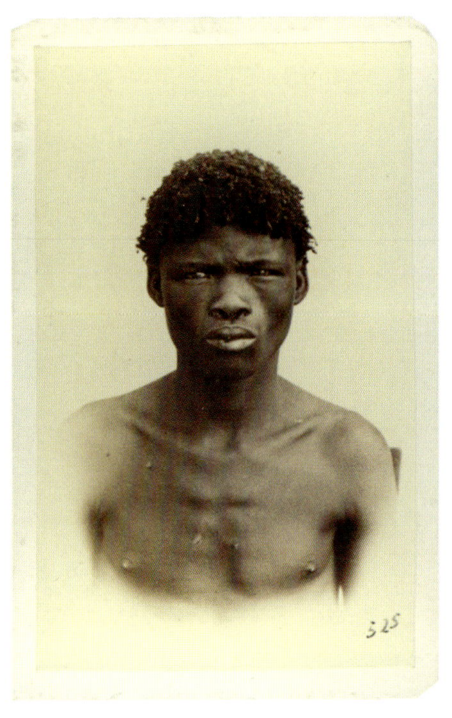

Figs. 229-230 ▲ ▼ (EM-SMB/32/1057-1058)

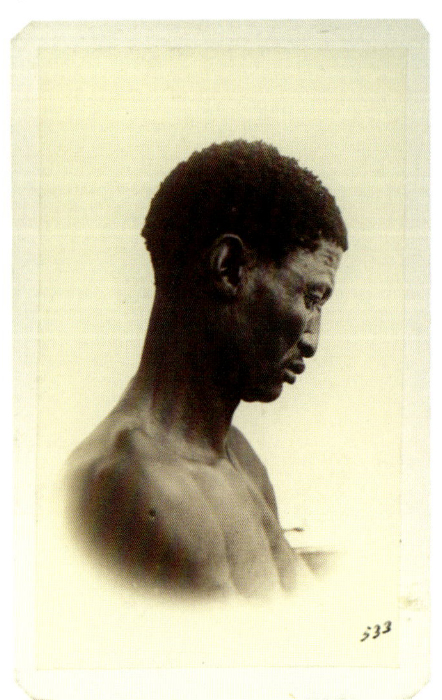

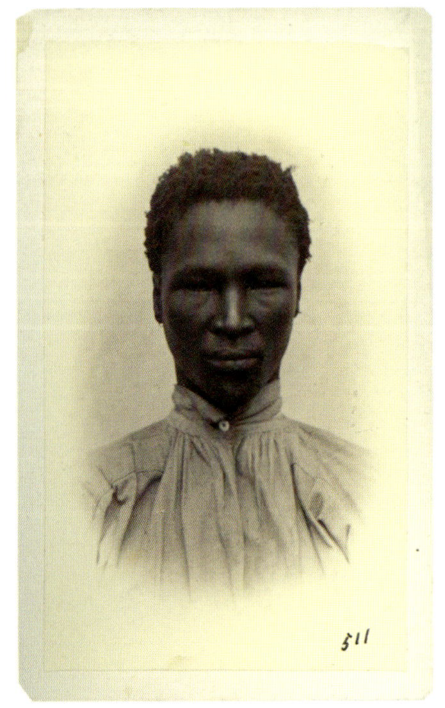

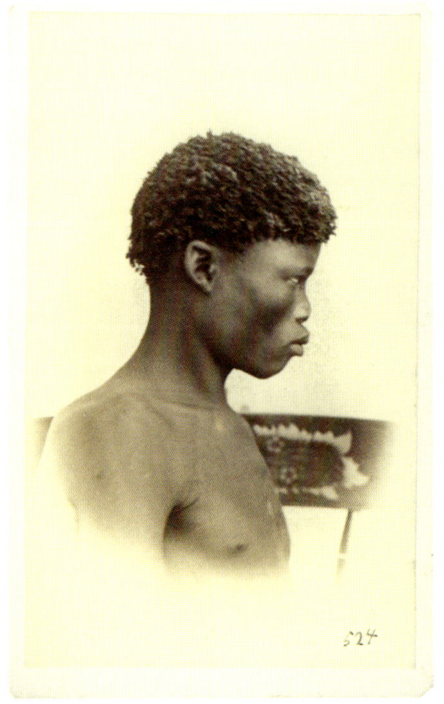

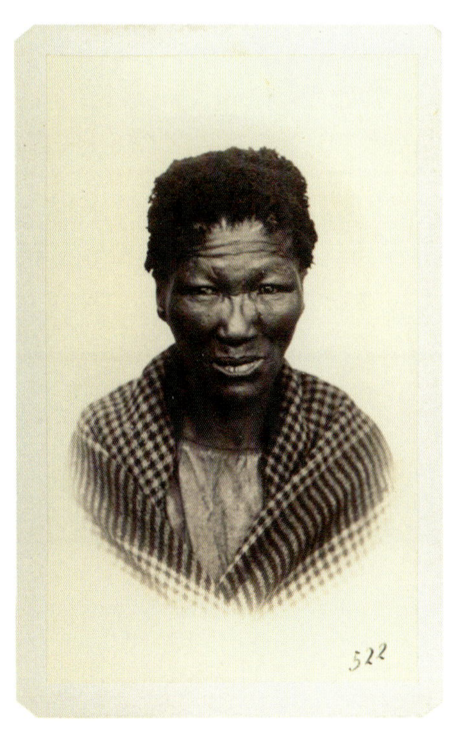

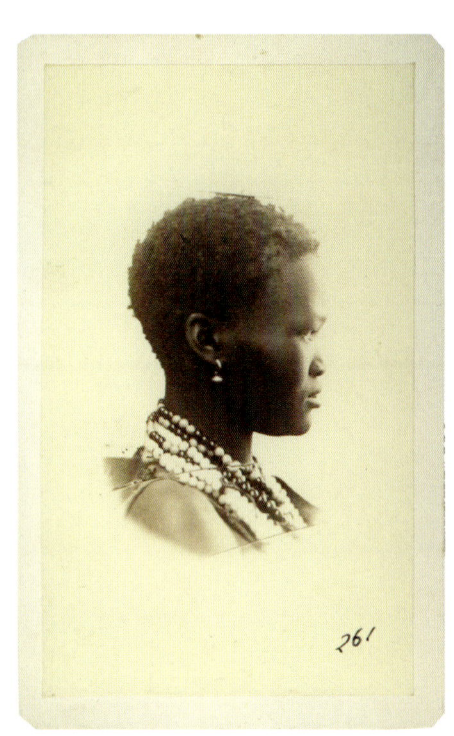

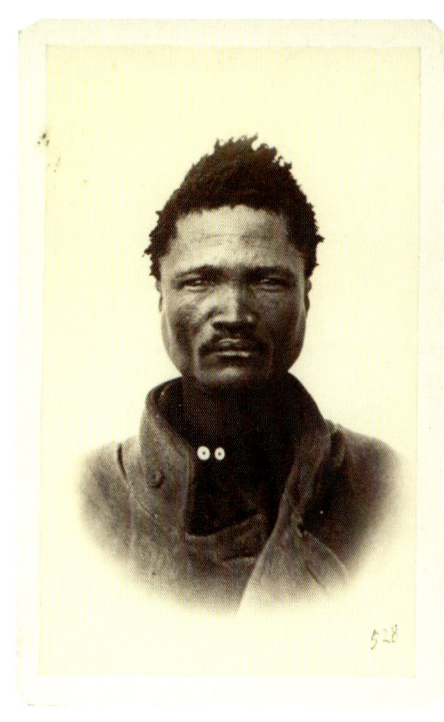

Figs. 231-232 ▲ ▼ (EM-SMB/32/1060-1059)   *Figs. 233-234* ▲ ▼ (EM-SMB/32/849-848)   *Figs. 235-236* ▲ ▼ (EM-SMB/32/1053-1054)

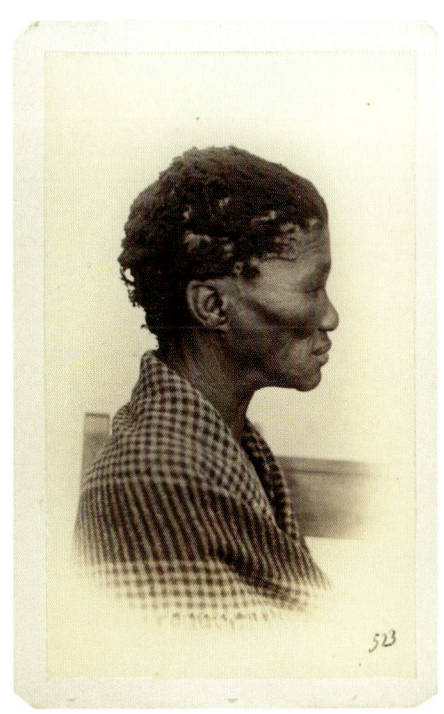

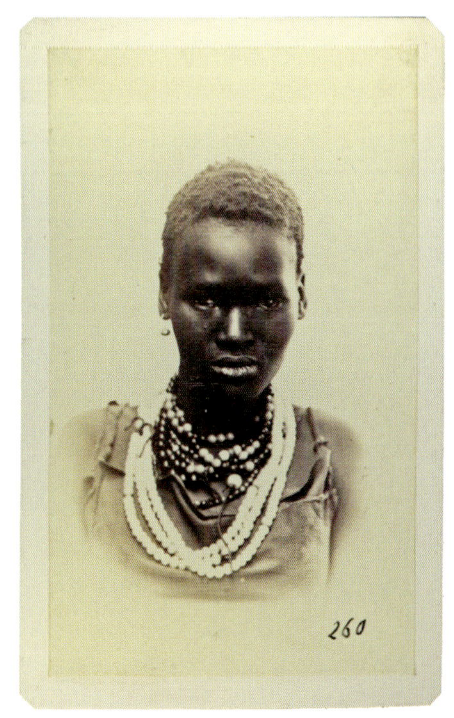

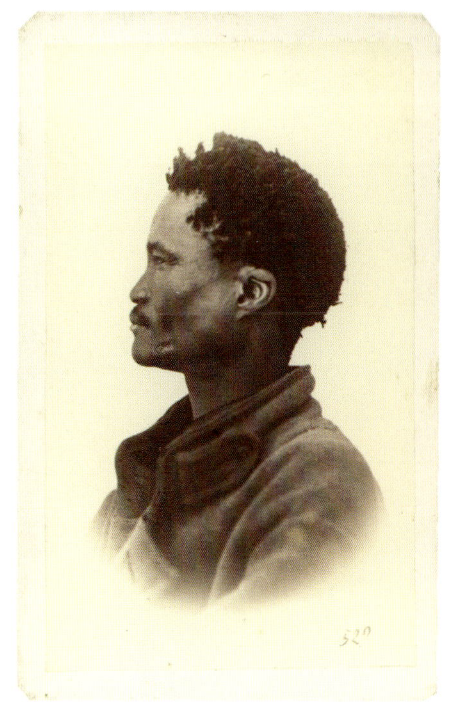

Anatomical and ethnographical studies

In his book *Die Eingeborenen*, Fritsch provided a number of wood engravings depicting anatomical studies of naked people, three of whom he photographed. He discussed the well-proportioned body of a young, naked Mfengu woman from Döhne as being an exception to other individuals depicted in *Die Eingeborenen*, though he commented that the exceptional qualities were not particularly noticeable in the photograph (Fig. 237). As the woman could speak some English, Fritsch ascribed her healthy condition to her working for an English family in Stutterheim and to having grown up in what he refers to as 'civilised' conditions.[146] Fritsch also took a full-length, naked photograph of a San man, Job, from Colesberg (Fig. 238). In *Die Eingeborenen* he discussed the wood engraving reproduction of this photograph in the context of anatomical features related to diet.[147] The third study was of a Khoikhoi woman from Boshof (Fig. 239). Fritsch described her breasts as being firm for her age, and noted that this was not uncommon for a woman of 35 years. He discussed her condition of steatopygia in anatomical detail, and especially how it affected the posture of the back and the position of the pelvis. Fritsch observed that the tendency towards steatopygia could be described as a normal characteristic among Khoikhoi women, and that in their social environment they were in no way seen as 'monstra', being viewed as curiosities only by Europeans who were not used to this condition. In his view, a truer depiction of the 'Hottentot Venus' could be found in his photographic portraits, whereas Le Vaillant's illustrations belonged to the fantasy images of this author and could not lay claim to correctness.[148] In his *Atlas* Fritsch remarked that, because of various obstacles, he did not succeed in photographing naked people apart from the few mentioned. He stated that only in the minority of cases did shyness or shame prevent people from undressing. In most cases, particularly with chiefs and students from mission schools, people were extraordinarily proud of 'the rags with which civilisation has clad them', and for this reason they appeared clothed. At times, it was so cold that they would shiver when posing for their photographs, while in a few cases undressing was refused on account of prejudice.[149]

In addition to his portraits and anatomical studies of naked people, in *Die Eingeborenen* Fritsch also provided a number of ethnographic studies of Zulu, Xhosa and Damara people, which range from group studies to posed studies demonstrating cultural activities and practices (such as dressing hair, fighting with sticks, smoking *dagga*). Whereas he acknowledged using James Chapman's photographs of Damara people, it remains unclear where he obtained the other photographs that form part of Album 32, as there is no evidence that he took them while in South Africa. Some of these are the same photographs (see, for example Figs. 240 and 241) as those presented to the South African Library (Grey Ethnological Album) and catalogued as 'Natives of Natal … presented by the late Capt Walmsley'. Captain Joshua Walmsley was a retired British army officer and border agent on the Tugela River employed by the Natal government. There is no other evidence of the origin of these photographs. Dr Wilhelm Bleek also probably provided Fritsch with photographic material for *Die Eingeborenen*, as Fritsch acknowledged Bleek's photograph of a San man (Fig. 242) which he used as a source for one of the wood engravings.

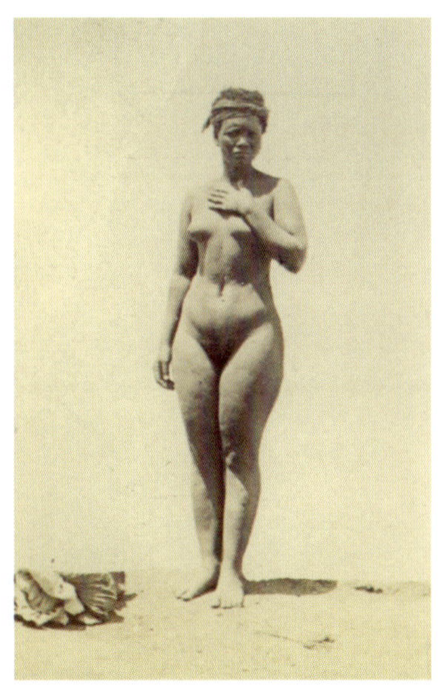

Mfengu girl, Döhne, British Kaffraria.
(EM-SMB/13/462)

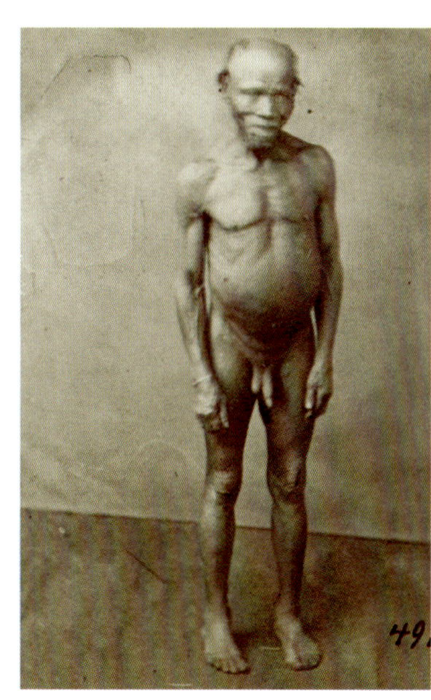

Job, San, Colesberg, Cape Colony.
(BGAEU/274)

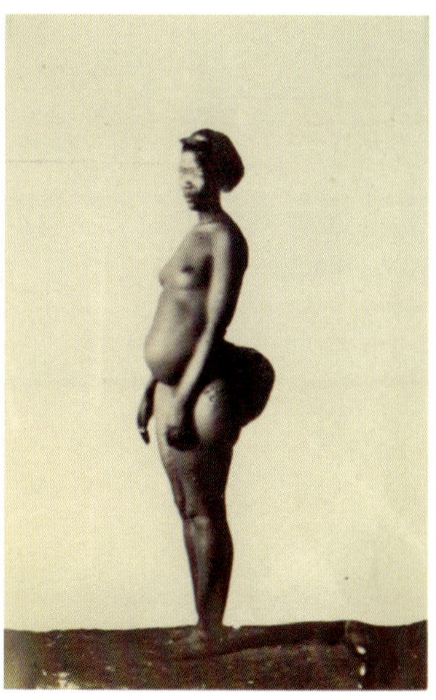

Gonaqua Khoikhoi, Boshof, Orange Free
State. (EM-SMB/13/463)

[Capt Joshua Walmsley], Zulu maidens,
Natal. (EM-SMB/32/1024)

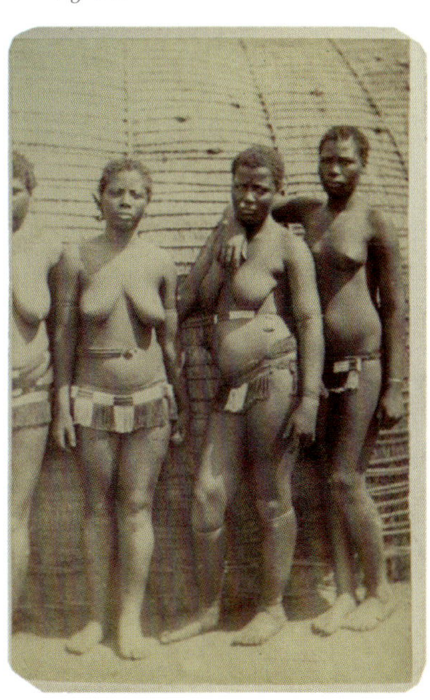

[Capt Joshua Walmsley], Zulu hair-dressers,
Natal. (EM-SMB/32/964)

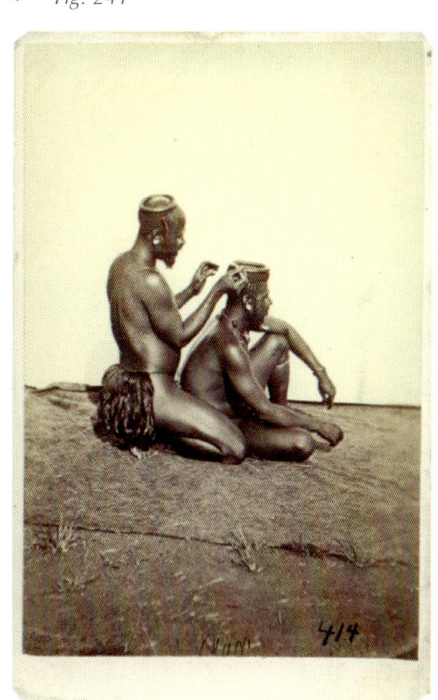

[Wilhelm Bleek], San man, Cape Colony.
(BGAEU/275)

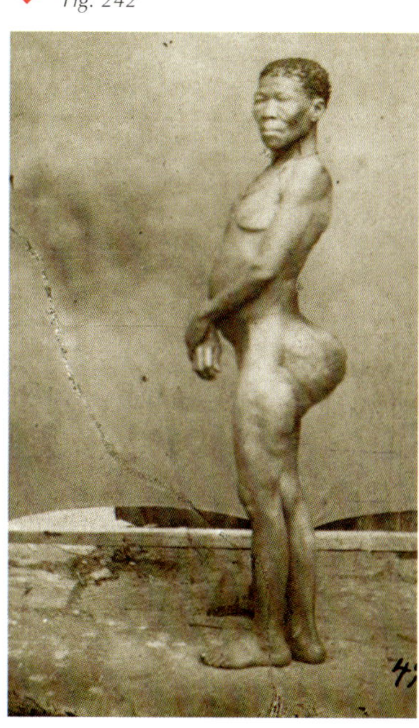

Because half-tone printing was still in its infancy at the time Fritsch published his books on South Africa, he was unable to have his portraits reproduced in these works. The illustrations were therefore translated from his photographs into wood engravings, etchings and lithographs. Fritsch did not describe the processes used to transform the photographs into printed illustrations, apart from the fact of his appointing Professor Hugo Bürckner, illustrator, woodcutter, engraver and etcher from the Academy of Arts in Dresden, to supervise the quality of the prints. Most of the illustrations were closely and accurately based on Fritsch's collection of photographs and are some of the most skilfully executed mass-produced illustrations of the period. The images were photographically transferred to the woodblocks, etching plates and lithographic stones, to which a photosensitive coating was applied. The reproduction process was called photoxylography (facsimile wood engraving),[150] whereby contact exposures were made from the negatives on to the blocks and plates. After the image had been developed and fixed, the engraver, etcher or lithographer would manually reproduce the image without the intervening process of a draughtsman to redraw the picture. Figs. 243 and 244 show an example of a photograph and the etching reproduction from the *Atlas*.

Wood engraving was the preferred means for book illustration at the time Fritsch published his works on South Africa. Because they were printed in relief, like raised type, it was possible to print the illustrations alongside the text. Wood engraving was, however, costly and time-consuming, and with photoxylography photographs could be photochemically transferred to the wood blocks for engraving. This was the process employed to engrave the wood-block illustrations for Fritsch's *Drei Jahre* and *Die Eingeborenen*. The illustrations for the *Atlas* which accompanied *Die Eingeborenen* were executed as etchings, while lithography was used for the illustrations of bones and skulls at the back of *Die Eingeborenen*.

Although Fritsch pioneered the role of photography in anthropological study, he recognised the drawbacks of photographic images and advocated a combination of photography and illustration where corrections could be made to images in the illustrations. This is certainly evident in some of the etchings from his *Atlas*, such as the alterations to the breast in the portrait of the San woman Rose from Bainsvlei. The full print of the photograph reproduced in the Dammann *Album* (Fig. 245) shows the unclear nipples of the woman, which were altered in the *Atlas* etching (Fig. 246). The etching of Job's portrait in Fritsch's

Atlas (Fig. 248) depicts him without clothing. Either Fritsch took two separate sets of photographs of Job, one with and one without clothing, or the head from the portrait (Fig. 247) was superimposed over the naked body of the full-length photograph (Fig. 238) to produce a photographic image for reproduction in the *Atlas* (Fig. 248).

Of interest to this study is Fritsch's awareness of the problems of visual material illustrating Africans that was produced by European engravers who had not personally observed the people they depicted. His constant references to misconceptions and erroneous interpretations in travel illustrations on South Africa support his contention that accurate ethnographic knowledge was not possible before photographic means of documentation. However, in spite of his obsessive reliance on photographic documentation (transformed into wood engravings and etchings as illustrations in his books), even Fritsch's 'objective' visual material does not provide an exact depiction of the people he photographed. Compared to the travel and ethnographic illustrations that originated as field sketches, however, the photographic process revealed nuanced traces of individual persons that we can read today in an entirely different context. Although Fritsch's portraits were subject to his anthropological project undertaken in the context of his studies on race, the camera itself makes no hierarchical choices. It does not 'see' people, and makes no distinction between 'native' (*Eingeborenen*) and 'civilised' (European). In contrast to Thomas Baines's illustrations, for example, in which the viewer is confronted with a disembodied picture of the colonising process of Africa, the people depicted in Fritsch's photographs are curiously watching themselves being observed. The spectacle is therefore not only Africa, but also the 'impartial observer' (*unbefangene Beobachter*) behind the camera. There is a sense of an encounter between Africa and Europe, with the observer and the observed engaged in looking and counter-looking, mediated by the camera.

Almost one and a half centuries ago, the light that reflected from the faces of the individuals who sat in front of Gustav Fritsch's camera, was fixed on glass plates coated with collodion emulsion and printed and preserved on paper. Having retrieved these portraits from the archives of the Berlin Society for Anthropology, Ethnology and Prehistory in the Ethnological Museum in Berlin, and having reconstituted them in a new archive, we trust that by making them accessible to the South African public these portraits may now be reclaimed as part of our own cultural heritage.

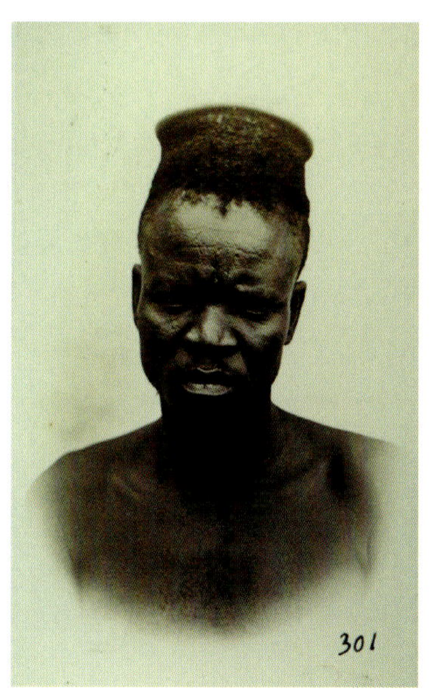

Fig. 243 ▲

Umsungune, Zulu, Harrismith, Orange Free State. (EM-SMB/32/897)

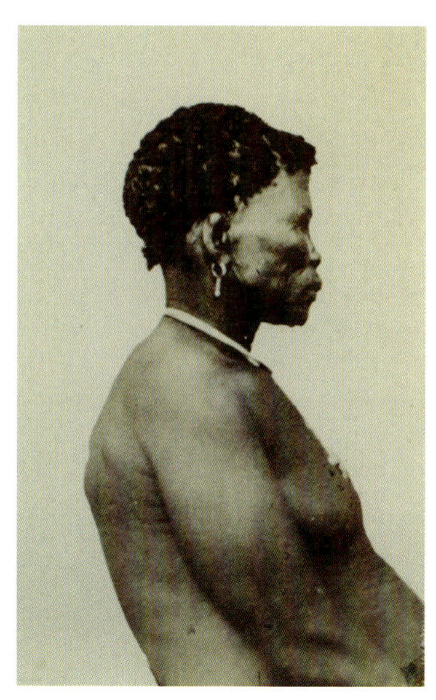

Fig. 245 ▲

Rose, San, Bainsvlei, Orange Free State. (EM-SMB/13/Plate XIII, 469)

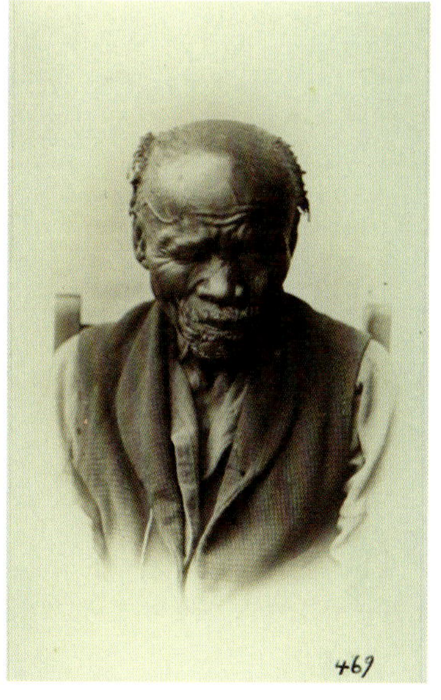

Fig. 247 ▲

Job, San, Colesberg, eastern Cape. (EM-SMB/28/689)

Umsungune, Zulu, Harrismith, Orange Free State. Etching. (Fritsch, *Atlas*: Plate I)

Fig. 244 ▼

Rose, San, Bainsvlei, Orange Free State. Etching. (Fritsch, *Atlas*: Plate XXVIII)

Fig. 246 ▼

Job, San, Colesberg, eastern Cape. Etching. (Fritsch, *Atlas*: Plate XXVII)

Fig. 248 ▼

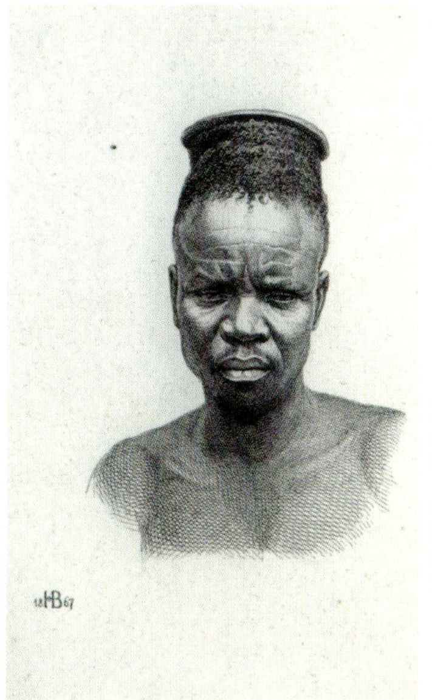

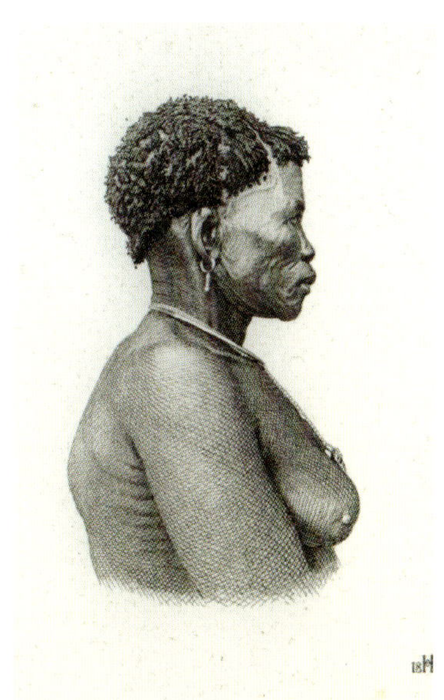

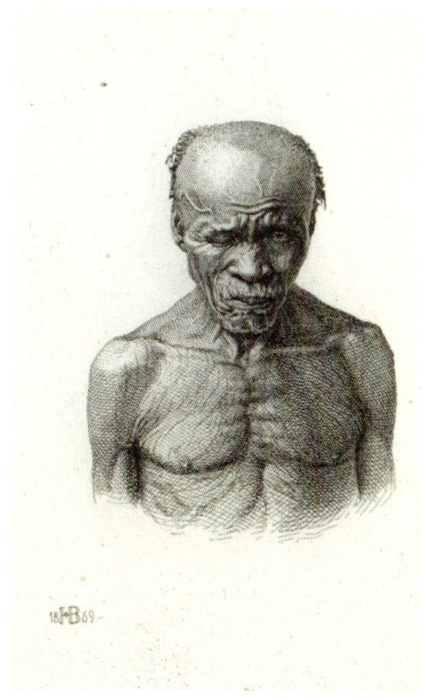

ENDNOTES

1   G.T. Fritsch, *Die Eingeborenen Süd-Afrika's ethnographisch und anatomisch beschrieben* (Breslau: Ferdinand Hirt, 1872), 10.

2   Fritsch, *Die Eingeborenen Süd-Afrika's*, ix.

3   G.T. Fritsch, *Die Eingeborenen Süd-Afrika's: Atlas* (Breslau: Ferdinand Hirt, 1872), 4, III.

4   Fritsch, *Atlas*, 4.

5   Fritsch, *Atlas*, 3.

6   Fritsch, *Die Eingeborenen Süd-Afrika's*, 27–28; Fritsch, *Atlas*, 3.

7   A stereoscope is a device for viewing a photograph three-dimensionally.

8   See the chapter by A. Lewerentz in this volume.

9   G.T. Fritsch, *Drei Jahre in Süd-Afrika. Reiseskizzen nach Notizen des Tagebuchs zusammengestellt* (Breslau: Ferdinand Hirt, 1868), 31.

10   Fritsch, *Drei Jahre*, 35.

11   Fritsch, *Drei Jahre*, 73.

12   Fritsch, *Drei Jahre*, 165.

13   Fritsch, *Atlas*, 4.

14   A.W. de Wiveleslie, *Photography with Emulsions: A Treatise on the Theory and Practical Working of the Collodion and Gelatin Emulsion Processes*, reprint of 1885 edition (Adamant Media Corporation, 2005), 208–210; B.E. Jones (ed.), *Cassell's Cyclopaedia of Photography*, reprint of 1911 edition (London: Ayer Publishing, 1973), 120–121.

15   Jones, *Cassell's Cyclopaedia of Photography*, 82–83.

16   Jones, *Cassell's Cyclopaedia of Photography*, 74–75, 99.

17   Jones, *Cassell's Cyclopaedia of Photography*, 14–16.

18   De Wiveleslie, *Photography with Emulsions*, 281–282.

19   De Wiveleslie, *Photography with Emulsions*, 295.

20   H. Deacon, 'The British prison on Robben Island 1800–1896' in H. Deacon (ed.), *The Island: A History of Robben Island 1488–1990* (Cape Town: David Philip, 1996), 39.

21   Deacon, 'The British prison on Robben Island 1800–1896', 49–52; J.B. Peires, *The Dead Will Arise: Nongqawuse and the Great Xhosa Cattle-Killing Movement of 1856–7* (Bloomington: Indiana University Press, 1989), 300–303.

22   Fritsch, *Drei Jahre*, 34.

23   Fritsch, *Atlas*, Plates VI and VII; C. Dammann, *Anthropologisch-ethnologisches Album in Photographien herausgegeben mit Unterstützung aus der Sammlung der Berliner Anthropologischen Gesellschaft* (Berlin, 1874), 316, 316a, 317, 317a, 318, 318a, 321, 321a, 322 and 322a.

24   Fritsch, *Drei Jahre*, 33.

25   Fritsch, *Drei Jahre*, 33.

26   Fritsch, *Drei Jahre*, 34–35; H. Deacon, 'The medical institutions on Robben Island 1846–1931' in H. Deacon (ed.), *The Island: A History of Robben Island 1488 – 1990* (Cape Town: David Philip, 1996), 66.

27   Fritsch, *Drei Jahre*, 71.

28   Fritsch, *Drei Jahre*, 73.

29   Fritsch, *Atlas*, Plate XII; Dammann, *Anthropologisch-ethnologisches Album*, 314, 314a, 327 and 327a.

30   R. Elphick and T.R.H. Davenport, *Christianity in South Africa: A Political, Social, and Cultural History* (Cape Town: David Philip, 1997), 75.

31   Fritsch, *Drei Jahre*, 91.

32   Peires, *The Dead Will Arise*, 67.

33   J.B. Peires, *The House of Phalo: A History of the Xhosa People in the Days of their Independence* (Johannesburg: Ravan Press, 1981), 150–155.

34   Peires, *The Dead Will Arise*, 12; P. Gon, 'The Last Frontier War', *Military History Journal*, 5, 6 (1982), http://rapidttp.com/milhist/vol056pg.html [6 June 2008].

35   Fritsch, *Drei Jahre*, 92.

36   Fritsch, *Atlas*, Plates VIII and IX; Dammann, *Anthropologisch-ethnologisches Album*, 311, 311a, 313, 313a, 319, 319a, 324, 324a, 331 and 331a; National Library of South Africa, National Library Visual Collection, Cape Town Campus (hereafter NLSA), Grey Ethnographic Album 167 (14162).

37   Fritsch, *Drei Jahre*, 93.

38   Fritsch, *Die Eingeborenen Süd-Afrika's*, 26.

39   Peires, *The Dead Will Arise*, 297.

40   Fritsch, *Die Eingeborenen Süd-Afrika's* 21.

41   Fritsch, *Atlas*, Plates VIII and IX; Dammann, *Anthropologisch-ethnologisches Album*, 320, 320a, 323, 323a, 332 and 332a.

42   Fritsch, *Atlas*, Plate L.

43   Fritsch, *Drei Jahre*, 103.

44   *The Moravian Church Miscellany*, 4, 2 (Bethlehem: Church of the United Brethren, 1853), 243, 247.

45   B. Krüger, *The Pear Tree Blossoms: The History of the Moravian Church in South Africa 1737–1869* (Genadendal: Provincial Board of the Moravian Church in South Africa, 1966), 240-241.

46   *The Moravian Church Miscellany*, 5, 1 (Bethlehem: Church of the United Brethren, 1854), 362.

47   Krüger, *The Pear Tree Blossoms*, 105.

48   Krüger, *The Pear Tree Blossoms*, 132.

49   Krüger, *The Pear Tree Blossoms*, 170–171.

50   A. Jones (ed.), *Africa in German Mission Archives: Herrnhut II* (Leipzig: Unitätsarchiv der Brüdergemeine Herrnhut, 2000), 32.

51   Fritsch, *Atlas*, Plates IX, XXI and XXII; Dammann, *Anthropologisch-ethnologisches Album*, 310, 310a, 328, 328a, 329, 329a, 330, 330a, 426a, 428, 428a, 429, 429a,

52   P.E. Raper, *A Dictionary of Southern African Place Names* (Johannesburg: Jonathan Ball, 1987), 101.

53   Fritsch, *Drei Jahre*, 109.

54   Fritsch, *Drei Jahre*, 110.

55   Fritsch, *Atlas*, Plates X, XXI, XXVII and XXIX; Dammann, *Anthropologisch-ethnologisches Album*, 427, 427a, 325, 325a, 340, 340a, 461 and 461a,

56   Fritsch, *Drei Jahre*, 110.

57   Fritsch, *Die Eingeborenen Süd-Afrika's*, 404–405.

58   Fritsch, *Drei Jahre*, 96–97.

59   Fritsch, *Drei Jahre*, 113.

60   Fritsch, *Drei Jahre*, 119.

61   Fritsch, *Drei Jahre*, 119–120.

62   J.A. Engelbrecht, *The Korana: An Account of Their Customs and Their History* (Cape Town: Maskew Miller, 1936), 4.

63   Engelbrecht, *The Korana*, 151–154.

64   Fritsch, *Atlas*, Plates XIV and XXVI; Dammann, *Anthropologisch-ethnologisches Album*, 333, 333a, 346, 346a, 347, 347a, 430, 430a, 431, 431a, 465, 468, 468a, 470 and 470a.

65   Fritsch, *Drei Jahre*, 121.

66   Fritsch, *Drei Jahre*, 123.

67   Fritsch, *Atlas*, Plates X, XI and XV; Dammann, *Anthropologisch-ethnologisches Album*, 308, 308a, 312, 312a, 326, 326a, 343, 343a, 344, 344a, 345 and 345a.

68   Fritsch, *Drei Jahre*, 124.

69   Fritsch, *Drei Jahre*, 127.

70   Fritsch, *Drei Jahre*, 129.

71   Engelbrecht, *The Korana*, 38–39; E.J. Verwy (ed.), *New Dictionary of South African Biography*, vol. 1 (Pretoria: HSRC Press, 1995), 110–111.

72   Fritsch, *Drei Jahre*, 129; Verwy, *New Dictionary of South African Biography*, 111.

73   Fritsch, *Drei Jahre*, 131.

74   Fritsch, *Drei Jahre*, 132; Fritsch, *Atlas*, Plates XXIV and XXV; Dammann, *Anthropologisch-ethnologisches Album*, 433, 433a, 434, 434a, 456, 456a, 457, 457a, 458, 458a, 459 and 459a.

75   Fritsch, Die *Eingeborenen Süd-Afrika's*, 370.

76   Fritsch, Die *Eingeborenen Süd-Afrika's*, 280.

77   Fritsch, *Drei Jahre*, 134.

78   Fritsch, *Drei Jahre*, 135.

79   Fritsch, *Atlas*, Plates XXVII, XXVIII, XXXIX and XXX; Dammann, *Anthropologisch-ethnologisches Album*, 464, 464a, 466, 469, 469a, 471, 471a, 472, 472a, 463, 473a, 474, 474a, 475 and 475a.

80   Fritsch, *Drei Jahre*, 138.

81   Fritsch, *Drei Jahre*, 136; W.W. Collins, *Free Statia* (Cape Town: C. Struik, 1965), 174.

82   Fritsch, *Drei Jahre*, 184.

83   Fritsch, *Drei Jahre*, 185.

84   Fritsch, *Drei Jahre*, 185.

85   Fritsch, *Atlas*, Plate III.

86   Fritsch, *Drei Jahre*, 185; Fritsch, *Atlas*, Plates I, III, XVI and XXIV; Dammann, *Anthropologisch-ethnologisches Album*, 301, 301a, 302, 302a, 303, 303a, 342, 342a, 348, 348a, 432 and 432a; NLSA, Grey Ethnographic Album, 167 (14140).

87   Fritsch, *Drei Jahre*, 185.

88   Fritsch, *Drei Jahre*, 195–196.

89   Fritsch, *Drei Jahre*, 199.

90   Fritsch, *Drei Jahre*, 211–212.

91   Fritsch, *Die Eingeborenen Süd-Afrika's*, 126.

92   Dammann, *Anthropologisch-ethnologisches Album*, 307.

93   Fritsch, *Atlas*, Plate II; Dammann, *Anthropologisch-ethnologisches Album*, 300.

94   Fritsch, *Atlas*, Plate II; Dammann, *Anthropologisch-ethnologisches Album*, 299.

95   Fritsch, *Die Eingeborenen Süd-Afrika's*, 126–127.

96   Fritsch, *Atlas*, Plate I; Dammann, *Anthropologisch-ethnologisches Album*, 298.

97   Fritsch, *Die Eingeborenen Süd-Afrika's*, 127.

98   Fritsch, *Atlas*, Plates I and II; Dammann, *Anthropologisch-ethnologisches Album*, 298, 298a, 299, 299a, 300, 300a, 307 and 307a; NLSA, Grey Ethnographic Album 167 (14200, 14201 and 14202).

99   Fritsch, *Drei Jahre*, 215–218.

100 Fritsch, *Drei Jahre*, 252–254.

101 J. Campbell, *Travels in South Africa Undertaken at the Request of the Missionary Society* (London: Black and Parry, 1815), 349.

102 H. Lichtenstein, *Travels in Southern Africa in the Years 1803, 1804, 1805 and 1806*, vol. 2 (Cape Town: Van Riebeeck Society, 1930), 238, 301–306; N. Mostert, *Frontiers: The Epic of South Africa's Creation and the Tragedy of the Xhosa People* (London: Jonathan Cape, 1992), 416–417.

103 Fritsch, *Atlas*, Plates XVII and XVIII; Dammann, *Anthropologisch-ethnologisches Album*, 417, 417a, 418, 418a, 419, 419a, 420 and 420a; F. Morton, 'Slave-raiding and slavery in the western Transvaal after the Sand River Convention', *African Economic History*, 20 (1992),108.

104 Fritsch, *Drei Jahre*, 259.

105 Fritsch, *Drei Jahre*, 262.

106 Fritsch, *Drei Jahre*, 268–269.

107 K. Dietrich, 'Of salvation and civilisation: The image of indigenous southern Africans in European travel illustration from the sixteenth to the nineteenth centuries' (DLitt et Phil thesis, Unisa, 1992), 213, 256.

108 Fritsch, *Drei Jahre*, 276–277.

109 Dammann, *Anthropologisch-ethnologisches Album*, 423, 423a, 224, 424a, 425 and 425a; NLSA, Grey Ethnographic Album 167 (14196).

110 Fritsch, *Drei Jahre*, 280–283.

111 N. Parsons, *King Khama, Emperor Joe, and the Great White Queen: Victorian Britain through African Eyes* (Chicago: University of Chicago Press, 1998), 43.

112 Fritsch, *Drei Jahre*, 305.

113 Fritsch, *Drei Jahre*, 311–312; Fritsch, *Atlas*, Plate XIX; Dammann, *Anthropologisch-ethnologisches Album*, 422 and 422a.

114 Fritsch, *Drei Jahre*, 323.

115 J. Ramsay, B. Morton and T. Mgadla, *Building a Nation: A History of Botswana from 1800 to 1910* (Gaborone: Longman Botswana, 1996), 88–90.

116 S.A. Hughes, *Tshomarelo Ngwao: The Museums of Botswana Celebrate Twenty-five Years of Independence* (Gaborone: National Museum, Monuments, and Art Gallery, 1991), 14–16.

117 Fritsch, *Drei Jahre*, 323–324.

118 Fritsch, *Drei Jahre*, 324–326.

119 Fritsch, *Drei Jahre*, 332.

120 M. Wilson and L. Thompson (eds.), *The Oxford History of South Africa* (Oxford: Oxford University Press, 1969), vol. 1, 439; Parsons, *King Khama, Emperor Joe, and the Great White Queen*, 39–40.

121 Parsons, *King Khama, Emperor Joe, and the Great White Queen*, 41.

122 G.Y. Okihiro, *A Social History of the Bakwena and Peoples of the Kalahari of Southern Africa, 19th Century* (Lewiston, NY: Edwin Mellen, 2000), 42, 52.

123 Parsons, *King Khama, Emperor Joe, and the Great White Queen*, 40.

124 Fritsch, *Drei Jahre*, 430; Fritsch, *Atlas*, Plates XVIII and XX; Dammann, *Anthropologisch-ethnologisches Album*, 305, 305a, 421 and 421a; NLSA, Grey Ethnographic Album 167 (14181).

125 Fritsch, *Atlas*, Plate XVIII.

126 Fritsch, *Drei Jahre*, 341–346.

127 Fritsch, *Drei Jahre*, 341–346.

128 Fritsch, *Drei Jahre*, 347, 364.

129 Fritsch, *Drei Jahre*, 364–365.

130 Fritsch, *Drei Jahre*, 365.

131 G.H. Anderson, *Biographical Dictionary of Christian Missions* (Grand Rapids: Wm B. Eerdmans Publishing, 1999), 360.

132 Fritsch, *Drei Jahre*, 377–379.

133 Fritsch, *Drei Jahre*, 378–379.

134 Parsons, *King Khama, Emperor Joe, and the Great White Queen*, 46.

135 B. Bennett, '"Suppose a black man tells a story": Dialogues with John Mackenzie the missionary and Sekgoma Kgari the king and rainmaker', *PULA Journal of African Studies*, 11, 1 (1997), 45.

136 M. Chirenje, 'Church, state, and education in Bechuanaland in the nineteenth century', *International Journal of African Historical Studies*, 9, 3 (1976), 401–418.

137 Parsons, *King Khama, Emperor Joe, and the Great White Queen*, 46–47.

138 Fritsch, *Drei Jahre*, 379.

139 Bennett, '"Suppose a black man tells a story"', 44–45.

140 Fritsch, *Drei Jahre*, 381–382.

141 Fritsch, *Atlas*, Plates XVIII and XX; Dammann, *Anthropologisch-ethnologisches Album*, 306; NLSA, Grey Ethnographic Album 167 (14184).

142 Fritsch, *Drei Jahre*, 380.

143 Fritsch, *Drei Jahre*, 383–384.

144 Fritsch, *Drei Jahre*, 382.

145 Fritsch, *Drei Jahre*, 394, 399.

146 Fritsch, *Die Eingeborenen Süd-Afrika's*, 26.

147 Fritsch, *Die Eingeborenen Süd-Afrika's*, 404–405.

148 Fritsch, *Die Eingeborenen Süd-Afrika's*, 280–281.

149 Fritsch, *Atlas*, 4.

150 S.P. Rice, 'Photography in engraving on wood' in *Common-place: The Interactive Journal of Early American Life*, http://www.common-place.org/vol-07/no-03/rice/ [12 May 2008].

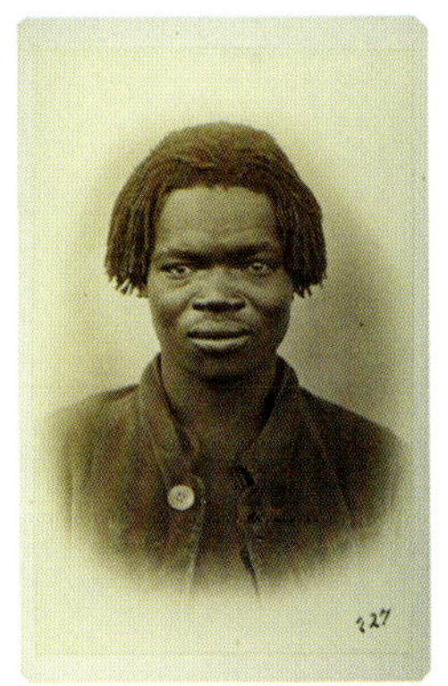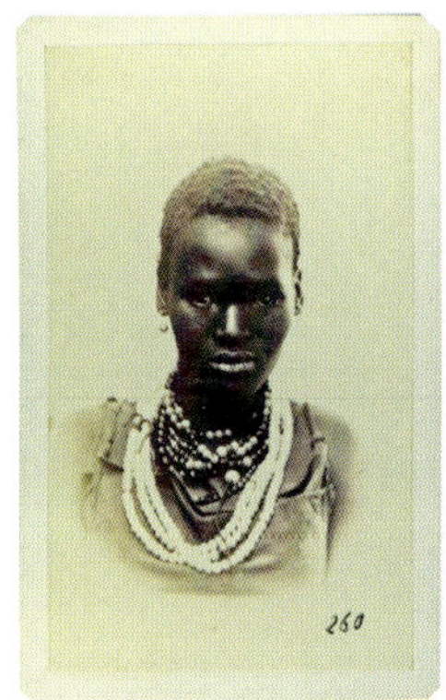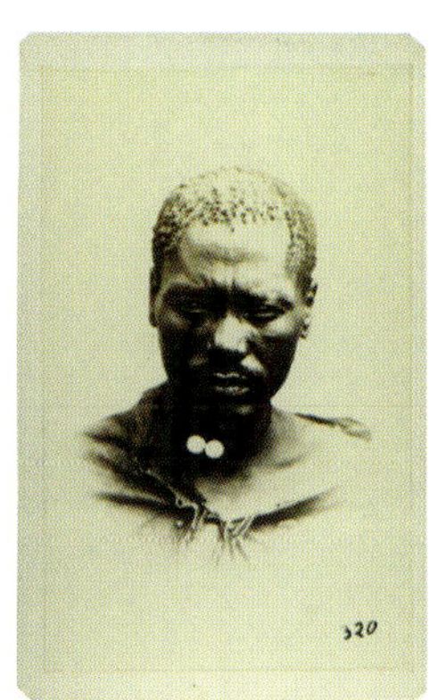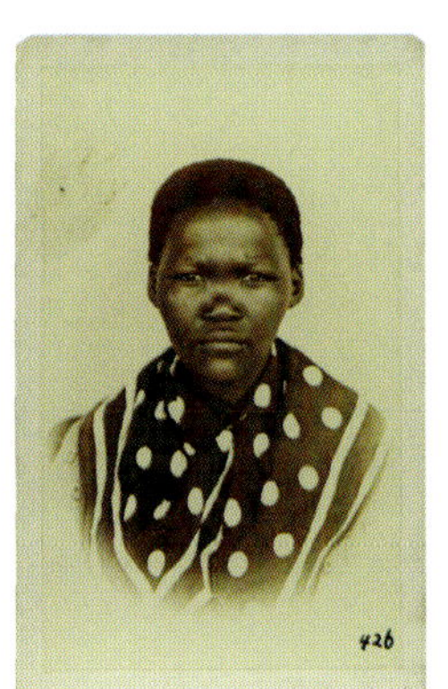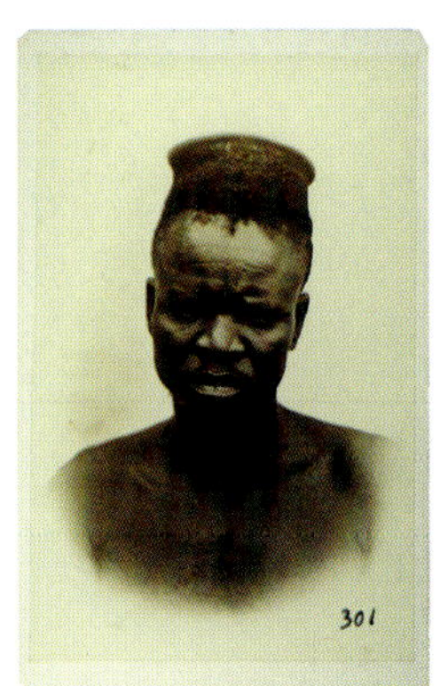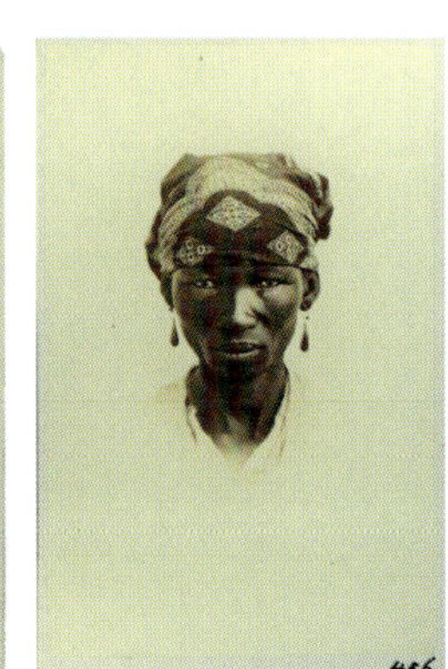

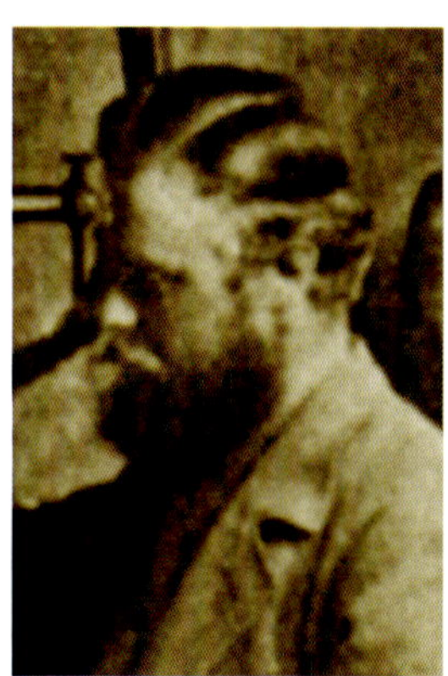

Part Two

Michael Godby
Andrew Bank
Andreas Broeckmann
Annette Lewerentz
Michael Hagner
Lize van Robbroeck

The art history of an anthropological image: Gustav Fritsch's 'Collection of photographic native portraits', 1863–1866

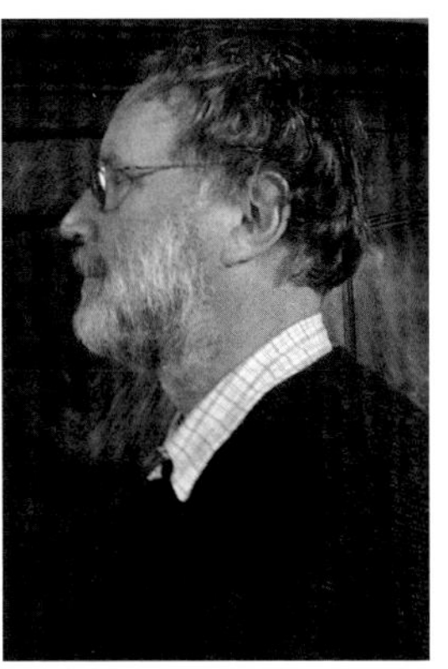

Michael Godby

In *Drei Jahre in Süd-Afrika* (1868), Gustav Fritsch describes his expedition through southern Africa between 1863 and 1866.[1] Fritsch was 25 years old when he left for the Cape and had recently completed his studies in the natural sciences and medicine at the universities of Berlin, Breslau and Heidelberg.[2] He travelled from Berlin to Plymouth via Paris and London, in both of which cities he studied material that he considered important for his journey before embarking on the *Saxon* on 6 August. Arriving in Table Bay on 8 September in the middle of a south-easter, he was confronted by a variety of racial types working in the harbour that he felt would keep any comparative anatomist occupied for a long time. On the very first page of his memoir, Fritsch defined the principal purpose of his journey as 'Anthropological studies, whereby I wished to form opinions based on my own observations of the nature of the natives, enabling me to advance my own views among those of various conflicting authors.'

Fritsch's visit to the Cape, therefore, was situated within the European debate on the relationship between the several racial types that had been observed in southern Africa, notably what were then called Kaffirs, Hottentots and Bushmen.[3] And he soon did advance his own views on this subject in the major scientific product of his visit, *Die Eingeborenen Süd-Afrika's ethnographisch und anatomisch beschreiben* (1872).[4] At the time of Fritsch's visit, the Cape presented the enigma of manifestly different peoples living in the same geographical area, with the tantalising suggestion that they embodied distinct stages in evolutionary history. In the wake of Darwin's *On the Origin of Species* (1859), the Cape seemed to offer European scientists a unique laboratory for research through evolution to the very origins of humankind. In Fritsch's time the scientific methods devised to prise open these secrets were linguistics, which was the specialisation of Dr Wilhelm Bleek, who was then Librarian at the Cape, and Fritsch's field of comparative anatomy. Fritsch in fact got to

know Bleek at some stage during his studies – they were, of course, both Germans working in the same area – but their methodological differences, and profound differences of understanding, seem to have prevented a friendly relationship.[5]

Fritsch was obviously committed to the European scientific method, not only in the emerging field of physical anthropology but also in zoology and botany, which feature throughout *Drei Jahre*. Fritsch's chief methods for 'anthropological studies' in his expedition were, on the one hand, to take measurements whenever he could of what were then considered key features of human anatomy and, on the other, to 'compile a collection of photographic native portraits'.[6] His remarks on early photographic encounters demonstrate his general approach to the project. Before leaving Cape Town, he went with friends to Robben Island where, amongst other things, he photographed Maqoma and other Xhosa chiefs who were imprisoned on the island.[7] As we shall see, his account of Maqoma reveals strong racial prejudice, and he complained sarcastically that Maqoma's reluctance to keep still meant that 'some of the pictures, therefore, still left much to be desired'. Tellingly, however, he concluded this story with the remark that 'at least they showed up the facial structure well enough for scientific use'. It is an extraordinary fact that neither the photograph itself nor its reproduction as a wood engraving in *Drei Jahre*[8] from this encounter reveals either the overt prejudice of the operator or the scientific application that he had in mind (Fig. 249). In this chapter I want to explore the extraordinary contradiction of Fritsch's images which, while patently the product of a superior, racist attitude, nonetheless seem to offer a genuinely humanist view of their subjects. The original photographs are reproduced elsewhere in this volume. Because the technology of the time prevented Fritsch from reproducing the photographs themselves in either of his publications, I have chosen to work in this chapter with the wood engravings he

Michael Godby is Professor of History of Art at the University of Cape Town. He has lectured and published on a wide range of topics, including Early Renaissance Italian art, eighteenth-century English art, especially the work of William Hogarth, nineteenth-century South African art, contemporary South African art, and the history of photography in South Africa. He has also curated a number of exhibitions, most recently 'Is There Still Life? Continuity and Change in South African Still Life Painting' at the Iziko Museums, Cape Town.

authorised for the text volumes of *Drei Jahre* and *Die Eingeborenen* and the copper etchings of the *Eingeborenen Atlas*.

A further early example of Fritsch's understanding of his photographic subjects as little more than scientific specimens is apparent in his discussion of people he came across in Swellendam, soon after leaving the Cape. 'The mixed race of this locality mainly shows the Hottentot type in greater or lesser clarity, with protruding cheekbones, sharply pointed chin, flattened nose and pale, yellow-brownish complexion. However, the difficulty of distinguishing the pure race from the half-caste deterred me from taking photographs of them, perhaps unjustly, as better specimens of this stock are difficult to locate.'[9] Not surprisingly, this attitude is accompanied by plentiful evidence of Fritsch's sense of innate superiority over everything he encountered in South Africa. He complained about the state of commerce in the Cape, and the high prices; he was derisory about the condition of the South African Museum collection, and the excuses of E.L. Layard, its curator; and he was scathing in his comments on the indigenous people. His account of his meeting with Maqoma and other prisoners on Robben Island, for example, is typically sarcastic: 'In return for some tobacco and 1 shilling per head, they readily allowed themselves to grant me their worthy presence for a while.'[10] Nor was he more sympathetic to the Boers, who were then widely understood in colonial circles to represent a degenerate breed of Europeans: 'The mental horizon of these good people is extraordinarily confined; even if much is exaggerated that is reported about them, what is sufficiently vouched for is quite enough to pass an unfavourable verdict on their intellectual abilities.'[11] And, doubtless also drawing on clichés of conventional wisdom, Fritsch lamented the lack of industriousness at the Cape in general and amongst coloured people in particular who, he said, 'find it more comfortable to lie on the ground and let themselves be warmed by the sun rather than work'.[12] After attending service at

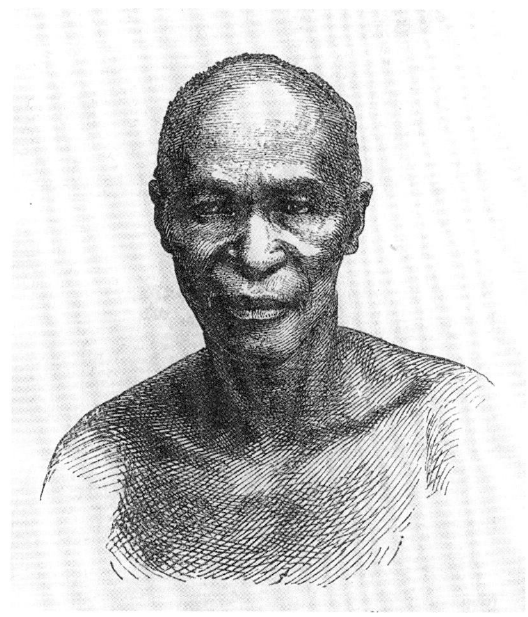

▲ *Fig. 249* 'Macomo, Chief of the Gaika'. (*Drei Jahre*, Fig. 5)

the coloured church in Worcester, Fritsch concluded: 'This race will probably always remain subordinated inasmuch as it subordinates itself and does not know any aspiration to rise in the world, which is so acutely stamped into the European stock.'[13]

The extraordinary thing about these comments is that they claim to be the result of first-hand observation when in fact they are demonstrably the product of a thoroughgoing racial prejudice. Amongst his references in *Die Eingeborenen*,[14] Fritsch lists no less than 35 published accounts of travel in southern African in which all these negative opinions, and more, were circulated. Like his scientific project itself, Fritsch doubtless brought these prejudices with him, only to find ready confirmation for them *in situ*.

It is relevant to this essay to explain the apparent contradiction between the thoroughgoing racism of these attitudes and the beauty of Fritsch's images, both originals and reproductions, that he also brought the very conventions of representing South African peoples and their landscape with him from Europe. Fritsch himself gives a very clear indication of his own understanding of appropriate subject matter for his camera, and appropriate methods of representing that subject matter, in the story of his attempt to take photographs on Table Mountain.[15] At the outset one might note a certain Romantic ambition in this enterprise on the part of a photographer whose project was actually to 'compile a collection of photographic native portraits', but the outcome of the expedition is even more revealing. In ascending the mountain, Fritsch had noted the beauty of the view through the Platteklip valley and determined to record it on his way down. When he returned, however, he found women washing clothes in the river, which, for him, spoilt the scene and threatened to rob him of his picture: in the event, he did photograph this view and had his engravers remove the offending washerwomen.[16] Obviously some visual artists at this time, both painters and photographers, would have delighted in the genre possibilities of this scene, but Fritsch seems to have been set on a sublime view of the landscape, which the presence of mundane working people would obviously destroy. On another occasion on Platteklip, however, Fritsch had found precipices and vertiginous rockfaces that clearly did fit with his idea of what mountain landscape should look like. He described the scene in *Drei Jahre*[17] and composed a photograph of the view that would similarly communicate the immensity and terror of the sublime (Fig. 250).[18] For Fritsch, as for Thomas Baines at the Victoria Falls at much this same time, the idea of the sublime derived ultimately from the theories of Edmund Burke.[19] But for the German scientist climbing Table Mountain – or, subsequently, encountering such scenes as the Umgeni Falls in Natal[20] – the visual image of the sublime would very obviously derive from artists such as Caspar David Friedrich.

Friedrich's project had been to overwhelm his viewer with the sense of the grandeur of Nature, in scenes of mountains, forests and

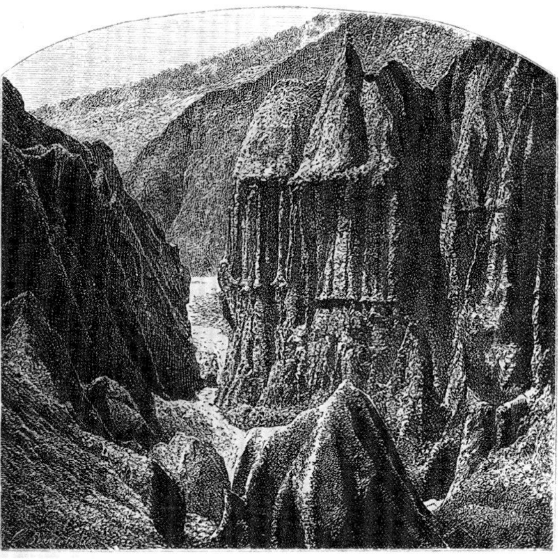

▲ *Fig. 250* 'Ravine on Table Mountain'. (*Drei Jahre*, Fig. 1)

▼ *Fig. 251* 'Ferns on the Banks of the Wit-Els River'. (*Drei Jahre*, Fig. 11)

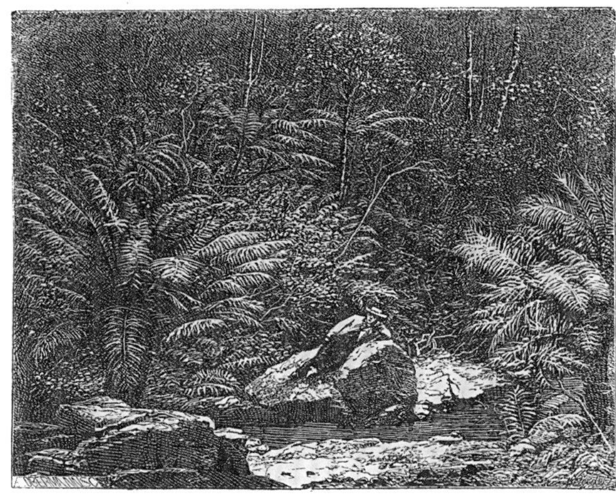

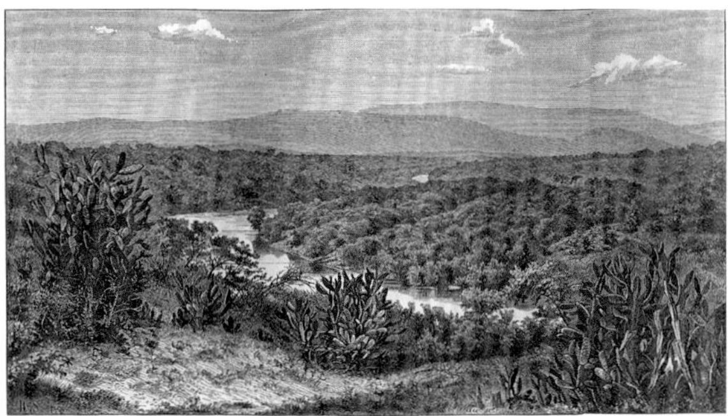

▲ *Fig. 252 'View of the Great Fish River'. (Drei Jahre, Fig. 14)*

▼ Fig. *253* 'Francolins, Guinea Fowl and Other Birds'. (*Drei Jahre,* Fig. 57)

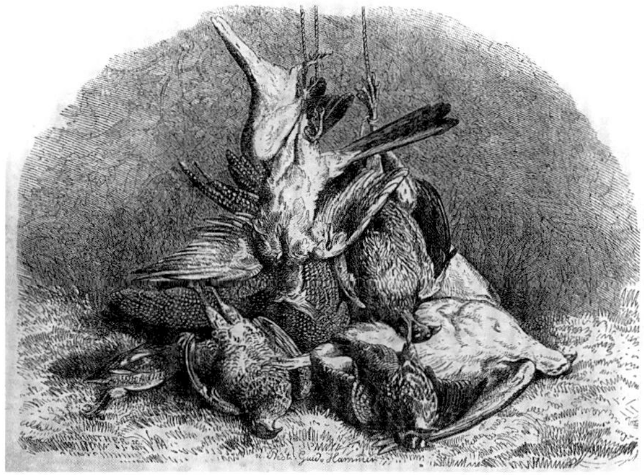

▼ Fig. 254 'After Thomas Baines, "Fingo Village near Fort Beaufort"'. (*Die Eingeborenen,* Fig. 21)

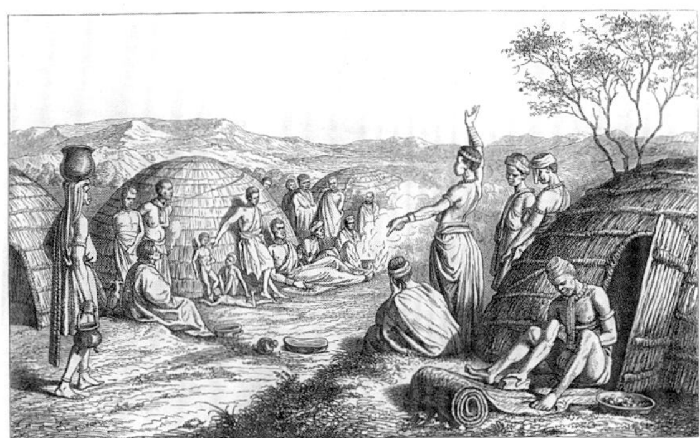

sea-shores. Like other Romantic artists, such as Goethe and Schubert, Friedrich would regularly use the device of the traveller to suggest the effects of Nature on a man of true feeling. Fritsch's ascent of Table Mountain was obviously undertaken in this spirit and, in fact, much of his journey through Africa can be understood as an extension to this continent of the trope of the sensitive traveller immersing himself in Nature: as Cornwallis Harris put it in his *Portraits of the Game and Wild Animals of Southern Africa* (1840), 'to wander through … scenes never before paced by civilized foot, is in itself [so] truly spirit-stirring and romantic'.[21] Fritsch clearly sought out typically Romantic scenery such as cliff-faces,[22] lighthouses on desolate promontories,[23] waterfalls[24] and forests, even designating the Knysna and Natal forests 'Urwald'[25] to evoke their primeval character. And, in the manner of Friedrich, he would occasionally position a traveller apparently absorbing the scene. In fact, Fritsch's only reference to such figures was to 'give a sense of dimensional proportions' to the scene,[26] but he cannot have been unaware of their poetic function also: the figure employed to indicate the huge size of the 'Ferns on the Banks of the Wit-Els River' (Fig. 251)[27] is arranged in the pose of Tischbein's celebrated portrait of *Goethe in the Campagna*, which long remained an icon of the poet immersing himself in Nature. To some extent, Fritsch's approach to the indigenous peoples of South Africa shared the same search for primitive beauty and unspoiled Nature. Thus his dismay at the appearance of the washer-women in Platteklip Gorge was not just because they were people, but because their occupation and clothing would have indicated to Fritsch their degeneracy from some pristine original: when he came across a Bushman dwelling in a cliff-face in Griqualand,[28] Fritsch's description seems to suggest that the wildness of the site was entirely appropriate for the savagery of its inhabitants.

Obviously the sublime was just one of the frames through which Fritsch both experienced and represented his African adventure. Like Thomas Baines and other artist-travellers of his time, Fritsch also drew upon the model of Claude Lorrain, particularly for the representation of extensive views. This model, which Fritsch, like Baines, might have derived directly but, more likely, indirectly from Claude's innumerable imitators, pervaded both verbal and visual descriptions. Thus Fritsch described the scene on the Berea: 'a splendid vista opened up on the other side to the Umgeni below, flowing gently through a charming valley on its course to the sea close by. On both banks of the river extensive sugar-cane plantations stretched forth, the mills rising between the light-green fields where numerous workers were busy cutting the cane and taking it to the mills for processing. The slopes next to the house were covered with coffee plantations, which were a mass of white star-like petals, and also with banana and orange groves.'[29]

And scenes such as 'The Great Fish River' (Fig. 252)[30] and 'The Groote Rivier'[31] are clearly constructed in the familiar repoussoir method to show the river in serpentine movement stretching towards the distant horizon: significantly, James Chapman composed a very similar view in his photograph of the Botletle River during his expedition through South West Africa a year or so before.[32] By Fritsch's time, evidently, Claude's method had become the standard formula for representing extensive views and was exported, along with the conventions of the sublime, to Africa and other exotic sites, to help make sense of unfamiliar landscape and incorporate it into the European knowledge system.

The point that Fritsch (like other travelling artists) represented his South African experience through the mediation of European artistic conventions is made most clearly, perhaps, through the extraordinary sequence in *Drei Jahre* of compositions of dead birds and animals. Fritsch was an enthusiastic hunter and he studiously labelled all the creatures he shot with their taxonomic classification. When he came to represent them in photographs which were to be used in wood-block engravings in his travelogue, however, he dropped the scientific mode and visualised them in the somewhat morbid terms of European Still Life with Game paintings. Thus his 'Duiker and Birds',[33] 'Striped Mongoose, Spring Hare and Other Animals',[34] and 'Francolins, Guinea Fowl and Other Birds' (Fig. 253),[35] amongst others, are presented in the manifestly contrived and bizarre arrangement of pictorial compositions of Desportes, Landseer and other painters of dead animals.

As for the representation of indigenous people in portrait photographs, at first glance there would seem to be no pictorial precedent or, indeed, any need for one: it should have been obvious to position the subject in front of the camera and just shoot. Painters, of course, would bring a whole vocabulary of visual conventions to bear on their African subjects and so create images that would resonate with their European spectators: the obvious example is the image of the Noble Savage that would refer to various works of antique sculpture. In *Die Eingeborenen* Fritsch occasionally drew upon the work of painters to illustrate his text and, in reproducing an engraving after Thomas Baines's lithograph *Fingo Village, Fort Beaufort* (1848) (Fig. 254), he imported the manifestly classical image of Baines's chief figure (notwithstanding that his engraving after another Baines lithograph, *Kafirs Having Made Their Fortune Leaving the Colony*, shows the opposite, degraded view of the African subject). In fact Fritsch himself, in certain descriptions of African people, clearly invokes the idea of classical sculpture, for example when he compares the Xhosa style of wearing a blanket with a Roman toga;[36] and his appreciation, albeit often begrudging (as is indicated in his use of the double negative), of the beauty of some Xhosa people seems to be couched in classical terms: thus some men are described as 'not lacking in a certain natural grandeur'; and Fritsch commended Sazini, the councillor to Chief Anta, as a 'beautiful example of a well-formed Kaffir', noting that the 'facial contours are even, certainly not ignoble, the hands are small, the fingers slender and pointed, of a real aristocratic character'.[37] Significantly Fritsch,

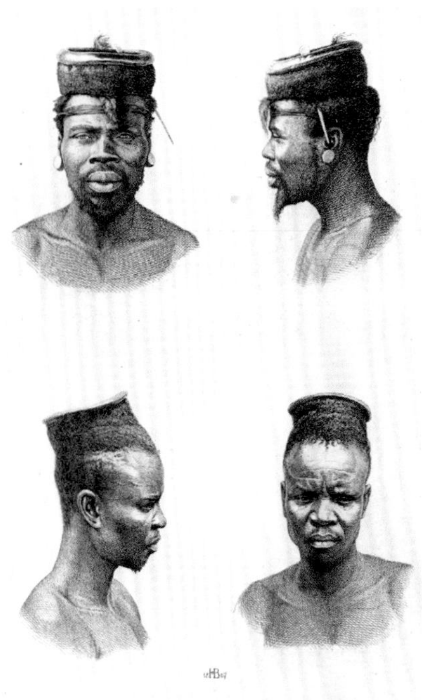

Fig. 255 ▶

'Ama zulu'. (*Atlas*, Plate I)

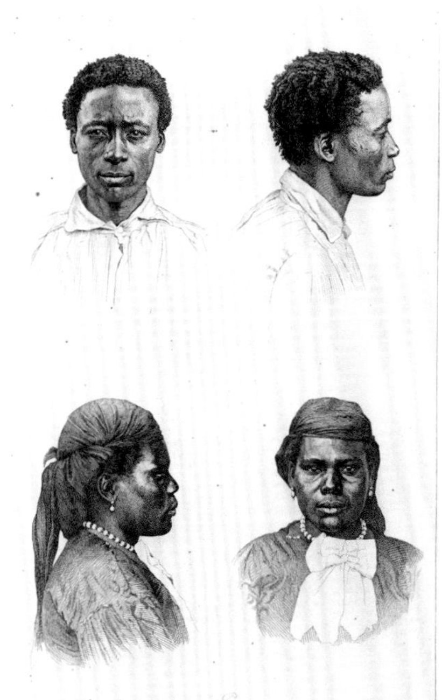

Fig. 256 ▶

'Ba suto, Ama fengu (Fingoe)'. (*Atlas*, Plate XII)

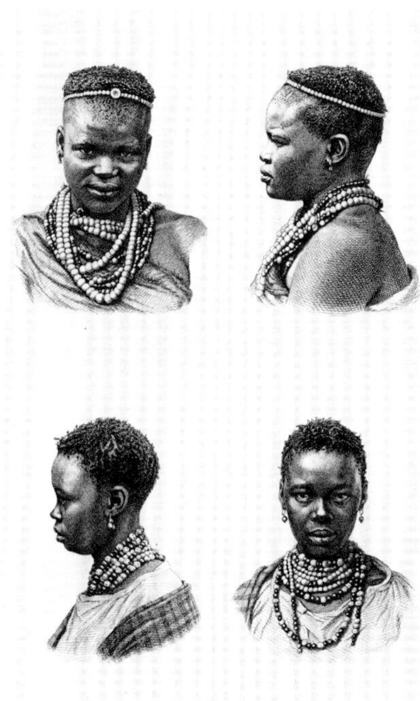

◀ *Fig. 257*

'Ba kuena, Ba rolong'. (*Atlas*, Plate XX)

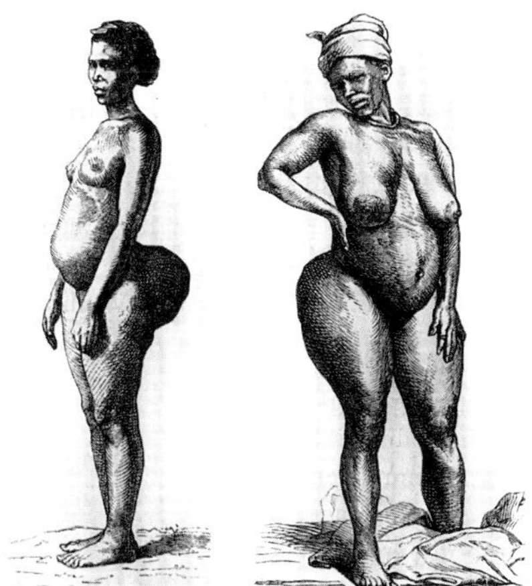

◀ *Fig. 258*

'Hottentot Women'. (*Die Eingeborenen*, Figs. 54–55)

like Barrow and other colonial travellers before him,[38] claimed that nobility in deportment, at least, resulted from 'freedom and lack of restriction in lifestyle' by which he contrasted the elegant Bakalahari with their enslaved cousins, the Makalahari.[39]

But while Fritsch could indulge in creating word pictures of his subjects in these terms, his reason for bringing a camera to South Africa to further his 'anthropological studies'[40] in the first place was, as he said, to 'compile a collection of photographic native portraits'.[41] For this project Fritsch decided to take full-face and profile views of his subjects whose regularity he could ensure by having the sitter positioned at a fixed distance from the camera (Figs. 255, 256 and 257). As Andrew Bank has indicated, Allan Sekula distinguishes this type of 'repressive' portrait photography, which was developed for anthropological and police work around this time, from what he terms the 'honorific' method of conventional, commissioned portraiture.[42] But, in his attempt to explain the contradiction between the apparent beauty of the original photographs and their subsequent use as scientific evidence, Bank proposes that Fritsch conceived his portrait subjects in the field in the individualistic, honorific tradition of portraiture, but shifted them when they were published in *Die Eingeborenen* towards the institutional, repressive style of representation. Bank relates this transformation from a supposed ethnographic-cultural treatment in the field to an understanding of the subject in the cold terms of physical anthropology, to Fritsch's ambition on his return to Berlin to succeed in the prevailing conditions of German anthropology.

In fact, notwithstanding the occasional rhetorical image of noble African types, both *Drei Jahre* and *Die Eingeborenen* leave absolutely no doubt that Fritsch was committed to the project of physical anthropology from the beginning of his visit. His account of his meeting with Maqoma, who was the first African subject to sit for him, is unambiguous in this regard. And only this interest can explain both his preparedness to undress certain of his photographic subjects[43] who were reproduced in *Die Eingeborenen* (Fig. 258); and his macabre hunt for human remains, on the site of recent massacres and in graves (Fig. 259).[44] *Die Eingeborenen* has many plates comparing sets of crania, on the one hand, and pelvic structures, on the other, many of which were obviously collected in the field (Fig. 260). Moreover, Fritsch obviously subjected many of his subjects, including all that appear in the *Atlas*, to the invasive process of taking detailed measurements of their anatomy. In this connection, his apparent predilection for elderly Bushman and Hottentot subjects[45] may be explained by the obvious fact that these subjects offer relatively good views of cranial and other bone structure. From the beginning, therefore, Fritsch's project most definitely involved the exercise of power over the bodies of his indigenous subjects, which he clearly felt his innate superiority as a European gave him the right to perform.

And yet, the photographs that Fritsch made under these patently 'repressive' conditions are extraordinarily beautiful images, and this anomaly demands explanation. Obviously, part of the answer lies in their superb technique, both photographic prints and wood engravings and copper etchings, which Keith Dietrich sets out elsewhere in this volume.[46] As far as Fritsch himself is concerned, he was clearly a meticulous personality: he claimed to have calculated the number of revolutions of the propeller of his ship the *Saxon* on his journey between Plymouth and Table Bay: 2,720,000![47] And he was certainly both careful with his materials and knowledgeable enough in chemistry to experiment with the photographic process.[48] But he also evidently had a very fine eye that he both brought to bear on the technical aspects of his own work and used in assembling his aesthetic vocabulary. As we have seen, Fritsch was clearly familiar with a range of pictorial conventions through which he made sense of his diverse experiences in South Africa. Although it may not be immediately obvious, it can be shown that he brought this educated eye even to his 'collection of photographic native portraits'.

Elizabeth Edwards dates the invention of the full-face and frontal views of photographic subjects, which was developed in ethnographic studies in Paris and St Petersburg, precisely to the decade in which Fritsch was working in southern Africa.[49] This would mean, surprising as it may seem, that although Fritsch undoubtedly knew of these ethnographic developments – he had stopped off in Paris on his way to Plymouth – he is unlikely to have seen any precise photographic precedent for his work. Within a very short time, needless to say, ethnographic and forensic demands had created an avalanche of 'repressive' portrait records in this style, which led, inevitably, to the most dehumanising images. In 1869, both Thomas Huxley and John Lamprey devised systems of photographing anthropological specimens precisely to introduce some kind of order into this mass of material.[50] Thus, for the moment, for this very short moment, Fritsch had absolutely no photographic model on which to base his images. But, if there was no precedent in photography for images that offered the human face as a subject for scrutiny, there was a long history of 'honorific' portraiture of this type. The pastel portraits of the mid-eighteenth-century French painters Jean-Baptiste Perroneau and Maurice Quentin de La Tour, and their followers, tended to shed the entire Baroque apparatus of the genre in order to concentrate on the most fleeting facial expressions. And, however scientific their intentions, travellers in Africa on either side of 1800 were constrained by this tradition to attribute some idea of animation to the faces of their ethnographic subjects. As we have seen, Fritsch listed no less than 35 travel accounts amongst his references in *Die Eingeborenen*. From Captain Gardiner, for example, whose *Journey to the Zoolu Country* (1836) provided the illustration of Dingane's capital for *Die Eingeborenen*,[51] Fritsch could have learned the use of full-face and profile

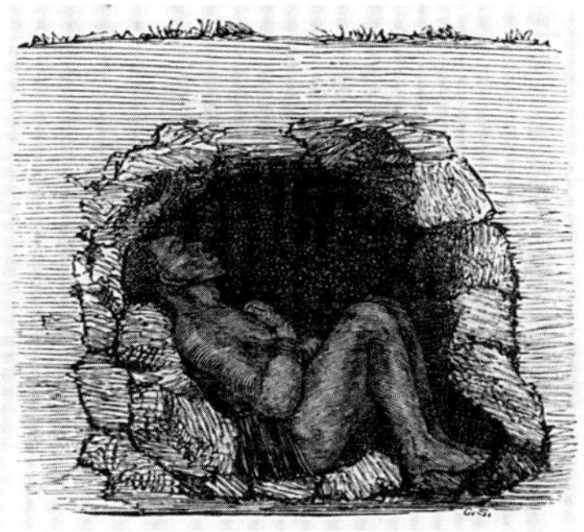

Fig. 259 ▶
'A Zulu Grave'. (*Drei Jahre*, Fig. 44).

▼ *Fig. 260* 'Crania'. (*Die Eingeborenen*, end plate 31)

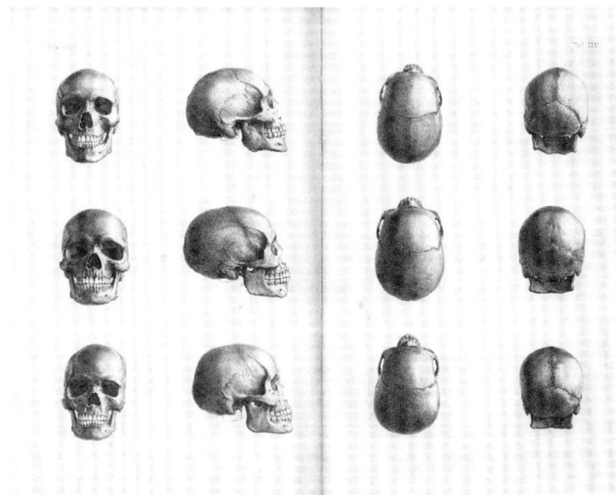

▼ *Fig. 261* 'Heads of Zoolu: Amahoash, Amaponda, Men and Women'. (Allen F. Gardiner, *Narrative of a Journey to the Zoolu Country*, 286)

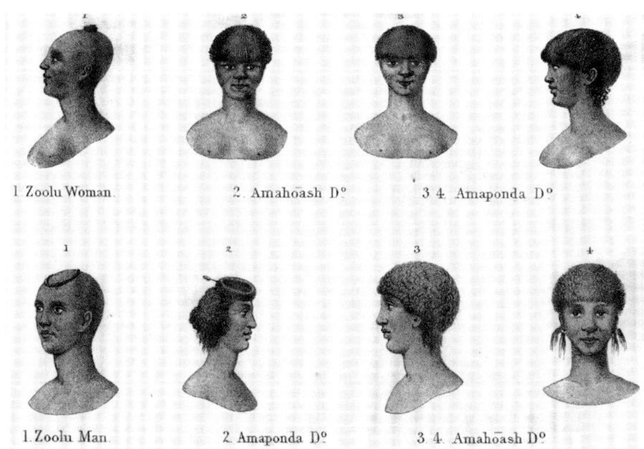

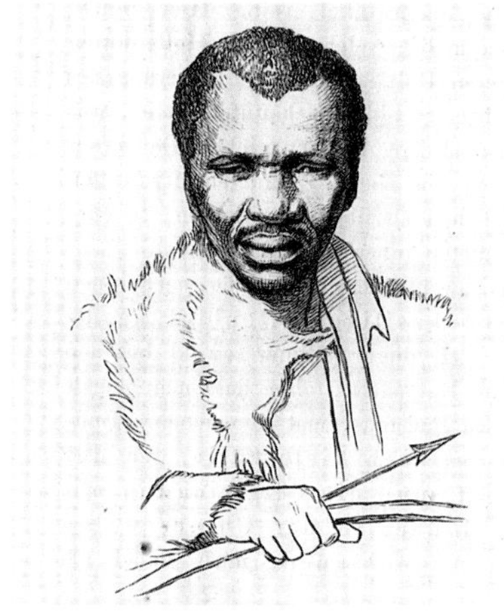

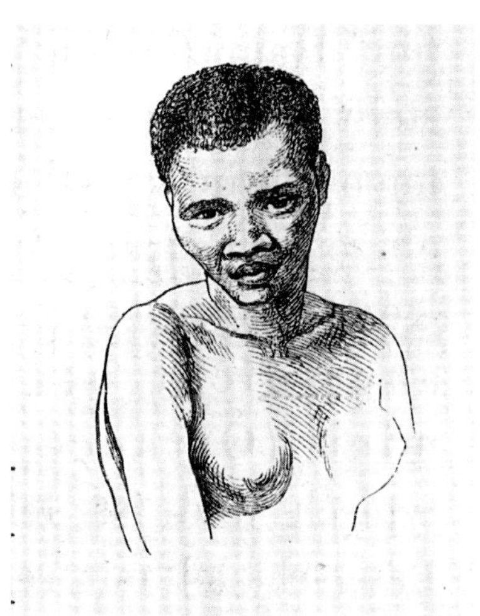

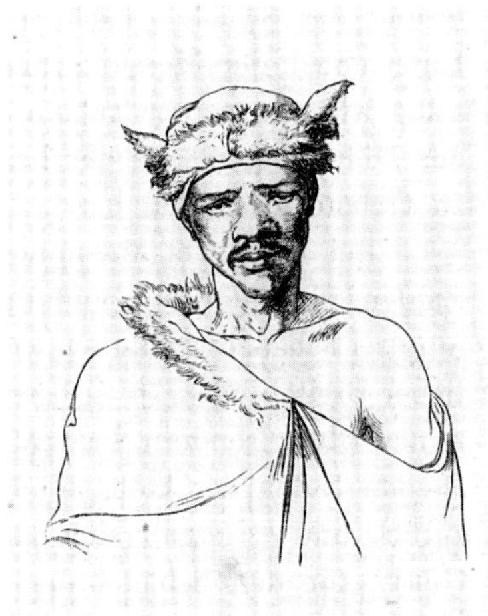

◀ *Fig.* 262

'Hottentots', after Samuel Daniell.
(*Die Eingeborenen*, Figs. 58–60)

views although, in Gardiner (Fig. 261), they are used with some charm simply to illustrate different types of hairstyle.[52] More significant for the retention of the 'honorific' quality of his portrait photographs is Fritsch's demonstrable dependence on the work of Samuel Daniell, who had clearly been inspired by the Enlightenment ideas of Nature and Liberty and who invariably communicated genuine respect for his indigenous subjects. In *Die Eingeborenen* (Fig. 262),[53] Fritsch actually reproduced three of Daniell's drawings of 'Hottentots' from *Sketches Representing the Native Tribes* (1820) and, although he might complain that it was anatomically inaccurate, he cannot have been insensitive to the true humanist qualities of Daniell's work.[54] There is, then, a very mixed collection of images of African people, both visual and verbal, in *Die Eingeborenen*, but for the formulation of the photographic portraits themselves, Daniell's example appears to have been influential. Technically, Daniell's images would seem to have suggested the consistent size of the portraits, the empty backgrounds, the acceptance of whatever dress the subject happened to be wearing and, most telling, the masking of the portrait into an oval format, which, in itself, serves to distinguish the 'honorific' from the 'repressive' style of portraiture. And, conceptually, Fritsch appears to have derived from Daniell a sense of real communication between artist and subject that suggested the fundamental notions of empathy and respect.

Travellers like Samuel Daniell and John Barrow at the turn of the nineteenth century distinguish themselves from others on Gustav Fritsch's list of references by their relatively straightforward view of their indigenous subjects: left to Nature, the peoples of South Africa presented a noble and dignified view of humankind. As 'civilisation' took hold over the following half-century, however, the image of indigenous people became more ambiguous mainly, but not exclusively, around the issues of subjection and acculturation. Thus writers like Cornwallis Harris, Thomas Baines and James Chapman, who all appear on Fritsch's list, composed both verbal and visual images of indigenous people that were, at one moment, heroic and romantic and, at the next, sarcastic and demeaning: and these contradictions are maintained through Baines's painted work, for example in the two lithographs that Fritsch used in *Die Eingeborenen*. In a work such as George French Angas's *Kafirs Illustrated* (1849), which is not actually on Fritsch's list, there is a complete contradiction between the demeaning image in the letter-press and the heroic language of the lithographs:[55] the point here is that the Romantic qualities of the Noble Savage in the African landscape would have been understood by its mid-century viewers to be self-evidently primitive, in its negative rather than positive sense. This, surely, is the condition in which Fritsch worked: on the one hand, he represented genre scenes of indigenous people in word or in image that veered between classicising beauty and degraded abjection; and, on the other hand, he made apparently

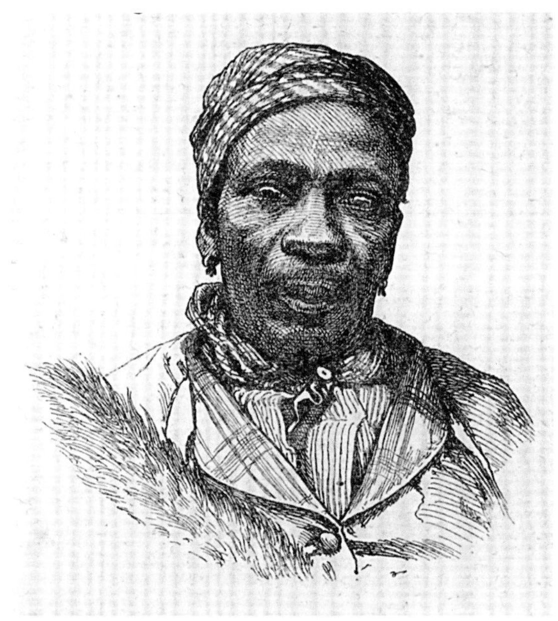

'Mosielele, Chief of the Bakatla'. (*Drei Jahre*, Fig. 62)

respectful full-face and profile portraits while simultaneously subjecting his sitters to the invasive system of measurements. Put another way, Fritsch's visual language for representing the indigenous South African subject, notably his many portrait studies, had not yet shaken off the conventions of past portrait traditions to communicate his scientific conviction that the several African races he encountered constituted distinctly inferior species.

There is perhaps one last reason why Fritsch's image of South African people retained so much of the honorific tradition of portraiture. Like many of the travel writers he cites in *Die Eingeborenen*, Fritsch regarded his expedition to Africa as an investment that he sought to recoup through writing books on his travels. Like his predecessors, Fritsch could look to offer a narrative of his adventures to the general public; or he could seek to promote his career by producing a work of science. In the event, of course, Fritsch did both – and he used similar portrait material for these very different publications. Thus the images he extracts from his 'collection of photographic native portraits' for *Drei Jahre* (Figs. 249 and 263) are put to a very different use from the anatomical purpose for which they were made – and as their kin appear in the *Atlas* of *Die Eingeborenen* (Figs. 255, 256 and 257). The profile views of Maqoma, Sandile and others are dispensed with; the measurements are not mentioned; and the image is presented in the honorific style of portraiture with some focus on the sitter's expression within an aesthetically masked format. Moreover, the portraits he chose for *Drei Jahre* were portraits of named individuals, not specimens or representative types. In fact, it was important for Fritsch's purpose in his travelogue that the portraits he illustrated should be of chiefs:

this status in his sitters would lend substance to his narrative and, even, some reflected glory for himself, which would obviously assist his sales. Given these demands for the portraits in *Drei Jahre*, it is hardly surprising that they retained some of the honorific quality of the original photographs. Having accepted this conventional sense of human dignity in the images of his travelogue, notwithstanding that, as in Angas, it is actively contradicted in much of the accompanying narrative, Fritsch had no option but to retain it in the *Atlas* of *Die Eingeborenen*, even though, tellingly, no portrait of a chief is included in this collection. In this later publication, which was aimed at an academic rather than commercial market, however, this humanistic quality is constantly negated not only by the grouping of the portraits for purposes of comparison, but also by their association with patently demeaning representations in the text and, in fact, by the nature of the entire scientific project that they illustrate.

ENDNOTES

1   Gustav Fritsch, *Drei Jahre in Süd-Afrika. Reiseskizzen nach Notizen des Tagebuchs zusammengestellt* (Breslau: Ferdinand Hirt, 1868). Three chapters of Fritsch's travelogue have been published in English as *A German Traveller in Natal: Three Chapters from Drei Jahre in Süd-Afrika*, translated by Gerlind Lyttle and introduced by Ian Hilton (Durban: Killie Campbell Africana Library, 1992). And a translation of the first fifty pages of *Drei Jahre* by Karlin Feurstein-Hartman is kept amongst the Van Riebeeck Society papers in the Cape Town campus of the National Library of South Africa. Translations from these sources have been cited in this text. Other translations have been made by myself with the assistance of

Nadja Daehnke.

2   For Fritsch's biography see Ian Hilton's 'Introduction' to *A German Travel-ler in Natal*, 9–15, and Andrew Bank, 'Anthropology and portrait pho-tography: Gustav Fritsch's *Natives of South Africa*, 1863–1872', *Kronos: A Journal of Cape History*, Special Issue: Visual History, 27 (November 2001), 43–76.

3   On this debate, see Saul Dubow, *A Commonwealth of Knowledge: Sci-ence, Sensibility and White South Africa* (Oxford: Oxford University Press, 2006); Andrew Bank, 'Evolution and racial theory: The hidden side of Wilhelm Bleek', *South African Historical Journal*, 43 (November 2000), 163–178; and G.W. Stocking, *Victorian Anthropology* (New York: The Free Press, 1987).

4   Gustav Fritsch, *Die Eingeborenen Süd-Afrika's ethnographisch und anato-misch beschreiben* (Breslau: Ferdinand Hirt, 1872).

5   Andrew Bank, *Bushmen in a Victorian World: The Remarkable Story of the Bleek-Lloyd Collection of Bushman Folklore* (Cape Town: Double Storey Books, 2006), 89, interprets Fritsch's inscription on a copy of *Drei Jahre*, which he is likely to have presented in Berlin in 1869, 'Dedicated by the Author to his Esteemed Friend, Dr Bleek', to suggest that 'relations between the two scholars were warm'. It is more likely that this was a conventional salutation, for Fritsch, in fact, made no reference to Bleek during the first of his three stays in Cape Town, even though he records that he twice visited Edgar Layard in the museum, which then shared the same premises as the library. Moreover, Bleek's recollection in his review of *Die Eingeborenen* in the *Cape Monthly Magazine*, 6 (March 1873), 173, of Fritsch regularly using the Grey Collection in the library, which must have been during his second or third visit to Cape Town and on which Fritsch made absolutely no comment, suggests a complete absence of contact between the two men. Fritsch referred just once to Bleek's work on South African languages in *Drei Jahre* (375), even though Bleek's magisterial *On the Origin of Language: Linguistics and Evolutionary Theory* had been published in German in 1867. Later, in 1872, however, Fritsch composed the entire fifth chapter of *Die Eingeborenen* on Bleek's *Comparative Grammar* (1862). But in his review of this book, while applauding the project, Bleek noted that he did not 'agree with him on every point', particularly Fritsch's reluctance to distinguish adequately between Hottentot and Bushman peoples.

6   Fritsch, *Drei Jahre*, 40.

7   Fritsch, *Drei Jahre*, 32–34.

8   Fritsch, *Drei Jahre*, Fig. 5.

9   Fritsch, *Drei Jahre*, 48–49.

10   Fritsch, *Drei Jahre*, 33.

11   Fritsch, *Drei Jahre*, 15.

12   Fritsch, *Drei Jahre*, 12.

13   Fritsch, *Drei Jahre*, 20.

14   Fritsch, *Die Eingeborenen*, 510–511.

15   Fritsch, *Drei Jahre*, 35–6.

16   Fritsch, *Drei Jahre*, Fig. 7.

17   Fritsch, *Drei Jahre*, 11.

18   Fritsch, *Drei Jahre*, Fig. 1.

19   Michael Godby, 'Thomas Baines on the Victoria Falls: A contest between science and art in the career of a British explorer in Africa' in Michael Stevenson (ed.), *Thomas Baines: An Artist in the Service of Science in South Africa* (London: Christie's, 1999), 30–39.

20   Fritsch, *Drei Jahre*, 195 and Fig. 38.

21   William Cornwallis Harris, *Portraits of the Game and Wild Animals of Southern Africa*, reprint (Alberton: Galago Publishing, 1986), 1.

22   Fritsch, *Drei Jahre*, Fig. 1.

23   Fritsch, *Drei Jahre*, Fig. 9.

24   Fritsch, *Drei Jahre*, Fig. 38.

25   Fritsch, *Drei Jahre*, Figs. 12 and 37.

26   Fritsch, *Drei Jahre*, 214.

27   Fritsch, *Drei Jahre*, Fig. 11.

28   Fritsch, *Drei Jahre*, Fig. 50.

29   Fritsch, *Drei Jahre*, 213.

30   Fritsch, *Drei Jahre*, Fig. 14.

31   Fritsch, *Drei Jahre*, Fig. 18.

32   Michael Godby, 'The interdependence of photography and painting on the South West Africa expedition of James Chapman and Thomas Baines, 1861–62', *Kronos: A Journal of Cape History*, Special Issue: Visual His-tory, 27 (November 2001), 30–42. Fritsch commended Chapman's work in *Die Eingeborenen* (1872), but since he does not mention him in *Drei Jahre*, it is not possible to say quite when he came across it. See also Bank, 'Anthropology and portrait photography', 47.

33   Fritsch, *Drei Jahre*, Fig. 23.

34   Fritsch, *Drei Jahre*, Fig. 26.

35   Fritsch, *Drei Jahre*, Fig. 57.

36   Fritsch, *Drei Jahre*, 70.

37   Fritsch, *Drei Jahre*, 95.

38   John Barrow, *An Account of Travels into the Interior of Southern Africa in the Years 1797 and 1798* (London: Cadell and Davies, 1801 and 1804); and Nigel Penn, 'Mapping the Cape: John Barrow and the First British Occupation of the Colony, 1795–1803', *Pretexts*, 4, 2 (1993).

39   Fritsch, *Drei Jahre*, 294–295.

40   Fritsch, *Drei Jahre*, 1.

41   Fritsch, *Drei Jahre*, 40.

42   Allan Sekula, 'The body and the archive' in Richard Bolton (ed.), *The Contest of Meaning: Critical Histories of Photography* (Cambridge, Mass.: Harvard University Press, 1989), 345; Bank, 'Anthropology and portrait photography', 44–45.

43   For example, Fritsch, *Die Eingeborenen*, 280–281.

44   Fritsch, *Die Eingeborenen*, Fig. 44.

45   For example, Fritsch, *Atlas*, Plate 27.

46   See also Bank, 'Anthropology and portrait photography'; and Annette Lewerentz, 'Der Mediziner Gustav Fritsch als Fotograf. Dokumentation seiner anthropologisch-ethnografischen Untersuchungen in Fotografien der Berliner Gesellschaft für Anthropologie, Ethnologie und Urgeschich-te', *Baessler-Archiv*, New Series, 48 (2000), 271–306: I am grateful to Andrew Bank for this reference. And Tanja Hemme, *Streifzüge durch eine fremde Welt*, Missions-geschichtliches Archiv 7 (Stuttgart: Franz Steiner, 2000), 103–118: I am grateful to Günther Packendorf for this reference.

47   Fritsch, *Drei Jahre*, 2.

48   Fritsch, *Drei Jahre*, 31.

49   Elizabeth Edwards, 'Photographic types', *Visual Anthropology*, 3, 2–3 (1990), 243, in Bank, 'Anthropology and portrait photography'.

50   Edwards, 'Photographic types'; Michael Godby, 'Images of //Kabbo' in Pippa Skotnes (ed.), *Miscast: Negotiating the Presence of the Bushmen* (Cape Town: University of Cape Town Press, 1996), 115–127.

51   Fritsch, Die Eingeborenen, Fig. 27.

52   Allen F. Gardiner, *Narrative of a Journey to the Zoolu Country in South Africa* (London: William Crofts, 1836), 286: 'Heads of Zoolu: Amahoash. Amaponda, Men and Women': I am grateful to Sandra Klopper for draw-ing my attention to this image.

53   Fritsch, *Die Eingeborenen*, 290–1 and Figs. 58–60.

54   *Sketches Representing the Native Tribes, Animals and Scenery of South-ern Africa, from Drawings Made by the Late Mr Samuel Daniell, Engraved by William Daniell* (London: William Daniell and William Wood, 1820). Bank, 'Anthropology and portrait photography', 55, notes Fritsch's disap-proval of Daniell's inaccuracies.

55   George French Angas, *The Kafirs Illustrated in a Series of Drawings Taken among the AmaZulu, AmaPonda, and AmaKosa Tribes, etc.* (London: Hogarth, 1849). For the contradiction in Angas's work, see Sandra Klop-per, 'George French Angas's (re)presentation of the Zulu in *The Kafirs Illustrated*', *South African Journal of Cultural and Art History*, 3,1 (1989), 63–73.

From the 'honorific' to the 'repressive': Gustav Fritsch's portraits of 'The natives of South Africa', 1863–1872

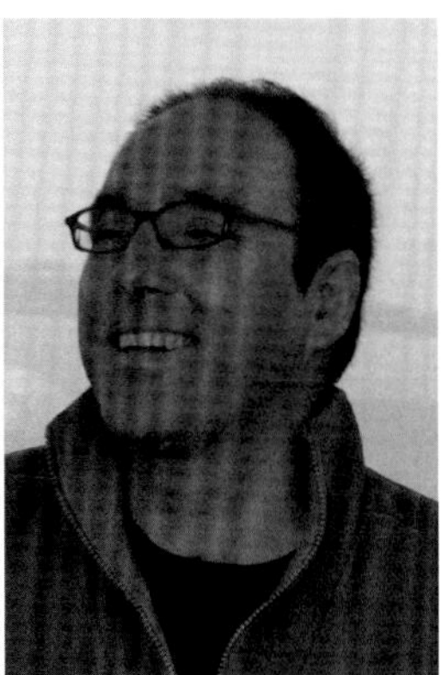

Andrew Bank

In a seminal article published in the 1980s, the visual theorist Allan Sekula wrote of an emerging tension in portrait photography during the mid- to late nineteenth century: a tension between what he described as the 'honorific' and 'repressive' functions of portraiture. 'We are confronting, then, a double system of representation capable of functioning both honorifically and repressively … On the one hand, the photographic portrait extends, accelerates, popularises, and … provid[es] for the ceremonial presentation of the bourgeois self … At the same time photographic portraiture began to perform a role no painted portrait could have performed in the same thorough and rigorous fashion. This role derived, not from any honorific portrait tradition, but from the imperatives of medical and anatomical illustration. Thus photography came to establish and delimit the terrain of the other, to define both the generalised look – the typology and the contingent instance of deviance and social pathology.'[1]

In this essay[2] I apply Sekula's notion of a tension between 'honorific' and 'repressive' uses of portrait photography to a particular case study: that of the portrait photographs of 'the natives of South Africa' (*Die Eingeborenen Süd-Afrika's*) taken by the medically trained German traveller and anthropologist, Gustav Theodor Fritsch, in southern African between 1863 and 1865. I argue that when Fritsch was in 'the field' (to adopt the terminology of a later era), he conceived of his portraiture primarily within the honorific tradition. This is evident from the way in which he selected his portrait subjects (from African chiefs, their wives and councillors to well-dressed mission converts) and the typically aestheticised and culturally oriented way in which he chose to portray them. The most appropriate framework within which to locate these 'honorific' portraits is the travel narrative that Fritsch published for a German readership in 1868, just two years after his return home. This narrative was based on notes recorded on site in his journal, as the title of his book makes explicit: *Drei Jahre in Süd-Afrika: Reiseskizzen nach Notizen des Tagesbuchs zusammengestellt* (Three Years in South Africa: Travel Sketches Compiled from Notes in a Journal).[3]

When a selection of these portrait photographs were re-presented in a technically modified form just four years later, in his first major anthropological study, *Die Eingeborenen Süd-Afrika's ethnographisch und anatomisch beschreiben* (The Natives of South Africa Ethnographically and Anatomically Described), they performed a very different function. Here the emphasis now shifted emphatically towards Sekula's 'repressive' pole of portrait photography. The focus of the selection of portraits that featured in the separate *Atlas*, as a kind of illustrative appendix to the major body of his weighty volume, was firmly on the physical configuration of different 'racial types' rather than on the cultural diversity of the indigenous peoples of southern Africa. By 1872 the emphasis was on using photography to 'delimit the terrain of the other', to create a 'typology' – in this case, one of racial rather than criminal types. Here again my evidence is drawn from a combination of a close visual reading of the portraits themselves, as they appear in hierarchically arranged form in his *Atlas* running from the 'A-bantu' down to the 'Bushmen', as well as the framing text with which they are most closely associated – in this case, *Die Eingeborenen*.

Given the absence of an archive of private papers, the precise reasons for this marked shift in emphasis in Fritsch's use of his portrait photographs can only be a matter of conjecture. My own interpretation is that the change can be attributed primarily to his integration within a newly institutionalised German anthropological community, in which physical anthropology was particularly dominant, and to his desire to establish his intellectual credentials within this new disciplinary space. I am also inclined to attribute some weight to his active military involvement in the intervening years, as a soldier rising through the ranks during the Austro-Prussian and Franco-Prussian wars. There are

Andrew Bank studied at the universities of Cape Town and Cambridge. He is now an Associate Professor of History at the University of the Western Cape and editor-in-chief of the journal *Kronos: Southern African Histories*. He is currently working on a history of women anthropologists in southern Africa.

hints in his later study which suggest that his intense military experience contributed to a heightened sense of racial 'othering'.

The 'honorific' portraits: southern Africa, 1863–1865

Fritsch indicated right at the outset of his expedition that his aims were 'ethnographic' or 'anthropological', terms that he used loosely and almost interchangeably in his 1868 travel narrative. He saw the creation of a 'picture gallery' of 'natives' as his most important objective. During his two expeditions through southern Africa, stretching across a period of three years, he photographed some 130 individuals, both in front and side profile form.[4]

The most striking feature of Fritsch's portrait photographs is undoubtedly their enormous diversity. The most prominent category of subjects to sit before Fritsch's lens was African chiefs and their associates. Fritsch's attempts to capture nobility on camera began not long after his arrival in Cape Town, when in the first week of November 1863 he embarked on an expedition to Robben Island, armed with his 'photographic equipment'. His travelogue suggests that there was, initially, a marked degree of ambiguity in his attitudes towards African leaders and, in particular, the exiled Xhosa chiefs whom the British kept imprisoned on the Island for their role in the Xhosa Cattle-Killing of 1856–1857. Fritsch stayed overnight and photographed Maqoma, Xhoxho, Siyolo, Stokwe and Dilima the following day (see Figs. 2–11), with an offering of 'a little tobacco and 1 shilling per head' by way of inducement.[5] His portraits of these Xhosa chiefs are probably his best known images. His photograph of Maqoma appears on the front cover and in the text of a recent edited volume on the history of Robben Island.[6] His side-profile view of Stokwe is reproduced in the body of the book. This was presumably one of the photographs he had in mind when he reflected on the difficulties in inducing his subjects

to sit still and that 'some of the pictures therefore left somewhat to be desired'.[7]

Fritsch's interest in photographing Xhosa chiefs was again evident in his tour of the eastern districts of the Cape Colony in January 1864. Here he photographed both Xhosa chiefs and their senior councillors: Sandile and Somi in Stutterheim (Figs. 17–20), and then Anta and Sazini in Windvogelberg (modern Cathcart) (Figs. 30–33). Fritsch's front-profile view of Sazini was reproduced in three-quarter-page format in Karel Schoeman's *The Face of the Country: A South African Family Album, 1860–1910* (1996). As Schoeman suggests, it is 'one of the finest of the Fritsch photographs … It is typical of this sequence of portraits in concentrating on the face of the sitter, only a minimum of distinguishing clothing or ornaments being shown or indicated, in this case a blanket draped over one shoulder, a necklace and a single eardrop'.[8]

On his journey through Bechuanaland in the latter part of 1865, Fritsch again focused his photographic efforts on African chiefs and their associates. At almost every site where he spent time, he photographed the Tswana chiefs and their families: Gaseitsiwe and 'his favourite wife' Motuane at Kanye, Mosielele at Moshupa, Sechele and his son Sibele at Ntsweng, and Khama, son of the chief of the Ngwato, at Shoshong (see Figs. 164–167, 175–176, 179–182, 197–198). In his travel narrative (and therefore one might assume in the travel notes recorded on site), Fritsch had much more to say about this new cast of chiefly characters than he had said about the Xhosa chiefs on Robben Island. Arguably this was not merely the result of differences in the degree of his interest in Tswana and Xhosa cultures, but evidence of how his three years of travel through southern Africa had produced a more complex and curious picture of African cultures. The sense one gets from reading the narrative at this point is of a much more active engagement with the subjects that sat before his lens. In the case of the christianised Khama, Fritsch seems to have felt a particular degree of affinity, commenting that 'the simple, modest, and at the same time noble deportment of this son of a chief evoked a delightful feeling'.[9]

On other occasions he photographed a Korana leader, Zwart Jaan, and his father, Gerrit, and Mapotla, the son of the Ndebele chief Mzilikazi (see Figs. 94–97, 187–188). The most striking omission in his collection of photographs of African notables is the absence of any portraits of Zulu chiefs or councillors. Instead, his portraits of the Zulu attempt to document a distinctive cultural practice: that of hairstyling. These are among the most aestheticised of all his portraits (see Figs. 135–142). His travel narrative suggests that he chose to photograph this cultural practice in order to highlight the relatively 'civilised' status of those whom he saw as the most 'noble' of southern African peoples. 'One is soon aware that one finds oneself here amongst a thriving group of natives when one sees the muscular bodies and the beautiful men of stately build. The powerful development of the body is the rule amongst the Zulu ... This favourable impression is heightened by the distinctive hair-dress of most of the armed men.'[10]

The second most prominent category of individuals to sit before Fritsch's camera was the inhabitants of mission stations. Fritsch took photographs of African converts at the Moravian mission station of Shiloh (near modern Queenstown), at the Berlin Missionary Society's station at Bethany (near Bloemfontein) and at the London Missionary Society's station at Kuruman. His portraits of Africans on these mission stations typically depict the impact of Westernisation, and particularly Western dress, on indigenous peoples. A series of portraits that he took at Shiloh, for example, portray three adult 'Hottentot' converts – Carl Stompjes, A. Minell and R. Schlinger – in jacket, shawl and dress (Figs. 40–45). This was one of the rare instances where the Africans he photographed had surnames. These were presumably given them subsequent to their conversion.

Fritsch's portrait of the 'Mosuto native teacher' at Shiloh, Johannes Nakin, presents a more complete example of cultural change on the missions (Figs. 38–39). In this frontal portrait Nakin appears in the accoutrements of the European gentleman: his waistcoat peeking out beneath the neatly buttoned-up jacket and his carefully tied dark cravat thrown in relief against his white shirt. The contrast of light and dark clothing is skilfully mirrored in Nakin's visage, with a dark outline framing and highlighting the teacher's fine facial features. Fritsch chose this portrait to illustrate the impact of Westernisation to his anthropological colleagues back in Berlin in later years. 'I will pass around a picture of the Chief Moshesh whose clothing indicates the influence of civilisation on him; so too in the case of this photograph of a Basotho, who grew up on the mission station at Shiloh and excelled in intellect.'[11] The 'picture' of Moshesh was not, however, one of Fritsch's own. He wrote of his wish while in the Orange Free State to journey

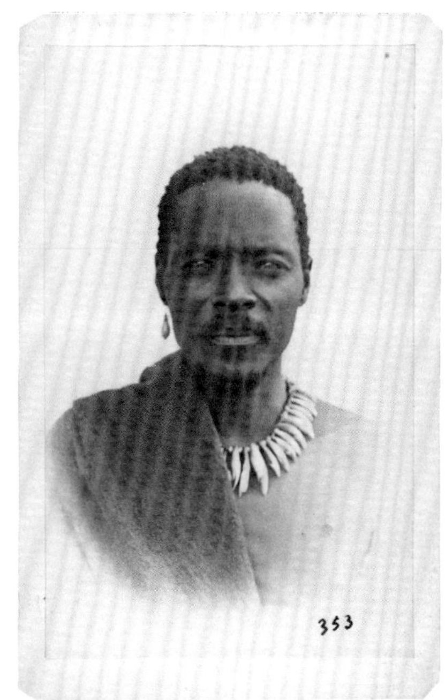

Fig. 264 ▶

Sazini, first councillor of Anta, Windvogelberg. (EM-SMB/32/928-927)

across to visit the Sotho chief, but regretted that it was too difficult to get there. This reinforces the argument that his was a systematic attempt to capture African nobility in photographic form.

There was a very practical reason for Fritsch's partiality for mission subjects. In his travelogue he made frequent reference to the fear with which African subjects viewed his imposing photographic technology. In order to win the trust of potentially fearful or reluctant sitters, Fritsch had to enlist the support of intermediaries. The missionaries were obvious candidates, given their close contact with Africans and knowledge of African cultures and languages. Fritsch expressed gratitude to Robert Moffat for his hospitality and assistance with 'photographic labours', and it was with Moffat's assistance that captured a portrait of 'Malitabe, a Morolong' living at Kuruman (Figs. 155–156). Indeed, Moffat himself agreed to sit before Fritsch's lens; and his is the only portrait of a European subject in the entire Fritsch collection (Fig. 154). Significantly, Fritsch only took a frontal portrait view. Was this partly his way of expressing his own sense of gratitude for the services in photographic mediation performed by Moffat? Did Moffat himself not perhaps request a portrait for posterity?

Fritsch's rapport with the German missionaries at Bethany, the Revd C.F. Wuras and Mr Meiffert, accounts for his success in capturing portraits of four mission subjects there. He records his gratitude at being 'given a very friendly reception at Mr Meiffert's house and ... assisted in every respect by the missionaries in my [photographic] work'. Not all missionaries were equally accommodating. Fritsch

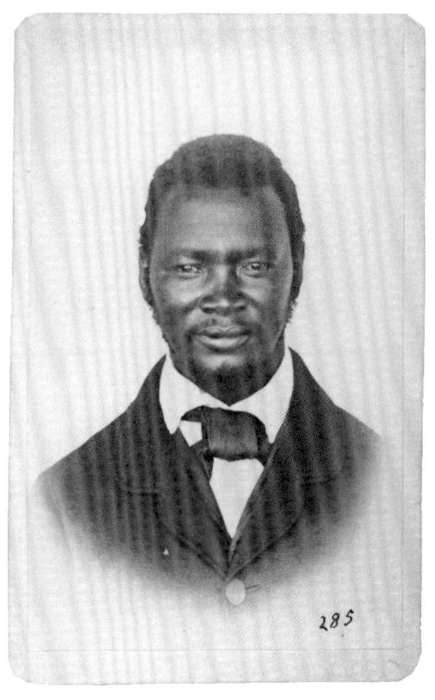

◀ *Fig. 265*

Johannes Nakin, Shiloh, eastern Cape. (EM-SMB/32/946-945)

reports on an earlier incident where the reluctance of a missionary to assist him prompted him to induce compliance by other means. 'I hoped to obtain some material for my anthropological studies from a sizeable Fingo settlement near Port Elizabeth. I took my apparatus out and approached the appointed missionary, but he would do nothing for me. Some of the natives showed great fear of the bulky apparatus. Others were bold enough to sit before the camera for 20 seconds in exchange for 5 shillings.'[12]

The importance of mediators is a theme that resurfaces regularly in the travel narrative, but is one that, significantly enough, he chose to efface in adopting the more authoritative voice of the scientist in his anthropological study of 1872. Apart from the missionaries, his photographic work drew on the labours of a diverse cast of African 'auxiliaries and intermediaries'.[13] Some of this help was technical. He wrote of his use of 'an assistant' while experimenting with photography in Cape Town before he set out on his first expedition, noting that this was 'the first time' (suggesting there were others) that 'I used the services of a coloured helper'.[14] In Durban he indicated that he used a Zulu assistant for the purposes of 'carrying my [photographic] apparatus'. When in Pietermaritzburg, he was unable to procure adequate assistance for his photographic work, though here it seems likely that a white settler rather than an African labourer was the type of 'middleman' he had in mind. 'Among the large number of Zulus wandering the streets of Pietermaritzburg, I saw many beautiful specimens that I wanted to add to my "gallery", but in the absence of

a middleman (*Mittelsperson*) I was unable to capture them.'[15] Whether he required this *Mittelsperson* for the initial purposes of persuasion or for translation in guiding his fearful potential subjects through the rituals of the photographic event is left unstated.

White settlers had certainly played an important role as mediators in his earlier photographic work in the Orange Free State. Thus, for example, the Scotsman Andrew Hudson Bain, who had a farm near Bloemfontein, permitted Fritsch first 'to gaze upon his rarities ... Bushmen of the purest origin that can be found in the land'[16] and then to photograph them: a process in which Bain himself would have had to serve as mediator. A woodcut image in Fritsch's travel narrative suggests that there were eight Bushmen living at Bainsvlei, and we have surviving portrait pairs of seven of them (see Figs. 106–120). In keeping with the collection of curiosities on the farm,[17] Fritsch seems to have emphasised their unusual items of attire. The 'Bush woman' Sanna is shown with a cloth blanket around her shoulders, a necklace and striking strings of white beads in her hair. Her son Carlo was photographed with a traditional bead necklace and metal chain slung across his chest, symbolic perhaps of the blend of cultural influences on the farm. Fritsch related an improbable tale, derived presumably from Bain, of how this unimposing teenager had killed a hyena with his bare hands.[18] The attire of the old man Boessek is particularly odd. Like many of the other portrait originals, it is of a remarkably fine quality, and the details of the wrinkles on his torso and neck, as well as the veins on his forehead, are very clearly visible. But the viewer's attention is drawn, above all, to his highly exotic headgear: a swathe of white feathers almost entirely covering the head.

Another locationally specific group of portraits is that of 'coolies from Madras', whom Fritsch photographed in Durban in October 1864. Unfortunately, we have no contextual information about the photographic venue or the potential 'middlemen' involved in persuading these Indian men to sit before the camera. It is worth noting, though, that here too we have a very rare photographic record. These are perhaps the only surviving images of individuals from the first wave of immigrant indentured labour brought to Natal. Between 1860 and 1866 over six thousand Indians were shipped to Natal and ended up working variously on sugar plantations, in the households of settlers and in government departments. Almost all of these early immigrants were from Madras or Calcutta and some 85 per cent of them were Hindu.[19]

A final and more scattered 'group' of portrait originals that warrants mention comprises the photographs that Fritsch took of young African women. While African women were often the subject of focus in earlier travel writings, Fritsch was the first southern African traveller to compile an extensive portfolio of images of them. His front profile view of Mickie, a 'Gona Hottentot' (see Figs. 121–122), is also reproduced in three-quarter-page format by Karel Schoeman in his *South African Family Album*. As Schoeman notes, 'artistically it is a fine composition with the contrasting patterns formed by lighter and darker colours and the dramatic silhouette of the women's large eardrops'.[20] In his frontal portrait of 'Cuenyone' (Figs. 157–158), the traditional culture of the Rolong is the point of focus. Here the viewer's attention is drawn particularly to her long bead necklace and its fine alterations of colour and bead size. The young woman looks at the camera with an intense gaze (perhaps accentuated by the use of a flash). He also photographed Motuane, 'the favourite wife' of the Tswana chief Gaseitsiwe, who is variously adorned with an animal skin around her shoulders, light and dark rings of two large-beaded necklaces, and beadwork in her hair. He later noted that her hair had been 'stuck together with metallic glitter and brill-cream'.[21]

Taken collectively then, the most striking characteristic of Fritsch's portfolio of original photographic portraits, apart from their fine quality, is their diversity and individuality. In keeping with the 'honorific' tradition of portraiture, derived from aristocratic and then bourgeois painting, the images compel attention to the particular, the specific. This sense of specificity, whether the subjects of his portraiture were nobles or not, comes primarily from the remarkably varied range of cultural adornments worn by his African subjects – whether leopard tooth necklaces, felt hats, feathers, chains, waistcoats and cravats, earrings, beads, horns, blankets and karosses, hairpins stuck through elaborately styled heads of hair, or handkerchiefs worn on the head.

The picture of African ethnic identities in his field notes-turned-travel narrative of 1868 was still a relatively fluid one. While he certainly wrote of his quest to record 'pure racial types' (or 'specimens' in the scientific language of the travelling anatomist), his narrative reveals that this ambition was often frustrated. Thus, for example, in an area where 'the mixed race is mostly of the Hottentot type', he conceded that 'it was difficult to identify the pure race and get photographs of them'. At his 'first opportunity to get pictures of the coloureds who call themselves "Griqua"', he reported that 'I could not really describe the individuals as particularly characteristic of this tribe. While the hair remained short and curly, there was an undeniable mixing of white blood.' Even in the case of those he viewed as the most noble of African peoples, the Zulu, he was forced to concede that their 'external appearance is so diverse that it is difficult to fix an exact type ... There is great diversity in skin colour; [and] while [it is] usually deep dark-brown, some have lighter, more reddy-brown tones although the overall physical make-up rules out any possibility of mixing with white blood.'[22]

Finally, a few points of qualification are necessary to my argument for an 'honorific' reading of Fritsch's portraits in the field and in the travel narrative with which I most closely associate them. To begin with, he took the photographs in portrait pairs in a format that was typical of the 'native type' portraiture just beginning to emerge at the

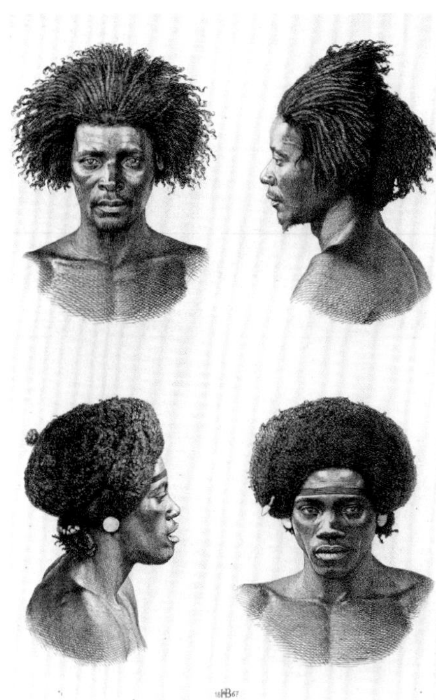

Fig. 266 ▶

'Plate 2: Ama-zulu'. (*Die Eingeborenen,* vol. 2)

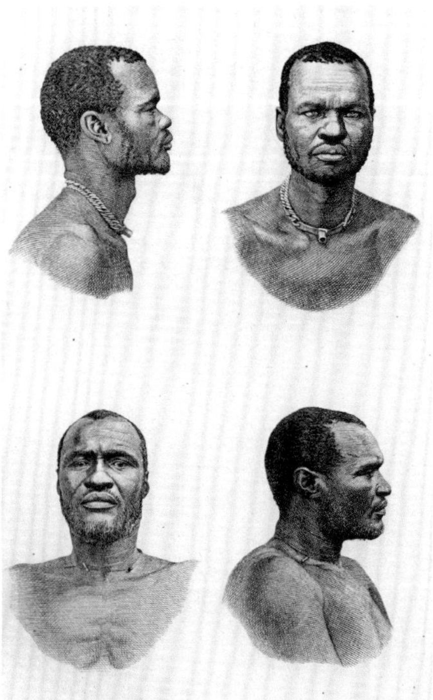

Fig. 267 ▶

'Plate 6: Ama-ngqika'. (*Die Eingeborenen,* vol. 2)

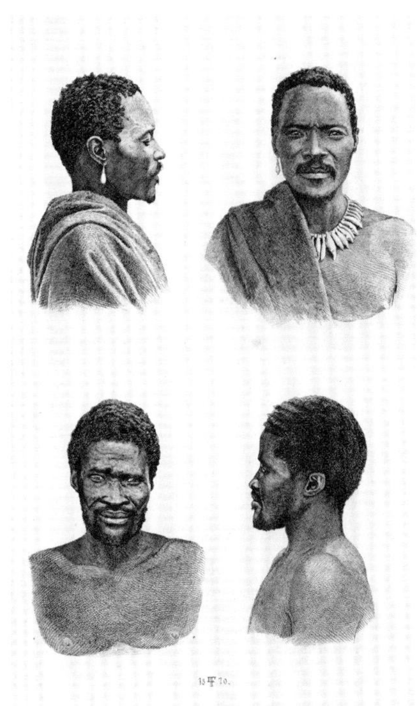

◀ *Fig. 268*

'Plate 7: Ama-ngqika'. (*Die Eingeborenen,* vol. 2)

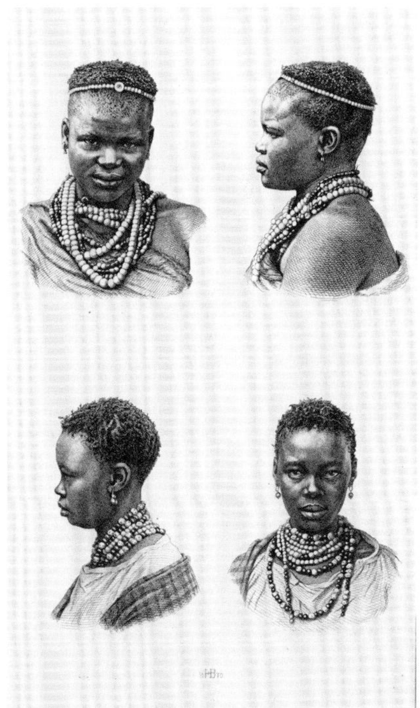

◀ *Fig. 269*

'Plate 8: Ama-mbalu and Ama-tembu'. (*Die Eingeborenen,* vol. 2)

time he was travelling.[23] Secondly, as a trained doctor and anatomist, Fritsch did take physical measurements of his photographic subjects, data which he came to foreground when he later published his scientific study, *Die Eingeborenen Süd-Afrika's*. Thirdly, there is occasional evidence that he photographed subjects naked, as for example in the case of his full-body frontal portrait of the Bushman Job (see Figs. 62–63). Fourthly, there is undoubtedly a discernible ambiguity in the racial attitudes he expressed in the travel narrative. The emphasis in my analysis so far has been on their relative fluidity, especially when read across the full volume and in comparison with the tone of his later study. However, as other authors in this volume emphasise,[24] there is also much evidence of expressions of irritation, impatience and frustration towards (uncompliant) African subjects, as well as at times dismissive and ethnocentric comments towards the Africans he met on his travels. My overall impression remains, however, that the newly trained doctor who came out to southern Africa at the age of 25 was curious and engaged, at times outright sympathetic towards the peoples he encountered, and in a way that the 34-year-old author of the scientific study simply was not. What is it that might explain such a relatively swift change in tone and attitude?

The 'repressive' use of portraits: Breslau, 1872

The answer, I believe, lies on the title and opening pages of his 1872 study, *Die Eingeborenen Süd-Afrika's*. The Preface begins in the following stridently nationalist terms: 'We live in a great age. The German Reich has defiantly triumphed against its mighty enemies after difficult battles. Even the author of the forthcoming study willingly followed the call of the Fatherland.'[25] Fritsch explained that he had enlisted in the German army a mere eight days after returning from southern Africa. In the curriculum vitae he compiled in later life, the section on his 'Military Career' looms large. Here he reported that he rose to the position of Second Lieutenant in the Prussian Army during the Austro-Prussian War of 1866, and proudly lists the military honours that were bestowed upon him after the war: 'Rothe Adlerord. II, Hohenzoll. Hausord. II, Eisernes Kreuz, Militar Dienstkreuz I'. In 1870 Fritsch once again took up arms, this time in the Franco-Prussian War. He recalled that he took part in the sieges of Strasbourg and Paris, defining moments in the making of the newly unified German nation under Otto von Bismarck in 1871. Two years after the war he was awarded the rank of First Lieutenant.[26]

The heightened sense of national identity and pride that went with this military career had a major impact on how Fritsch viewed not only his Prussian fellows, but also those Austrian, French, and African 'others' whom he would write about in the very years in which he was most intensely involved in warfare. As we shall see below, there is explicit evidence of the shaping role of this new national consciousness in his 1872 study.

The other important development in Fritsch's career is recorded in the list of his qualifications and appointments on the book's title page: medical doctor and assistant at the Royal Anatomical Institute in Berlin. When he was not fighting for the Prussian Army, Fritsch was building a scientific career in Berlin. Fritsch had been appointed as an assistant anatomist at the Royal Anatomical Institute in 1867. In 1873, presumably partly as a result of the publication of his southern African study, he secured a permanent post as a lecturer in the Department of Anatomy at Berlin University. During the intervening years he had played an active role in the institutionalisation of anthropology in Berlin. Fritsch was a founder member of the highly influential Berlin Society for Anthropology, Ethnology and Prehistory (BGAEU) in 1869. He served as the acting secretary of this fast-growing organisation in its early years.[27] Minutes of the Society's meetings, published in its journal *Zeitschrift für Ethnologie* (also founded in 1869), indicate that Fritsch was a vocal and highly respected member of this emerging anthropological community. During the 1870s and 1880s, he became their acknowledged expert on photography and its anthropological applications, as well as one of the experts on the indigenous peoples of Africa.[28]

A few aspects about the general character of the German anthropological tradition are of particular relevance here. Historians of anthropology have contrasted the strong physical emphasis in the Continental, and especially German, anthropological traditions with the more philosophical and evolutionary approach of British (and American) anthropologists of the mid- to late nineteenth century.[29] While the latter typically plotted non-European societies according to their stage of development in what was seen as the universal path of 'progress in civilisation', the German anthropologists drew a much starker line between those peoples they classified as *Kulturvölker* (cultural peoples) and those they classified as *Naturvölker* (natural peoples). In his incisive study on this intellectual tradition, Andrew Zimmerman demonstrates that the Berlin anthropologists played a particularly dominant role in the new national tradition. They focused on the *Naturvölker* to an even greater extent than their colleagues elsewhere, and visual modes of representation like photography were accorded an especially prominent place in the making of German anthropological knowledge.[30]

It was within this new intellectual space (and seemingly puffed up with national pride) that Fritsch published his scientific study of 1872, *Die Eingeborenen Süd-Afrika's*. The book appeared in two volumes, one textual and one visual. The first volume, running across more than 500 pages, presented a detailed physical anthropological and ethnographic analysis of the indigenous peoples of southern Africa, with a series of lithographic plates appended comparing the skulls,

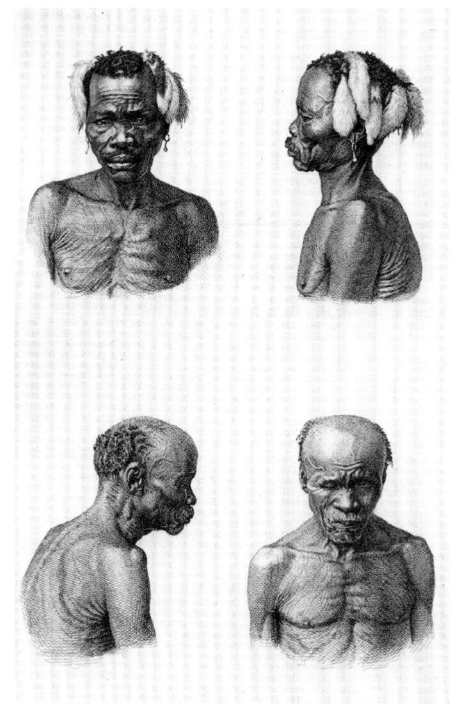

Fig. 270 ▶

'Plate 27: Buschmänner'. (*Die Eingeborenen*, vol. 2)

skeletal features and skin colours of the different 'races'.[31] Fritsch was somewhat apologetic about the limited number of measurements that he had taken of living bodies in the field, and, perhaps partly by way of compensation for his specialist scientific audience, made hugely detailed measurements of the skulls presented in his lithographic tables, to which he had access in the collection of the Berlin Anatomical Museum. While no match for the German-speaking Hungarian Aurel von Turok, who took 5371 measurements of a single skull in 1890,[32] his 55 separate measurements of each individual skull do suggest a rather obsessive preoccupation.

It was in the second volume that a selection of 30 of his more than 130 portrait pairs were featured in what he called an 'Atlas of Racial Types'. Before we consider the way in which the selected portraits featured in this *Atlas*, it is necessary to say something about the technical process involved in converting the original photographic plates and prints into the copper etchings that were reproduced in the book. As Andreas Broeckmann indicates in this volume, Fritsch worked in very close collaboration with his colleague in Dresden, Hugo Bürckner, to ensure the kind of accuracy appropriate to a scientific publication. On the eve of the book's publication, Fritsch explained his motivations to his colleagues in the Berlin Society for Anthropology, Ethnology and Prehistory. 'Mr. Fritsch placed a portrait collection of South African racial types before the Society that belongs to a larger work on the natives of South Africa and explained the principles that guided the

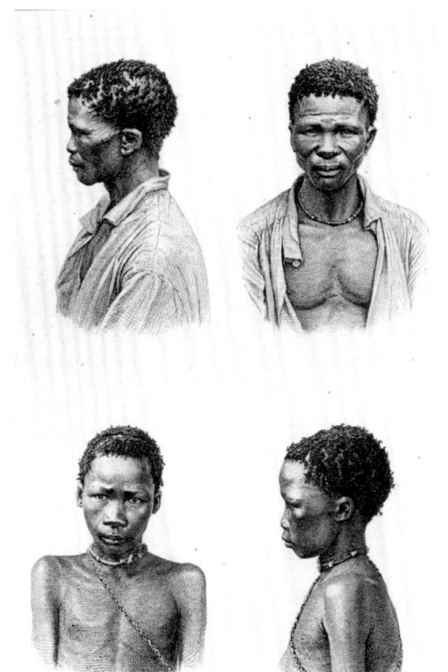

◀ *Fig. 271*

'Plate 29: Buschmänner'. (*Die Eingeborenen,* vol. 2)

presentation of this collection of portraits with special *retrospective* attention to their physiological characteristics ... [He said that] The further use of photographic portraits required careful consideration. It was, unfortunately, not advisable to use the photographic originals themselves as illustrations and on the following grounds. It was not possible with the changeable external circumstances and difficulties of [photographing] on the expedition to obtain negatives of sufficient quality from which proper and consistent copies could be made. Further, the original prints, even in cases when the plates have been well washed, deteriorate rapidly when reprinted in books and become yellowed. A single, poorly reproduced photograph ... can distort the integrity of an entire collection.'[33] [My emphasis]

His reference to 'retrospect' is significant in my view, suggesting the changing motivations of Fritsch the travelling photographer and Fritsch the scientific author. The difference between the originals and the published version involved very much more than technical alteration, however. The ways in which Fritsch came to select, order and frame these copper-etched versions of his portraits encouraged a physical anthropological reading that diverged, I believe, from the spirit and emphasis of the original photographs and photographic occasions. In choosing the 30 portraits for his *Atlas*, Fritsch was careful to streamline the collection in such a way that evidence of racial mixing was excised. The omission of Robert Moffat or the three Indian indentured labourers from Durban is scarcely surprising in a portrait

collection of 'natives of South Africa', but his decision to leave out portraits like that of 'Piet, Griqua' (see Figs. 191–192), or 'Nelleka, Bastaard' (see Figs. 27–28) suggests that he was now anxious not to muddy the impressions of racial purity that his *Atlas* sought to convey. He also went out of his way to downplay evidence of cultural hybridity. This explains why mission converts, Africans in Western dress, and those more acculturated Africans like transport-riders or servants in European households, feature far less prominently in the *Atlas* than they do in the wider collection. He was well aware that images of the likes of Johannes Nakin might have threatened to unsettle the idea of 'racial purity' implicit in the notion of 'racial types'.

In his attempts to encourage a physical reading of the portraits, Fritsch showed a strong preference for those portraits where the head and chest were exposed. His expressions of 'retrospective' regret in the prefatory text in the *Atlas* are again suggestive to me of the discrepancy between the spirit of the originals and those of the republished photographs. 'With retrospective consideration to the clear presentation of anatomical features, the head and chest of the individuals should probably have been exposed.'[34] In his defence, he told his scientific peers that many of his photographic subjects had not wanted to be photographed without their shirts or items of cultural adornment. It seems unlikely, though, given the great frequency with which these items appear in the original photographs, that he felt as strongly about this issue in 1865 as he did in 1872.

Like the lithographs of skulls, skeletal features and skin colour in the plates appended to the first volume, the portraits in the second volume were presented in hierarchical order. Rather than following the geographical distribution of the peoples of southern Africa as he encountered them on his travels, he graded his portraits in descending racial rank from 'A-bantu' (a term he borrowed from the philologist Wilhelm Bleek but invested with a physical anthropological meaning)[35] down to the 'Khoikhoin' (a term he used to include Khoi and San subjects). Within this wide racial typology the various 'tribes' were also presented in 'descending' racial order, Thus, the 'A-bantu' sequence began with the Zulu and the Ndebele before proceeding 'down' to the Xhosa and Sotho-Tswana peoples. The 'Khoikhoin' sequence began with the (colonial) 'Hottentots' and proceeded via the 'Korana' down to the lowly 'Bushmen'.

The prefatory table to the *Atlas* highlights the fact that Fritsch was now interested in the physical rather than the cultural characteristics of his portrait subjects. For each of the individuals photographed, the table records their name, their 'tribe' (*Stamm*), their approximate age, their height and two head measurements: the height of their head and the width of the face across the jaw. These had been taken in the field, a process which met with resistance from numerous potential subjects.

The other framing context is of course the text presented in the first volume. The tone here contrasts markedly with that of the travelogue: any hints of ambiguity or even empathy for African subjects have now simply been excised. In the case of the Zulu, for example, the contrast with 'the noble Zulu' of his travel narrative could hardly be greater. The emphasis now falls not on the skilful craftsmanship involved in the elaborate hairstyling and the exoticism that it lent to the appearance of the Zulu, but rather on the 'bizarre' character of this custom as yet another sign of African 'wildness'. 'A national characteristic that is evident in viewing the portraits is the artistically constructed hairstyles, whose bizarre forms add much to the wild expressions on their faces.'[36]

In the portraits of the Xhosa chiefs that Fritsch re-presented in the *Atlas*, there is little sense of the 'honorific'. The lack of cultural adornment and focus on the body are the most striking features of the portraits of the chiefs Xhoxho, Anta, Siyolo and Dilima (shown in Figs. 267 and 268). The text in the first volume made explicit the new 'repressive' reading of these images. In the case of Xhoxho and Anta, for example, it was now the 'deviant' development of the lips and nose that elicited comment. 'This table gives a good example of how important it is to have two views of the same individual. No one would have believed that the weakly developed nose in the profile view could convert into such a hideous, almost ape-like nose in the front view ... Another characteristic of the Xhosa that diverges from the facial configuration of the European is the mouth. The lips are flattened and protruding (Plate 6 Hanta [Anta]).'[37]

While his portraits of the councillors Sazini and Somi (the former shown in Fig. 268) do retain something of the cultural emphasis of the originals, even here the effect is largely negated by the more clinical and greyer rendering of the images in engraved form and their location within a square grid.

In the case of the Xhosa portraits, as elsewhere in the text, the European head and body serve as the implicit model that points up the deficiencies of the African physique. The European is in a sense the 'shadow archive' that runs through the text.[38] Those who are inclined to idealise the African physique, Fritsch suggested, 'should as a corrective visit the [Prussian] military swimming school where they would soon become convinced that the healthy, normal German, in the proportions, strength and extent of the form, in fact the entire build, is superior to the A-bantu man'.[39] Here in the strident new language of Fritsch the Prussian lieutenant, we have an explicit indication of the extent to which his military experience had reshaped his racial ideas, as well as a suggestion of the way in which German racial science was buttressed by a discourse of masculinity. Robert Gordon argues that the obsession with African genitalia among a later generation of German anthropologists studying the Khoisan was related to a growing crisis of masculinity in Germany in the years preceding the First World War.[40]

As regards the portraits of the Sotho-Tswana in the *Atlas* – diversely classified as 'Basuto', 'Bamantitisi', 'Barolong', 'Gamalete', 'Maaue', 'Bakhatla', 'Bakuena', 'Babidiji' and 'Bawanketsi' – Fritsch's commentary once again drew attention to the physical rather than the cultural. Of the portraits of two Kgatla men, for example, Fritsch simply noted that 'The crown and back of the head in the profile view provides a favourable illustration of the "hypsisteno-cephalic" skull.'[41] Where the six portrait figures (Maqoma, Sandile, Gaseitsiwe, Mosielele, Sechele and Khama) reproduced in his travelogue were exclusively shown in the frontal view, all of them chiefs, five of them dressed, here it was the side profile view that commanded attention.

Likewise, the portraits of the 'Khoikhoin' are read in the text in anatomical terms, with attention drawn variously to the 'pepper-corn hair', shoulders, skull configuration, skin wrinkling or facial features. As regards the 'Bushman' boy Carlo, for example, Fritsch now drew exclusive attention to the features of his body. 'The characteristically wrinkly, leathery appearance of the skin is already evident in the 13-year-old boy that I photographed near Bloemfontein. The narrow shoulders of the young boy are exactly characteristic [of the Bushmen] ... although the muscles have not yet taken on the character of those of the adults.' As for the old man Bosseck, Fritsch suggested a reading that diverged markedly from the impression created by the original photograph. He interpreted the published portrait, not in terms of the strikingly exotic cluster of feathers draped over the subject's head, but as an illustration (again in profile view) of the characteristic formation of the 'Bushman' nose and degree of 'prognathy'.[42] Along with the cephalic index already mentioned, this was a concept that Fritsch borrowed from the influential Swedish racial scientist, Gustav Anders Retzius.

Given their framing and these textual promptings, it is hardly surprising that Fritsch's portraits were read by his contemporaries in physical anthropological terms. Even liberal intellectuals like Wilhelm Bleek, Rudolf Virchow and E.B. Tylor came out in praise of the book, all of them commenting in particular on the scientific value of the *Atlas*. Bleek praised the 'magnificent Atlas' and drew the attention of his Cape readers to Fritsch's 'excellent photography' in that part of the work illustrative of 'the different races'. Rudolf Virchow described Fritsch's book as a *Prachtwerk* ('beautiful work') and of great importance for the 'ethnology of the primitive peoples of South Africa'. Tylor wrote of the study more generally as an example of how 'the closer appreciation of race-types, which is now supplanting the vaguer generalities of twenty years ago, is in no small measure due to the introduction of photographic portraits'.[43]

Fritsch's overwhelming emphasis on 'race types' in his scientific study was, I have argued above, an expression of a shift to the 'repressive' pole of portrait photography. I have suggested that his original portrait photographs of 'natives' taken during his two expeditions through southern African between 1863 and 1865 were conceived in an 'honorific' tradition. Here I emphasised Fritsch's very choice of subjects (notably African chiefs, their associates and mission converts), the strong ethnographic orientation of these original portraits with their highly diverse range of items of cultural adornment, and the relatively open and engaged (albeit still highly ambiguous) attitudes towards Africans expressed in his 1868 travelogue, *Drei Jahre in Süd-Afrika*. I have speculated that the reasons for the very marked shift in tone between his two books, and the associated ways in which he conceived the portraits in relation to them, most likely derive from a shift in his racial attitudes as a result of his active involvement in the Prussian wars of 1866 and 1870, and his integration into an emerging anthropological community in Berlin with its strong orientation towards physical anthropology.

ENDNOTES

1   A. Sekula, 'The body and the archive' in R. Bolton (ed.), *The Contest of Meaning: Critical Histories of Photography* (London and Cambridge, Mass., 1989), 345.

2   This essay is an abbreviated and adapted version of the article I had published in the 'Visual History: Special Issue' of the journal *Kronos*. See A. Bank, 'Anthropology and portrait photography: Gustav Fritsch's "Natives of South Africa", 1863–1872', *Kronos*, 27 (November 2001), 43–76. My thanks to Patricia Hayes for her extensive and incisive commentary on the draft versions of that article, and to Keith Dietrich for his comments on this reworked essay.

3   I have, unfortunately, been unable to trace a copy of this original field diary.

4   See Keith Dietrich, this volume.

5   Gustav Fritsch, *Drei Jahre in Süd-Afrika. Reiseskizzen nach Notizen des Tagebuchs zusammengestellt* (Breslau, 1868), 32. Here and elsewhere the translations from the original German are my own.

6   H. Deacon (ed.), *The Island: A History of Robben Island, 1488–1990* (Cape Town, 1996).

7   Fritsch, *Drei Jahre*, 33. The figure numbers in the text refer back to the portrait reproductions in Keith Dietrich's essay in Part I of this volume.

8   K. Schoeman, *The Face of the Country: A South African Family Album* (Cape Town, Pretoria and Johannesburg, 1996), 23.

9   Fritsch, *Drei Jahre*.

10   Fritsch, *Drei Jahre*, 190.

11   'Proceedings of the Berlin Gesellschaft für Anthropologie, Ethnologie und Urgeschichte (BGAEU)', 14 June 1873, *Zeitschrift für Ethnologie*, 5 (1873), 105.

12   Fritsch, *Drei Jahre*, 73.

13   J. Fabian, *Out of Our Minds: Exploration and Madness in Central Africa* (Chicago, 2000), 28–35.

14   Fritsch, *Drei Jahre*, 12.

15   Fritsch, *Drei Jahre*, 199.

16   Fritsch, *Drei Jahre* , 134.

17   For details, see Keith Dietrich, this volume.

18   Gustav Fritsch, *Die Eingeborenen Süd-Afrika's ethnographisch und anatomisch beschreiben* (Breslau, 1872), 321.

19   J. Brain, 'Indentured and free Indians in the economy of Colonial Natal' in B. Guest and J.M. Sellers (eds.), *Enterprise and Exploration in a Victorian Colony* (Pietermaritzburg, 1985). I am grateful to Uma Mesthrie for this reference and for pointing out to me to the novelty of these photographs.

20   Schoeman, *A South African Family Album*, 67.

21   Fritsch, *Die Eingeborenen*.

22   Fritsch, *Drei Jahre*, 49, 186, 199.

23   See E. Edwards, 'Photographic "types": The pursuit of method', *Visual Anthropology*, 3, 2–3 (1990), 235–256.

24   See M. Godby, this volume, for a reading of the travel narrative as 'dismissive' towards Africans; and L. van Robbroeck, this volume, for an emphasis on his anxiety and aversion in relation to the Africans he encountered on his journey. My own reading here is very much more in keeping with the emphasis in the Dietrich essay in Part I, which does, I think, demonstrate exactly this: a marked degree of curiosity and engagement in Fritsch's wide-ranging cultural encounters.

25   Fritsch, *Die Eingeborenen Süd-Afrika's*, vii.

26   This information about Fritsch's military careers is drawn from his Personal File in the Humboldt University Archive: Registry, F, no. 51, vol. 1.

27   It had attracted 120 members by 1872, a number that grew to over 500 by the turn of the century, 300 of whom were based in Berlin. See B. Massin, 'From Virchow to Fischer: Physical anthropology and "modern race theories" in Wilhelmine Germany' in G.W. Stocking (ed.), *Volksgeist as Method and Ethic: Essays on Boasian Ethnography and the German Anthropological Tradition* (Madison, 1996), 83–87.

28   See Andreas Broeckmann, this volume.

29   G.W. Stocking (ed.), *A Franz Boas Reader: The Shaping of American Anthropology, 1883–1911* (Chicago, 1974), 9.

30   See A. Zimmerman, *Anthropology and Antihumanism in Imperial Germany* (Chicago and London, 2001), 38–61. For an alternative interpretation regarding the place of photography in German anthropology in this period, see Andreas Broeckmann, this volume.

31   Historians of physical anthropology in South Africa have identified this as one of the first systematic studies in the field, and it was certainly extensively cited by physical anthropologists of the early twentieth century.

32   Massin, 'From Virchow to Fischer', 82.

33   'Proceedings', 9 December 1871, Meeting of the BGAEU, *Zeitschrift für Ethnologie*, 4 (1872), 11. See Keith Dietrich and Andreas Broeckmann, this volume, for more detailed accounts of the process of conversion and Fritsch's supervisory role in it.

34   Fritsch, *Die Eingeborenen*, 3–4.

35   On Wilhelm Bleek's coining of the concept 'Bantu' (in collaboration with George Grey), see R. Thornton, '"That dying out race"'

36   Fritsch, *Die Eingeborenen*, 126.

37   Fritsch, *Die Eingeborenen*, 28.

38   Sekula, 'The body and the archive', 345.

39   Fritsch, *Die Eingeborenen*, 18.

40   R. Gordon, 'The rise of the Bushman penis: Germans, genitalia and genocide', *African Studies*, 57, 1 (1998), 30–32.

41   Fritsch, *Die Eingeborenen*, 162.

42   Fritsch, *Die Eingeborenen*, 399, 404.

43   W.H.I. Bleek, 'Dr Fritsch's "Natives of South Africa"', *Cape Monthly Magazine*, 7 (1873), 172; Rudolf Virchow in 'Proceedings of the BGAEU', 14 December 1872 in *Zeitchrift für Ethnologie*, 4 (1872), 275; Tylor cited in M. Godby, 'Images of //Kabbo' in P. Skotnes (ed.), *Miscast: Negotiating the Presence of the Bushmen* (Cape Town, 1996), 121.

Gustav Fritsch:
Facialising the anthropological matrix

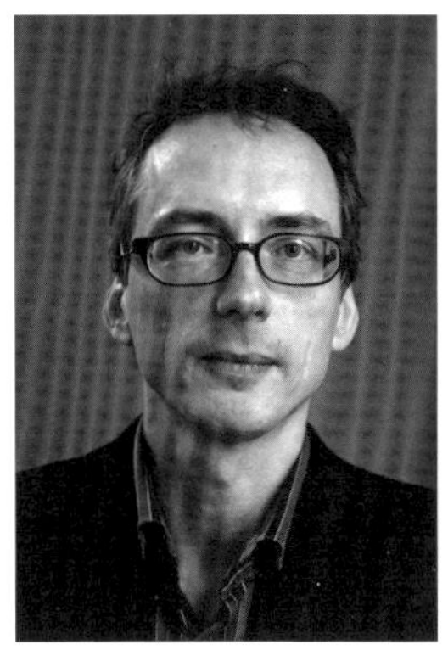

Andreas Broeckmann

Gustav Fritsch was one of the first anthropologists to make use of photography consistently, and in his publications from the early 1870s he presented a coherent theory of photographic representation. This essay offers a detailed reading of these texts, summarising the role that photography played in the discipline of anthropology in the nineteenth century. The analysis aims not only to contribute to an understanding of the motivations of the photographer, but to offer an insight into the radical changes that the interpretation of images can undergo. Whereas for Fritsch photographs were primarily records of racial types, their publication today presents the portrayed subjects as individuals with a personal history and a local identity.

Fritsch began his research when there was a growing scientific interest in human variety, an interest that cannot be separated from the context of colonialism and European imperialism. In his time, anthropology was a physically oriented cross-discipline that united different strands of the nineteenth-century inquiry into the nature of Man. In a more narrowly defined sense, it was conceived as the study of the human races, of their physical and cultural characteristics, and was divided into physical anthropology and ethnography. For most of the nineteenth century, physical anthropology had higher scientific credentials. The highly influential French anthropologist Paul Topinard called it *anthropologie proprement dite*, 'anthropology proper', while ethnography was relegated to second place, along with other *sciences accessoires*, such as history, archaeology, comparative mythology and demography. Despite this hierarchical difference, however, physical anthropology and ethnography were seen as interdependent. 'The two have to be reunited under the general term anthropology because they complement and cannot live without each other.'[1] The imbalance in favour of physical anthropology was gradually reversed until, by the middle of the twentieth century, it had turned into a mere side branch, while ethnography became the legitimate anthropological science: *social* anthropology, stripped of as much of its biologistic foundations as possible.

As regards physical anthropology, laboratory work concentrated on inanimate parts and representations of the body, on skulls, bones, hair, anthropometric data and photographs. The exactness of this work derived from silence and order; it was achieved by means of direction and balance. In contrast, the research domain of ethnography was problematic, especially given the unscientific ethos of the traveller, as opposed to the calm determination of the laboratory anthropologist: 'The traveller has generally other objects which occupy his attention. He sets out with certain erroneous opinions, allows himself to be influenced by the events of the day and his own preconceived notions; or he ignores what he ought to observe, and passes by facts which possibly might clear up questions long in dispute.'[2] Yet it was the activity of travelling which provided the necessary material for anthropological study, and which was instrumental in constituting its locale of intervention. In the first edition of *Anleitung zu wissenschaftlichen Beobachtungen auf Reisen* (Guidelines for Scientific Observation during Travels), a German project edited by Georg von Neumayer (published in three consecutive editions in 1875, 1888, 1906), which combined natural scientific, naval and anthropological interests, one contributor wrote: 'The traveller should never forget the main rule that his task on the journey is only to collect material which he himself or others shall later work on scientifically and in calm concentration. He has to observe and represent facts. This requires open senses and an open mind which can approach anything that is noteworthy and which can faithfully and sharply take in the given; and then a clear and untainted documentation has to be secured.'[3] The traveller described here requires no professional identity or ethos. He is an exchangeable collecting and observing apparatus: very much like a camera, he merely records for future development and analysis in the quiet darkroom of the study.

Andreas Broeckmann holds a PhD in art history from the University of East Anglia. He lives in Berlin and lectures internationally on the history of modern art, media theory, machine aesthetics and digital culture, and has curated exhibitions and festivals in major European venues. He is working on a study of twentieth-century machine art.

When we come to consider Fritsch's detailed discussion of photography, we should keep in mind that even before the shift of emphasis from physical anthropology to ethnography, photography played no major role in the toolbox of anthropology. Photography hardly featured either in the seminal British handbook, published by the British Association for the Advancement of Science, *Notes and Queries* (1874, 1892, 1899), or – with the exception of Fritsch's own article – in Neumayer's *Anleitung*. Even in the 1906 edition of the *Anleitung*, and despite the recurring claim that the use of photography had become so prevalent that it hardly needed justification, practical suggestions were made for only a handful of applications: for determining time and place through astronomical photography, for the recording of topographical situations, for plant geography and zoology. In the chapter on anthropology, a brief reference was made to the use of photography in physical anthropology when taking straight profile and frontal views of the head.

The practical obstacles to using photography in anthropology, the problems of transporting unwieldy equipment, the time-consuming procedures of photographing and measuring, and what was seen as the lack of intelligent co-operation on the part of the subjects, seriously restricted the medium's application in the field. Photography thus remained of minor importance throughout the nineteenth century, and for both of the main anthropological disciplines. It was deemed to be vital neither in the natural historical context of physical anthropology, nor in the cultural and sociological studies of ethnography. There were, however, some powerfully argued attempts at installing photography as an integral part of the scientific apparatus of anthropology. One of the most comprehensive of these was that made by Gustav Fritsch who, in the early 1870s, formulated what amounts to a theory of photographic portraiture for anthropology.

Fritsch had travelled to southern Africa in the 1860s and published the results of his studies in a number of texts from 1868 onwards.

He was a member of the Berlin Society for Anthropology, Ethnology and Prehistory and showed, at the beginning of his career, a lively interest in modern representational technologies, claiming as early as 1870 that recent progress made in the science of anthropology was largely due to the improvement of representational methods. Fritsch presented photography as a key device in the positivist scientific method, complementing the requirements of measuring, mechanical reproduction, and the tabulation of data. He generally believed in truth claims based on facts: 'The present work may thus be recommended to all those who strive to progress in the understanding of truth guided by facts rather than by feeble speculations, and may they be forbearing with regard to the *positive data* if here or there a *mistake* has sneaked in.'[4] At the same time, Fritsch was very tentative about the interpretative value of such data. He pointed to the difficulties of measuring living people, especially when they were 'uncivilised', and to the unavoidability of mistakes and inaccuracies. In his view, the only way of eliminating the effect of such mistakes was extensive tabulation of data, which were, however, often not readily available and difficult to obtain. Fritsch suggested that the value of measurements, when conducted under normal conditions, might not justify the effort: in the economy of collecting information, anthropometry could be too costly.[5]

In a contribution to the *Zeitschrift für Ethnologie* written in 1870, Fritsch compared the manual device of the Lucae apparatus, which recorded the outline and profile of objects, with photography. Johann C.G. Lucae (1814–1885) was a zoologist and anthropologist whose writings included 'The morphology of racial skulls' (1861–1864). The apparatus he invented was later improved as the 'diagraph' and 'dioptograph' by the physical anthropologist Rudolf Martin (1864–1925). For Fritsch, the Lucae apparatus was an important step forward from free drawing because it was a mechanical representational tool that provided straight views from a fixed viewpoint and eliminated perspective. However, use of the apparatus posed a number of problems. Irregularities of the object could cause inexactitudes, so that 'it seems desirable to have measurements alongside the drawing'.[6] Further imprecision could arise through hasty work, and the apparatus was time-consuming to use and could strain the eyes. Finally, the resulting representation did not match the 'image of natural perception'. 'The drawing produced with the Lucae apparatus is therefore a graphically represented figure table rather than an image, especially as it is more or less limited to the outline, while further elaboration has to be trusted to the judgement of the draughtsman.'[7] Fritsch conceived of an image as a full representation analogous to visual perception, an iconic sign, while the outline or contour provided by the Lucae apparatus was a gridlike, two-dimensional matrix. Its dependence on the draughtsman's interpretation for filling in its visual content robbed it of any scientific exactitude. Fritsch concluded: 'With photographs, this is not the case. Here the perspective is retained in the image, one gets outlines and planar views simultaneously, and the representation therefore gives a natural impression.'[8] Although photography was a generally superior representational medium, this superiority was qualified by the fact that 'obviously, photography also has its great flaws'.

Fritsch's most extensive discussion of photography appeared in his contribution to Neumayer's research manual, *Anleitung*. His chapter, 'Praktische Gesichtspunkte für die Verwendung zweier technischer Hülfsmittel: Das Mikroskop und der photographische Apparat' (Practical aspects of the use of two technical instruments: The microscope and the photographic apparatus),[9] is the last in the volume and the only chapter entirely devoted to technical instruments. Changes to the text made for the second (1888) and third (1906) editions were minor and will, where relevant, be pointed out. Their insignificance further supports my hypothesis of the relative unimportance of photography to the discipline of anthropology, which could live with a thirty-year-old account. In this chapter Fritsch claims that what is a single occupation for the scholar in his study – microscopic photography – falls, because of 'difficulties in the field', into two distinct areas for the traveller. He therefore deals with each instrument individually, starting off with the microscope and discussing different types and particular uses. The second part, entitled 'Photographische Aufnahmen', contains sections on anthropological photography (subdivided into physiognomy, ethnology and zoology), botanical, and geological and geographical photography, reproduction and other technical aspects. In the third edition of 1906, Fritsch added a bibliography and a list of companies which dealt in photographic equipment.

Fritsch started his account with a section on the importance and general use of photographs during travel. 'There are today probably only a few people who have not recognised the great significance of photography, and especially for the traveller it has become highly important. If he does not only want to see for himself, but wants to make permanent use of what he observed for a wider circle and advance the progress of knowledge, it is necessary that, where description is not sufficient, he offers proofs which may serve as material evidence for the uninformed, replacing direct observation, and simultaneously as a corrective for the subjective notions of the traveller. Such demands are best met by photographic images.'[10]

Fritsch raises some of the key issues of scientific photography. As regards temporality, its ability to arrest vision allows for the 'permanent use' of the derived visual data. At a semiotic level, the photographic representation surpasses verbal description and can replace unmediated observation by its ability to mimic the material object. As an externalised, objectified perception it can balance out subjectivist inaccuracies and make the evidence available to the wider scientific community, thereby shifting analytical authority away from the observer.

The various obstacles and problems posed by graphic representations, especially the frequent lack of skill and time for execution, can easily be countered. 'Photography completes the image there and then in the shortest span of time, it inscribes all details visible to the gaze with admirable sharpness, gives a representation of the relations which is precisely controllable, and at least some indications of the local tonalities.'[11] Fritsch thus inscribes photography into the economy of science on a number of levels: the medium can serve to help other scientists and further the utility and progress of science, and also improve the time economy of collecting data. Its corrective function is directly connected to the positivist claim of controllability through which the qualities and relations of objects can be visually determined.

Despite this clear commitment to the evidential value of photography, Fritsch is critical of its limitations. Nevertheless, he maintains that problems like those caused by the absence of colour or often clumsy equipment can be overcome by using photography in conjunction with other media and data. No scientific field has, according to Fritsch, shown the deficiencies of hand-drawn images as clearly as anthropology, for which the minute comparison of physical features is a paramount task. 'The application of photography has therefore to be pointed out as vital for the production of reliable and generally comparable representations of foreign tribes.'[12]

The problems of photographic representation are those of technological complexity and semiotic abundance, rather than of visual scarcity and exactitude. 'Finally it should be noted that the flaw of photography in giving too many inessential details in relation to the structure of the surface and showing colour variations in the same way as shadows is certainly a very problematic one, especially if one wants to use such representations as models for the draughtsman.'[13]

Fritsch makes particular reference to portrait photographs when he points out that they may become hard to recognise as the result of aestheticising or unusual viewpoints, wrong lighting or inappropriate lenses. Satisfactory results depend on the right choice of focus, distance and size, and comparability can only be achieved between images taken with the same lens. The epistemological status of photographs, Fritsch seems to imply, hinges on their perceptual effect rather than on the ontological nature of their production process.

'Natural impression'– the correlate of human visual perception – is both an important feature of an image and a factor undermining the scientific usefulness of the representation. The perspectival distortions in photographs become obvious, especially when they are compared to images made with the Lucae apparatus. In order to overcome this difficulty, Fritsch suggests combining the two techniques: 'It is advisable, and the present speaker has already realised this practically, to combine the two methods dealt with here in such a way that the photographically reproduced geometric outline is filled with a photographic image of the same view.'[14] This system – the photograph is copied into a photographically reduced, mechanically derived outline – is superior because it produces no measurable flaws and still maintains features of the 'natural impression'.

When Fritsch made these statements it was still assumed that photographs would not be printed directly in books but would appear in engraved reproductions. This transposition did not pose an epistemological problem, but one of legibility. 'Yet one learns very soon to recognise the images [i.e. the photographs] correctly in order to eliminate the problem, and even if in the beginning some unfortunate attempts were made, the writer has in the end always found artists who were able to meet the requirements and who sometimes completed their task with admirable facility.'[15] Ultimately, artisanal skill and the judgement of the author were sufficient for an accurate decoding of the visual matrix of the photograph. The problem – if there was one – lay in the accuracy of the production process; it was neither inherent in the process of transposition, nor was it, ultimately, a restriction imposed by human perception. On the contrary, the authorial, perception-based control of the production process secured the evidential value of the visual representation. The disjunction between objectively truthful representations and images which appear natural and truthful to the human eye is bridged by the informed judgement of the photographer-anthropologist.

In 1872, Fritsch published his magnum opus, *Die Eingeborenen Süd-Afrika's ethnographisch und anatomisch beschrieben* (The Natives of South Africa Ethnographically and Anatomically Described). Over 500 pages, the author gives accounts of South African tribes, each dealt with individually under three categories of: physical and religious development (outer appearance, the skeleton, capability (*Leistungsfähigkeit*)); dress, weapons, tools and dwellings; and mores and customs. These accounts are accompanied by a general chapter on indigenous languages. The text is illustrated with 77 engravings which, according to the title page, were 'executed in woodcut, mainly after original photographs and drawings by the author'. Of these, 11 are head and shoulder portraits, 16 show individual standing figures, 18 are group portraits, and the remainder are depictions of scenes, mainly of everyday activities (18) as well as of tools and landscapes (14). In an appendix, there are twenty lithographic plates illustrating parts of the skeleton (skull, pelvis, feet), colour samples, and of 'Bushman drawings', and tables giving measurements of skulls (28 samples), pelvises (16) and skeletons (7).

Alongside this volume, Fritsch published an *Atlas* which, in the words of the subtitle, contains '30 plates of racial types. Sixty portraits, taken from the front and from the side, etched in copper by Professor Hugo Bürckner after original photographs by the author.' The images in this volume are derived from photographs which come from the same series as those used for the portraits illustrating the main text. However, the serialised juxtaposition of *en face* and profile views in rectangular frames produces a distinctly different effect from the presentation of individual *en face* images placed straight on the page. The latter have captions giving the name and social position of the sitter, while the *Atlas* gives two pairs of images, one under the other on one page, with details underneath of the tribes to which the individuals belonged. In a table placed between the introduction to the *Atlas* and the illustrations themselves, Fritsch lists, in the order of the plates, the details of the individuals represented: name, tribe, approximate age, height, two anthropometric measurements (to facilitate the establishment of other exact measurements from the illustrations), the place where the photograph was taken, and notes, especially of sociological interest.

In his attempt to describe the population of southern Africa, Fritsch deploys both physical anthropological and ethnographic methods. While his main concern is to provide a cultural definition of the different tribes, he also seeks to describe their variations on a physical-racial level. The positive data in Fritsch's account are detailed descriptions of bodies and body parts. While these seem to remain on firm ground as long as trunk, arms and legs are concerned, Fritsch admits that the description of the face is more problematic. 'What remains now is the discussion of the facial formation, with regard to which, however, the examination of the added copper plates made after photographs will have to do most for providing understanding, as it is hardly possible to create, through a description, an accurate image of totally alien features for those who are unaccustomed to them. Each of us sees with different eyes and we lack a shared standard, while photography sufficiently counteracts this problem and provides an appropriate base for the scientific comparison of objects like those under consideration here.'[16]

The main obstacle to the precise description of faces is the absence of a shared physiognomical semiotic. Fritsch locates the problem at the point where the reader has to decode a given description. But, he adds, not only does the cognitive translation of verbal into mental images differ; seeing itself differs from one observer to the next. The merit of photography is that it sets a standard of visuality and thus provides a (graphic) base for scientific comparison. Photography's epistemological advantage lies precisely in its ability to abstract from natural vision, which seems incapable of pinning down the precise individual differences of features, a problem that is particularly pressing with representations of the human face. 'Nevertheless, it cannot be ignored that a certain equivalence is to be found even in wider areas through the comparison of the portraits, although it is often difficult to express them in words. However, in order not to lose oneself in vagueness completely and to be as positive as possible, it is necessary to stick to the individual tribe more strictly than has been done so far.'[17]

More than anything, this passage reveals Fritsch's sense of frustration about the inability to describe the observed physiognomies in a useful way. His own accounts of faces are vague and imprecise, and it is only when he turns to skulls that he can make detailed and self-assured statements about their structure, measurements and angles. In a methodological twist that is frequently encountered with the typological use of portraiture, the samples of faces from certain tribes are tautologically presented by Fritsch as the basis for distinguishing between the typical physiognomies of tribes. Like Francis Galton, who used selected rather similar images for his composite portraits, Fritsch extrapolates from selected individuals to define the types to which these individuals are assumed to belong.

The extraordinary typological significance of the head, and of the face in particular, for anthropological analysis is challenged by a special difficulty in representation: the positive data embodied in the individual head are neither easily extracted nor communicated. Photographic portraiture therefore poses a particular challenge to Fritsch. 'The impression of inadequacy which I got from studying even the best portraits of foreign peoples made after hand drawings was the original stimulus for me to produce ... models by using photography in order to reduce in a controlled way the draughtsman's tendency to resort to European forms.'[18] The tendency towards 'Europeanisation' appears to be, for Fritsch, an unavoidable feature of hand-drawn images: humans are inherently inaccurate and subjective representational machines, while photography provides superior, that is controllable, models once its inherent problems are overcome. The photographic production process is authorial in all its phases: Fritsch emphasises that he took all photographs himself on location, and asserts that the execution of the engravings for reproduction took place under his own oversight and guidance.[19] This effectively affirms not only the validity of the representations, but also the position of the photographer-anthropologist as a continuous subject across the planes of presentation.

Contemporary techniques for reproducing photographs were, Fritsch claims, not advanced enough to achieve satisfactory results from negatives. 'In addition, I have learnt through extended observation that it is not at all easy for everybody to see photographs correctly, as the dark areas brought about by specific local, especially yellow, colours appear to be shadows for many, and that some training is necessary to avoid such illusions. Yet the draughtsman who has accustomed himself to the "mode" [*Manier*] of photography finds in it a perfectly clear model from which to transpose the shapes into another, commonly understandable representational medium, and without difficulty he can adjust for the missing regularity in the sitter's attitude.'[20] The problem of reading images, which Fritsch referred to previously in the context of the primacy of visual evidence over verbal description of perceptions, is now deployed to maintain the greater objectivity – understood as legibility – of a skilfully executed engraving over the easily misread photograph.

Altogether, Fritsch introduces an impressive list of fault lines in his account of anthropological photography: the practical and technical problems of photographing and printing, the idiosyncratic reading of the photograph by the artist, the limitations of the engraving, the necessary changes made during transposition, the idiosyncratic reading of the printed illustration. Partly, these problems are bridged by the expertise acquired by the artist and, more importantly, by the guidance of the author-cum-anthropologist-cum-photographer, who is the crown witness of objectivity and whose expertise is the 'most adequate basis for scientific comparison'.[21]

Fritsch proposes a classification of photographic portraiture in which the visual field of anthropology is considered from the point of view of the purpose of representation. 'The method will differ according to whether one is concerned with the facial features or the body forms (physiognomical photographs), or whether one wants to fix the general impression of the persons, picture them in their way of life and occupation, their clothes, weapons and tools (ethnographic photographs).'[22]

The semantic relationship constructed between the photographer and the object of representation gives important hints about the status of the different subjects of the photographic process. In the first case, the relation is dual: the photographer confronts the physical formation. In ethnographic photography, there is a discursively conceived triad consisting of the photographer, the sitters, and their habits, clothes and tools. The image circumscribes the sitters by focusing on their 'spiritual', social and material surroundings. While physiognomic photographs are of the body, the ethnographic photography envisaged by Fritsch depicts culture. In neither case is portraiture construed in the sense of 'capturing the characteristic features of an individual', the notion that dominated European studio portraiture of the time.

The types of reception related to this classification are equally stratified and related to the representational means. 'It is impossible for images of the first category to be as picturesque and entertaining as those of the second, but for science they are of greatest use and have to be placed first in line here as only photography can provide them in a sufficient way, whereas for the second category the draughtsman will often do.'[23] Scientific accuracy is linked to physiognomic photography and opposed to the picturesque and entertaining tasks to which both graphic means and ethnographic photography can cater. The dichotomy is replicated in the doubling of scientific disciplines (physical anthropology; ethnography), of image types (photograph; drawing), and of receptive attitudes and effects (analysis; pleasure).

Fritsch gives detailed instructions about the way in which photographs should be taken, which predate Alphonse Bertillon's guidelines for anthropometrically useful portraiture by ten years, and rival their consistency: straight projection, *en face* and profile views, size of the lens, constant focus and distance, uncovered head and breast, light background. The resulting superiority of Fritsch's photographs when compared with those of his contemporaries can be seen from the plates of the *Anthropologisch-ethnologisches Album in Photographien*, which Carl Dammann published in Berlin in 1873–1874. Initiated by the Berlin Society for Anthropology, Ethnology and Prehistory, this album was intended to give a structured overview of the Society's photographic collection, and to present a classificatory tableau of the human races of the five continents. Dammann ordered hundreds of photographs according to their geographical region of origin, mostly in an unstructured mix of straight portraits, studio photographs, genre scenes and so on. There is a clear representational break in the section on Africa when, from the seventh (of ten) instalments onwards, Fritsch's systematic shots begin to dominate the plates. In comparison with the rest of the *Album*, these photographs are clearly the most visually structured attempt at producing a physical anthropological record. The images which in Fritsch's *Die Eingeborenen Süd-Afrika's* (1872) appear as woodcuts and engravings are here included as photographic prints.

In the instructions Fritsch provides for taking accurate portraits, hardly any reference is made to the corporeality of the sitters. The subjects of this photography are shapes that can be turned into measurements and thus become operational for statistical calculations. 'One should always choose straight projections, i.e. one should take each head as precisely as possible from the front and from the side in a natural attitude, while at the same time the camera is also placed horizontally and positioned at such a height from the ground that the prolongation of the optical axis of the lens runs approximately through the middle of the head.'[24] The parallel instruction for taking pictures of the full figure reads: 'The body should again possibly be uncovered, the posture straight and upright. Asymmetrical positioning of the body members should be avoided, as they bring far-reaching alterations in the individual parts of the body with them. As an exception, the placing of one hand on the breast with the arm bent at a right angle can be recommended, in order to represent clearly the relations of the fingers. One has then to make sure, however, that the arm is not held too tightly, that the nipples remain visible, and that the position of the shoulder is not altered. At least one arm has to remain in a natural hanging position.'[25] Here the body is conceived of as an ensemble of parts which have to be arranged in such a way as to provide a rational tableau: symmetrical posture, rectangularity of body members, an unaltered trunk structure. Greatest attention is paid to the mathematical legibility of the body so as to enable precise measurements to be made from the photographs.

Reference to the sitters as social personae is made only in the context of a plea for good technical equipment. 'In the case of physiognomic photographs (portraits as well as full figures), where the task is often to photograph individuals of little intelligence, or even resistant ones, brevity of time of exposure is one of the most important demands on the lens.'[26] In this account, the sitter appears as one of a series of obstacles. These include technical difficulties, unfavourable weather conditions, and the natural clumsiness of the natives. Fritsch claimed that apart from the skill needed to tackle technical problems, there were also the anxieties and fears of the subjects, some of whom 'fled the uncanny measuring instrument out of superstition'.[27] In fact, there is little actual ethnographic evidence for the frequently reiterated belief that non-European people resisted portrait photography for fear of putting their souls at risk. Although this may have been true at times, the trope is more interesting as a European projection about 'native people' than as an anthropological insight. David Freedberg[28] has suggested that the reaction might be rooted in general patterns of human cognition, rather than being culturally specific. For now, it seems best to treat it as a complex of animistic beliefs, fears and projections germane to the modern European history of cognition.

Whenever Africans resisted the request to bare their breasts, this was, in Fritsch's opinion, especially with chiefs and mission students, the result of pride in their 'by no means prepossessing rags'. Similarly, uncovering the head was resisted because of 'prejudice'. Considerable attention to local religious beliefs and a rather critical view of Christianity did not stop Fritsch from making such judgements. The derisory tone in some sections suggests that he was more or less willing to grant that such beliefs were 'religious' in nature, depending on the degree of empathy he felt for certain tribes: he found nobody as stubbornly superstitious as the Khoikhoi who would more often than others refuse to let him take their photographs. The evaluation of people as 'superstitious' and 'prejudiced' seems to suggest more the dissatisfaction of the photographer, than the dogmatism of the Christian ethnographer. As the photographic practice becomes prominent in the researcher's project, it also comes to influence his ethnographic judgement.

In Fritsch's contribution to the volume *Anleitung zu wissenschaftlichen Beobachtungen auf Reisen* (1875), the section on ethnological photography is considerably shorter than the one on anthropological photography and mainly gives a number of suggestions for recommended types of photographs: in addition to the face, Fritsch lists weapons and tools, dwellings, scenes of private and public life, transport and human activities. 'While the strict norms, the forced uniformity, in the mode of representation lend few attractive aspects to the works discussed above, ethnographic photographs leave more room for the artistic leanings of the photographer. That is why one can be sure to find a hundred of these images more easily than one of the other type; one must not forget, however, that the one may outweigh all hundred in its scientific value ... Ethnographic photographs have to be highly varied in character, which is why little can be said about them in general. Each picture belongs to this category, which is related to Man and his environment in so far as he has formed it through his own activity.'[29] The photographer, disciplined and restricted when taking physiognomic images, can turn himself into an artist and explore the variety of human creation when taking ethnographic photographs. Man, the creator of his environment, seems, however, to stand in an accessory relation to the costumes, the instruments, the architecture, even to his own preferred postures. 'One should try to achieve photographs which can complement the physiognomic ones. As in the latter the posture is predetermined and the body should be uncovered, the former have to represent the preferred attitude of the body and the dress of the people, in which case one has to notice how it changes for special occasions as festive decoration, for religious celebrations, as war equipment (warriors' body decoration), etc.'[30]

In the European art tradition, the notion of portraiture refers to the representation of individual character as expressed by physiognomy, pose, dress and accessories. Since the middle of the nineteenth century, the modern European individual – *homo photographicus* – has found expression in the photographic studio portrait. In contrast, the ethnographic portrait is seen as an anti-individualistic map of cultural and ethnic particularities; it articulates a culture or race, rather than individuals. In anthropometric portraits, this means of articulation is radicalised in terms of its abstraction from the visual information: the represented face is construed as a grid of measuring points which serves the computation, statistical analysis and virtual reconstitution of the body as a natural, historically relevant, racial structure. However, rather than indicating a subtraction of individual characteristics, the anthropometric example suggests that portraiture constitutes, in each case, a mapping process in which bodies and cultural formations are deterritorialised into characteristics, types, and series of identical units, which are reterritorialised on photographic images.

Fritsch's accounts of anthropological photography feature a variety of subjects involved in the process. The most prominent figure is the authorial photographer and scientist, who appears to determine the production as well as reproduction of the images. Decisions about the types of photographs to be taken are made partly on the basis of formal categories, which are ordered hierarchically according to their scientific value and their scarcity, and partly according to their aesthetic qualities. The status of the anthropologist-photographer is clearly different from that of a mechanically collecting traveller. Secondly, the draughtsmen and etchers compete with the photographer for producing the most characteristic representations of foreign people, or lend their skill to the reproduction of the superior photographs in order to make them accessible to a wider public, but they remain constantly subordinated to the photographic author. Finally, the subjects of Fritsch's portraits emerge as individuals in his discourse when they put up resistance to being photographed, or when their behaviour complicates the photographic process. Otherwise they are made part of the photographic scheme and dispersed into the grids of scientific analysis.

For anthropologists who engaged in photography, taking images of the head and face was regarded as both the most important and the most difficult task. The scientific significance and the semiotic complexity of portraits posed a particular challenge to the attempt to facialise the anthropological matrix. The process was conceived in strongly authorial terms, making the objectivity of the photographic document dependent on its legibility. This was guaranteed by the photographer-anthropologist, who engineered and supervised the production process of visual representations. His authorial position was not undermined or even called into question by reflections on constructive and cognitive processes which crucially challenged the authorial position in other fields and which, ultimately, highlighted the authorial position of the human scientist as being subject to the same forces that constituted the 'typical' sitters of scientific portraits. Rather than a one-dimensional relation between the observer, armed with the camera, and the observed, victim of the mechanised gaze, we should consider the scientific subject as a conditioned site of the constitution of knowledge and a guarantor of truth.

Among today's historians of photography and of anthropology there are divergent opinions about the status of photography within the scientific discipline of anthropology in the nineteenth century. Andrew Zimmerman argues for a strong visual focus among the Berlin and German anthropologists of this period.[31] Similarly, Elizabeth Edwards has emphasised the importance that photographic evidence had for anthropologists of the time.[32] My own impression is that in a broader perspective, photography was taken seriously only by a small number of scientists, and its effective use was in fact marginal. All seem to agree, however, that the role of photography was deemed much more significant in the 1860s and 1870s, than after 1880. This is also in accordance with the findings of a comparative study of the use of portrait photography in the human sciences in the nineteenth century.[33]

Nélia Dias confirms this observation in an essay on the role of photography in nineteenth-century French anthropology, which shows that the basic currents of the debates were similar in Germany, Britain and France.[34] Dias focuses on portrait photography and proposes two reasons for the decline of anthropological portraiture as a scientific tool after around 1880. She claims that portrait photography failed because it was first unable to provide convincing representations of ethnic *types*, and because, when the concepts of race and type themselves came under attack, the discipline was methodologically unable to take representations of individuals into account.

Christopher Pinney has described this phenomenon as part of what he calls the 'parallel histories of anthropology and photography'.[35] Explaining the gradual disappearance of photographs from anthropological monographs alongside the rise of ethnographic field research, Pinney writes: 'The anthropologist's exposure to data ... occurred during a period of inversion from his normal reality, a stage which is formally analogous to the photographic negative when the all-important rays of light which guarantee the indexical truth of the image are allowed to fall on the negative's emulsion ... Photography is thus revealed to be much less and much more important than we thought. The anthropologist has taken on to his own person the functions of a plate of glass, or strip of film which, having been prepared to receive and record messages in negative form during a moment of exposure in "the field", is able, after suitable processing, to present them in a "positive" state in the ethnographic monograph.'[36]

Through memorisation, the ethnographer becomes the collector and analyst, camera, plate and darkroom of anthropological knowledge. To the degree that the interior representational devices of field notes and the ethnographic narrative were gradually established as the prime source of anthropological truth, the superficial and precarious evidence offered by photography disappeared from this logocentric epistemological tableau.

ENDNOTES

1   P. Topinard, *Eléments d'anthropologie générale* (Paris: Delahaye and Lecrosnier, 1885), 215.
2   P. Topinard, *Anthropology*, translated by R.T. Hawley Bartley (London: Chapman and Hall, 1878), 204.
3   G. von Neumayer (ed.), *Anleitung zu wissenschaftlichen Beobachtungen auf Reisen* (Berlin: Oppenheim, 1875), 551.
4   G. Fritsch, *Die Eingeborenen Süd-Afrika's ethnographisch und anatomisch beschrieben, nebst einem Atlas* (Breslau: Ferdinand Hirt, 1872), IX–X.
5   Fritsch, *Atlas*, 22.
6   G. Fritsch, Untitled paper on the Lucae apparatus and photography, read in Berlin, 12 March 1870, *Zeitschrift für Ethnologie*, 2 (1870), 172–173.
7   Fritsch, Untitled paper on the Lucae apparatus and photography, 173.
8   Fritsch, Untitled paper on the Lucae apparatus and photography, 173.
9   Neumayer, *Anleitung*, 591–625.
10 Neumayer, *Anleitung*, 605.
11 Neumayer, *Anleitung*.
12 Neumayer, *Anleitung*, 606.
13 Fritsch, Untitled paper on the Lucae apparatus and photography, 174.
14 Fritsch, Untitled paper on the Lucae apparatus and photography.
15 Fritsch, Untitled paper on the Lucae apparatus and photography.
16 Fritsch, *Atlas*, 26.
17 Fritsch, *Atlas*, 27.
18 Fritsch, *Atlas*, 3.
19 Fritsch, *Atlas*, 5.
20 Fritsch, *Atlas*, 4–5.
21 Fritsch, *Atlas*, 26.
22 Neumayer, *Anleitung*, 606.
23 Neumayer, *Anleitung*, 607.
24 Neumayer, *Anleitung*, 607.
25 Neumayer, *Anleitung*, 609–610.
26 Neumayer, *Anleitung*, 611.
27 Fritsch, *Atlas*, 4.
28 David Freedberg, *The Power of Images: Studies in the History and Theory of Response* (Chicago: University of Chicago Press, 1989), 278–282.
29 Neumayer, *Anleitung*, 612.
30 Neumayer, *Anleitung*, 613.
31 Andrew Zimmerman, *Anthropology and Anti-Humanism in Imperial Germany* (Chicago: University of Chicago Press, 2001).
32 Elizabeth Edwards, *Anthropology and Photography, 1860–1920* (New Haven: Yale University Press, 1992).
33 A. Broeckmann, 'A visual economy of individuals' (PhD thesis, University of East Anglia, Norwich, 1995).
34 'Photographier et mesurer: les portraits anthropologiques', *Romantisme*, 84 (1994), 37–49.
35 C. Pinney, 'The parallel histories of anthropology and photography' in Edwards, *Anthropology and Photography, 1860–1920*, 82.
36 Pinney, 'The parallel histories of anthropology and photography'.

The racial theories and nude photography of Gustav Fritsch, 1870–1910

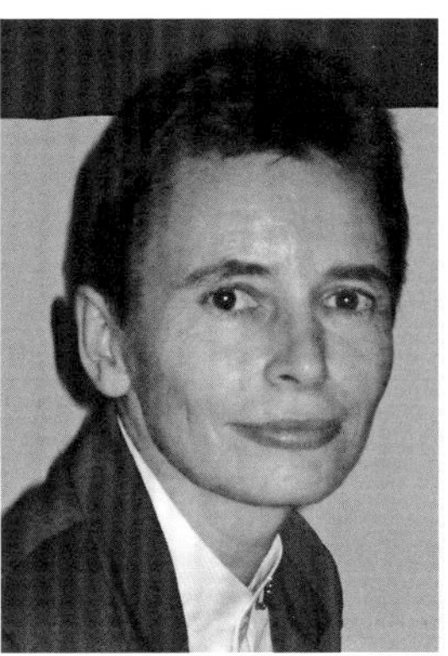

Annette Lewerentz

By the late nineteenth century physical anthropology had emerged as a field of study distinct from cultural anthropology in Wilhelmine Germany. While cultural anthropology explored the intellectual and cultural achievements of humans from diverse geographical regions and eras, physical anthropology examined the distinguishing physical characteristics of peoples classified as 'races'. Gustav Fritsch was among the leading practitioners of German physical anthropology from the mid-nineteenth to the early twentieth century. This essay traces Fritsch's changing ideas about the use of photography in anthropology, and focuses in particular on his use of nude photography in his later work. I will show how his emphasis shifted from the scientific to the aesthetic in his theories about the use of photography in anthropology. In the 1870s Fritsch, a great champion of photography as a tool for anthropologists, had insisted that the strictest scientific rules be followed in the taking of nude photographs, in particular of non-European 'races'. By the 1890s and 1900s, however, he came to lay greater emphasis on the aesthetic use of nude photography in anthropology, expressed in a language of ideal proportions and 'racial beauty', which applied as much to the German Self as to the non-European Other. In conclusion, I draw attention to the influence of these concepts and his advocacy of nude photography in anthropology on his contemporaries, notably the physician and fellow racial scientist Carl Heinrich Stratz (1858–1924).

The concept of racial classification was something Fritsch inherited from his Continental forebears. Like earlier scientists such as the French naturalist Georges Cuvier, Fritsch distinguished between three human types: what he termed the white, yellow and black 'races'.[1] Like his predecessors, too, he defined 'race' in terms of common physical characteristics, which were associated with levels of cultural and intellectual development. The underlying assumption was that the white 'race', especially the European, represented the highest stage of cultural and biological development while the lower stages of racial development were referred to by terms such as 'primitive', 'rudimentary' and 'progressive'.[2]

Technological advances in the late nineteenth and early twentieth centuries brought new possibilities for the use of visual evidence in anthropology. Traditional methods used in anthropological studies, such as drawings, statistical tables and texts, were complemented, or rather superseded, by photographs as sources of anthropological data. As earlier essays in this volume have emphasised, Fritsch gave a particularly prominent role to the use of photography in the emerging discipline of anthropology. At his first public address on the subject, at a March 1870 meeting of the Berlin Society for Anthropology, Ethnology and Prehistory, Fritsch insisted that 'progress in anthropology comes to a great degree from improving methods of documentation'.[3] Over the following decades he came to use numerous types of photographs in his anthropological work: from travel illustration, landscape and portrait photography,[4] he turned to micro-photography,[5] and then increasingly to nude photography. At first he insisted on the 'objective nature' of anthropological photographs. In his 1870 address Fritsch suggested that photographs were superior to drawings as a form of scientific evidence. He argued that drawings were 'subjective' in that a drawing showed an object as the eye of the draughtsman would see it. The pencil stroke depended on the artist's talent and, as such, offered a personal interpretation. The anthropological photograph, by contrast, could provide a direct and exact representation and was therefore objective.[6] In this sense, it was also superior to written descriptions.[7]

Fritsch's positivist claims for the objectivity of photography stand in direct contrast with the claims and concerns of the non-figurative art movements of the time. At the beginning of the twentieth century, ideas about objectivity in visual imagery were under considerable revision in modern art movements from Jugendstil and Expressionism to Symbolism and Cubism. It was, indeed, the art of 'primitive socie-

Dr. Annette Lewerentz studied classical archaeology, art history and prehistoric archaeology at the universities of Kiel and Heidelberg, and obtained her doctoral degree from the University of Heidelberg. Since 2002 she has worked in the Department of Research at the Free University of Berlin. Her current research interests are in the areas of cultural history and the history of science in the nineteenth and twentieth centuries.

ties' that had provided much of the impetus for these challenges to objectivity made by contemporary European artists like Emil Nolde, Paul Gaugin and Max Pechstein.[8]

In an essay published in 1875 Fritsch elaborated on his understanding of the 'objectivity' of anthropological photography by outlining a set of 'scientific' rules for prospective scientific travellers to follow.[9] For Fritsch, standardising the photographic process would assist in the measurement of human proportions and the creation of a database for the comparison of human 'types'. He claimed that photography alone could provide the necessary 'scientific' evidence for anthropologists. Fritsch tried to follow these rules on his travels, including his three-year-long journey through southern Africa between 1863 and 1865. But his portraits of the people he encountered there show other concerns and approaches. For example, he photographed indigenous people with their cultural accessories or dressed in European clothes (see Fig. 80),[10] which ignored his own set of rules about the way people should be presented for purposes of measurement and comparison. On the basis of this material, Fritsch wanted to document and elucidate biological variables and determine how far these could be traced back to racial influences. Consequently he began to call, with increasing urgency, for the systematic collection of a database of photographs of naked people as a means of grounding anthropological studies. 'I must at the same time, though, not suppress the urgent admonition to all who have the opportunity not to neglect to make every effort to contribute to the collection of extensive photographic material of nude figures from all over the world as long as the opportunity presents itself to collect racial characteristics, which are stable to a degree.'[11]

By the 1890s and 1900s nude photography had come to dominate Fritsch's photographic work. His own nude photographs can be divided into two categories: those of Europeans and those of non-Europeans. Different photographic forms were employed for these two groups. In photographing non-Europeans, he followed the set of rules he had first advocated in his 1875 essay by portraying the naked body in a standardised form (Fig. 272). His portraits of non-European cultures were intended to illustrate their 'otherness' and to classify them into diverse 'races'. Fritsch's nude photographs of Europeans, on the other hand, were used to illustrate the development of what he came to term 'the ideal body'. These portraits belong to the genre of 'nude studies' and, as I argue below, followed the conventions of art rather than of science.

In his 1893 study, *Die Gestalt des Menschen* (The Human Form), Fritsch defined 'the ideal white body' (Fig. 273) with the help of a theory of proportions derived from antique sculpture and first enunciated by Polyclitus, the Greek sculptor of the classical period (Fig. 274).[12] On this basis, Fritsch developed what he termed a 'canon of proportions' (Figs. 275 and 276),[13] which he then deployed as a yardstick to compare the anatomical proportions of different racial groups. This canon of proportions was used to illustrate Fritsch's theory that 'the white race' came closest to the anatomical 'ideal' in its bodily proportions (Figs. 277, 278, 279 and 280).[14] While measurement was the standard method for racial research at the time, indeed a method Fritsch himself had used during earlier fieldwork expeditions in southern Africa and Egypt, he advocated this more abstract 'proportional canon' as the most 'scientific' instrument for biological race classification. Fritsch believed that anthropometry had become 'swamped with numbers' and claimed that photographs when viewed in terms of his canon of proportions were the most useful means of examining racial difference.[15]

Fritsch constructed what he described as a 'norm' for the human body – and he explicitly used the term 'normal' in the captions to many of his photographs of the 'European body'.[16] Soft and delicate compositions of women (Fig. 281) and forcefully staged compositions of male bodies (Figs. 282 and 283) expressed the balance of anatomical proportions that he saw as the aesthetic ideal. Fritsch's choice of

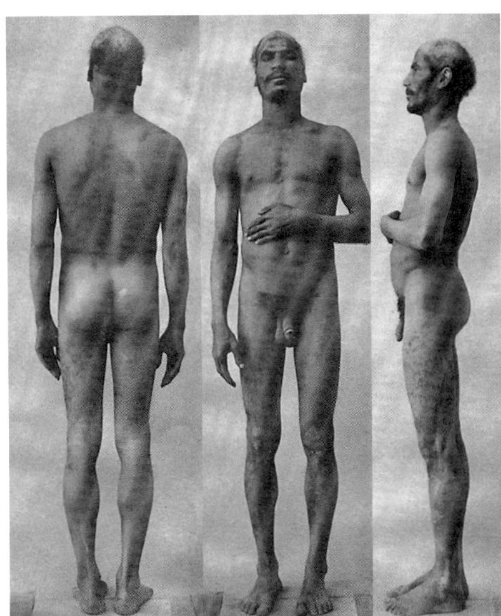

▲ *Fig. 272*

Egyptian from Cairo. Photo G. Fritsch. (BGAEU/218)

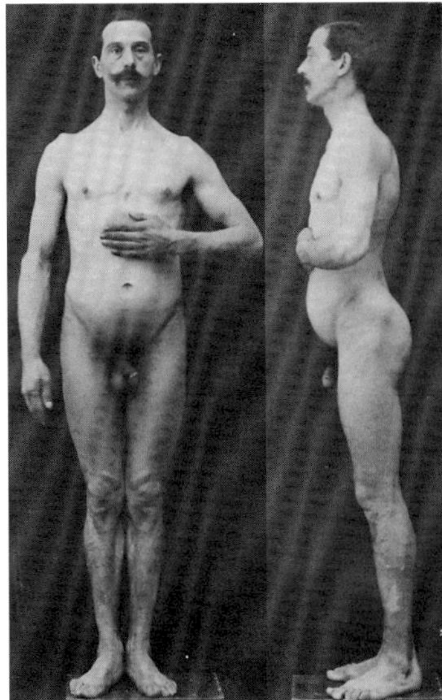

▲ *Fig. 273*

Gym teacher from Hanover. Photo G. Fritsch. (BGAEU/354)

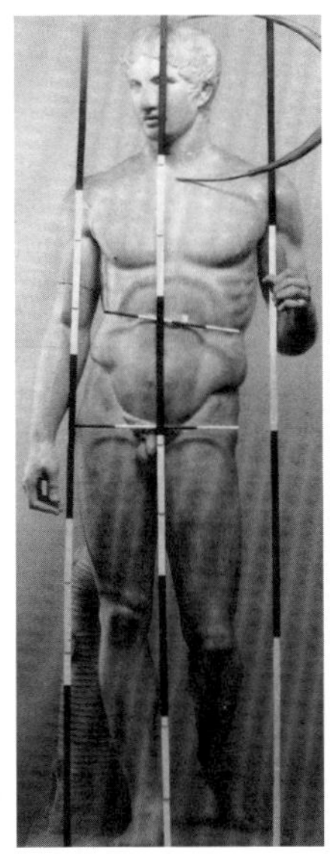

▲ *Fig. 274*

Statue by Polyclitus, with yardstick and dividers. (MVFB 13762/13)

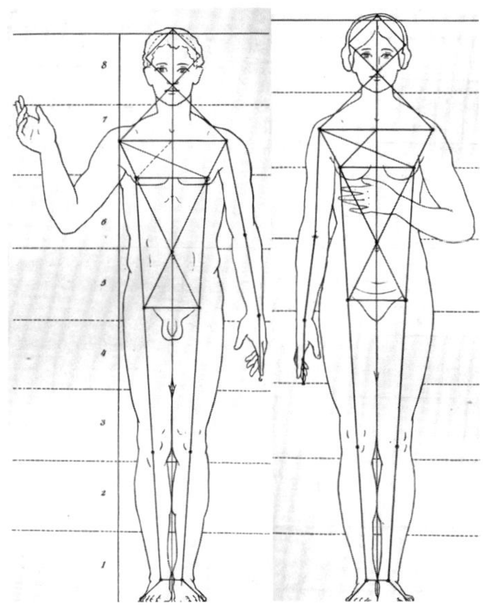

▲ *Figs. 275 and 276*

Canon of male proportions by G. Fritsch. (*Stratz, Naturgeschichte des Menschen,* 200, Figs. 152 & 153)

subjects to be photographed was highly selective. For the ideal male body, he chose German athletes who, by the very nature of their invigorating activities, came closest to his ideal. For Fritsch, these (male) forms embodied 'the standard-ideal human being, just the same as a civilised being has reached a certain maximal degree of perfection ... The human being is the outcome of a natural aptitude under the influence of culture which appeared in the region of a race we ... would like to call Aryan in countries around the Mediterranean.'[17]

This anatomical standard, defined by an ideal canon of proportions, was then applied to non-European 'races', whom Fritsch found to be biologically deficient. 'Incidentally, it should be mentioned here that the body posture of darkly coloured Africans, for instance, often undeservedly praised, contravenes the aesthetic requirements because of the rib cage … rather abruptly falling away.'[18] Fritsch used further examples to illustrate what he considered to be the anatomical deficiencies of non-European bodies – of those he called 'wild tribes', who stood in contrast to 'normal civilised man'.[19] He argued that such defects were evident in the 'unbalanced' body proportions in the sculptures of non-European peoples, which provided evidence of disproportionately elongated limbs (Fig. 284).[20]

Fritsch's nude photographs of the Akka, taken in 1893,[21] are prominent examples of his use of photography to illustrate anatomical

difference. In German physical anthropology at the time, the Akka, a group often described by contemporaries as a 'pygmy race', were a recurrent object of interest. Fritsch was asked by the Berlin Society for Anthropology, Ethnology and Prehistory to photograph two Akka girls who were visiting Berlin (Fig. 285).[22] He later used these photographs in his published work, comparing the bodily proportions of the Akka with the ideal model that he had developed to represent the 'normal' European body. This comparison highlighted the 'large heads and small stature' of the Akka, something they were seen to share with the Khoikhoi of southern Africa.[23] The Akka and the Khoikhoi, Fritsch argued, were among the lowest peoples in the hierarchy of human races, lumped together under the category 'dwarf negroes' and dismissed as having a 'stunted human form'.[24] Likewise, Australian Aboriginals and Papuans were also regarded as occupying a particularly low status on the racial hierarchy 'on account of the accumulation of primitive characteristics' (Fig. 286).[25] In these cases, too, Fritsch used his canon of proportions as the benchmark for racial ranking, and nude photographs as his main form of visual evidence.[26]

Another subject of interest in Fritsch's racial studies was the so-called 'borderline areas' brought about through cultural exchange and migration, where white and black 'races' mixed with each other and developed racial hybrids.[27] The Egyptians were one prominent example

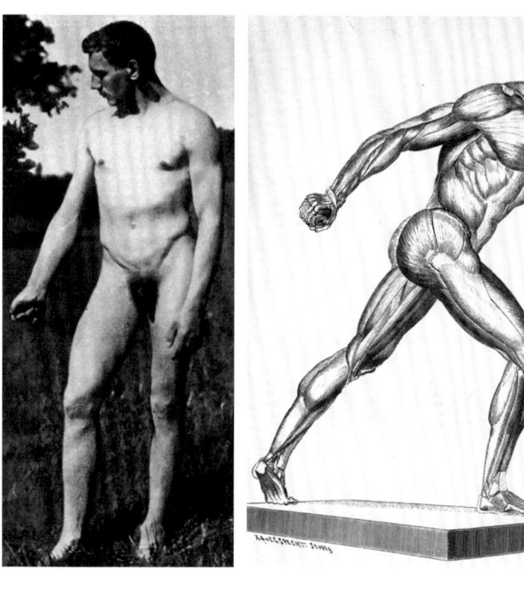

▲ *Fig. 277*

Young man with 'antique' pelvic cross-section. (Stratz, *Die Darstellung*, 71, Fig. 51)

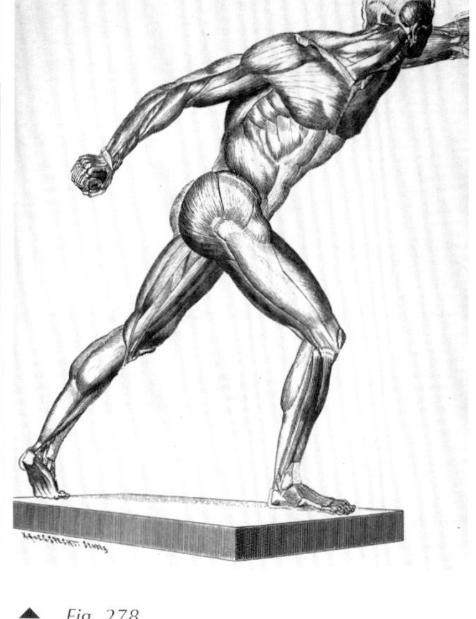

▲ *Fig. 278*

Drawing with indications of muscles of the so-called Borghese fencer. (Fritsch, *Die Gestalt des Menschen*, Plate VIII)

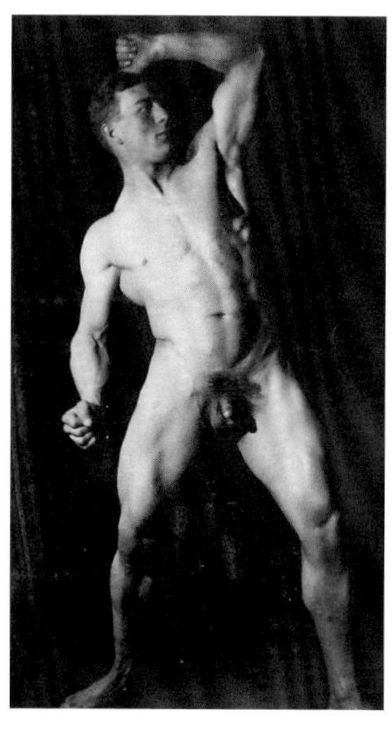

▲ *Fig. 279*

Lionel Strongfort, artist as pugilist. Photo G. Fritsch. (Gustav Fritsch album, BGAEU/358)

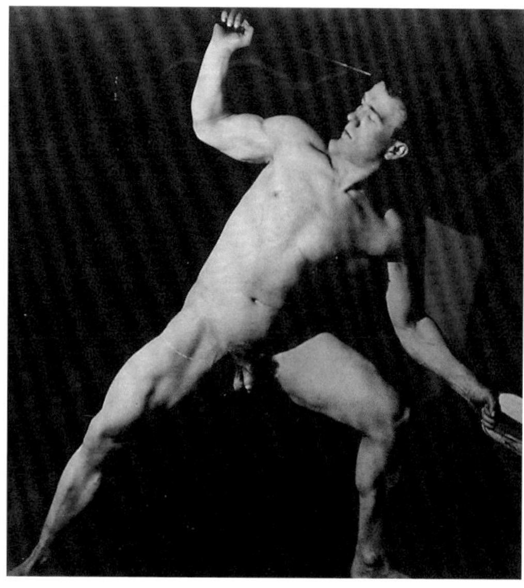

▲ *Fig. 280*

Lionel Strongfort, artist as Theseus in the Battle of the Amazons. Photo G. Fritsch. (Gustav Fritsch album, BGAEU/357)

of a hybrid race and culture that attracted Fritsch's interest. In 1898 and 1899 Fritsch visited Egypt. The visual evidence he accumulated on his travels, notably his collection of full-body nude photographs of different 'races' in the region, he used in his 1904 study, *Ägyptische Volkstypen der Jetztzeit. Nach anthropologischen Grundsätzen aufgenommene Aktstudien*. In this book Fritsch argued that North Africans, and especially Egyptians, embodied a proportional balance that came close to that of the 'white race'.[28] Though he nowhere defined it, Fritsch also saw culture as a prerequisite for a high level of biological development. The Egyptians, as descendants of an early advanced civilisation, were well qualified for attaining this level, even though their ethnic type was difficult to establish on account of their history of racial mixing.[29] As evidence, portraits of Egyptians were compared with ancient Egyptian sphinx heads.[30] Using the close physiognomic proximity that he saw between indigenous North Africans and Egyptian sculpture, Fritsch argued that there was a constancy of 'racial type' over a long period and presented photographs of fellahin, Nubians, Bedouins and Egyptians as characteristic examples of the Egyptian *volkstypen* (Figs. 272, 287, 288, 289 and 290).

In this 1904 study he also made extensive use of sculpture as illustrative material in the service of anthropology, arguing that 'the colourful melange of peoples of North Africa, especially Egypt, has inspired artists to portray the most interesting characters they could observe there; polychrome figures executed in various techniques best befitting the model, are examples of it; the "painters of the Orient" enliven our exhibition halls and galleries with magnificent works which also in respect of the human figure lay claim to being true to nature.'[31] For Fritsch, the sculptures of ancient civilisations, such as Egyptian, Assyrian or Greek, provided an historical basis for physiognomic studies. From these sculptures Fritsch deduced that certain racial characteristics and physiognomic features had been passed down through the generations. Even though he acknowledged that the idealisation of pictorial representation in classical Greek sculpture rendered them problematic in anthropology, he claimed that Egyptian and Assyrian sculptures had a greater physiognomic likeness to the indigenous people of those regions – almost having the character of portraits – and were therefore useful as anthropological evidence.[32]

As the significance of Fritsch's nude studies[33] within the context of anthropology lay at the border between science and art, we need to examine the theories he developed from his nude photographs for the evaluation of races. The majority of Fritsch's own nude photographs, as well as those he acquired from other sources, do not meet the necessary standards as anthropological images (see Figs. 238, 239 and 242). He was constantly concerned to highlight the anatomical

155

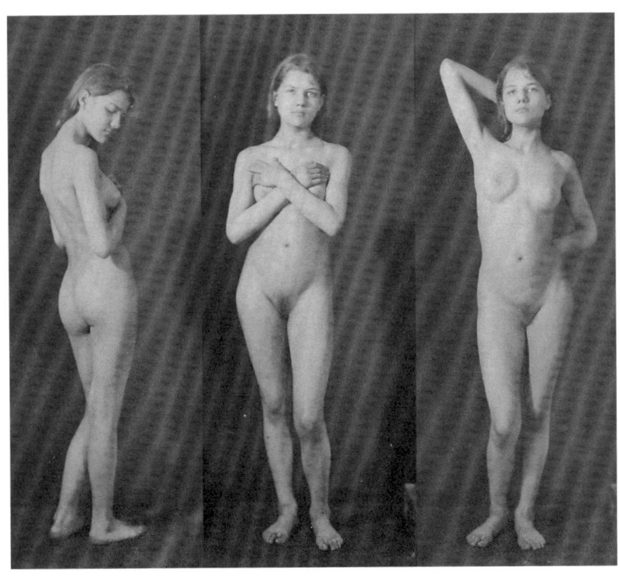

Berlin woman. Photo G. Fritsch. (Gustav Fritsch album, BGAEU/374)

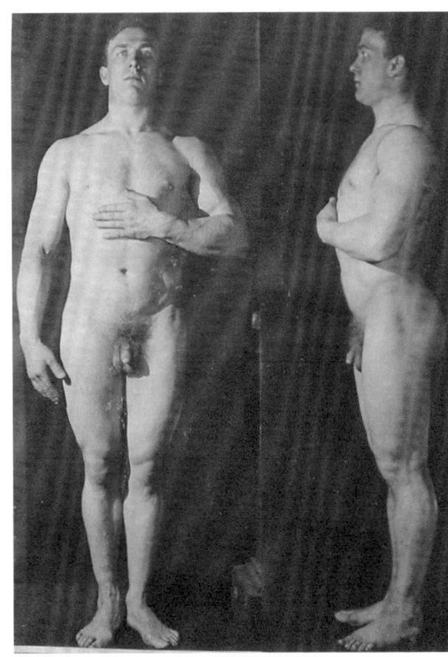

Artist from Berlin. Photo G. Fritsch. (Gustav Fritsch album, BGAEU/347)

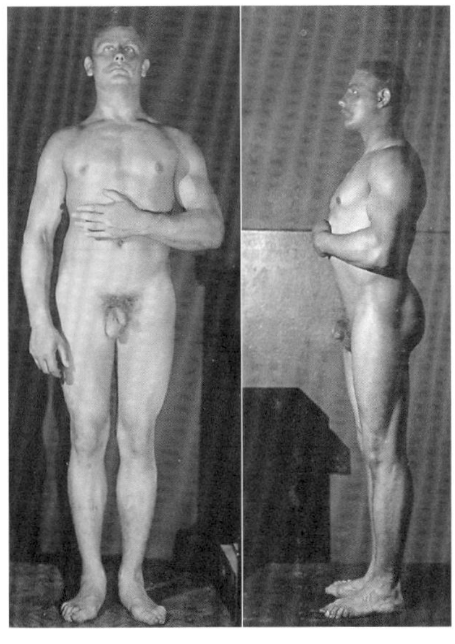

Professional wrestler from Berlin. Photo G. Fritsch. (Gustav Fritsch album, BGAEU/347)

deficiencies of particular ethnic groups, so that he could draw inferences about the stage of their biological development. Furthermore, his nude studies were posed in artificially constructed environments. Popular themes included East Asian 'bathhouse scenes',[34] especially in those photographs depicting Japanese women.

The artistic dimension of nude studies was important to Fritsch, serving both anthropological research and art. He insisted that photographers and artists should acquire in-depth anatomical knowledge in order to portray the body in its correct compositional form.[35] Photographic techniques had to be used to 'mould the body' optically. For Fritsch, physiognomic features carried both scientific and artistic connotations. This distinguished him from most of the anthropologists of his time who worked with photographs. In his view, slender bodies were appropriate to show a perfect anatomy,[36] and in this respect he followed the ideal proportions of antique sculpture, especially for the male body.[37]

In his later writings, notably his study *Nackte Schönheit* (Naked Beauty), Fritsch came to attach particular importance to the concept of 'beauty', which he defined as the degree of biological perfection of an ethnic group as measured by its anatomical defects or merits. Along with his theory of proportions, the concept of 'beauty' became an additional criterion for racial evaluation. A healthy physiology and an ideal anatomy were prerequisites for 'beauty'. It was not the anthropologically standardised photograph that was needed to illustrate 'beauty', but the artistic nude study. Like his canon of proportions, this concept was deeply Eurocentric, once again drawing on classical Greek forms. In order to illustrate imperfections or near-perfect bodies, and to formulate racial classifications, Fritsch compared nude photographs of different ethnic groups with classical Greek sculpture, which he felt best represented an ideal physical beauty (Fig. 292). Statues of male athletes, for example, expressed vitality and health, while images of Aphrodite reflected the harmony of female forms. These, in his view, constituted models for the visual arts, nude photography and the ideal body.[38] Nude photographs of the 'white race', with its high level of cultural development, approximated the idealised body of antique sculptures and his own canon of proportions. While the European 'race' represented the 'standard type' (Fig. 293), the 'black races' with their disproportional and deficient anatomies expressed a lower stage of physical development.

For Fritsch, it was only the Europeans who, since antiquity, had reached an almost perfect stage of physical development and cultural progression.[39] In respect of both the body and art, Europeans constituted the norm as opposed to non-Europeans. Outside Europe, only Egyptian sculptures exhibited a similar level of development and could be seen

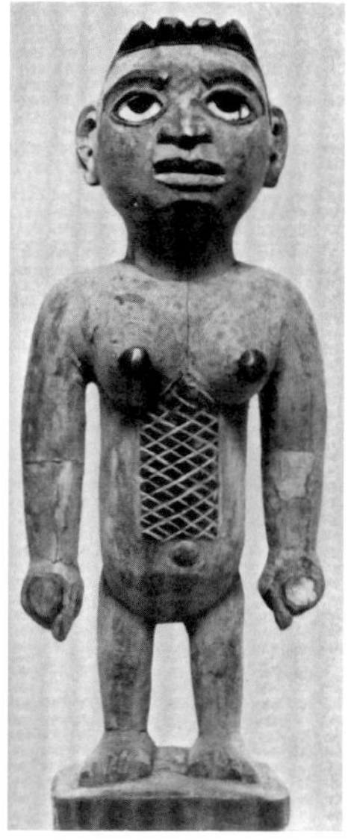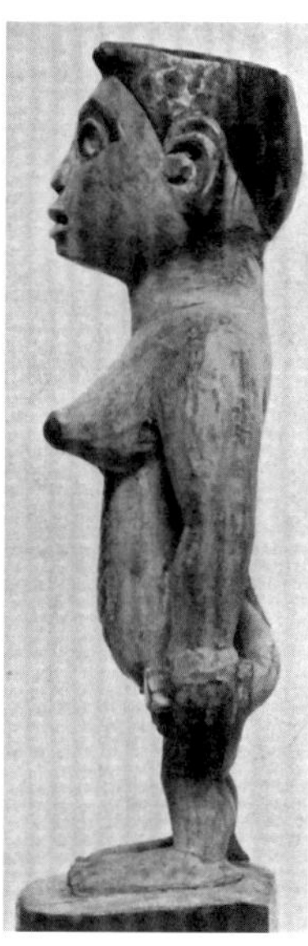

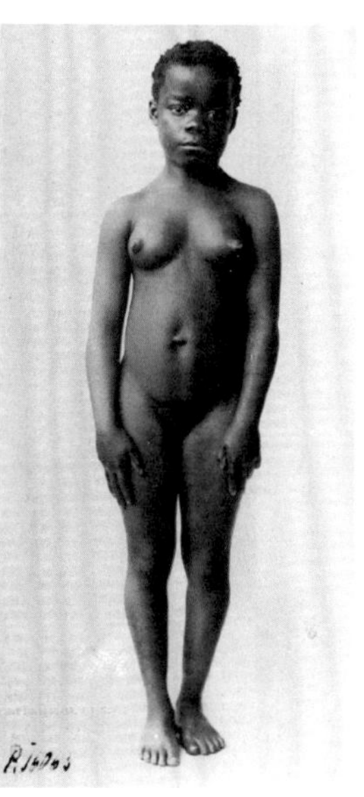

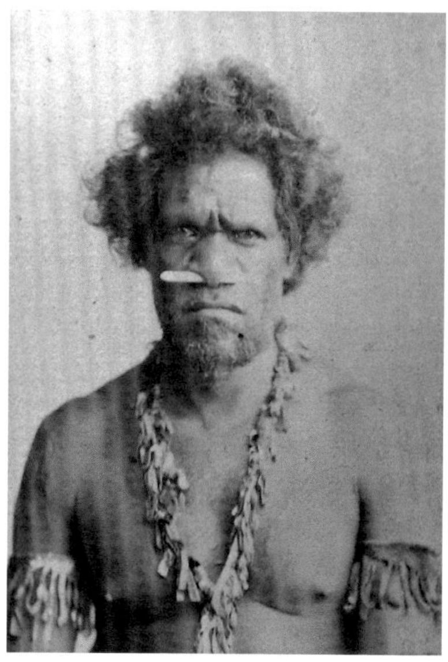

▲ *Fig. 284*

Female fetish from western Africa. Ethnographical Museum, Leiden. (Stratz, *Die Darstellung*, 39, Figs. 24a, 24b)

▲ *Fig. 285*

Akka girl, 1893. Photo G. Fritsch. (BGAEU/P 16063; EM-SMB/24)

▲ *Fig. 286*

Australian from north-east Australia. Photo Carl Günther. (Gustav Fritsch album, BGAEU/314)

as records of an early high culture. Physical and artistic characteristics were therefore mutually dependent, and human beings in advanced civilisations possessed a high degree of 'racial beauty'.

By the early 1900s, Fritsch had begun to define 'races', not by means of standardised photographs or proportional figures, but through the use of artistic nude studies. This clearly ran counter to the kind of objectivity that he had claimed for anthropological photography in his earlier writings. Proportions and the art of antique high cultures defined in Fritsch's theories the developmental stage and 'beauty' of a race. The body closest to nature was thought to be 'beautiful'.[40] 'Regularity', according to Fritsch, 'would become beautiful and the beautiful regular.'[41] Nude studies of Europeans revealed their anatomical beauty and embodied the norm of what was regarded as 'beautiful'. Non-European 'races', by contrast, lacked this natural regularity, and their beauty was consequently questioned.

The different portrayals of the unclothed body in Fritsch's photographs, anthropologically evaluated and artistically positioned as nude studies, document a change in anthropological images and a new development in German society of the day.[42] In *Nackte Schönheit*, Fritsch commented on contemporary attitudes towards nakedness and tried to counter moral objections to nudity.[43] In his book Fritsch used photographs of naked men, women and children, both

as groups and as individuals, taken predominantly in nature. Some of the compositions are inspired by themes from antiquity, such as depictions of Venus or Prometheus chained to a rock. Others show nude male figures involved in sport, or female and male nudes in staged environments (Figs. 292 and 295). An iconographic distinction is made between a male and a female nude. Whereas the male studies embody the athletic and energetic, the female studies express delicateness and softness. These images mirror the notions of male and female prevalent at the time.

In the captions to the photographs in *Nackte Schönheit*, Fritsch analyses the technical and compositional elements of the photographs. Men have athletic, muscular bodies while women are chosen for their youthful forms. In both instances the healthy young body expressing male vigour or female grace served as the criterion for selection. As well as providing scientific interest, enabling Fritsch to comment on anatomical defects, the photographs were intended to be seen as works of art. In them Fritsch attempted to bring art and science together without explicitly naming the anthropological aspect.

In *Nackte Schönheit* there is a noticeable discrepancy between text and image. The descriptive text hardly ever refers to the photographs; only the captions describe the pictures, showing that Fritsch had come to attribute a significantly higher value to image than to

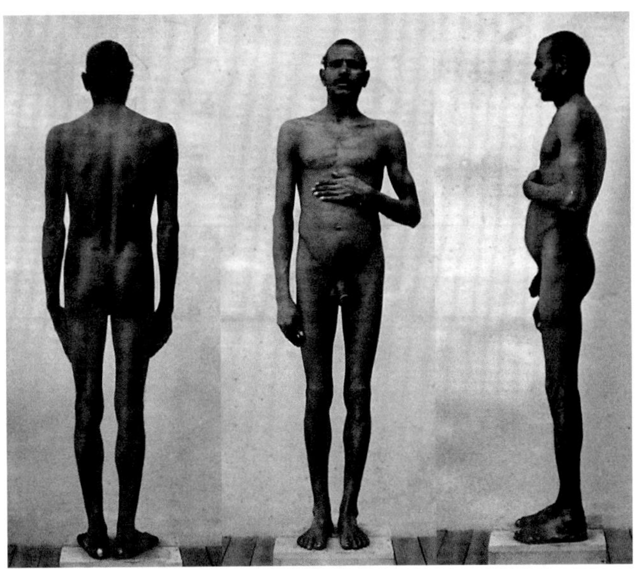

Fig. 287

Fellah from Cairo. Photo G. Fritsch. (Gustav Fritsch album, BGAEU/217)

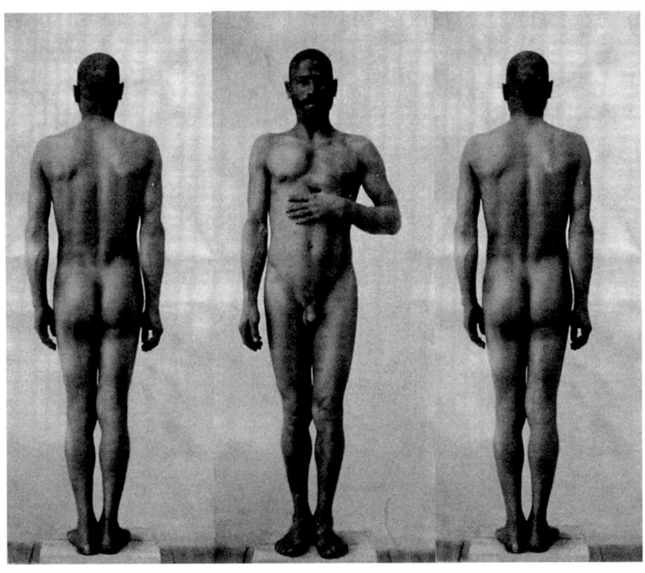

Fig. 288

Fellah from Cairo. Photo G. Fritsch. (Gustav Fritsch album, BGAEU/221)

text. At the same time the book provides evidence of a new spirit of the time and society. Around 1900 a changed attitude towards the body and its public presentation had developed in Germany. The object was to keep the body healthy and free from the prudish bourgeois constraints of the nineteenth century, to remove restrictive clothing, and to expose the body to nature. This change can be seen in the emergence of various movements at the beginning of the twentieth century, such as nudism, the *Lebensreform* ('life reform' or 'back to nature') movement, and vegetarianism,[44] which strove to create a 'New Man' as the foundation for a reformed society. Nude photography reflected these developments through its staging of the body, as an idealised form, in nature.[45] In his own photography and writing, Fritsch demonstrated his closeness to the ideas animating the *Lebensreform* movement, which he saw as expressing the 'progress of the new time'.[46]

Fritsch was not alone in his approval of nude studies and use of nude photography to support racial theories. The physician and gynaecologist Carl Heinrich Stratz (1858–1924) sought to demonstrate that barely clad ethnic groups could produce anatomically better sculptures because of their visually alive 'models' than could clothed or tattooed ethnic groups.[47] The Greeks, for example, could form their sculptures naturally because they had naked athletes in gymnasiums as live models for anatomical studies.[48] Stratz drew heavily on Fritsch's racial theories, his model of ideal proportions and even the racial application of his more abstract concept of 'beauty'. In his 1922 study, *Naturgeschichte des Menschen* (Natural History of Man), he adopted the proportional model that Fritsch had set out in *Die Gestalt des Menschen* and argued that 'the body proportions of the Europeans, which are judged as normal, coincide exactly with Fritsch's scheme of measurements'.[49] Following Fritsch's model, Stratz viewed Europeans as representatives of the highest level of human development, while those cultural groups with the least exchange with other cultures, both physically and culturally, represented the lowest stages of development.[50] On the evidence of photographs of these 'lower races' – Africans, Australians and Asians – Stratz found them 'unbalanced' when set against the Fritsch's proportional ideal.[51] Stratz wrote: 'The works of Fritsch ... come closest to the ideal aimed at in modern anthropological documentation.'[52]

Stratz also adopted Fritsch's concept of 'racial beauty'. His central criterion for the evaluation of beauty and the developmental stage of a 'race' derived from Fritsch's canon of physical body proportions. On the basis of such proportional comparisons, he ranked white, African, Australian and Asiatic 'races' on a scale from high to low. In this table, the biological stage of development of an Akka female

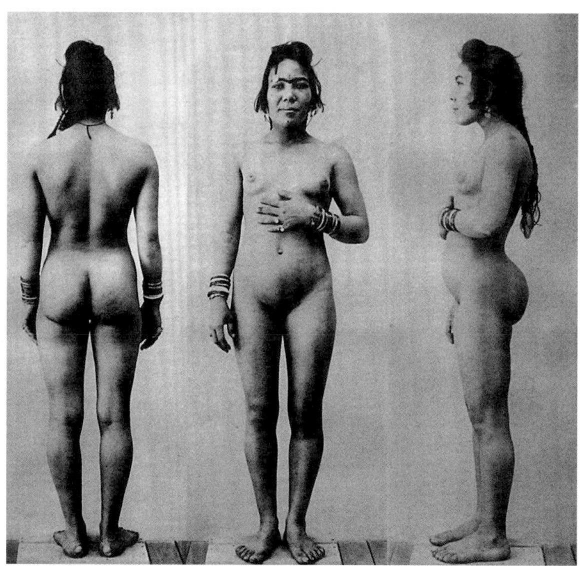

▲ *Fig. 289*

Female fellah from Cairo. Photo G. Fritsch. (Gustav Fritsch album, BGAEU/228)

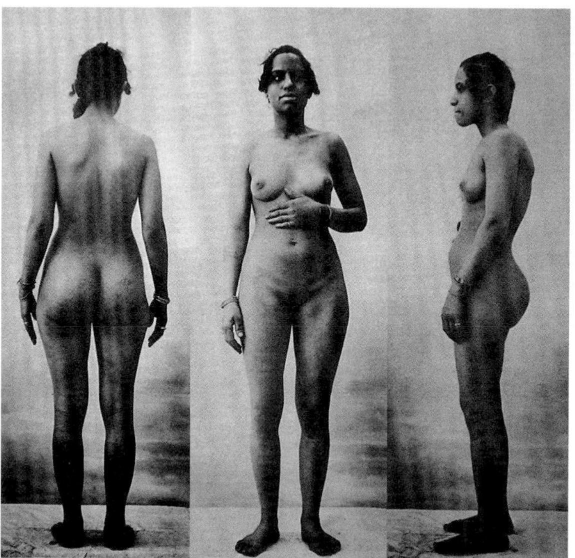

▲ *Fig. 290*

Egyptian woman from Alexandria. Photo G. Fritsch. (Gustav Fritsch album, BGAEU/232)

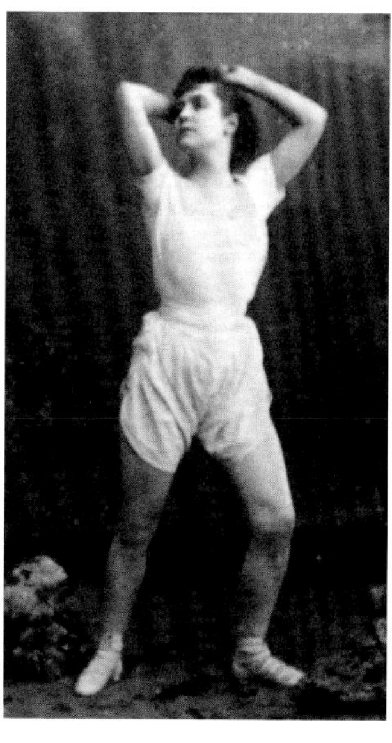

▲ *Fig. 291*

American female artist. Photographer unknown. (Gustav Fritsch album, BGAEU/345)

in respect of bodily proportions and height was equated with that of a six-year-old European girl, while the developmental stage of a Japanese woman (Fig. 294) was on a par with that of a twelve-year-old European girl.[53] Stratz made extensive use of nude photographs (primarily of women) to illustrate his theories, many of which were taken from Fritsch's own collections.[54]

The photographic depiction of naked bodies in Wilhelmine Germany heralded a new attitude towards the body. Fritsch saw nude photography, as well as the photograph itself, as art and at the same time as a medium of science. It could be used for the comparative study of cultural groups in which evaluations might be made for a history of civilisation and evolution. Fritsch's anthropological methods and associated classifications of humans were adopted by many others in anthropology at the time.

ENDNOTES

1   G. Fritsch, *Geographie und Anthropologie als Bundesgenossen* (1881); G. Fritsch, 'Ueber die Anwendung des von G. Fritsch veröffentlichten Messungsschema in der Anthropologie', *Zeitschrift für Ethnologie*, 34 (1902), 36–37; G. Fritsch, 'Die Entwicklung und Verbreitung der Menschenrassen', *Zeitschrift für Ethnologie*, 42 (1910), 580–586.

2   C.H. Stratz, *Naturgeschichte des Menschen. Grundriss der somatischen Anthropologie*, 3rd edn (Stuttgart, 1922), 207–252; Fritsch, 'Die Entwicklung und Verbreitung der Menschenrassen'.

3   G. Fritsch, 'Verhandlung der Berliner Gesellschaft für Anthropologie, Ethnologie und Urgeschichte', *Zeitschrift für Ethnologie*, 2 (1870), 172.

4   Gustav Fritsch in a letter from Cape Town to his mother dated 1 February 1865 (private collection, Maria Schwabe).

5   Fritsch used microphotography of human hair for the differentiation between races: G. Fritsch, 'Neuere Beobachtungen zum Studium der Rasseneigentümlichkeiten des menschlichen Haupthaares', *Zeitschrift für Ethnologie*, 47 (1915), 232–233; G. Fritsch, 'Buschmannhaar im Gegensatz zu gestapelten Spirallocken', *Zeitschrift für Ethnologie*, 48 (1916), 1–7; G. Fritsch, 'Die Anthropoiden und die Abstammung der Menschen', *Zeitschrift für Ethnologie*, 50 (1918), 1–11; G. Fritsch, 'Verwertungen von Rassenmerkmalen für allgemeine Vergleichungen', *Zeitschrift für Ethnologie*, 43 (1911), 274–277; see also M. Hagner, 'Mikro-Anthropologie und Fotografie. Gustav Fritschs Haarspaltereien und die Klassifizierung der Rassen' in P. Geimer (ed.), *Ordnungen der Sichtbarkeit. Fotografie in Wissenschaft, Kunst und Technologie* (Frankfurt am Main, 2002), 267–268; L. Jankau, 'Die Photographie im Dienste der Medizin' in L. Jankau (ed.), *Internationale medizinisch-photographische Monatsschrift*, vol. 1 (Berlin, 1894), 2.

6   G. Fritsch, *Die Eingeborenen Süd-Afrika's. Atlas enthaltend dreissig Tafeln Racentypen* (Breslau, 1872), 3, on the advantages of photography versus drawings. Fritsch wrote to his mother from Bloemfontein on 29 April 1864: 'I have always had a great preference for photographs, and even though they are unpretentious, they are nevertheless reliable and 'true to nature.' (Private collection, Maria Schwabe)

7   G. Fritsch, 'Sonst und Jetzt der menschlichen Rassenkunde vom morpho-

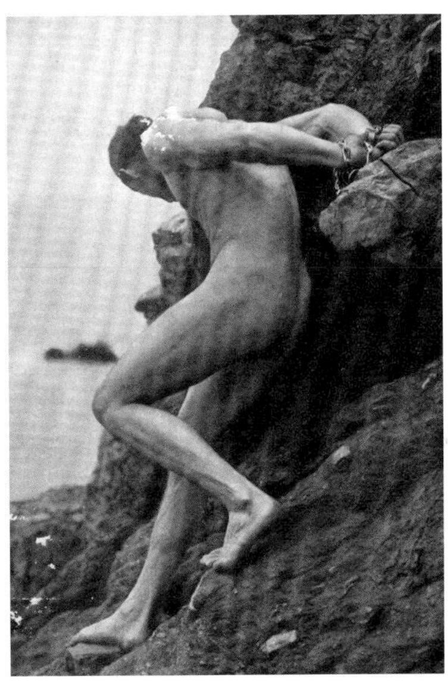

▲ *Fig. 292*

Prometheus, chained to a rock. Photo E. Schneider. (G. Fritsch, *Nackte Schönheit*, 10)

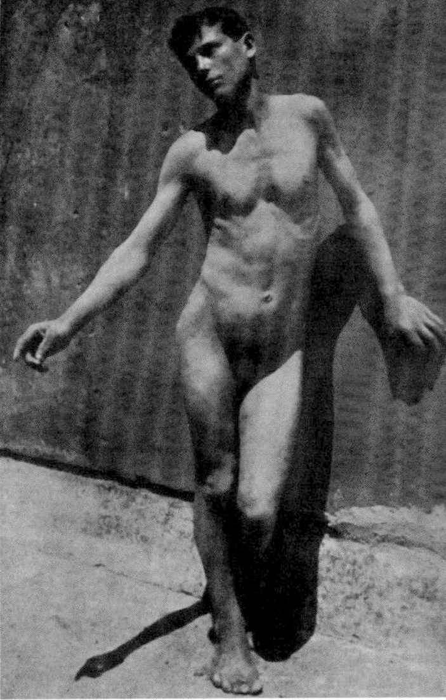

▲ *Fig. 293*

'Normal' male body, Italian. Photo by Plüschow. (Stratz, *Naturgeschichte des Menschen*, 172, Fig. 121)

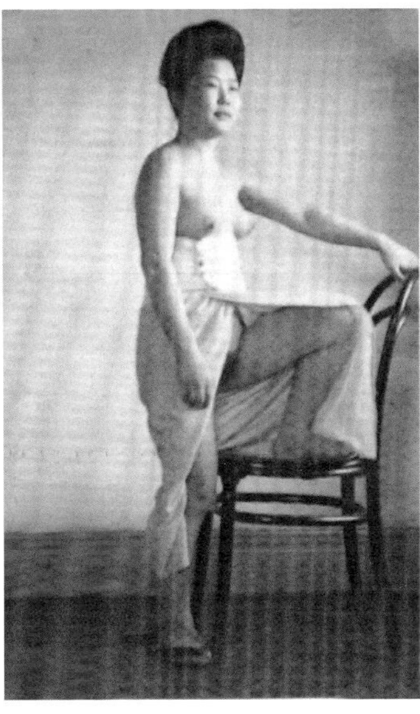

▲ *Fig. 294*

Japanese girl. Photographer unknown. (Gustav Fritsch album, BGAEU/345)

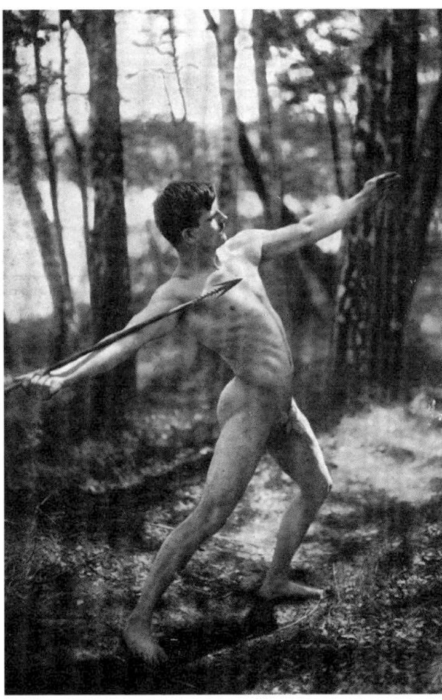

▲ *Fig. 295*

Javelin thrower. Photo E. Schneider. (G. Fritsch, *Nackte Schönheit*, 24)

logischen Standpunkt', *Zeitschrift für Ethnologie*, 13 (1881), 214.

8 E. Nolde, *Welt und Heimat* (Cologne,1965), 57; Pechstein for example travelled to Palau in 1914 and with a few strokes sketched human scenes.

9 G. Fritsch, 'Praktische Gesichtspunkte für die Verwendung zweier dem Reisenden wichtigen technischen Hilfsmittel: Das Mikroskop und der photographische Apparat' in G. von Neumayer (ed.), *Anleitung zu wissenschaftlichen Beobachtungen auf Reisen*, vol. 2, 3rd edn (Hanover, 1906), 731–814; on anthropological-physiognomic photographs, see 764–777; on ethnographical photographs, 777–779.

10 G. Fritsch, *Drei Jahre in Süd-Afrika* (Breslau, 1868); G. Fritsch, *Die Eingeborenen Süd-Afrika's*; G. Fritsch, 'Vorlage einer Portraitsammlung südafrikanischer Rassentypen', *Zeitschrift für Ethnologie*, 4 (1872), 11–13. In a letter from Cape Town to his mother dated 1 February 1865 (private collection, Maria Schwabe), Fritsch mentioned that he had produced an album of portraits with 179 photographs, 52 stereo views and 60 landscape views which he wanted to use for studies about South African tribes.

11 G. Fritsch, *Die Gestalt des Menschen. Mit Benutzung der Werke von E. Harless und C. Schmidt für Künstler und Anthropologen dargestellt von Gustav Fritsch* (Stuttgart, 1899), 148.

12 On the antique theory of proportions and Polyclitus' canon, see C.H. Stratz, *Die Schönheit des weiblichen Körpers. Den Müttern, Ärzten und Künstlern gewidmet*, 45th edn (Stuttgart, 1941), 44–62; E. Berger, 'Zum Kanon des Polyklet' in P.C. Bol (ed.), *Polyklet. Der Bildhauer der griechischen Klassik. Ausstellungskatalog* (Mainz, 1990), 156–184; H. Philipp, 'Zu Polyklets Schrift "Kanon"' in P.C. Bol (ed.), *Polyklet. Der Bildhauer der griechischen Klassik. Ausstellungskatalog* (Mainz, 1990), 135–155.

13 On the calculation and theory of Fritsch's canon, see Stratz, *Naturgeschichte des Menschen*, 197–198; G. Fritsch, 'Die graphische Methode zur Bestimmung der Verhältnisse des menschlichen Körpers', *Zeitschrift für Ethnologie*, 27 (1895), 172–188; Fritsch, 'Ueber die Anwendung des von G. Fritsch veröffentlichten Messungsschema', 36–37.

14 On the basis of measurements in Fritsch's canon, see Stratz, *Die Schönheit des weiblichen Körpers*, 48–50; C.H. Stratz, *Die Darstellung des menschlichen Körpers in der Kunst* (Berlin, 1914), 9–32; 13, Fig. 3 (construction of Fritsch's canon).

15 Stratz, *Naturgeschichte des Menschen*, 396.

16 Stratz, *Naturgeschichte des Menschen*, 381–386, figure of German male nudes. On so-called normal male and female bodies of Europeans, see 172–173, Figs. 121 and 122.

17 Stratz, *Naturgeschichte des Menschen*, 147.

18 Stratz, *Naturgeschichte des Menschen*, 91.

19 Stratz, *Naturgeschichte des Menschen*, 90.

20 C.H. Stratz, *Die Rassenschönheit des Weibes*, 15th edn (Stuttgart, 1922), 37–38.

21 The naming of ethnic groups refers to definitions of the time. See Stratz, *Naturgeschichte des Menschen*, 246–252.

22 Photographs in the picture library of the African collection of the Ethnological Museum Berlin, album no. 24, neg. P 16062–16066. See G. Fritsch, 'Akka-Mädchen', *Zeitschrift für Ethnologie*, 28 (1896), 544–545.

23 Stratz, *Naturgeschichte des Menschen*, 302–313, on the Khoikhoi, compared with the canon of proportions; on the Akka, 337–338, with figure of an Akka girl by Fritsch; *Die Rassenschönheit des Weibes*, 84–86, Figs. 46–57 (photo of Akka girl by Fritsch).

24 Stratz, *Naturgeschichte des Menschen*, 246, for quote by Fritsch; the anthropologist Johannes Ranke classified the Khoikhoi similarly (246). On the classification of African ethnic groups according to Fritsch and Stratz, 255–257.

25 Stratz, *Naturgeschichte des Menschen*, 257–287.

26 Stratz, *Naturgeschichte des Menschen*, 313.

27 G. Fritsch, 'Die Verbreitung australoider Merkmale in Melanesien und den Philippinen', *Zeitschrift für Ethnologie*, 48 (1916), 114–116.

28 Stratz, *Die Rassenschönheit des Weibes*, 308, Fig. 238 of an Arabian girl, photo by Fritsch.

29 Stratz, *Die Rassenschönheit des Weibes*, 314–323, Fig. 240 of a woman from Middle Egypt, photo by Fritsch.

30 Quoted Stratz, *Die Rassenschönheit des Weibes*, 316. Comparison of an Egyptian woman with the Giza Sphinx, 314–315, Figs. 240 and 241; G. Fritsch, 'Portraitcharaktere der altägyptischen Denkmäler', *Zeitschrift für Ethnologie*, 15 (1883), 188, on the portrait character of sphinxes.

31 Fritsch, *Die Gestalt des Menschen,* 148. On photography and art in the 'Gründerzeit', see U. Peter, *Stilgeschichte der Fotografie in Deutschland 1839–1900* (Cologne, 1979), 213–273.

32 Fritsch, 'Sonst und Jetzt der menschlichen Rassenkunde'; 'Portraitcharaktere der altägyptischen Denkmäler', esp. 184–185.

33 R. Steiger and M. Taureg, 'Körperphantasien auf Reisen. Anmerkungen zum ethnographischen Akt' in M. Köhler and G. Barche (eds.), *Das Aktfoto. Ansichten vom Körper im fotografischen Zeitalter* (Munich and Lucerne, 1985), 116–136.

34 Stratz, *Die Rassenschönheit des Weibes*, 239, Fig. 178; 240, Fig. 79 (bathhouse scenes of Japanese women).

35 G. Fritsch, 'Beiträge zur Kenntnis unserer Körperformen', *Zeitschrift für Ethnologie*, 26 (1894), 23–31; *Die Gestalt des Menschen*, V–VII, 144–148 on the application of the canon of proportions to artworks, the correct ratio of body proportions and their analogous representation in sculptures as the Greek sculptor Polyclitus calculated it in his 'canon'. See G. Fritsch, *Unsere Körperformen im Lichte der modernen Kunst* (Berlin, 1893).

36 M. Köhler, 'Jeder sein Michelangelo oder: Der Körper als Kunstwerk' in M. Köhler and G. Barche (ed.), *Das Aktfoto. Ansichten vom Körper im fotografischen Zeitalter* (Munich and Lucerne, 1985), 282–288.

37 For instance, the antique statue of the Borghese fencer: Fritsch, *Die Gestalt des Menschen*, 87–91.

38 Fritsch, *Die Gestalt des Menschen*.

39 Similarly Stratz, *Die Darstellung des menschlichen Körpers in der Kunst*.

40 On beauty in its dependence on natural truth, see Fritsch, 'Die graphische Methode zur Bestimmung der Verhältnisse des menschlichen Körpers', 173–174.

41 Fritsch, 'Die graphische Methode zur Bestimmung der Verhältnisse des menschlichen Körpers', 176.

42 M. Wiener, *Ikonographie des Wilden. Menschen-Bilder in Ethnographie und Photographie zwischen 1850 und 1918* (Munich, 1990), 136–144; J. Kohlenbrock-Netz, 'Kunst und/oder Pornographie. Ein Beitrag zur Diskursgeschichte der Zensur im 19. und 20. Jahrhundert' in I. Lindner, S. Schade and S. Wenk (eds.), *Blick-Wechsel. Konstruktionen von Männlichkeit und Weiblichkeit in Kunst und Kunstgeschichte* (Berlin, 1989), 493–499.

43 G. Fritsch (ed.), *Nackte Schönheit. Ein Buch für Künstler und Ärzte*, vol. 1 (Stuttgart, c.1907), 1–41. On the validity of using nude photographs to show human beauty and assign it to certain races, see also Stratz, *Die Schönheit des weiblichen Körpers*, 3–10, 484.

44 On the *Lebensreform* movement, see C. Klose-Lewerentz, 'Natürliche Körper? Zwischen Befreiung und disziplinierender Norm. Diskurse zur Lebensreformbewegung und das Aufkommen des Wunsches nach Geschlechtsumwandlung' (unpublished master's thesis, Humboldt University, Berlin, 2007), 9–14, 15–19; on nudism, see M. Köhler, 'Lebensreform durch Körperkultur. "Wir sind nackt und nennen uns du"' in M. Köhler and G. Barche (eds.), *Das Aktfoto. Ansichten vom Körper im fotografischen Zeitalter* (Munich and Lucerne, 1985), 289–303.

45 Richard Ungewitter (ed.), *Die Nacktheit in entwicklungsgeschichtlicher, gesundheitlicher, moralischer und künstlerischer Bedeutung* (Stuttgart, 1909).

46 Fritsch, *Nackte Schönheit*, 31–32, 36.

47 Stratz, *Die Darstellung des menschlichen Körpers in der Kunst*, 36–44.

48 Stratz, *Die Darstellung des menschlichen Körpers in der Kunst*, 57–85.

49 Stratz, *Die Darstellung des menschlichen Körpers in der Kunst*, 199.

50 Stratz, *Die Darstellung des menschlichen Körpers in der Kunst*, esp. 224.

51 Stratz, *Naturgeschichte des Menschen*, esp. 175–206, 207–252, 253–394.

52 Stratz, Naturgeschichte des Menschen, 394.

53 Stratz, Naturgeschichte des Menschen, 39–40.

54 Stratz, Naturgeschichte des Menschen; Stratz, *Die Rassenschönheit des Weibes*; Stratz, *Die Schönheit des weiblichen Körpers*.

Anthropology and microphotography: Gustav Fritsch and the classification of hair

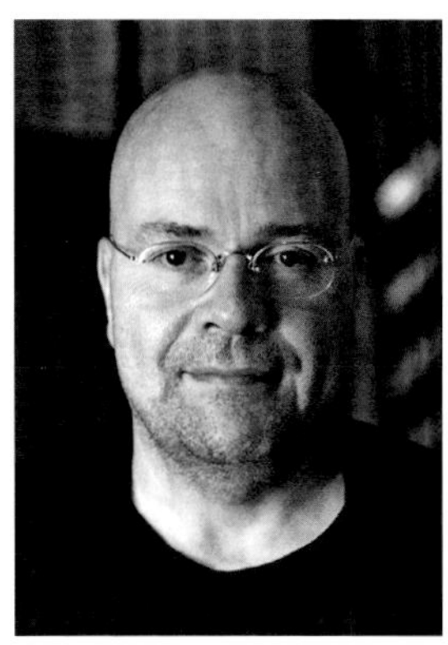

Michael Hagner

In his long career as a scientist, Gustav Fritsch published on a variety of topics, but two subjects occupied him consistently: microphotography and the photographic representation of the human body.[1] He contributed extensively to the theory and practice of scientific photography from the 1860s onwards, made suggestions for technological innovations, and argued again and again for the mechanical objectivity as well as for the vividness of photography. In this essay, I want to show that Fritsch's interest in photography went far beyond his beautiful portraits of South African natives. He used photography for the representation of microscopic tissue, for an aestheticising display of the nude body and for anthropometric measurement of the body parts. Despite this variety, Fritsch was mainly searching for bodily characteristics for the anthropological classification of *race*.[2] As I will argue, Fritsch's goals culminated in his *Atlas* on the racial classification of hair, which connected his work on microphotography and the representation of the human body. The second purpose of this work was to defend the value of photography for anatomical and anthropological purposes. This value was contested by other forms of representation such as drawings and statistics, and Fritsch was well aware that each of these representations had its merits and its limitations. In his defence of photography, Fritsch emphasised both epistemological and aesthetic reasons, and this bipolar approach integrates his entire work on micro-photographic anthropology. Before going into more detail, I will give a brief overview of Fritsch's contributions to photography in relation to his work as an anatomist and physical anthropologist.

In 1911 Karl Wolf-Czapek published a comprehensive work on *Applied Photography in Science and Technology*, in which several scholars gave an overview of the use of photography in their respective disciplines. Fritsch, who was 73 years old at the time, wrote the two chapters on anatomy and on anthropology, in which he had to admit that the triumph of photography was far from complete. As an anatomist, he had been among the first to recognise the importance of photography for the study of microscopic tissue. In particular, the microscopists's difficulties with stereoscopic vision intrigued him, and hence he introduced a technological device for stereoscopic microphotography in 1873 (Fig. 296).[3] To Fritsch's disappointment, however, stereoscopic microtypes did not become a standard method in anatomy.[4] He also complained that in the macroscopic representation of the body and its parts, photography had all the disadvantages of 'inexorable faithfulness' in emphasising unwanted problems in presenting the body and the unavoidable signs of decay.[5] The situation was different in micro-anatomy and bacteriology. Here photography played an important role, although it had by no means completely replaced drawings. Thus Fritsch criticised the popularity of drawings because of the subjective attitudes of the draughtsmen and complained about the traditional visual habits of anatomists. His main argument for photography was its mechanical objectivity. Microphotographs delivered an 'incontestable document' and enjoyed the justified trust of the observer.[6] As we will see below, these programmatic reflections were not entirely matched by Fritsch's own use of microphotography. In his work on the classification of hair, the experience and intuition of the observer were as important as the objectivity of photography.

When assessing Fritsch's achievement as an anthropological photographer, we have to bear in mind that he travelled abroad for almost ten years between 1863 and 1905. His expedition to South Africa in the early 1860s was the first in a series of at least six expeditions that led him to most regions of the world, with the exception of North and South America. Not all these expeditions were devoted primarily to anthropology, but from the outset Fritsch travelled with photographic equipment. Thus it comes as no surprise that for Fritsch the emergence of anthropology in the second half of the nineteenth century was so closely linked to photography that he preferred to speak of an 'anthropological photography' or 'photographical anthropology' in his review article for Wolf-Czapek's anthology. Before the inception

Michael Hagner studied medicine and philosophy at the Free University in Berlin and worked in London, Lübeck and Göttingen before he moved to the Max Planck Institute for the History of Science in Berlin. Since 2003, he has been Professor of Science Studies at the ETH, Zürich. His current research projects include the history of cybernetics and the history of sexuality.

of photography, anthropology (in Fritsch's view) had been anecdotal and produced contradictory results, and any attempt to develop an exact science had therefore been in vain. Photography presented reliable documents and preserved data, which the anthropologist had not always recognised while he was in the field.[7] The most important use of anthropological photography was in the measurement of the body and its parts in order to compare and classify human races.

As early as 1872, Fritsch had differentiated between ethnological photography, which showed humans in their cultural environment and documented clothing, ornament, hair-style and tattoos, and physiognomic photography (or to be more exact, anthropometric photography), which was based on the standardisation of the images.[8] An ideal triad was front-view, side-view and back-view. These three perspectives were necessary for undertaking comparative measurements of bodily proportions. For this purpose Fritsch had developed a so-called *Proportionsschlüssel* (key of proportions) of the human figure, which was a reference system for the main proportions of the body (Fig. 297). This ideal measure could be applied to the real body, so that actual measurements would show whether, for example, arms or legs were too short or too long, or whether the pelvis and the shoulders were too broad.[9] Fritsch's claim that this kind of photography was an effective 'simplification of measurement'[10] and could replace the body itself for gaining reliable data did not go uncontested. Critics expressed their concern that the photographic perspective led to mensural errors and that it was almost impossible to define exact reference points for the measurement of the pelvis, skull and the bones of the limbs.[11]

When Fritsch published his voluminous atlas with anthropometric photographs of the nude bodies of 52 Egyptian, Ethiopian and other African men and women, which he had taken on his expedition to Egypt in 1898 and 1899, he was aware that his practice of measuring the photograph instead of the body itself was questioned by certain of his scientific peers.[12] Thus in his comments on the photographs he also focused on characteristics such as the gaze, the lips, the breasts and hair. All of these were subject to personal experience and aesthetic preferences rather than to quantitative measurement. That Fritsch's fascination for the nude body went far beyond anthropometry is clear from two photographic books he co-edited, which celebrated the nude bodies of young European women and men. In them he contributed essays in which he defended the public presentation of the beautiful naked body as providing a kind of role model for the preservation of health.[13] In the first years of the twentieth century, Europeans became preoccupied with the body and concerned about degeneration. Praise of healthy, athletic and erotic bodies was one of the strategies for coping with these anxieties. Fritsch's celebration of the nude body was in fact much more successful than his anthropometry (Fig. 298).

For more than 40 years, Fritsch had contributed extensively to various fields of photography. But by the end of his career, he had to accept that the new optical medium had not replaced other forms of visual representation. Indeed, Fritsch's use of microphotography can be seen as a means to save the anthropological value of photography. Whereas the measurement of the skull, brain, skin or pelvis had traditionally dominated physical anthropology – and Fritsch also contributed to this effort – late-nineteenth-century anthropologists were searching for new criteria and shifted from the investigation of the macro-level to the micro-level. For instance, the components of blood and blood groups in particular became a fashionable research object for racial classification in the early twentieth century. Before then, however, the true domain of micro-anthropology was the comparative examination of the structure and texture of hair. Its use for racial classification is one of the more ominous chapters in the history of physical anthropology, because it implied the accessibility of the scalps of dead people from all over the world. Fritsch worked on this subject for several decades, and it comes as no surprise that he was an ardent collector of scalps on his scientific travels in Africa and elsewhere.

Although no one went deeper into the classificatory examination of hair, Fritsch was not the first naturalist to become interested in this topic. In fact there was a nineteenth-century tradition of classifying hair, which began with the French naturalist Isidore Geoffroy Saint-Hilaire, who differentiated between races with woolly hair and those with smoother hair. This kind of binary classification can be seen in the tradition of late-eighteenth-century anthropological dichotomies: the brain is lighter or heavier, more or less excitable, more wet or more dry; the facial angle is larger or smaller; the skull is shorter or longer and more or less spacious. Dichotomies like these legitimated social hierarchies and valuations. Accordingly, woolly hair was regarded as being typical of 'lower races', whereas smooth hair was ascribed to 'higher races'. This racist classification was further refined in the wake of evolutionary theory. In his book on *The Descent of Man*, Charles Darwin compared the hair-growth of man and apes in order to clarify the genealogy of man. He also mentioned that the texture of hair in various races was as different as the capacity of the lungs and the convolutions of the brain.[14] But whereas Darwin drew no conclusion from this comparison, his follower Ernst Haeckel combined the idea of evolution with racial hierarchies. He argued firstly that if human hair was woolly and was similar to the hair of animals, this supported the idea of a continuity between animals and humans. Secondly, if woolly hair was mainly found in black people, then this supported the assumption of their inferiority: they were closer to animals than peoples with smooth hair. Thomas Huxley was more modest in his claims: he restricted himself to the division of human races into straight-haired and woolly-haired though he was also convinced that the latter were racially inferior.[15]

Evolutionary thinking, racist hierarchies and the search for a new, robust criterion for racial classification led to a remarkable growth in the anthropological study of hair in France, Germany and Britain.[16] For example, the *Zeitschrift für Ethnologie*, the official organ of the Berlin Society for Anthropology, Ethnology and Prehistory, published 42 articles on this topic between 1870 and 1910, 16 of them by the famous pathologist and anthropologist Rudolf Virchow, who was the editor of the journal until his death in 1902. When Fritsch published his *magnum opus* on this topic in 1912, *Das Haupthaar und seine Bildungsstätte bei den Rassen des Menschen* (Scalp Hair and Its Origins among the Human Races), he listed 113 titles in his bibliography. With one exception, all of them were published after 1860. An important step in the classification of hair was undertaken by the French anthropologist Pruner-Bey, who microscopically examined the cross-section of hair. According to him, hair with an elliptic cross-section was mainly to be found in black Africans; a circular cross-section was to be found in Asians and in Native Americans: and finally, in between these two extremes, an oval cross-section was to be found in Europeans.[17] These findings were more or less in accordance with

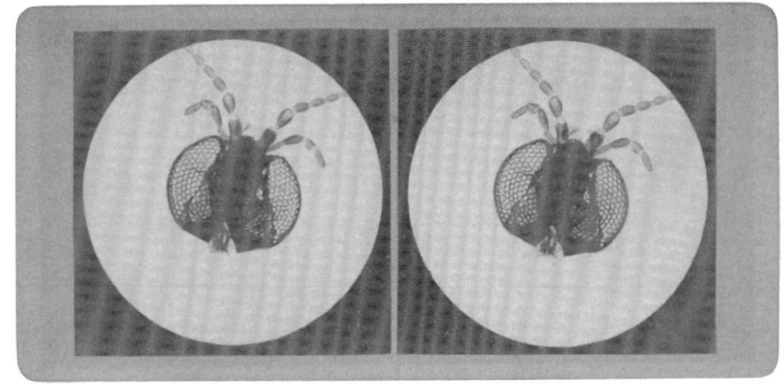

▲ *Fig. 296* G. Fritsch, *Ueber das stereoskopische Sehen im Mikroskop und die Herstellung stereoskopischer Mikrotypieen auf photographischem Wege* (1873), Plate 3.

▼ *Fig. 297* G. Fritsch, *Die Gestalt des Menschen*, 2nd. edn (1905), 140.

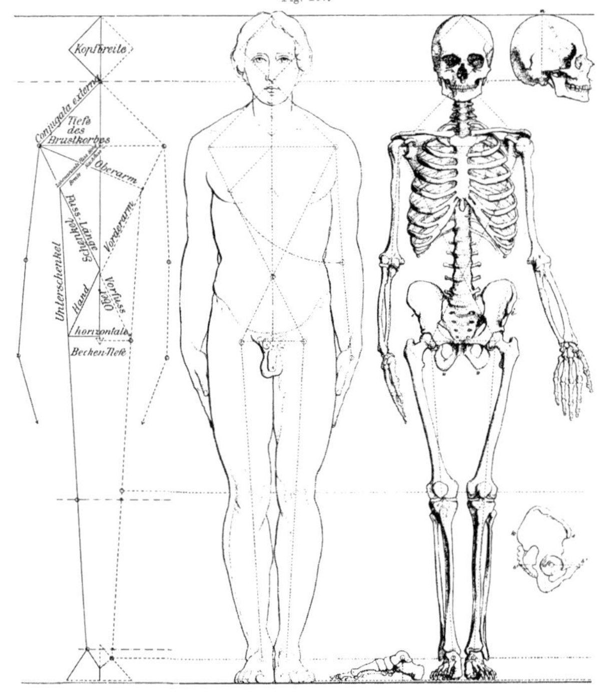

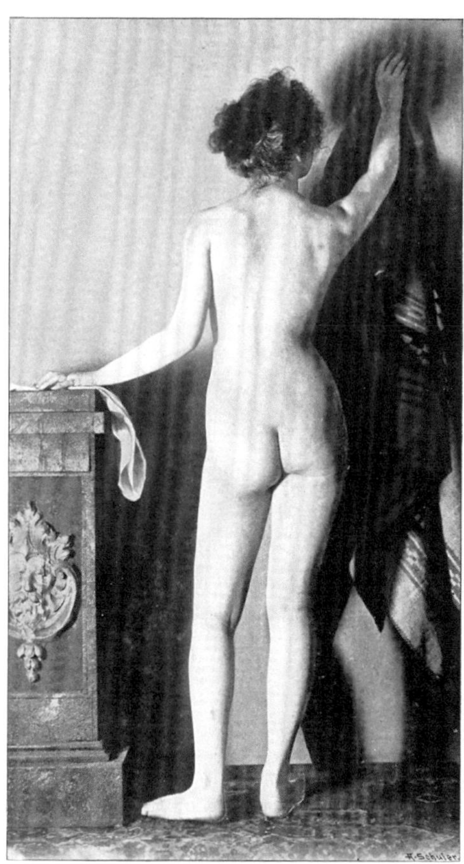

Fig. 298 ▲ . C.H. Stratz, *Die Schönheit des weiblichen Körpers,* 6th edn (1900), 183

Fig. 299 ▼ W. Waldeyer, *Atlas der menschlichen und tierischen Haare* (1884), Plate XII.

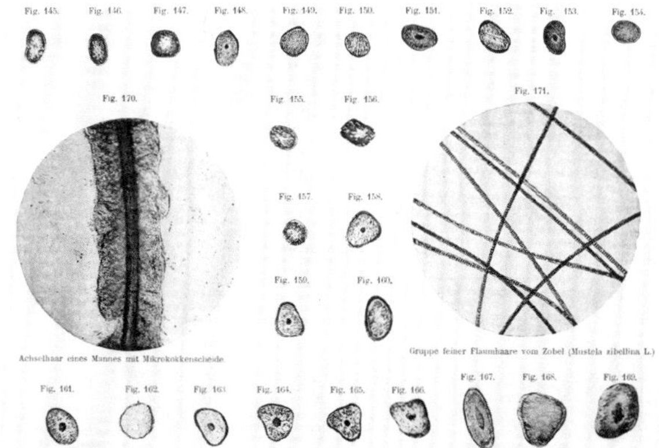

the macroscopic appearance of hair: the circular form with smooth or tight hair, the elliptic form with woolly hair.

This taxonomy was refined by Paul Topinard, one of the leading French anthropologists, who linked Pruner-Bey's classification of hair with the well-known binary classification of skulls and with the colour of hair.[18] Although this connection was not generally accepted, the German anatomist Wilhelm Waldeyer admitted that Topinard provided a sound approach to the anthropological classification of hair.[19] Around the same time, members of the Berlin Society for Anthropology, Ethnology and Prehistory set up a Committee for the Scientific Investigation of Hair. Rudolf Virchow and Gustav Fritsch were among its founding members. The intention of the committee was to establish guidelines for collecting, preparing and examining hair, and to define rules, a terminology and rough classifications as the starting point for further research.[20] At the same time, anthropological societies in Paris and London also discussed various classifications of hair. In Paris, anthropologists approved five divisions, while their colleagues in London approved three.[21]

The attempts to find reliable criteria for further research can be seen against the background of the frustrating situation with which the anthropologists were confronted. In his *Atlas der menschlichen und tierischen Haare* (Atlas of Human and Animal Hair), Waldeyer produced a micro-photographic illustration of racial classification, in which he relied on Pruner-Bey's criterion of the cross-section of hair (Fig. 299). It is not difficult to see that this plate undermined Pruner-Bey's classification. The visual representation of the hair of a 'brunette Jew', of 'brunette and blond Germans', of 'a negro' and of 'a Japanese' showed remarkable individual variability. For example, the cross-section of the African's hair was oval, almost circular and square-edged, whereas the hair of the Japanese was rather elliptical and square-edged than circular. The hair of the German and of the Jew was characterised by all possible forms. In his comments on this illustration, Waldeyer had to admit to the enormous variability of the shape of hair, but he was not willing to reject cross-section as a useful category for racial classification. Instead he proposed taking into consideration 'all physical and anatomical properties of hair of the various peoples',[22] including their scalps.

Fritsch had already started to collect hair on his expedition to Egypt and other eastern Mediterranean countries in 1881. In subsequent years Fritsch gave a number of talks at the Berlin Society, in which he took sides with Waldeyer. He proposed an expansion of research and hoped to include even those amateur anthropologists who were not specialists in microscopy or microphotography. According to Fritsch, any interested anthropologist might collect material and contribute to the clarification of terminology. He also warned of unjustified expectations about the value of hair as a determining criterion for racial differentiation and mused about the connection between the individual variability of textures of the cross-section and the mixed character of many races. Fritsch's lecture had a further aspect. When Waldeyer mentioned the importance of examining the scalp in order to better understand the origin of hair, he added that he was not very hopeful because of the difficulties of acquiring scalps. Fritsch was more optimistic and declared that all 'erudite travellers' would deserve well of anthropology if they 'collected stripes of hairy scalps or full scalps (which usually do not need to be taken from living humans). Even smaller pieces of hairy skin, dried or preserved in liquids, would be valuable, if their origin is exactly characterised.'[23] Proposals like these have to be seen as examples of the unscrupulousness of anthropologists, who were convinced that scientific progress justified practices which they would otherwise have regarded with distaste. Fritsch was a convinced spokesman of German colonialism. He expressed his willingness on several occasions to put his knowledge about South Africa to the service of German colonialism.[24] In turn, he hoped to receive samples of native scalps from the German colonies in Africa, but his hopes were in vain.

In 1894 Fritsch undertook another expedition to Africa, and spent his time systematically collecting African scalps. In none of his publications did Fritsch give detailed information about the circumstances under which he acquired these 'specimens'. He was certainly aware that such a venture faced many difficulties, and therefore he asked for support from his colleagues. But when he gave his first report about his new research results on the anthropology of hair at the Prussian Academy of Science in 1896, he expressed some indignation: 'If I had not have succeeded in acquiring specimens for examination from Africa, they would be lacking still today. Before and after my last journey to the East [in 1881], I have tried unavailingly to acquire useful material for investigation from our colonies.'[25] Inadvertently or not, Fritsch made it very clear that – if necessary – he was a hunter rather than a genteel academic. This ambiguity characterised his modus operandi as a travelling anthropologist. On the one hand, he attached great importance to being a respectable researcher with epistemological and moral standards. For example, his early use of photography was intended to establish his scientific credentials, compared with the dubious and unreliable anthropological adventurers who had preceded him. On the other hand, Fritsch had no moral scruples in hunting for what he thought was necessary for his scientific research.

The anthropological community was also ambivalent. Their members did not directly assist one another in this matter, but they were certainly interested in the scientific results. Fritsch presented his new results on the basis of criteria which had been suggested by Waldeyer and others, but no one before Fritsch had applied them to the study of hair. These included the arrangement of hair on the scalp, the implantation of hair in the follicle, the shape of the follicle, the shape of the papilla and the cross-section of hair adjacent to the scalp

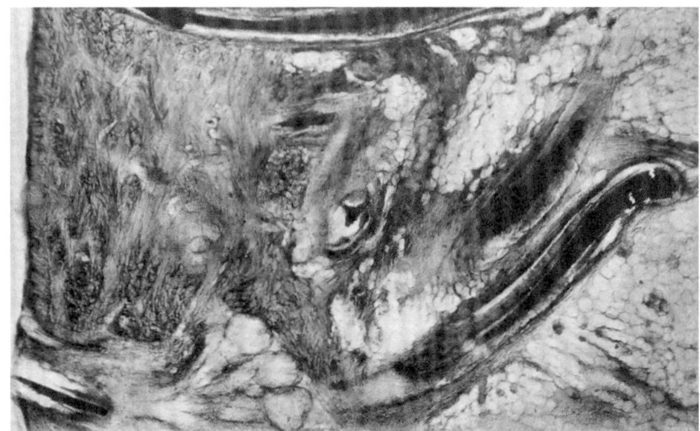

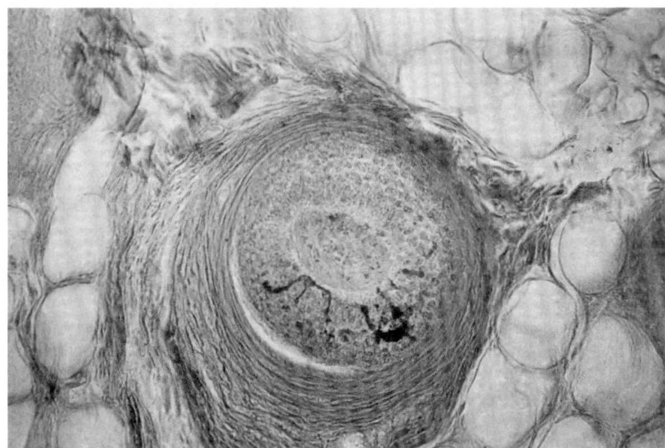

▲   *Fig. 300*

G. Fritsch, 'Über die Ausbildung der Rassenmerkmale des menschlichen Haupthaares' (1896), Plate 3.

(as compared to the cross-section at the peak of the hair). To begin with the cross-section, Fritsch was still convinced that it was useful for purposes of classification, although his results were as unsatisfactory as the earlier ones. Fritsch tried to reduce these problems by shifting the focus to the cross-section of the papilla, that is the origin of hair within the epidermis. The results more or less accorded with older assumptions: the papilla of hair of Europeans was circular, the papilla of Africans was oval or had the form of a kidney.[26] Fritsch concluded that the shape of the papilla determined the texture and form of hair. If the latter differed from the former or was more variable, then accidental reasons like climate, hair-care, disease or hygiene were responsible. A further encouraging result for Fritsch was the form of the follicles, which were mostly sickle-shaped in Africans. This revived the 1860s paradigm, with its distinction between straight and woolly hair.[27]

What strategies did Fritsch use to establish criteria like the follicle and the papilla? He was certainly aware that individual variability would

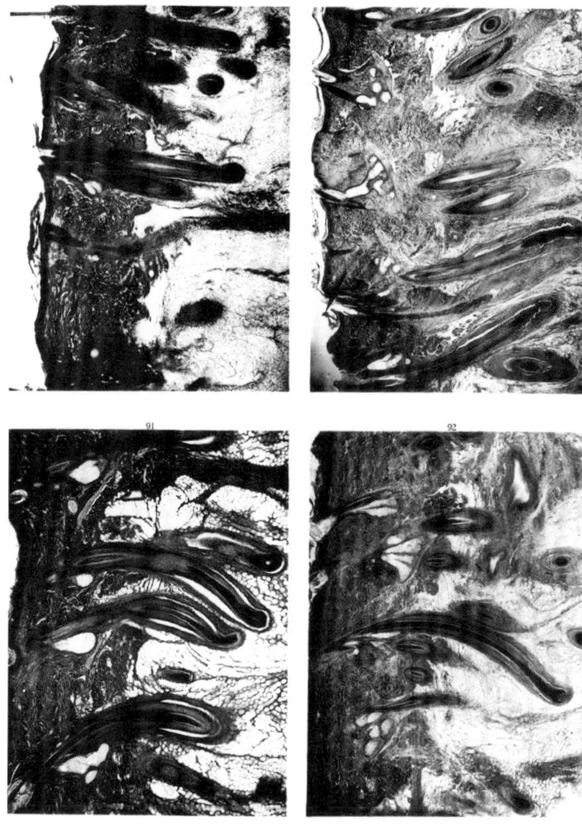

▲ *Fig. 301*

G. Fritsch, *Das Haupthaar und seine Bildungsstätte bei den Rassen des Menschen* (1912), Plate XXIII.

impair his claims. Therefore he avoided numbers, tables and statistics. He made no reference to the number of scalps he had examined, and did not say how many papillae and follicles he had compared in one individual. Instead of using quantitative methods, he relied on visual representation and used microphotography for the first time in his research into hair. Fritsch presented these photographs as his evidence. Unlike Waldeyer, he did not display several examples side by side, but selected a number of typical papillae or follicles. According to the explanation given in the published text of his lecture, Fritsch presented two figures of the same individual – a deceased female slave from Sudan. The first image displayed a number of sickle-shaped follicles, the other one displayed an oval papilla (Fig. 300). His abandonment of quantitative analysis went hand in hand with his trust in visual evidence. He assumed that his audience would trust him for two reasons: firstly, his subjective experience as a microscopist, and secondly, the objective conclusiveness of photography. This methodological

combination encouraged Fritsch to intensify his attempts to establish anatomical characteristics for the differentiation of races.

After his successful talk, Fritsch went back to his colleagues at the Society for Anthropology and renewed his invitation to make the inquiry of hair a collective enterprise.[28] Although he was not provided with scalps by his colleagues, his proposal was well accepted. It turned out that there were scalps available in anatomical collections, for example at the Anatomical Institute at the University of Strasbourg. When Jean Frédéric published his paper on the racial differences of human hair of the head, he had 32 scalps from three continents at his disposal.[29] Frédéric began his examination with the same criteria that Fritsch had proposed: the arrangement of hair on the scalp, the follicles, the cross-section of hair and the papilla. Yet he added further criteria and counted the number of hairs per square centimetre, measured the average diameter of hair, and the thickness of the cutis and the subcutis. While Frédéric confirmed and substantiated some of Fritsch's results, he was uncertain about others or even rejected them. The research methods Frédéric applied were radically different from Fritsch's emphasis on visual evidence. He relied on measurement and counting, comparison and tables. The methodological differences between these two approaches made it clear that photography was by no means superior to other forms of representation in anthropology. Though the visual approach and the quantitative approach could be used alongside each other, they represented two different research cultures.

When Frédéric published his paper in 1906, Fritsch had just returned from his last expedition, which took him to India, China, Japan and Australia. One of the main purposes of these travels was to acquire scalps in order to make a final effective statement on the anthropology of hair. This time Fritsch was apparently successful in his quest. He took home 45 pieces of scalps, and in subsequent years he analysed the specimens and worked on two carefully produced folio atlases, which were financially supported by the Prussian Academy of Science.[30] These prestigious publications were meant to be Fritsch's final contribution to the classification of races. The monograph on hair consisted of 70 written pages, 45 of which were devoted to an exhaustive explanation of 30 plates. Each of these plates contained between four and six micro-photographs (Figs. 301 and 302).

Fritsch attached great importance to the difference between his approach and that of Frédéric. Whereas Frédéric preferred numbers, he preferred images. Fritsch emphasised technical reasons for this difference: 'I worked with specimens of the scalp, carefully prepared histologically, so that the character of the material did not permit me to present clearly arranged numerical data of the hair.'[31] Whether Fritsch would have been able to produce quantitative data, his decision to treat the anatomical specimens in the way he did was a consequence of his longstanding preference for photography. But though he was an outspoken proponent of the visual method, Fritsch accepted for the first time two different methodological and representational ways for creating evidence. This concession was inevitable, because both methods led to the same results. In fact, Fritsch could not present any new findings that went beyond Frédéric's and his own earlier work. He conceded the fact of individual variation and warned against those 'hyperexact' sceptics who would put an end to the differentiation of races. Moreover, he confirmed once again the differences between smooth and spiral hair, between extended and sickle-formed follicles, and between circular and oval or kidney-shaped cross-section.

If the outcome of this ambitious research project, which had required so much time, energy and money, was so modest, why was such a spectacular publication necessary? And why did Fritsch highlight the differences between the two research methods? Two points seem to be relevant here. Firstly, the financial support of the state and of the Prussian Academy of Science demanded an appropriate and representative publication. The splendid folio volume with its costly plates was a symbolic repayment for his two-year expedition round the world. The second point seems to be even more important for an understanding of Fritsch's research strategies and publication practices. Although he was familiar with microphotography from the 1860s, he did not use it for the anthropology of hair before the 1890s; and it was only after Frédéric's publication that Fritsch felt the need to defend microphotography as a valuable method in anthropology. This was not merely an issue of defending an objective technology. Rather there was at stake a fundamental difference in the self-understanding of the respective researchers. The quantitative and the visual methods were marked by different skills, preferences and mentalities.

On the one hand, there was the anatomist, counting, measuring and comparing in his laboratory. He used illustrations, but he did not trust a single image. He did not believe that such an image could lead to a typical representation of the research object. Therefore he relied on evidence gained through comparative measurement. On the other hand, there was the anatomist and anthropologist who had spent many years of his lifetime on expeditions. Fritsch made it clear on several occasions that he was not interested in quantitative measurement of hair. He presented himself as a travelling adventurer and anthropologist, who relied on personal authority, experience and intuition. It is exactly at this point photography came into play. This was the medium that enabled Fritsch to combine adventure and intuition, objectivity and visual evidence. Anthropometric photography of the nude body was a strategy to get rid of the subjectivity of the draughtsman and to create a new research object, which allowed comparative measurement. This is how Fritsch approached the quantitative method. He was a proponent of objectivity, and he did not contest the value of measuring skulls, the pelvis and other body parts. On the contrary, he actively participated in anthropometry. But the more data anthropologists collected, the

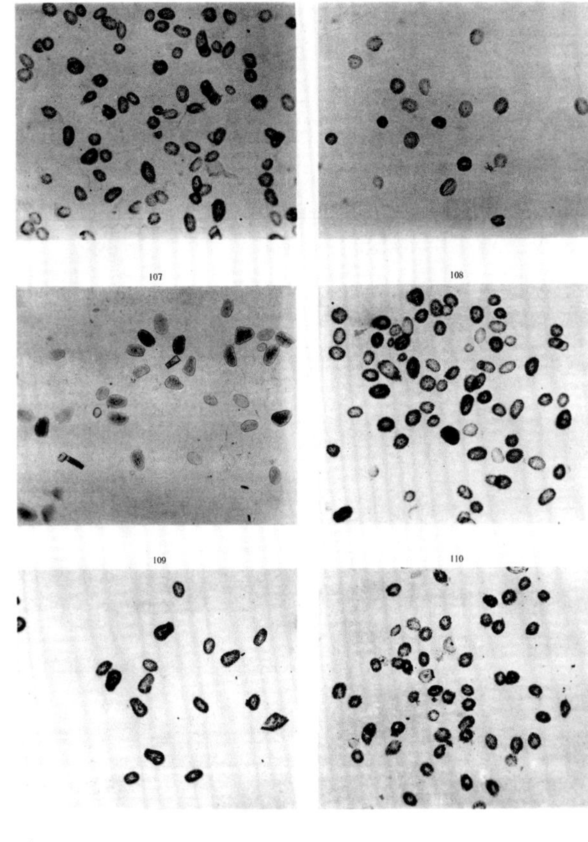

▲ Fig. 302

G. Fritsch, *Das Haupthaar und seine Bildungsstätte bei den Rassen des Menschen* (1912), Plate XXVII.

more confusing the situation seemed to be. Physical anthropologists had proposed so many categories for measurement that at least some of them started to doubt the usefulness of numbers and statistics in the 1890s. Fritsch was among these frustrated anthropologists, and in this situation photography served as an alternative to measurement.

The shift in Fritsch's views about the use of anthropological photography is evident in a review article on the microscope and photography which he contributed to a handbook on scientific expeditions and which he then revised for each new edition. In 1875, he saw the main purpose of photography as disciplining and correcting the subjectivity of the travelling anthropologist.[32] In 1906, he did not object to this value, but, more importantly, he celebrated photography for allowing the observer to gain an 'intuition of the living form', in contrast to the 'peripatetic tables with its mop of dead numbers'.[33] Understanding a photograph depended on the experience of the observer; and, in contrast to statistics, photography gave a vivid image of the body. The microphotographies of the scalp followed this logic. They relied on intuition and not on numbers and calculation, on visual aptness and not comparative tables. For amateurs, microphotography was certainly not as interesting as nude bodies, but for the experienced observer it provided a powerful image. Whereas Frédéric's measurements were objective and anti-individual, Fritsch's photographs were objective and subjective at the same time. Since both research strategies were accepted in anthropology around 1900, it is not possible to say that one proved superior to the other, that photography replaced drawings or that comparative measurements replaced subjectivity and intuition. Although Fritsch was a passionate proponent of photography for almost 50 years, by the end of his career he came to realise that it was not the medium as such that gave access to innovative scientific knowledge. The medium, rather, depended upon different audiences, specific research cultures, and the skills and mentalities of the observer. In the racial classification of hair, microphotography did not lead to any significant insight that was closed to other research strategies. Its main significance should be seen in its importance for nineteenth-century visual culture and in the shift from macroscopic to microscopic criteria in the massive but dubious anthropological project of finding determining characteristics for the classification of race.

ENDNOTES

1   This essay is adapted from my more detailed paper 'Mikro-Anthropologie und Fotografie. Gustav Fritschs Haarspaltereien und die Klassifizierung der Rassen' in P. Geimer (ed.), *Ordnungen der Sichtbarkeit. Fotografie in Wissenschaft, Technologie und Kunst* (Frankfurt am Main, 2002), 252–285.

2   Please note that *race* is not my category. It is the category of the historical actors, with whom I am dealing in this article, and therefore I italicise it at its first mention.

3   G. Fritsch, 'Zur Kenntnis der mikroskopischen Photographie', *Licht. Zeitschrift für Photographie*, 1 (1869), 140, 156–162, 174–177, 188–193, 205–208; G. Fritsch, *Ueber das stereoskopische Sehen im Mikroskop und die Herstellung stereoskopischer Mikrotypieen auf photographischem Wege* (Berlin, 1873).

4   G. Fritsch, 'Die Schwierigkeiten einer Wiederbelebung der Stereoskopie', *Internationale photographische Monatsschrift für Medizin und Naturwissenschaft*, 3 (1896), 193-208.

5   G. Fritsch, 'Anatomie' in K.W. Wolf-Czapek (ed.), *Angewandte Photographie in Wissenschaft und Technik* (Berlin, 1911), vol. 2, 67.

6   Fritsch, 'Anatomie', 69–72.

7   G. Fritsch, 'Anthropologie' in K.W. Wolf-Czapek (ed.), *Angewandte Photographie in Wissenschaft und Technik* (Berlin, 1911), vol. 4, 19.

8   G. Fritsch, 'Die Bedeutung physiognomischer Darstellungen'', *Zeitschrift für Ethnologie*, 4 (1872), 12.

9   G. Fritsch, 'Anthropologie', 21. See also G. Fritsch, *Die Gestalt des Menschen*, 2nd edn (Stuttgart, 1905), 134–142.

10 G. Fritsch, 'Ueber die Körperverhältnisse der heutigen Bevölkerung Ägyptens', *Korrespondenz-Blatt der Deutschen Gesellschaft für Anthropologie, Ethnologie und Urgeschichte*, 30 (1899), 137.

11 See T. Theye, 'Wir wollen nicht glauben, sondern schauen' in 'Zur Geschichte der ethnographischen Fotografie im deutschsprachigen Raum im 19. Jahrhundert' in T. Theye (ed.), *Der geraubte Schatten. Photographie als ethnographisches Dokument* (Munich and Lucerne, 1990), 92–94.

12 G. Fritsch, *Ägyptische Volkstypen der Jetztzeit. Nach anthropologischen Grundsätzen aufgenommene Aktstudien* (Wiesbaden, 1904).

13 G. Fritsch, 'Ist die Darstellung des Nackten anstößig?' in Eduard Daelen, Gustav Fritsch, Bruno Meyer, Ludwig Schrank and Konrad Wahr (eds.), *Die Schönheit des menschlichen Körpers* (Stuttgart, 1905), 1–14; Fritsch, 'Bekleidung und Sittlichkeit' in Fritsch (ed.), *Nackte Schönheit. Ein Buch für Künstler und Ärzte* (Stuttgart, 1907), vol. 1, 1–41.

14 C. Darwin, *The Descent of Man, and Selection in Relation to Sex* (London, 1871), vol. 1, 216.

15 See, for example, E. Haeckel, 'Natürliche Schöpfungsgeschichte. Zweiter Teil' in E. Haeckel, *Gemeinverständliche Werke*, vol. 2 (Leipzig and Berlin, 1924), 383–384; T.H. Huxley, 'On the methods and results of ethnology', *Fortnightly Review*, 1 (1865), 257–277.

16 For an informative overview, see M. Trotter, 'A review of the classification of hair', *American Journal of Physical Anthropology*, 24, 1 (1938), 105–126.

17 Pruner-Bey, 'De la chevelure caractéristique des races humaines d'après des recherches microscopiques', *Mémoires de la Société d'Anthropologie de Paris*, 2 (1863), 1–35; Pruner-Bey, 'Deuxième série d'observations microscopiques sur la chevelure', *Mémoires de la Société d'Anthropologie de Paris*, 3 (1864), 77–92.

18 P. Topinard, *Anthropologie* (Leipzig, 1888), 347–354.

19 W. Waldeyer, *Atlas der menschlichen und tierischen Haare* (Lahr, 1884), 47.

20 See G. Fritsch, 'Das menschliche Haar als Rassenmerkmal', *Zeitschrift für Ethnologie*, 17 (1885), 279.

21 Trotter, 'Review of the classifications of hair', 110.

22 Waldeyer, *Atlas der menschlichen und tierischen Haare*, 45.

23 Fritsch, 'Das menschliche Haar', 282.

24 See G. Fritsch, *Südafrika bis zum Zambesi* (Leipzig and Prague, 1885), vii–viii; Fritsch 'Frage, welche Methode der Negerbehandlung die beste sei' in F. Giesebrecht (ed.), *Die Behandlung der Eingeborenen in den Deutschen Kolonien* (Berlin, 1898), 76–81.

25 G. Fritsch, 'Über die Ausbildung der Rassenmerkmale des menschlichen Haupthaares', *Sitzungsberichte der Preussischen Akademie der Wissenschaften zu Berlin* (1896), 511.

26 Fritsch, 'Über die Ausbildung der Rassenmerkmale des menschlichen Haupthaares', 506.

27 Fritsch, 'Über die Ausbildung der Rassenmerkmale des menschlichen Haupthaares', 500.

28 G. Fritsch, 'Ueber die Entstehung der Rassenmerkmale des menschlichen Kopfhaares', *Korrespondenz-Blatt der Deutschen Gesellschaft für Anthropologie, Ethnologie und Urgeschichte*, 29 (1898), 161.

29 J. Frédéric, 'Untersuchungen über die Rassenunterschiede der menschlichen Kopfhaare', *Zeitschrift für Morphologie und Anthropologie*, 9 (1906), 249.

30 See G. Fritsch, *Das Haupthaar und seine Bildungsstätte bei den Rassen des Menschen* (Berlin, 1912); Fritsch, *Die menschliche Haupthaaranlage. Weitere Beobachtungen als Nachtrag zu: Das Haupthaar und seine Bildungsstätte* (Berlin, 1915).

31 Fritsch, *Das Haupthaar*, 2.

32 G. Fritsch, 'Praktische Gesichtspunkte für die Verwendung zweier dem Reisenden wichtigen technischen Hilfsmittel: Das Mikroskop und der photographische Apparat' in G. von Neumayer (ed.), *Anleitung zu wissenschaftlichen Beobachtungen auf Reisen*, (Berlin, 1875), 605.

33 G. Fritsch, 'Praktische Gesichtspunkte für die Verwendung zweier dem Reisenden wichtigen technischen Hilfsmittel: Das Mikroskop und der photographische Apparat' in G. von Neumayer (ed.), *Anleitung zu wissenschaftlichen Beobachtungen auf Reisen*, 3rd edn (Hanover, 1906), 771.

The 'problem' of difference and identity in the photographs of Gustav Fritsch

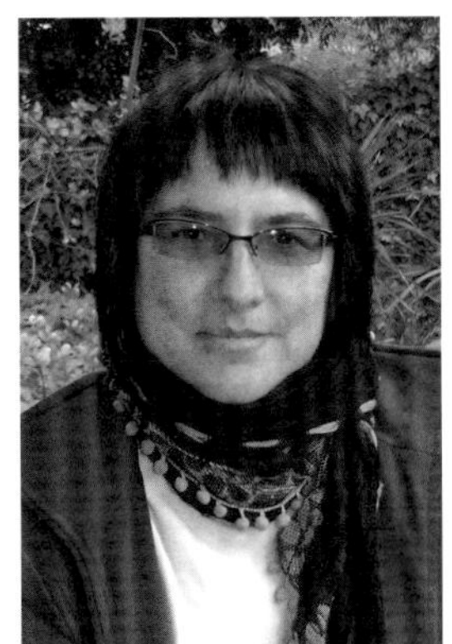

Lize van Robbroeck

Gustav Fritsch's anthropological objectives are recounted in this volume by Broeckmann and Bank, who situate his photographic practice within the context of the newly professionalised and rapidly expanding field of anthropology in the mid- to late nineteenth century. From these accounts, we know that Fritsch embraced the then common belief that surface characteristics signified essential differences – a belief that informed most of the new social sciences and pseudo-sciences of the second half of the nineteenth century, including craniology (the measurement of the human skull), phrenology (the mapping of protrusions and depressions on the cranium), criminology and, of course, physical anthropology.[1] Fritsch's attempt to identify, describe and quantify typological differences between South Africa's various peoples was aided by the concurrent development of photography, which revealed an optimistic (and, as it proved, ultimately short-lived) faith in the camera's power to record race typologies neutrally and objectively.

According to Glen Penny, nineteenth-century German anthropological practices were for the most part 'self-consciously liberal endeavors … guided by a broadly humanistic agenda and centered on efforts to document the plurality and historical specificity of cultures'.[2] The anthropological field was dominated by ethnology (with its emphasis on culture), and the prominence of this liberal humanist discipline meant that imperial ideology, with its essentialist emphasis on innate racial and national differences, was largely disdained. As Zimmerman confirms, physical anthropology struggled to find a foothold within this dominant liberal humanist sphere, and was practised largely by anatomists and medical professionals such as Gustav Fritsch.[3] Fritsch's physical anthropology was informed by the liberal ethnologists' concept of static cultural 'types'. His aim was to document, through his photographs of selected individuals, the typical physical characteristics of South Africa's various indigenous 'tribes', on the understanding that physical appearances encoded the complete human being, including moral, cultural and intellectual qualities. In order to achieve these aims, Fritsch had to uncover the similarities (the samenesses by which identity is constituted) between individual members of a given group, so as to establish the broad differences between the various ethnic types. The ultimate aim of this exercise was to finally uncover, beneath the multiplicity and plurality of human types, the underlying, universal human principles. Fritsch's obsession with surface differences formed part, therefore, of a humanist quest to establish the constants and givens of human identity.

In this essay, I look at Fritsch's anthropological project from a perspective that falls somewhere between the disciplines of philosophy and visual studies. In particular, I employ Fritsch's South African photographs as a vehicle to explore a central 'problem' in both modern and postmodern philosophy, namely the 'problem' of the relationship between difference and identity in the constitution of the human 'family'. I put the word 'problem' in inverted commas because I hope to demonstrate that the relationship between these two apparent opposites need not necessarily be seen as problematic at all, and that a non-oppositional reading of their relationship might, in fact, open up opportunities for a new appreciation of Fritsch's photographic oeuvre.

From a perspective informed by postmodern theories about language, representation and human subjectivity, Fritsch's deceptively simple portraits are encoded with a complex semantics that flow from a pronounced ambiguity at the heart of modernist Western discourse. This ambiguity, I hope to demonstrate, is the result of the essentially conflicting demands posed by the simultaneous belief in totalising universalism, liberated individualism and strictly fixed (and hierarchically ordered) human difference. I finally interrogate how Fritsch's portraits resonate with the modern viewer and suggest that they reveal, in our current context, both an absence of Fritsch's

Lize van Robbroeck studied art history at the universities of the Witwatersrand and South Africa and obtained her doctoral degree from Stellenbosch University. She is a Senior Lecturer in the Department of Visual Arts, Stellenbosch University, and her current research interest is in the area of nationalism and the visual arts.

intended meaning and an excess of signification that spills entirely beyond their intended frame.

Since the demise of Western colonialism and the emergence of the linguistic turn, the foundational principles and practices of anthropology have been the focus of sustained criticism.[4] In the wake of the racist excesses of the Nazi Holocaust, physical anthropology in particular has come under attack. This field's preoccupation with physical differences and the interpretation of these differences as signs of deep-seated inequality between races and nations has been thoroughly discredited. This postmodern questioning of nineteenth-century anthropology forms part of a much larger critique of the perceived arrogance of modernist positivist science and philosophy, which, it is proposed, served to impose and entrench Western power and values across the globe. These critiques largely centre on the way the human subject has been represented and theorised in the West, and particularly take issue with the way in which the ideal Enlightenment subject of modernity has been constituted at the expense of his non-European Other.

In many respects, Fritsch can be regarded as an arch exemplar of the Enlightenment ideal of the rational subject who, driven by curiosity about the world he inhabits, sets out to contribute towards the scientific project to complete the book of human knowledge. Penny points out that nineteenth-century educated Germans attached enormous value to the ideal of *Bildung*, which can be described as 'intellectual and moral self-cultivation'.[5] The concept of *Bildung* clearly derived from an Enlightenment perspective on the infinite capacity for human self-improvement. It cultivated an eagerness to gather information from numerous sources and from a wide variety of fields, encouraged a cosmopolitan and worldly outlook, and regarded travelling as an important component of self-cultivation. Fritsch, in his capacity as physician, anatomist, physical anthropologist, scientific traveller, amateur botanist and photographer, clearly subscribed to

the ideals of *Bildung*, and exhibited a quintessential Enlightenment faith in the infinite scope of autonomous rational subjectivity. Pippin defines this autonomy as 'the possibility that human beings can regulate and evaluate their beliefs by rational self-reflection, that they can free themselves from interest, passion, tradition, prejudice and autonomously "rule" their own thoughts, and that they can determine their actions as a result of self-reflection and rational evaluation'.[6]

It was perhaps this concern with ideal human subjectivity that also motivated Fritsch's interest in human anatomy, not only as a scientist, but also from an aesthetic point of view. In 1907, Fritsch edited a book titled *Nackte Schönheit. Ein Buch für Künstler und Ärzte.*[7] This book of highly aestheticised photographs of the naked (European) human form (most of them of the male figure and charged with homo-erotic tension) indicates a typical late-nineteenth-century German obsession with health and beauty.[8] This cultish preoccupation with physical beauty is not only representative, one could argue, of the German tradition of progressive positive idealism (as exemplified by Kant and Hegel and to which Fritsch clearly subscribed), but posits, in material form, the transcendental human ideal underlying Western humanism. It indicates the inevitable need for a normative, prescriptive base against which Otherness (not only non-European otherness, but otherness within, such as criminality and mental illness) could be measured. This normative base, as Annette Lewerentz suggests in this book, was supplied by antique classical sculpture, which was felt to embody the aesthetic values of beauty, proportion, harmony and moderation.

Today the 'scientific detachment' and blatant Eurocentrism of Fritsch's projects (and of physical anthropology and modernist science as a whole) tend to repel and alienate us. We justifiably feel that the singularity of Fritsch's individual subjects is violated by the instrumentalist purposes to which they are put – whether a leader or a follower, naked or clothed, noble or degenerate; all are regarded as specimens of a type. This dehumanising and objectifying effect is exacerbated by the fact that we associate the convention of full-face and profile shots with criminality and aberration. Paging through these faces, we feel like witnesses hunting through police mug-shots for a suspect. We feel uncomfortably like voyeurs and, in viewing these images, feel implicated in the dehumanising and objectifying effects of physical anthropology and Western science as a whole. The cold distancing implied by the programmatic repetition of the same poses and profiles suggests a scientist at work who is dissociated from his own empathetic and ethical responses to others. The fact that Fritsch experimented on live dogs in his neurological research confirms the extent to which he suspended empathetic response in the service of the 'greater good of science'. But we must remember that this detachment was (and still is today) regarded as a requirement for objective empirical research, and that it is pointless and even hypocritical to condemn Fritsch for taking this injunction seriously. A more fruitful reaction on our part would be to apply insights gained from our postmodern vantage point to understand the subjective mechanisms at play in this suspension of empathetic response to the Other.

Postmodern theories suggest that a dichotomy between the subject (the 'I' that thinks, investigates, interprets and represents) and the object (that which is thought about, investigated, interpreted and represented) lies at the root of modernist discourse. The subject as 'thinking thing' must be withdrawn even from his own body, which he regards as an object of quasi-scientific manipulation and control. Since the subject inhabits both sides of the body–mind duality, he is divided from within: on the one side, the transcendental 'thinking thing'; on the other, the physically embodied and socially constituted object.[9] Fritsch thus also objectified *himself* as disembodied consciousness that neutrally observes, calculates, measures, weighs and names.

This split consciousness is also evident in Fritsch's writings in which he described encounters with his subjects. In keeping with his scientific quest, he refers to the subjects of his photographs as 'specimens' and at times barely disguises his contempt for their undisciplined fidgetiness, for their superstitious fears, their laziness and stubbornness. In his *Die Eingeborenen*, Fritsch argued that his own account was superior to those of missionaries, whose familiarity with the people they described compelled them to 'prettify' their accounts.[10] Yet Fritsch's written accounts are significantly undercut by ambivalence, suggesting that his objectification of the Other was accompanied by an uncomfortable repression of his empathetic faculties. He compliments some of his subjects (albeit begrudgingly, as Michael Godby suggests in this volume) by commenting on their noble bearing, pride and beauty. In one poignant passage recounted by Keith Dietrich, Fritsch writes about the ease and enjoyment he experienced in the company of Khama, the christianised son of the ruler of the Ngwato. In this passage, Fritsch confesses to his prejudice

against the 'Ethiopian race' and clearly feels greatly moved and curiously relieved about the 'delightful feeling' of friendship evoked by contact with Khama. 'I am glad by my acquaintance with Khama, to have the opportunity of mentioning a black man whom I would under no circumstances be ashamed to call my friend.'

Today, in the postmodern intellectual climate of radical doubt, ambivalence is not only tolerated, but even celebrated. We accept that our own responses to the visual image are ambiguous and we revel in the challenge to decode the complexity of feeling and thought they evoke. Schooled in postmodern scepticism and aware of the crisis in representation that underpins it, we do not share Fritsch's optimistic faith in the camera (and, by extension, language) to represent the world truthfully. But what we lose in confidence, we gain in creative response. The radical destabilisation of the relationship between the signifier and its referent opens up space for a more creative and self-reflexive encounter with images.

As human beings, with sight as our primary sense, we tend to respond first and foremost to the affective register of images. When the human face is portrayed, this affective response is even more pronounced because our survival, as social animals, depends on an accurate reading of the faces surrounding us. But despite the universality of this fact, contemporary scientific inquiry into facework interaction suggests that there are distinct cultural differences in the interpretation of faces.[11] Cross-cultural readings of faces are considerably more complicated than inter-cultural readings, largely because the interpretation of, and value attached to, facial characteristics and expressions vary from culture to culture. Our response to Fritsch's photographs is complicated not only by cultural difference, but also by time. We are not coeval with the people caught in Fritsch's camera or with Fritsch himself, and our responses to these photographs are bound to reveal significant shifts in the values attached to them.

Despite postmodern protestations against the universalism of humanism, we know that we respond, first and foremost, to the humanity and individuality contained in each photograph. If we contemplate them one by one, we form a distinct and even uncanny sense of the person behind the camera. From the scant evidence provided by the moment captured in the full-frontal photograph, our imaginations embroider complex empathetic responses. We read some of these faces as proud and defiant, others as abject and miserable, yet others as tantalisingly impassive and resistant to interpretation. Our knowledge of the traumatic effects of the colonial encounter supplies additional material for our imaginations. As Keith Dietrich's research in this book makes clear, the historical moment of Fritsch's encounter with the subjects of his photographs was immensely devastating to indigenous populations. The decimation of entire societies, the ravaging and divisive effects of missionary Christianity on families and cultural traditions, the scourge of alcoholism, the genocide of hunter nomads, inter-tribal wars and conflicts as populations were unsettled, all contribute material for a sympathetic response to Fritsch's subjects.

The postmodern philosopher Emmanuel Levinas proposes another reason why the human face affects us so deeply. For him, the confrontational nakedness of the face is first and foremost a call to ethics. The nakedness of the face makes it extremely vulnerable and affective. 'The face is exposed, menaced, as if inviting us to an act of violence.' Yet, it is precisely this vulnerability that, in most human encounters, prevents violence: 'At the same time, the face is what forbids us to kill.'[12] The face is a primary, immediate and eloquent statement: 'the face speaks. It speaks, it is in this that it renders possible and begins all discourse.'[13] In Levinian terms, the faces in Fritsch's photographs are affective because they arouse in us a profound ethical responsibility (response-ability).

For Levinas, however, the researcher's look (as encapsulated by Fritsch's scientific project) is a denial of the moral injunction of the face: 'the look [of the researcher] is knowledge, perception …You turn yourself toward the Other as toward an object when you see a nose, eyes, a forehead, a chin … The best way of encountering the Other is not even to notice the colour of his eyes. When one observes the colour of the eyes one is not in social relationship with the Other.'[14] Fritsch's resolute determination not to engage in social dialogue with the Other but rather, with instruments in hand, to take the Other's measure (literally and figuratively) is to deny the voice of the Other's face, and amounts, in Levinian terms, to a violent inversion of the primary ethical command. It is a refusal to answer the face's call to engage in dialogue. The violence of this repression of the ethical command is also a violence one does to oneself – it is dehumanising not only to the Other, but also to the self. Hence Fritsch's patent relief in submitting to the dialogue invited by Khama's face.

On the other hand, we are struck by the beauty of both the pattern of the archival collection and the individual photographs. Our response is distinctly aesthetic. The fine grain of the prints – their old-worldliness and tonal clarity – elicits in us nostalgic delight. The slight blurring of some areas, juxtaposed against other areas of crisp focal clarity, unmistakably dates these photographs to the nineteenth century, a period sufficiently distant from us to invite nostalgia, yet close enough to be legible. This legibility, however, is discomforting, since it raises the spectre of eugenics, the Nazi Holocaust, and all the other ethnic cleansings of the twentieth century which followed in the wake of Fritsch's modernist project. Unlike Fritsch, we know that the consequences of his modernist quest have not been the final closure of the book of human knowledge, as he anticipated, but horrors and depravities beyond imagining.

In part our interest in these images emanates from the questions they raise about photographic representation. From the distance afforded us, we know that the optimism engendered by the invention of photography – an optimism centred on the putative ability of the photograph to render neutrally and objectively – has been disappointed. The reasons for this are fascinating to contemplate, and photography becomes a metaphor of the (im)possibilities of the Enlightenment quest to finally quantify, name and place everything. Deborah Poole explores the irony of the photographic paradox. Precisely because cameras recorded everything they were pointed at unselectively and without discrimination, they recorded much more than was needed. The camera as a tool was briefly celebrated as the ideal instrument to capture difference because it was believed that it eliminated human selectiveness and bias, and recorded purely and truly. Yet, as Deborah Poole points out,[15] it was precisely this – the fact that the camera captured, unselectively, too much difference, too much diversity, too much contingency – that eliminated it as a reliable anthropological tool. More importantly, it threatened to undermine the very hierarchical difference it aimed to entrench by proving the coevality of the researcher and his subject: 'the same machine that had made it possible to imagine a utopia of complete transparency also introduced the twin menace of intimacy and contingency – and with them, the possibility … of acknowledging the coevalness and, thus, the humanity of their racial subjects.'[16] As much as Fritsch tried to erase the dialogics of his encounter with his photographic subjects, as much as he tried to render them objects or specimens, their singularity and agency speak to us across the years. Fritsch's photographs thus stand as evidence of an encounter, 'an encounter, in turn, contained within the specter of communication, exchange, and presence'.[17]

As Andrew Bank points out in this volume, it was precisely this surplus, the small bothersome details which caught the undesirable contingencies of the moment and the particularities of place, that destroyed the usefulness of the photograph. Physical anthropology was interested in capturing the general in order to place it in the frame of the universal (it aimed at identifying the broad characteristics of a particular 'tribe' or race in order to determine its place in the 'family of man'). The camera's unwelcome proof of human singularity and the complexity of the moment undermined this quest. Fritsch's attempts to eliminate contingencies and context by situating each of his subjects in the same position, and his erasure of background detail in the development process, become a metaphor for the entire selective blindness of the Enlightenment project. It becomes clear that the modernist relationship with the camera is ambiguous precisely because the modernist relationship with difference is ambiguous.

From a postmodern point of view, all representations, whether they are utterances, pictures or written texts, contain just such an excess of unintended meaning. The intended meaning is eclipsed by these excesses, and so excess is always, ironically, accompanied by absence (the absence of intended meaning). This paradox, more than any other, defeats Fritsch's object, and (ironically) retrieves his photographs for us as (unintended) statements about the fundamental singularity and irreducible unknowability of the individual human subject.

Fritsch's project is riddled with paradoxes. From the infinity of faces confronting him, he had to make selections. He selected in accordance with his predetermined supposition about the visual appearance of racial and ethnic types. In choosing faces that conformed to his predetermined idea of the typology belonging to a particular collective, he reified it through repetition. His photographs are, in that sense, self-fulfilling prophecies. Fritsch's selectiveness was determined by another logistical issue. Although his writings reveal that he was interested in recording 'authentic' types uncontaminated by Western influence, he was, of necessity, compelled to travel along established colonial routes. He needed interpreters since he did not speak the local languages. He thus settled, most of the time, on people who were accustomed to white men – leaders and their entourages, servants, Christian converts and prisoners. When he encountered peoples unaccustomed to Westerners, they were too fearful or hostile to allow themselves to be captured on camera. Just as he started to navigate terrain less touched by the colonial presence, he had to turn back because the photographic quest had become too difficult.

But does this mean that Fritsch's project was entirely misguided and fallacious to begin with? Not necessarily. The ordering impulse of science is not to be rejected on principle – that would be to throw the proverbial baby out with the bathwater. Clearly it would be extreme and counterproductive to suggest that we should do away with groupings altogether. If we had no general classes of things (predicated on samenesses between them), language could not exist and we would be floundering in an infinite sea of endlessly reverberating and proliferating differences. In his groundbreaking research, the philosopher Paul Cilliers applies complexity theory to the 'problem' of difference and identity in the social sciences. 'Difference', Cilliers suggests, 'is a necessary condition for meaning. For something to be recognizable as being that something, it must be possible to differentiate it from something else … The more differences there are, the more distinctions can be made. Meaning is the result of these distinctions, of the play of differences.'[18] But boundless or limitless difference poses problems. Difference can only generate meaning if there are boundaries – what Cilliers calls an *economy* of difference. It is identity (the relationship of relative sameness between entities) that provides those boundaries. Thus both difference and sameness are needed to create meaning. Hence, according to Cilliers, 'we cannot use the notion of difference without reference to the notion of identity. Identity, however, does not determine difference, it is the result thereof.'[19] While the irreducible singularity of the Other is ethically non-negotiable, no system (social, linguistic or biological) can exist without sameness. If there was no sameness, there would be no systems; language would fall apart and all communication would

cease. Cilliers concludes by stating that 'difference is thus a resource to be cherished, not a problem to be solved'.[20]

In an attempt to retrieve the possible value of anthropological photography, Deborah Poole makes a similar suggestion: 'perhaps what is needed is a re-thinking of the notion of difference itself …, a questioning of its stability as an object of inquiry and a new way of thinking about the temporality of the encounter as it shapes both ethnography and photography.'[21] Poole argues that the data provided by ethnographic photographs should not necessarily be dismissed as of dubious anthropological value. The problematic abstractions of race that we take issue with today, she says, were produced not by the photographs *per se*, but by the archive into which they were incorporated. Once the archive is seen as the dominant interpretative frame, the photograph is freed for re-interpretation and re-appreciation: 'to reframe the archive as itself a visual technology takes us a long way from early studies in which the "meaning" of particular photographic images was interpreted as being a reflection, or "expression", of racial and colonial ideologies formed elsewhere, outside the archive.'[22] Today, it is precisely the camera's stubborn insistence on capturing the 'noise' of small humanising details that provides photographic databases of the colonial era with their value. Once taken from their problematic site of interpretation (the colonial archive, where hierarchical values are attached to differences), these photographs produce ethnographic evidence of an entirely different nature from what was originally intended, confirming 'photography's unique capacity to reveal the particularities of moments, encounters, and individuals'.[23] These photographic details supply us with at least some of the information needed to undertake a 'thick description'[24] of the effects wrought by the colonial encounter on indigenous identities.

The postmodern critique of the modernist paradigm centres on the latter's conception of identities (nations, sexes, races, cultures and ethnic groups) as static, bounded and biologically determined, and hence as permanently fixed in the hierarchical positions afforded by their perceived strengths and weaknesses. Discourses about authenticity, contamination and acculturation (so familiar in apartheid South Africa) belong to this paradigm, since they assume that identity (whether cultural, ethnic, sexual or racial) is a pure and free-standing entity, the integrity of which must be protected from contamination and salvaged from the threats posed by the rapid changes wrought by modernity. The critique of this modernist perspective has, justifiably, led to radical scepticism about projects such as Fritsch's. Not only has the notion of essential ethnic types been rejected, but along with it the 'salvation paradigm', premised on the notion of the inevitable extinction of 'backward' societies, which motivated scientists such as Fritsch. In the process, the data generated by these projects have been relegated to obscurity and left to gather dust on remote shelves in forgotten archives. I want to argue, however, that the postmodern conception of identity as cultural and linguistic construct could invite too facile a celebration of hybridity, and too glib a jettisoning of the impulse to recognise and protect identity. This jingoistic, celebratory multiculturalism suggests a happy melting-pot and a level playing field where none exists. Such a superficial interpretation of postmodernism – also driven, in South Africa, by the demands of nation-building – often declines to respect the boundaries established by the samenesses (identities) without which difference becomes infinite and valueless.

To create a more dynamic and complex understanding of difference and identity in South Africa, much work still needs to be done on the historical and perpetually reverberating effects that the colonial encounter had on local identities, whether personal, cultural, ethnic or linguistic. While the ground has been prepared for this research on a theoretical level, the need exists for more intensive historical research to negotiate the complex psychological and social effects of the traumatic events set in motion by European colonisation and slavery. This would include encounters not only between coloniser and colonised, but also between South Africa's various indigenous populations in the wake of the massive dislocations wrought by the colonial presence. To this end, data would also have to be retrieved about social and language groups that have been virtually eradicated by the tsunami effect of this encounter. In addition, much more research needs to be done on the historical formation of new identities in the crucible of the traumatic colonial moment. Fritsch's photographs, which capture this moment, provide valuable evidence – not of the purity of racial types, as he had hoped – but of the dynamic and volatile interplay of sameness and difference in the formation of human identities, which are always involved in the process of becoming.

ENDNOTES

1 Johannes Fabian calls this phenomenon 'visualism', and suggests that 'the ability to visualize a culture or society almost becomes synonymous for understanding it'. J. Fabian, *Time and the Other: How Anthropology Makes Its Object* (New York: Columbia University Press, 1983), 106.

2 H.G. Penny, 'Traditions in the German language' in H. Kuklick (ed.), *A New History of Anthropology* (Oxford: Blackwell Publishing, 2008), 80–81.

3 A. Zimmerman, *Anthropology and Antihumanism in Imperial Germany* (Chicago: University of Chicago Press, 2001).

4 The most influential deconstructions of anthropology and ethnography are: J. Asad (ed.), *Anthropology and the Colonial Encounter* (Atlantic Highlands: Humanities Press, 1975); J. Boon, *Other Tribes, Other Scribes: Symbolic Anthropology in the Comparative Study of Cultures, Histories, Religions, and Texts* (Cambridge: Cambridge University Press, 1982); J. Clifford and G.E. Marcus (eds.), *Writing Culture: The Poetics and Politics of Ethnography* (Berkeley: University of California Press, 1986); J. Fabian, *Time and the Other: How Anthropology Makes Its Object* (New York: Columbia University Press,1983); C. Geertz, *The Interpretation of Culture* (New York: Basic Books, 1973); C. Geertz, *Works and Lives: The Anthropologist as Author* (Stanford: Stanford University Press, 1988).

5 Penny, 'Traditions in the German language', 81.

6 B.P. Pippin, *Modernism as a Philosophical Problem: On the Dissatisfactions of European High Culture* (Cambridge: Basil Blackwell, 1991), 12.

7 G. Fritsch (ed.), *Nackte Schönheit. Ein Buch für Künstler und Ärzte* (Stuttgart: Hermann Schmidts Verlag, 1907).

8 See, for instance, M. Hau, *The Cult of Health and Beauty in Germany: A Social History, 1890–1930* (Chicago: University of Chicago Press, 2003).

9 A.J. Cascardi, *The Subject of Modernity* (Cambridge: Cambridge University Press, 1992), 63.

10 Zimmermann, *Anthropology and Antihumanism*, 218.

11 See, for instance, S. Ting-Toomey (ed.), *The Challenge of Facework: Cross-cultural and Interpersonal Issues* (Albany: State of New York Press, 1994). This book explores cross-cultural variations in the conceptions of the face and facial expressions from a variety of disciplinary perspectives. The various contributors to this book demonstrate how personal and social phenomena that find expression in the face, such as embarrassment, politeness and aggression, to name but a few, elicit subtly varying interpretations not only between the sexes, but also between different cultures.

12 E. Levinas, *Ethics and Infinity: Conversations with Phillippe Nemo* (Pittsburgh: Duquesne University Press, 1985), 86.

13 Levinas, *Ethics and Infinity*, 87.

14 Levinas, *Ethics and Infinity*, 85.

15 D. Poole, 'An excess of description: Ethnography, race, and visual technologies', *Annual Review of Anthropology*, 34 (2005), 159–179, 164.

16 Poole, 'An excess of description', 164. An article by Michael Godby about photographs taken of the 'bushman' //Kabbo is very revealing in this regard. Godby explores how //Kabbo was first dehumanised in anthropometric photographs, but subsequently rehumanised as his researchers got to know him intimately. M. Godby, 'Images of //Kabbo' in P. Skotnes (ed.), *Miscast: Negotiating the Presence of the Bushmen* (Cape Town: UCT Press, 1996), 115–128.

17 Poole, 'An excess of description', 166.

18 P. Cilliers, 'Difference, identity and complexity: A philosophical analysis', Unpublished paper presented at the National Conference of the Philosophical Society of South Africa, 17–19 January 2007, University of Stellenbosch, 3.

19 Cilliers puts this succinctly ('Difference, identity and complexity', 6): 'In order to recognize a difference between A and B, they must in the first place be identifiable *as* A and B (in their singularity), and secondly, they must, even if only slightly, share something that makes a comparison possible (there must be an element of identity). Moreover ... it is not really possible to talk of the difference between A and B if A and B are the only two things under consideration. The difference between apples and pears can only be understood in terms of what they share, e.g. that both are fruit.'

20 Cilliers, 'Difference, identity and complexity', 1.

21 Poole, 'An excess of description', 172.

22 Poole, 'An excess of description', 162.

23 Poole, 'An excess of description', 165.

24 Here I refer to Clifford Geertz's famous formulation of an anthropological approach characterised by acknowledgement of the semiotic singularities and complexities of the various contexts in which anthropological inquiry takes place. See C. Geertz, 'Thick description: Toward an interpretative theory of culture' in *The Interpretation of Cultures* (New York: Basic Books, 1973).